PARTNERS NEVERTHELESS

*Canadian-American Relations
in the Twentieth Century*

Edited by Norman Hillmer

New Canadian Readings

PARTNERS NEVERTHELESS

Canadian-American Relations in the Twentieth Century

Edited by
Norman Hillmer

Copp Clark Pitman Ltd.
A Longman Company
Toronto

For Michael

ISBN 0–7730–4913–4

Editing: Kathryn Defries
Design: Kathy Cloutier and Susan Coull
Cover: Editorial cartoon by Vic Roschkov. Reprinted with permission
— The Toronto Star Syndicate
Typesetting: ECW Production Services
Printing and Binding: Alger Press Limited

Canadian Cataloguing in Publication Data

Main entry under title:

Partners nevertheless: Canadian-American relations in the twentieth century

(New Canadian Readings)
ISBN 0-7730-4913-4

1. Canada – Relations – United States.   2. United States – Relations – Canada.
I. Hillmer, Norman, 1942– . II. Series.

FC249.P37 1989   303.4'8271'073   C89–093392–8
F1029.5.U6P37 1989

Copp Clark Pitman
2775 Matheson Blvd. East
Mississauga, Ontario
L4W 4P7

Associated Companies:
  Longman Group Ltd., London
  Longman Inc., New York
  Longman Cheshire Pty., Melbourne
  Longman Paul Pty., Auckland

Printed and bound in Canada

FOREWORD

New Canadian Readings is an on-going series of inexpensive books intended to bring some of the best recent work by this country's scholars to the attention of students of Canada. Each volume consists of ten or more articles or book sections, carefully selected to present a fully-formed thesis about some critical aspect of Canadian development. Where useful, public documents or even private letters and statistical materials may be used as well to convey a different and fresh perspective.

The authors of the readings selected for inclusion in this volume (and all the others in the series) are all first-rank scholars, those who are doing the hard research that is rapidly changing our understanding of this country. Quite deliberately, the references for each selection have been retained, thus making additional research as easy as possible.

Like the authors of the individual articles, the editors of each volume are also scholars of note, completely up-to-date in their areas of specialization and, as the introductions demonstrate, fully aware of the changing nature of the debates within their professions and genres of research. The list of additional readings provided by the editor of each volume will steer readers to materials that could not be included because of space limitations.

This series will continue into the foreseeable future, and the General Editor is pleased to invite suggestions for additional topics.

J.L. Granatstein
General Editor

ACKNOWLEDGEMENTS

The literature on Canadian-American relations is disappointingly scattered and sparse, particularly in its historical dimension. I have written this book for my students, but I hope that in a larger sense it makes a contribution to a better overall understanding of the relationship in both countries.

I am grateful to J.L. Granatstein, the general editor of the *New Canadian Readings* series, for his support and suggestions. Ian M. Drummond corrected some of my misconceptions concerning the economics of the partnership, and my colleague Roger Sarty taught me much of what I know about the eighteenth- and nineteenth-century context. Larry Aronsen, Garth Stevenson and Graham Taylor assisted with ideas on the selection and organization of articles. I have learned a great deal over many years about Canadian-American relations from my good friends, Robert Bothwell, John English, and Basil Robinson. Gloria McKeigan, as always, was indispensable. My Copp Clark editor, Kathryn Defries, brewed just the right mixture of pressure and sympathy. My wife Anne, who is actually in the business of Canadian foreign policy, listened patiently to my wordy descriptions of the project, and retaliated with good advice and good sense.
I dedicate the book to my son, Michael.

N.H.
Ottawa
February, 1989

CONTENTS

INTRODUCTION

When John F. Kennedy visited Ottawa in 1961, on his first trip to a foreign country as president of the United States, the exchange of catch phrases about the cheery state of Canadian-American relations was already a well-established ritual. With his now-familiar Boston cadence, and his clipped rhetorical jabs, Kennedy told the parliament of Canada that "geography has made us neighbours. History has made us friends. Economics has made us partners. And necessity has made us allies. Those whom nature hath so joined together, let no man put asunder."[1]

For Canadians, there was no arguing about geography, economics, or necessity — the sheer overwhelming proximity of the United States, the easy access of its markets, the size of its population and gross national production, and the military threat to North America. All this meant, as a Canadian politician once put it with unconscious irony, that the United States was our best friend whether we liked it or not.[2] President Kennedy seemed to be saying just that. Canada and the United States were in it together for the duration — whether we liked it or not.

History was a different matter. A legacy of distrust and suspicion of the United States was every Canadian's inheritance. The past was a reminder that the United States could never be expected to be neutral or benign where its interests were concerned, and that the Canadian experiment was fragile, vulnerable, even somewhat unnatural. "The evolution of Canada," a Canadian soldier wrote in the 1930s, "has been a gigantic struggle against nature because the natural sea and land communications of North America run in a general north and south direction. When man drew an arbitrary line separating Canada and the United States, he defied nature. Canada has been bucking nature ever since. . . ."[3]

Whatever Kennedy might say, history has made Canada and the United States anything but friends.[4] From the beginning of the American War of Independence, the United States was the principal military threat to Canada's existence. One of the first actions of the American revolutionary troops was to invade Quebec in 1775–1776. On that occasion, and in subsequent smaller-scale campaigns, professional British troops — with support from Canadian militia, the rugged terrain, and the long brutal winters — turned back the Americans. That same combination, and the crushing dominance the Royal Navy was able to exert on the American seacoasts, saved Canada again when United States' forces invaded during the War of 1812. English-Canadian nationalist mythology fed throughout the nineteenth century on the glorious "Canadian" performance in the 1812 conflict and on the lessons learned about the grasping, dishonest, untrustworthy neighbour to the south.[5]

Although war did not break out again, there were repeated scares from the 1830s to the 1860s when disputes flared into confrontation or violence along the border. The most dangerous of these occurred during the American Civil War of 1861–1865, when the Union government, sometimes with good reason, charged Britain and Canada with aiding the Confederacy. Britain poured over 10 000 troops into Canada and greatly reinforced her naval squadrons in the western Atlantic. The vast size and power of the Union forces, however, brought British and colonial leaders to see that Great Britain could no longer confidently protect the North American colonies. This realization was perhaps the single most important impetus to the confederation of the colonies in 1867: united, the British North Americans could more adequately protect themselves.

Although both Britain and Canada pursued friendly relations with the United States after the Civil War, military staffs in all three nations continued to plan for hostilities. Only after 1900, when Britain faced increasingly powerful and dangerous enemies in Europe, did the possibility of armed conflict in North America recede. Even so, anti-Americanism was never far from the surface in Canadian politics. The unpopularity of the Alaska boundary settlement of 1903 and the defeat of Sir Wilfrid Laurier in 1911, after his government reached a freer trade agreement with the United States, are clear indications of this. As late as the First World War, fears of cross-border raids by the many Americans of German ancestry led the Canadian government to establish military garrisons along the international frontier, much as had been done in the 1860s.

By the 1920s and 1930s citizens of the two countries could forget much and agree on much. Horrified by the savagery of the First World War, protected from danger by two huge oceans, North Americans turned away from a world which they believed had nothing to teach them. In fact, they believed the reverse to be the case. Other continents, where boundary lines were real and war commonplace, could profit from the example of North America's lengthy undefended border and shared institutions, where statesmen talked their problems through. O.D. Skelton, an academic who became the head of the Department of External Affairs in 1925, wrote that "Canada lies side by side for three thousand miles with a neighbour fifteen times as powerful. . . . Her security lies in her own reasonableness, the decency of her neighbour, and the steady development of friendly intercourse, common standards of conduct, and common points of view. Why not let Europe do likewise?"[6] "We think of Canadians as fellow North Americans," the Chicago *Tribune* editorialized. "Italians do not think of Germans or Frenchmen as fellow Europeans in anything like the same sense. They are suspicious where we have confidence."[7] Economist and humourist Stephen Leacock added that North Americans had achieved an unwritten alliance which "holds as deep in the soil as a New England elm." Whatever may happen, he wrote, "don't let this continent go the way of Central Europe: let nothing and nobody betray us into that."[8]

The ties between Canada and the United States were of course not just moral or psychological. Thirty million border crossings took place in one year alone in the mid-1920s. United States investment was rolling into canada, and that already meant substantial foreign ownership of Canadian industry. In came American periodicals, American radio and American films as well. Despite the repeated rejections of reciprocity, trade flourished, so that during the 1920s the United States replaced Great Britain as Canada's top market; in these same years, the U.S. was already providing well over sixty percent of Canada's imports.[9]

Yet there were continuing doubts. Complaints surfaced about the flood of Canadians choosing to live to the south and about the pervasiveness of the U.S. economy and mass culture. Military planners in Canada (and in the United States, for that matter) allowed for the possibility of hostilities between their countries until at least the early 1930s. The "State or the United States," warned the Canadian Radio League in advocating a government-owned, country-wide broadcasting system to fight the dominance of American programming. "It is impossible in Canada," a university professor wrote in 1930, "not to be struck by the co-existence of two apparently contradictory phenomena — a network of intimate friendships between Canadians and Americans, and a widespread distaste for Americans in general. . . . The fact is that we constantly indulge in acrimonious criticism of things and persons American — a habit so ingrained in us that it passes without comment or justification."[10]

Canada, too, was still a British colony, part of the British Empire. The connection with the world's greatest empire encouraged Canadians to believe that the boundary which separated them from the United States was more than a fiction. The empire gave them something to brag about that was at least comparable to U.S. achievement and international status.

Prime Minister Mackenzie King, Canada's pivotal politician, was a passionate Anglophile, although he sometimes had a strange way of showing it. As he negotiated the 1935 reciprocity agreement (the first since 1854), King told the U.S. minister in Ottawa, Norman Armour, that the two countries ought to be brought closer together "in every way, politically as well as economically." Canada had a choice to travel either the American or the British road; King desired the former. Armour rejoiced that reciprocity would bring Canada "not only within our economic orbit but our political orbit."[11] But King did not wish an American Canada. Like many Canadians, he remained fundamentally distrustful of the United States. He preferred the British, who knew what true liberty meant. In 1939, English- and French-speaking Cabinet ministers and parliamentarians stood with the prime minister in supporting the mother country's war against Hitler. Their judgement, in the final analysis, was that no distinction could be made between what was good for Britain and what was good for Canada.

Canada's future, however, lay not in Britain but in North America, and it was the Second World War, more than any other event, which brought the fact home. For a while, as Great Britain hovered on the edge of defeat, it appeared that an isolated North America would be the last bastion of freedom. It was then that long-standing military and economic links were forged, and then that Canada truly entered the American orbit. Although they now had no other road to travel but the American, Canadians did so willingly and admiringly. By war's end, without quite having withdrawn their allegiance from the British, they thought of the U.S. as their best friend and closest ally.

In the new world created by the Second World War, nuclear weapons threatened both Canada and the United States. Communism seemed on the march, and directed ultimately at capitalist North America. The British were sufficiently diminished that it was harder than ever to resist the pull of the continent. The options, never considerable, had narrowed, and subtlety was not an easy commodity for Canadians to discover. We were committed cold warriors, but frequently frightened by U.S. methods and bluster. America's power to commit Canada to war, wrote L.B. Pearson in his memoirs, was "a hard fact which brought us anxiety as well as assurance."[12] Canadian diplomats in the Cold War era, by attempting to control the Americans and channel their enthusiasms, aimed to ensure that the peace was not threatened by their best friends. Canada strongly supported the United Nations and the North Atlantic Treaty Organization, which helped to extend and diversify the range of external relationships. In these institutions, it was hoped, others would share the burden of U.S.-watching. "We did not want," Pearson said revealingly, "to be alone with our close friend and neighbour. As a debutante on the world stage we were worried, not about rape, but seduction."[13]

Washington was annoyed and perplexed by the pinpricks of criticism from the north, but Canada was valued for its stability, economic strength, and strategic importance. The two countries co-operated in the construction of radar systems across the Canadian north. The most famous of these, the Distant Early Warning (DEW) Line, was built in the Arctic at American expense and completed in 1957. That same year NORAD, a combination of continental air defences under a single command structure, was agreed upon. The American Secretary of State of the 1950s, John Foster Dulles, told a group of senators that Canada was "a very important piece of real estate." You just had to humour Canadians along.[14]

The special relationship did not survive much longer. The Diefenbaker government could not be humoured through the Cuban missile crisis or the defence debacle of the early 1960s. The Vietnam War and Watergate soured Canadians. NATO and NORAD came into question, particularly among intellectuals. Serious reservations were voiced about the influence of U.S. culture and the level of American investment, which had greatly increased in the 1950s and further in the following decade. Polls showed that Canadians felt less compatibility with the United States, and that large numbers had little confidence in Washington's ability to cope with its international responsibilities. When President Nixon visited Ottawa in 1972, Public Works officials had to melt snow away with hot water so that demonstrators would not be tempted to throw snowballs.[15] Americans, for their own part, were not amused by the flow of Vietnam draft dodgers into Canada, or the tossing of lofty sermons of peace across the border. Nor were they pleased by the Trudeau government's professed desire to be more independent of the U.S. or by its moves in that direction, such as the 1974 Foreign Investment Review Agency and the 1980 National EnergyProgram.

Pierre Trudeau was followed by Brian Mulroney, whose Conservatives won votes with the cry that the Liberals had damaged Canada's vital American connection. The Mulroney government set about the work of repair and reconciliation and in 1985 the prime minister and President Reagan met warmly at the Shamrock Summit in Quebec City. There the free trade idea was floated; negotiations were soon launched leading to an agreement which was breathtaking in its scope. Canadians, as is their way, were perverse in their reaction to the Mulroney-Reagan era of good feelings. Many who had felt in 1984 that Trudeau "nationalism" had gone too far were complaining four years later that his successor had become too close to the Americans.[16] In the election of 1988, just as in 1911, the United States became *the* issue. Unlike 1911, however, enough Canadians supported the government and its free trade agreement to give the Conservatives a solid parliamentary majority.

There is a good deal more to Canadian-American relations than presidents, prime ministers, and public opinion. It is arguable, indeed, that what happens at the top does not change the essence of the relationship. Canada and the United States are so intimately and necessarily intertwined that neither nation could escape if it wanted to. As historian John Bartlet Brebner once put it, the two countries are the Siamese twins of North America who cannot separate and survive.[17] We are their best customer, and they ours. Our defences against aggression are indivisible. We share an endangered environment. Canadian energy is indispensable to the United States. Our bureaucracies cuddle and occasionally snap at one another: more than fifty U.S. federal departments and agencies deal on a regular basis with the Embassy in Washington, with offices in fourteen American cities, and with the many arms of Ottawa and the provinces.[18] This says nothing of the thousands of public and private sector contacts daily between businesses, unions, professional associations, clubs, and individuals. Canada and United States are unequal partners but partners nevertheless — whether they like it or not.

Notes

1. R.F. Swanson, ed., *Canadian-American Summit Diplomacy, 1923–1973* (Toronto: McClelland and Stewart, 1975), 201.

2. Lawrence Martin, *The Presidents and the Prime Ministers. Washington and Ottawa Face to Face: The Myth of Bilateral Bliss 1867–1982* (Toronto: Doubleday, 1982), 204. See also C.S.M. Girard, *Canada in World Affairs*, XIII: *1963–1965* (Toronto, 1980), ch. 2.

3. Lieutenant Colonel Kenneth Stuart, "Canada and Imperial Defence" [1932], Directorate of History, Department of National Defence (DHist) 74/256.

4. James Eayrs, "Sharing a Continent: The Hard Issues" in John Sloan Dickey, ed., *The United States and Canada* (Englewood Cliffs, N.J.: Prentice-Hall, 1964), 70.

5. Carl Berger, *The Sense of Power: Studies in the Ideas of Canadian Imperialism 1867–1914* (Toronto: University of Toronto Press, 1970), 90–1, 166.

6. Quoted in Norman Hillmer, "The Anglo-Canadian Neurosis: The Case of O.D. Skelton" in Peter Lyon, ed., *Britain and Canada: Survey of a Changing Relationship* (London: Frank Cass, 1976), 76.

7. Quoted in Eayrs, 57.

8. Stephen Leacock, *All Right, Mr. Roosevelt (Canada and the United States)* (Toronto: Oxford University Press, 1939), 3, 6.

9. Canada, Dominion Bureau of Statistics, *The Canada Year Book 1929* (Ottawa: King's Printer, 1929), 482–3.

10. P.E. Corbett, "Anti-Americanism," *Dalhousie Review*, X, 3 (October 1930), 295. Dr. W.J. McAndrew drew this source to my attention. See also Carl Berger, *The Writing of Canadian History: Aspects of English Canadian Historical Writing 1900–1970* (Toronto: Oxford University Press, 1976), 138–40.

11. C.P. Stacey, *Canada and the Age of Conflict*, II: *1921-1948, The Mackenzie King Era* (Toronto: University of Toronto Press, 1981), 173; Marc T. Boucher, "The Politics of Economic Depression: Canadian-American Relations in the

Mid-1930s" in *Canadian Society and Culture in Times of Economic Depression, Canadian Issues*, VIII (Ottawa and Montreal: International Council for Canadian Studies/Association of Canadian Studies, 1987), 29–30.

12. John A. Munro and Alex I. Inglis, eds., *Mike: The Memoirs of the Right Honourable Lester B. Pearson*, II: *1948–1957* (Toronto: University of Toronto Press, 1973), 31.

13. Ibid., 33.

14. Quoted in Robert Bothwell and John Kirton, " 'A Sweet Little Country': American Attitudes Toward Canada, 1925–1963," *Queen's Quarterly*, 90, 4 (Winter 1983), 1093.

15. Martin, *The Presidents and the Prime Ministers*, 19.

16. Interview with Michael Adams, Environics Research, "The Insiders," *The Journal* (CBC television), 3 Oct. 1988.

17. John Bartlet Brebner, *North Atlantic Triangle: The Interplay of Canada, the United States and Great Britain* (New Haven: Yale University Press, 1945), xii.

18. "Notes for Remarks by H.B. Robinson to Conference on the Canada-U.S. Economic Relationship, Toronto, June 10, 1982."

SECTION 1
OVERVIEWS

There are two serious schools of thought about Canadian-American relations. The first holds that both conflict *and* co-operation characterize the relationship: as the subtitle of a recent American Assembly volume put it, "Enduring Friendship, Persistent Stress." The second view is tougher, seeking to place in higher relief the degree to which Canada is dependent on the United States, or even a satellite of an American empire.

Arguments that an American imperialism has operated — and is operating — in Canada are usually as unsatisfying as easy phrases of the past celebrating good neighbourhood, the best of friends, and an undefended border. Gordon T. Stewart of Michigan State University gives the imperialism theme substance by focussing on American documents and points of view — an uncommon perspective in Canadian-American scholarship — and by rejecting the notion that the simple saying (or writing) of the word "imperialism" necessarily makes it so. There is little doubt, says Stewart, that U.S. policy and policy-makers aimed over a long period at encouraging continental integration and discouraging independent Canadian action. This, in the author's view, is imperialism, but he notes an extraordinary overlap in goals, expectations and values between metropolis and hinterland. Stewart's imperialism has a collaborator in the Canadian government, not an unwilling and unknowing victim.

This is a refreshing and disturbing interpretation. Stewart, however, covers a lot of ground quickly, and his account is not always a fair representation of Canadian attitudes. Mackenzie King did not, for example, wish to travel the "American road" after 1935. The Norman Hillmer-John English survey of Canadian-American relations from the 1930s to the 1980s shows that clearly. Even at the height of Canadian good feeling about the United States, their paper says, Ottawa frequently had reservations about American policies and tried to change them. By the 1960s, indeed, Canadians and their government were becoming so skeptical about the United States that a whole new attitude towards the relationship evolved: more critical, more anxious about American influence, more willing to assert national independence.

Robert Bothwell and John Kirton of the University of Toronto fit their analysis firmly into the co-operation-conflict mould. Like Stewart, they discuss the narrowness of the American perspective, and the difficulty Washington has had in understanding the ways of the "sweet little country" to the north. Like English and Hillmer, they emphasize the "far greater measure of equality, divergence and distance" which came into the relationship as it matured. However, the authors also have a great deal to say about the complex net of formal and informal co-operation, fuelled by close personal ties, which was built up over the years across a broad spectrum of government departments, agencies, groups, and subject areas.

Freer trade carries this section into the most contentious area of all. In a section of his article not printed here, J.L. Granatstein recounts the history of the 1854–1866 reciprocity treaty between Canada and the United States and its aftermath. Sir John A. Macdonald's Conservative governments of the late nineteenth century never stopped searching for a freer trade agreement. In 1891, however, the old politician was able to use Sir Wilfrid Laurier's advocacy of reciprocity — and therefore of an apparently diminished tie with mother England — to scupper the Liberals. The pattern continued into the twentieth century. Co-operation can and does flourish between two realistic and eager trading partners, but problems arise on the domestic front when the issue attracts public attention. For many Canadians, it seems, the political and emotional aspects of freer trade count for more than the arguments of economic advantage.

AMERICA'S CANADIAN POLICY†

GORDON T. STEWART

America's relations with Canada seem a deservedly neglected field in U.S. diplomatic history. Canada never has been the cause of basic definitions or basic shifts of U.S. foreign policy goals. America's relations with Canada retained a low priority, even when Canada became its most important market, its biggest field of foreign investment, and its closest military ally. Relations between the two countries always have seemed to be in a special category, uniquely determined by natureand geography. At times the relations were locally interesting; sometimes they were stirred by controversy, from the perennial fisheries dispute of the nineteenth century to the recent disagreements over energy policy. But the American-Canadian bilateral relationship usually is regarded as having little general or theoretical significance.

This relegation from the normally competitive system of international relations had a great deal to do with the publication in the 1930s and 1940s of the seventeen-volume Carnegie series on Canadian-American relations, which emphasized the theme of good neighbours willing to settle disputes through arbitration. The general editor of the series, Canadian-born James T. Shotwell, was a leading internationalist who hoped that Canadian-American diplomacy would set a salutary example to the international community of how to eliminate selfish national interest and bellicosity between nations.[1] The bilateral relationship thus was regarded as exceptional and exemplary rather than normative.

This benign view was never accepted by many Canadian scholars

† Gordon Stewart, " 'A Special Contiguous Country Economic Regime': An Overview of America's Canadian Policy," *Diplomatic History* VI, 4 (Fall 1982): 339–57.

who, by the 1960s, argued in various forms from studious monographs to popular diatribes that American economic and cultural expansion, along with the military defence integration of the two nations in the 1940s and 1950s, constituted American imperialism towards Canada.[2] Indeed, within the Carnegie series itself, Canadian authors had demonstrated their misgivings about the internationalist approach of Shotwell. Above all, Donald G. Creighton's *The Commercial Empire of the St. Lawrence* proposed a quite different conceptual framework, emphasizing competition between the two countries over North American resources and transportation routes.[3]

While this more critical, dynamic view gained ground in Canada, the old good-neighbour approach was never challenged in the United States by a major book, certainly not by a weighty multivolume series equivalent to the Carnegie effort. This situation was not so much due to the fact that American scholars stood by the good-neighbour arbitration approach but because the whole subject, so vital to Canadians, was only of marginal interest to American diplomatic historians and experts. Thoughtful American textbooks in diplomatic history backed off from the Panglossian optimism of Shotwell's model and added details of tensions between the two countries.[4] The conjunction of Richard Van Alstyne's view of the expanding American continental empire with William Appleman Williams's emphasis on the expansionist drives of the American industrial economy could be pieced together as a revisionist interpretation of America's Canadian policies.[5] But no textbook or monograph offered a systematic reappraisal of American-Canadian relations.

The subject finally received a conceptual jolt with the publication in 1980 of Robert Hannigan's analysis of the Taft reciprocity policy of 1911.[6] In this seminal article, Hannigan proposed that America's view of Canada was not sealed off from the rest of the world but could be placed illuminatingly in the context of general U.S. foreign policy goals. He argued that William Howard Taft and his advisers planned, in the short run, to gain an "open door" to Canada's market and raw materials and, in the long run, to prevent Canada from developing into a successful core state with a competitive industrial economy. By 1911 American policy-makers understood that urban and industrial America would require readier access to foreign markets and that the ability of the United States to remain self-sufficient in food production was questionable. Taft and Secretary of State Philander C. Knox therefore viewed reciprocity in terms of capturing the Canadian market and gaining access to Canadian grain production.[7] Hannigan placed Canada squarely in the midst of American open-door diplomacy of the early twentieth century. He brought American-Canadian relations in from the cold.

A problem arises, however, in treating the Canadian relationship in the same conceptual terms as America's relationship with China or the

Latin American states. The stubborn fact remains that Canada's geographical contiguity to and similarity with the United States in economic organization and expectations have given it a special place in U.S. policy formulation. At the time that Taft's advisers were writing about an open door, for example, the United States already controlled abut 60 percent of the Canadian market. On the one hand, the Carnegie series went too far in eliminating the possibility of a dynamic, competitive or exploitative relationship with the United States and Canada; on the other, it may be that Hannigan has gone too far in arguing that Canadian policy was simply another example of general open-door policy goals. In short, American-Canadian relations need to be assessed anew to bring into focus the basic structure of that relationship.

Analysis of U.S. congressional debates and committee hearings and of State Department correspondence reveals the existence of three basic American attitudes that remained consistent and formed the American view of Canada down to the early 1900s. The first was that Canada possessed a population similar to that of the United States, that it was operating in equivalent geographical conditions, and that Canada, of all the countries in the world, would be the first to follow the American pattern of economic and political development. Speaking before the Senate Foreign Relations Committee in 1888, H.V. Poor argued that "nothing is to stand in the way . . . of the 'Americanization' of the whole continent."[8] In 1890 the Senate Select Committee on Canada listened to a comprehensive account by Francis Glenn of how Canada "has been coming to us, and is coming to us steadily, more rapidly than ever before."[9] Another example occurred even earlier. As he sought to convince Congress to enter into new trade negotiations with Canada in 1876, J.W. Ward rested his case on the grounds that "Canada, from her geographical position and similarity of her people to our own, is the first with which we should seek an extension of our commence."[10] This standard view of Canadian-American similarity was given official sanction in 1892, when Secretary of State John W. Foster described Canadians as "our Northern neighbors, bound to us by so many ties of race and community of interest."[11]

The second American attitude, embracing a counterinterpretation of Canada's destiny, viewed the Canadian confederation, established in 1867, as part of England's policy of strengthening its empire to make permanent its influence and institutions in North America.[12] This view that Canada was still an integral and important factor in British imperial machinations took on substance as Americans perceived direct economic threats from Canada's transportation policies. In a report to Secretary of the Treasury Howell Cobb in 1860, Israel T. Hatch described the Grand Trunk Railroad as a systematic means of tapping the resources of the American heartland and opening it up to manufactured exports from Great Britain. The scale and the cost of the railroad, backed by British capital with its headquarters in London, proved that it was "less the struggle for temporary trade than for permanent empire."[13] Once the Canadian Pacific Railroad was completed in 1886, the American critique expanded to charge Canada with the attempt to divert American trade with China and Japan. The building of the Canadian Pacific, together with British admiralty subsidies to associated shipping lines on the Atlantic and the Pacific coasts, was regarded as a concerted effort to secure "the supremacy of the British flag upon the seas . . . and a scheme of British imperial supremacy over the commerce of the western side of this continent."[14]

While critics of Canada's railroad policies saw Britain as the main problem (without British capital and mercantile support, Canada posed little danger in itself), a third distinct attitude held that Canada, under the Conservative governments of John A. Macdonald, knowingly was using its position in the empire to cause problems for the United States. This attitude was expressed best by Joseph Nimmo, a spokesman for American railroads, when he told the 1890 Select Senate Committee that "Canada simply uses the British flag to play high-handed tricks upon the United States."[15] This was a long-standing complaint. In the 1860s Canada was accused of having disregarded utterly "the spirit and substance" of the 1854 reciprocity treaty, because it had raised tariffs against American manufactured goods.[16] In the late 1880s, at the height of the fisheries controversy, Canadian policy, with its strict enforcement of the 1818 Anglo-American treaty provisions on the fisheries, was denounced as "inhuman" and an "outrage."[17] Furthermore, as Canada arranged its canal tolls to discriminate against American ships passing through the Welland and St. Lawrence canals, congressional complaints increased to the point where President Grover Cleveland declared that the United States had been "imposed upon and humiliated."[18] The deep involvement of the Canadian government in British-subsidized transportation led American critics to decry Canada's "foreign policy as intensely commercial, which gives a very peculiar character to our Canadian relationship and renders it much more difficult for us to enter fair treaty arrangements with Canada than with any other nation on the globe."[19] In 1893, President Benjamin Harrison summed up this negative assessment of Canada as he insisted that in all major disputes between Britain and the United States — the Atlantic fisheries, the Bering Sea sealing question, transportation matters — Canada had "thwarted negotiations by unreasonable and unfriendly objections and protests."[20]

These three attitudes — that Canada was similar to the United States and would eventually conform to an American pattern, that Canada was still burdened by European institutions and represented direct imperial economic threats, and that Canada was a deceitful and troublesome diplomatic partner — constituted the American response to Canada in the mid- or late-nineteenth century. These attitudes could not lead to any consistent policy because they were essentially contradictory. For example, Republican railroad lobbyists like Nimmo made all manner of complaints about Canadian diversion of U.S. foreign and domestic commerce and about the imperial purpose behind the Grand Trunk and Canadian Pacific railroads; but when President Cleveland, in 1888, threatened to withdraw all bonding and transit privileges in retaliation for Canadian fisheries policy, the Republicans in Congress refused to support such draconian measures because of their negative impact on American shippers, insurers, and agents who handled the Canadian business.[21] Similarly, while eastern railroad interests objected to the unfair competition of Canadian railroads (unrestrained by Interstate Commerce Commission regulations), farmers and shippers in the midwest and northwest and manufacturers and consumers in New England all valued the additional capacity and cheaper rates thus made available. Occasionally action was taken, as in 1893 when Harrison and his secretary of state, James G. Blaine, retaliated against Canadian canal policy by raising charges on American canals;[22] but no comprehensive Canadian policy could be based on these conflicts among lobbyists, congressmen, and administration officials. Insofar as any policy operated, it was of the do-nothing variety, since all administrations from 1866 onward refused to alter U.S. tariff barriers to allow freer trade between the two countries.

Canada in these years was a genuine puzzle for American officials and politicians. As Nimmo told the Senate Select Committee in 1890, that country was "a riddle to the American mind."[23] Canada was close, similar in population and circumstances, heading supposedly in an American direction; but the two nations were, throughout the 1870s, 1880s, and 1890s, "in a state of commercial belligerency."[24] Moreover, Canada was playing an active, aggressive role in the expansion and direction of British commercial imperialism and in all major diplomatic dealings seemed intent on playing devious tricks on the United States. In short, Canada's public policies, with their "insane idea of empire,"[25] contradicted any American expectation that Canada was adjusting herself to a continent on which the United States was the preponderant power.[26] As Ward put it in 1876, when he wondered about Canada's "natural" place in North America and the actual state of economic antagonism between the two nations, relations between the United States and Canada were of "an exceptional and peculiar character."[27]

Beginning about 1906, however, these attitudes and actions began to be replaced by more considered policymaking. A key factor preparing the ground for a clearer assessment of American goals was the rapprochement with Britain, which reduced fears of British imperialism in North America, even though one U.S. senator as late as the 1930s objected to the proposed St. Lawrence Seaway because it would

be used "as an avenue of approach for their [British] warships."[28]
Another factor that altered the American view of Canada was a growing, informed awareness among U.S. officials that time and nature
indeed appeared to be working on their side. In 1906 departmental
special agent Charles M. Pepper reported to the secretary of commerce and labor that Canada's proximity and similarity in business
methods made it less a foreign market "than an extension [of] the
domestic market."[29] Using post–1898 trade statistics, he proceeded to
show that, in spite of imperial tariff preferences, Canada steadily was
importing more from the United States than from Britain, and he
forecast that all attempts to maintain an imperial economic system
would fail.[30]

A confirmatory assessment of these trends was made in 1908 by John
B. Osborne, chief of the State Department's Bureau of Trade Relations, who argued that "nature is a most powerful ally in the development of the commercial relations between the United States and
Canada."[31] Trade statistics showing that the United States had about
60 percent of the Canadian market were "pregnant with meaning,"
and Osborne believed the United States would continue to displace
Britain in the Canadian economy.[32] Yet another significant sign of the
times was identified in a 1910 report by Joseph F. Johnson to the
National Monetary Commission. An analysis of the Canadian banking and credit system showed the extent in which it was tied to New
York rather than to London. Quite simply, concluded Johnson, "Canada is financially part of the United States."[33]

In these circumstances, created both by rapprochement and by
favourable underlying economic trends, modern American policy
toward Canada was formed. The American goals were to continue to
detach Canada from the empire, increase the U.S. share of the Canadian market, gain readier access to Canadian natural resources, and
encourage, in general, Canadian integration into a unified North
American economy. It was not so much a case of obtaining an open
door as of taking the door off its hinges.

These goals were evident in President Taft's reciprocity policy. He
explained to Congress in January 1911 how the proposed trade treaty
with Canada would increase the supply of foodstuffs, enable the
United States better to control the international wheat market, and
further open the Canadian market for the products of urban America.[34]
In a phrase revealing his view of Canada, the president told the Illinois
legislature two weeks later that reciprocity would strengthen "our self-
supporting capacity."[35] Taft and Knox, encouraged by the arguments
of Pepper and Osborne, concluded that there was a definite possibility
in 1911 of shifting Canada from her previous imperial pattern of
development to a more "natural" pattern that would better fit the
needs of the American economy. This is why the president spoke of
Canada as being "at the parting of the ways," and why the British Tariff

Commission complained that the United States was trying to "develop conditions of disintegration" between Britain and its colonies.[36]

The goals of weakening Canada's ties to the empire and of developing an interlocking economic system in North America were not pursued with any sense of urgency after 1911. Canada never came near the top of the State Department's priority list and, in any event, the economic trends continued to work in the American interest. By the mid-1920s the United States had replaced Britain as the largest foreign investor in Canada.[37] But whenever issues did arise, U.S. officials made clear the role they expected their neighbour to play. In the early 1920s, for example, when the Canadians set duties and tariffs to encourage the establishment of pulp and paper factories at home, rather than simply exporting the raw pulpwood abroad, committees in both the House and the Senate complained that American paper mills would be forced to close "unless a reasonable supply of raw material could be kept flowing."[38] The controversy surfaced again in 1923, when Secretary of State Charles Evans Hughes, speaking to and through the U.S. chargé in Ottawa, warned that there would be American "retaliation of a far-reaching character" if Canada persisted in her attempts to limit the export of raw pulpwood.[39]

During the 1930s, as Canada desperately sought a new trade treaty with the United States, American officials became even more forthright in setting out their assumptions and aims with respect to that country. These were revealed in 1933 when the Conservative government of Richard B. Bennett, after fruitlessly seeking an imperial solution to Canada's trading problems, turned to the United States for tariff relief. When the Roosevelt administration moved slowly on these overtures, the Canadians became increasingly resentful, and in November 1934 the Canadian ambassador to Washington, W.H. Herridge, delivered a note that amounted to an indictment of American policy toward Canada.[40] Herridge pointed out that the Canadian market for American business was significantly larger than the Japanese, Chinese, French, German, and Latin American markets; that Canada had, since 1882, carried a trade deficit with the United States; and that between 1903 and 1933 about 70 percent of Canada's imports had come from the United States. He then drew attention to American investment in Canada, with a consequent annual outflow of an estimated $125 000 000 in interest payments. He pointed out further that Canada's only credits with which to pay for its interest outflow and trade deficit were gold and revenue from American tourists. As this was a restricting and unfairly dependent position for Canada, Herridge concluded bluntly that his nation should be allowed to increase its exports to the United States.[41]

The American response to this critique was revealing. A comprehensive analysis of Herridge's note was made by the U.S. minister to Ottawa, Warren Robbins, and accepted by the State Department.[42]

Robbins had advised that it was important for the State Department to reject a basic implication of the Herridge case; namely, that Canada was unfairly on the receiving end of the American-Canadian economic connection and that it therefore deserved better access to the American market. The basic objective, argued Robbins, should be "the restoration of normal trade between the two countries and its increase without reference to, or commitment regarding, any Canadian desire to have Canadian exports to the United States exceed their normal relation to American exports to Canada." It also was important to discredit the idea of closing the gap in American-Canadian trade, for if that principle were acknowledged by the State Department, even the Canadian Liberal party, traditionally friendly to the United States, might introduce it as a goal.[43] Robbins, in his reply, clearly illustrated the American view that Canada "normally" should be in a dependent position and should not become an exporter of manufactured goods to the U.S. market. American policy was neatly summed up in June 1935 by the U.S. chargé in Ottawa, Pierre De L. Boal, who devised a more accurate, if more cumbersome, phrase than "open door." The American aim, he wrote to Secretary of State Cordell Hull, was to fashion a "special contiguous country economic regime."[44]

The post–1945 years presented encouraging circumstances for American policymakers to pursue this end. The wartime co-operation and joint discussion on defence that had been taking place since the Ogdensburg agreement of 1940, combined with Canada's serious postwar trade difficulties and exchange problems, offered a rare opportunity.[45] Canada's position was critical by fall 1947, when it found itself unable to earn dollars from trade with a devastated Europe and so finance the country's traditional trade deficit with the United States. Canada faced an acute shortage of dollars. U.S. Ambassador Ray Atherton reported from Ottawa that the . . . Conservative opposition leader, John Bracken, was proposing a customs union with Britain to ease these trade problems. Given Prime Minister W.L. Mackenzie King's pro-American leanings and the atmosphere of co-operation between the two governments in the defence field, the Canadian economic predicament could be used as an opportunity for further economic integration and a final destruction of the imperial connection. As Atherton explained in October 1947, opinion in favour of "a closer integration of the economies of Canada and the United States . . . has reached probably an all-time high." In addition, the King government seemed ready to make wholesale changes that "clearly imply Canada's secession from the Empire trading unit" and "the expansion of the Dominion's economy along lines complementary to that of the U.S."[46]

During the winter of 1947–48, tariff discussions took place in Washington between Canadian and American "technicians." On the Canadian side were Hector Mackinnon, chairman of the Dominion

Tariff Board, and John Deutsch, director of economic relations in the Department of Finance; on the American side were Woodbury Willoughby, associate chief of the Division of Commercial Policy, and Willard Thorp, assistant secretary of state for economic affairs.[47] A plan was drawn up to phase out, over a five-year period, all tariff barriers between the two countries. In a top secret memorandum, Thorp explained how the plan met long-standing American policy objectives. The Canadians understood the far-reaching consequences and considered "the proposal, if implemented, to be one of the most momentous decisions in their history." Thorp urged that this golden moment be seized and advised the Truman administration to begin talking immediately to key congressional leaders in order to prepare political opinion; he emphasized to them "the vital significance of the plan from a strategic as well as an economic standpoint."[48]

The phasing out of tariffs, explained Thorp, "would result in the immediate elimination of all Empire preferences granted by Canada, with important economic and political implications for the United States." It was essential to move now on this, he added, because King was due to retire in August and "his successor may not be equally favourable to the plan." This was, concluded Thorp, "a unique opportunity of promoting the most efficient utilization of the resources of the North American continent and knitting the two countries together — an objective of U.S. foreign policy since the founding of the republic."[49]

While these assessments of American goals with respect to Canada were expressed only in secret documents in 1947–1948, they emerged in public during debate on the St. Lawrence Seaway agreement. Both President Franklin D. Roosevelt and Harry S. Truman were strong supporters of a joint American-Canadian route to the sea. Roosevelt had emphasized the energy aspect of the project, urging Congress in 1941 to view the seaway as an important additional electrical power source that would enable the United States to outstrip its enemies "in the race of production . . . that determines the rise and fall of nations."[50] Truman had drawn attention to the role of the Tennessee and Columbia River power projects in the development of the atomic bomb and argued that power from the St. Lawrence project would be equally significant.[51] Undersecretary of State Dean G. Acheson, in his arguments, emphasized the unusual needs of the American industrial heartland:

> Almost unique among the highly industrialized sections of the world, our middle western manufacturing areas have grown up far away from ocean transportation. . . . Since the first World War, this area has progressively grown into a surplus producing area which now must ship its products not only within the

United States but to foreign countries and which must procure its raw materials not only from within the United States but increasingly from abroad. For all this, a water route to the sea is needed.[52]

In spite of these pleas from Roosevelt, Truman, and Acheson, the opposition of affected American interests was strong enough to prevent any congressional action on the issue until the Canadians, in 1951, decided to proceed with an all-Canadian seaway.[53] Administration pressure was stepped up in Congress. Already in 1950 the National Security Resources Board had argued that the United States soon would be critically short of iron ore and that it was essential to gain easier access to ore deposits in Labrador.[54] In June 1953, Frank Nash, assistant secretary of defence, took the seaway issue before the House Committee on Public Works, impressing upon the representatives how serious the matter was to the president, the entire cabinet, and the Joint Chiefs.[55] Nash repeated the warnings about iron ore depletion and pointed out that the region north of the Gulf of the St. Lawrence seemed rich in other important raw materials. From a national security standpoint, Nash argued, it was necessary to prevent an all-Canadian route into the heart of the United States. Other proponents of the seaway added the arguments that "Canada's huge mineral resources in the vast St. Lawrence Gulf region will find an increasing market in our country," and that a joint route to the sea was "an economic matter of primary concern to the United States."[56]

Such economic benefits might follow even if the seaway were a purely Canadian project, but such autonomous Canadian control presented definite dangers to American interests. Critics, drawing on the deep historical suspicions of Canadian transportation policies, warned that Canada might well operate a discriminatory toll and regulating system. Since most incoming tonnage was expected to be in the form of raw materials for American industry, there were "compelling reasons why U.S. participation is of the utmost importance."[57] If the seaway were owned and operated by Canada alone, it would be run in Canada's own national interest, most obviously as "a revenue-producing investment, with U.S. interests continuing to pay rental for its use."[58] On the other hand, joint American-Canadian control not only would prevent any nationalist Canadian policy on the seaway but also would bring broader benefits since it would "augment integration of our economy with that of Canada."[59]

The St. Lawrence seaway agreement represents a high mark in Canadian-American good neighbourliness. In the communiqué announcing joint participation, both president and prime minister spoke of Canadian-American co-operation in NATO, Korea, and the Cold War in general.[60] At the signing ceremony, Congressman George A. Dondero of Michigan, key figure behind the legislation, talked of the joys of working with "our good neighbor to the north."[61] These are valid characterizations of the atmosphere in which the final agreement was made, and Canada, all along, had certainly worked for American participation in sharing the cost of construction and ensuring the commercial success of the seaway.[62] But public fanfare about good neighbourliness should not obscure the reality that the United States had acted to gain readier access to Canadian raw materials, to prevent Canada from pursuing an autonomous, nationalist policy on seaway matters, and to confirm physically, as it were, the complementary nature of the two economies. The seaway was like a huge economic zipper knitting these countries together. It was a fitting climax to the post–1906 policy goals of economically integrating the two countries and molding the "special contiguous country economic regime."

In assessing the American response to Canada and in searching for a phrase that might best sum up that response, one approach can be quickly dismissed. It makes little sense to use the good-neighbour concept as an explanatory device. This approach, which figured so much in the Carnegie series, has been undermined by many scholars since then, but it needs to be sealed firmly in its coffin. Its weakness is that rhetoric is mistaken for reality. It is possible to find good neighbour and similar sentiments expressed throughout the period, although they multiply by the 1930s; indeed, because the sentiment was expressed so often and so variously the rhetoric has taken on a life of its own. It would even be possible to trace the origins of the notion in both countries and show its changing content and impact. It could be argued effectively, for example, that Americans were always more partial to the phrase than Canadians and used it as a kind of euphemism when they hoped Canada would act in "American" rather than "imperial" ways.[63]

The geographical relationship between the two countries gave the good-neighbour concept a vitality that can be analyzed in terms of its influence on public opinion and government actions. An example of this special language between the two countries occurred in April 1951 when the American ambassador to Ottawa, Stanley Woodward, asked Lester Pearson, the . . . minister of external affairs in the Louis St. Laurent government, to explain what Pearson had meant in speeches apparently critical of American influence in Canada. He explained himself and then was told that Woodward had been invited to a Kiwanis Club dinner in Ottawa in honour of Canadian-American Friendship Day, a dinner at which Pearson was to deliver a speech. Pearson laughed and said that he supposed he had better talk about the undefended border and 135 years of peace. He then invited the ambassador to accompany him to the opening baseball game at Lansdowne Park.[64] This kind of jocular, familiar interchange is one of the hallmarks of modern Canadian-American relations and can be studied to weigh its impact on policy formation, but it does not constitute the substance of policy. The St. Lawrence Seaway decision culminated in an outpouring of good neighbourliness, but U.S. policy was rooted in quite different considerations. The good-neighbour rhetoric is part of the superstructure, not the foundation.

When describing that foundation, there is a problem with conventional terminology. It is easy to charge that American policy was "imperialistic," as many Canadian scholars have done and as Hannigan has argued persuasively with reference to the 1911 agreement. Placing American policy in the setting of Immanuel Wallerstein's model of world development (as Hannigan does) certainly makes more sense than accusations that the United States was embarked on a course of "capitalist imperialism" against a country as developed as Canada.[65] In this more considered view of American policy, the object was to prevent Canada from growing into a core state with a complex industrial economy that might rival that of the United States. In this schema, American policy aimed at incorporating Canada into the core economy of the United States as a source of raw materials and as a market for exports.[66] This did not mean that the United States would try to prevent any diversified growth in its neighbour, for growth and prosperity were required if Canada was to remain an attractive and important field of sales and investment, but it did mean that from about 1911 on U.S. policymakers tried to fashion Canadian development to fit American needs. Such is the case made by Hannigan, and it is a plausible one for 1911 and beyond, as the pulpwood affair of the 1920s clearly shows.

Some awkward facts, however, have to be dealt with before that interpretation can be accepted. The biggest question is whether Canada could have become a core state irrespective of U.S. policy. From the seventeenth into the twentieth century Canada's economy always had been tied to a metropolitan market and an outside source of capital. With its small population, difficult geographical setting, and fragmented domestic market, it could well be argued that Canada never had the capability of developing into a core state.[67] Indeed, if one is looking for destructive American tactics, it makes more sense to go back to 1783 when Canada was cut off from the Ohio Valley. Had Canada retained control of the entire Great Lakes basin, it might have been able to develop into a significant, competitive core economy. Insofar as any American policy thwarted Canada's core-state possibilities, it was not a policy embraced by the corporate lawyers, academic experts, and business lobbyists who advised the State Department after 1900. It was, instead, the more innocent diplomatic policy of the founding fathers. To make the case either way requires a more sophisticated and sustained economic analysis, but it is reasonable to suggest that this fundamental issue requires careful discussion before concluding that the United States prevented the emergence of a Canadian core state after 1911.

Related to this basic consideration is the role assigned to Canadian policies throughout the period. Canadian governments from 1867 onward, sometimes deliberately, sometimes as a by-product of other goals, encouraged much of the economic integration between the two countries. Even Macdonald's national policy, with its avowed purpose to develop Canada along east-west lines and thus forestall absorption into the United States, contributed to the long-term trends by encouraging American investment across the border.[68] Once the post–1921 Liberal governments of King and St. Laurent were in office, they encouraged U.S. investment down into the 1950s. Moreover, at the time it was rejecting American complaints about its pulpwood export policies in the 1920s, Canada also was encouraging U.S. investment in its papermaking business, to the point where 69 percent of the Canadian pulp and paper industry was controlled by Americans.[69] After King returned to power in 1935, he immediately called on Norman Armour, U.S. ambassador to Ottawa, and told him how anxious he was to take Canada down "the American road."[70] It is clear, too, that during the 1940s Canada participated willingly in military and defence integration with the United States.[71] Therefore, it is inaccurate to regard American policy as being imposed on an unwilling and unknowing country. If the United States is judged guilty of imperialism, then Canada must accept a ruling of contributory negligence.

Another important complication is the extent to which American-Canadian relations were shaped by factors outside the control or purview of officials of either government. Over the years a whole host of interactions have taken place between the United States and Canada that makes their relationship unusual. The intermingling of populations is a special conditioning factor.[72] Since the turn of the century, links have multiplied in a wide range of fields. The close banking ties between the two countries, established as early as 1910, had little to do with policy on either side of the border. In more recent years, ties have multiplied in the fields of business, labour, and professional organizations as well as in education, entertainment, media and communications, voluntary service agencies, and professional sports. In most cases of such bilateral relations, it can be assumed as axiomatic that those relations can be assessed best by examining the interactions of major government departments in terms of economic and strategic goals. In the case of America's relations with Canada, it might well be argued that the complex array of interactions below the national government level constitutes the real shapers of the relationship.

Such an hypothesis has been proposed by John H. Redekop who has invented the useful phrase "sub-system dominance" to describe the phenomenon.[73] There are some loose ends in the theory, particularly on where to draw the line between normal government interaction and the sub-system, but it is a timely reminder of the peculiarities of the

American-Canadian relationship. However, even if the sub-system model is given full weight, it will not alter the arguments advanced in this paper. Indeed, the multiplying of such ties fitted neatly and easily into the State Department's view that Canada should be integrated as variously and extensively as possible into the American economy and the American view of the world.

All this makes it tempting to view America's relationship to Canada as unplanned, but that leads to the kind of analysis that fails to get at the foundation of the U.S. response to Canada. It makes the relationship seem a benign growth, as though it were geographically determined and required the United States to have no need of a policy. But even amidst the sea of nineteenth-century rhetoric, the United States took some actions to push Canada in a particular direction, and from about 1906 onward, State Department and other administration officials advocated policies with specific goals in mind. These approaches rested on the old American attitude that Canada was part of the North American continent and that it ought to be "naturally" an economic extension of the United States. Because of its imperial connection, American administrations in the late nineteenth century were distrustful of Canada and refused to enter into close commercial ties for fear that Britain thereby would gain more influence in the U.S. economy. As the imperial factor was reduced, American officials concluded that Canada was beginning finally to follow the "natural" path of economic co-operation and integration. American policy after 1906 was designed to break the final links with Britain and bring Canada down this American road.

In so doing the United States was pursuing conventional foreign policy goals — protecting strategic interests, promoting exports and investments. But in the peculiar circumstances of the two countries, these conventional goals directly threatened to circumscribe Canadian autonomy. American officials ignored this adverse impact on Canadian nationalist values and aspirations. Just as Canada was a riddle to nineteenth-century Americans, so it remained a puzzle in the post–1945 years. State Department officials in 1951 believed that anti-American feelings in Canada were the product of a narrow intellectual circle with a disproportionate influence in the Department of External Affairs.[74] By 1958 a congressional delegation finally awoke to the fact that there were strong and pervasive anti-American values in Canada.[75] From that point on, administrations and Congress have tried to be more sensitive to Canadian nationalism, but as Mark MacGuigan, present secretary of state for external affairs, has noted recently, the United States reacts quite sharply to any Canadian efforts to reduce the integration already achieved in the fields of business and energy.[76] This failure to comprehend the impact of American policies on Canada justifies the use of the word "imperialism" but only if the special conditions of Canadian complicity are borne in mind.

The negative American response in 1934 to the Bennett government's complaint that Canada was suffering unfairly under prevailing economic relations and the determination from 1951 to 1953 not to permit autonomous Canadian control of the seaway both confirm that U.S. policy was to keep that country in a dependent relationship. In such policy formulations lies the imperialism of the American response to Canada. The United States always has been concerned lest Canada become "a producer rather than a consumer, and sufficient unto herself."[77] It had been concerned from the 1850s to the 1890s that Canada would be used as part of Britain's imperial designs. As President Taft explained in 1911, Canada's post–1900 prosperity might crystallize into a rival economic power.[78] The task was to make Canada accept the preponderant economic position of the United States on the continent and run its economy to meet the needs of that reality. Both advocates and opponents of reciprocal trade with Canada from 1854 to 1911 expected Canada, in the long run, to become part of the U.S.-controlled North American economy.[79] Taft assumed too easily that the course finally could be set in 1911. State Department officials in the 1920s and 1930s made clear their expectation that Canada should become an economic adjunct of the United States. The Truman administration, between 1947 and 1949 and from 1951 to 1953, was expressly interested in encouraging more integration of Canada into "our military industrial pattern."[80]

American imperialism in Canada was not only different from American economic expansion and its accompanying ideology in China or Latin America but also different from British imperial expansion in Africa, India, or even in Ireland because there was so much overlap in values, expectations, and general economic goals between the United States and Canada. These two circles intersected deeply. Here, then, is an exotic growth rather than an example of a common or garden variety of open-door imperialism. To repeat Ward's phrase of 1876, relations between the United States and Canada always have been of "an exceptional and peculiar character."

Notes

1. In his preface to Charles C. Tansill's *Canadian-American Relations 1875–1911* (New Haven, 1943), Shotwell wrote that the relationship presented an example "of the way in which statesmanship and common sense have ultimately built up a technique for the settlement of disputes . . . which can and should furnish a model to all the world." The final volume (and one that has stood the test of time) in the series, John B. Brebner's *North Atlantic Triangle:*

The Interplay of Canada, the United States and Great Britain (New York, 1945), lists all the monographs in the Carnegie project. See also Harold Josephson, *James T. Shotwell and the Rise of Internationalism in America* (Cranberry, N.J., 1975).

2. Carl C. Berger, "International, Continentalism and the Writing of History: Comments on the Carnegie Series on the Relations of Canada and the United States," *The Influence of the United States on Canadian Development*, ed. Richard A. Preston (Durham, N.C., 1972), 32–54. Other examples of works on this theme include Ian Lumsden, ed., *Close the 49th Parallel* (Toronto, 1970); D.W. Carr, *Recovering Canada's Nationhood* (Ottawa, 1971); Philip Sykes, *Sellout: The Giveaway of Canada's Resources* (Edmonton, 1973); John W. Warnock, *Partner to Behemoth: The Military Policy of Satellite Canada* (Toronto, 1970); and Abraham Rotstein and Gary Lax, eds., *Getting It Back: A Program for Canadian Independence* (Toronto, 1974).

3. Donald G. Creighton, *The Commercial Empire of the St. Lawrence* (Toronto, 1937). An earlier study, which was not part of the Carnegie series, had drawn attention to the economically competitive dimension to the relationship. See Hugh L. Keenleyside, *Canada and the United States: Some Aspects of their Historical Relationship* (New York, 1942).

4. For example, Thomas A. Bailey, *A Diplomatic History of the American People*, 10th ed. (Englewood Cliffs, N.J., 1980), 685–86.

5. William Appleman Williams, ed., *From Colony to Empire: Essays in the History of American Foreign Relations* (New York, 1972), 39–202. There are many books and articles that deal with aspects of American-Canadian relations. All books on Anglo-American diplomacy in the nineteenth century treat Canadian issues. Writings on the theme of manifest destiny invariably include discussion of U.S. expansion and its impact on Canada. See, for example, Frederick Merk, *Manifest Destiny and Mission in American History* (New York, 1963); Kendrick A. Clements, "Manifest Destiny and Canadian Reciprocity in 1911," *Pacific Historical Review* 42 (1973): 32–52; and James G. Snell, "The Frontier Sweeps Northwest: American Perceptions of the British-American Prairie West at the Point of Canadian Expansion," *Western Historical Quarterly* 11 (1980): 381–400. Excellent monographs such as Alvin Gluek, *Minnesota and Manifest Destiny* (Toronto, 1965); and Robin Winks, *Canada and the United States: The Civil War Years* (Baltimore, 1960) have analyzed aspects of American policy with regard to Canada. Donald F. Warner, *The Idea of Continental Union: Agitation for the Annexation of Canada to the United States 1849–1893* (Lexington, Ky., 1960), has provided an overview of annexationist sentiment, but there has been no systematic reappraisal of American goals.

6. Robert Hannigan, "Reciprocity 1911: Continentalism and American Weltpolitik," *Diplomatic History* 4 (Winter 1980): 1–18.

7. Ibid., 2–3, 18.

8. U.S. Congress, Senate, *Select Committee on Relations with Canada Submitted by Mr. Hoar, July 21, 1890*, 51st. Cong., 1st sess., 1890, Sen. Rept. 1530, pt. 2, 951–53 (hereinafter cited as Sen. Sel. Com., 1890). Poor was a lawyer and a railroad lobbyist. His 1888 testimony was reprinted in the 1890 report.

9. Ibid., 774–81; Francis Glenn to George Hoar, Brooklyn, 7 June 1890, ibid., 877–83. Glenn also wrote periodical articles on this theme. See *American Economist* 6 (31 Jan. 1890): 68–71.

10. U.S. Congress, Senate, *Report of J.W. Ward*, 62nd Cong., 1st sess., Sen. Doc. 80, 1361 (hereinafter cited as Ward Report, 1876).

11. John W. Foster to Michael Herbert, Washington, 24 Aug. 1892, U.S., Department of State, *Foreign Relations of the United States 1892* (Washington, 1893), 304 (hereinafter cited as *FRUS*).

12. U.S. Congress, Senate, *W.H. Derby Report 1867*, 62d Cong., 1st sess., Sen. Doc. 80, 992 (hereinafter cited as Derby Report, 1867); Derby Report, 1869, ibid., 1230, 1238; Rice Report, 1880, ibid., 1385; Sen. Sel. Com., 1890, 787, 886, 944. H.V. Poor told the 1890 committee that Britain's objective in Canada was "the erection on this continent of a new or second empire to hold in check the United States."

13. Israel T. Hatch to Howell Cobb, Secretary of the Treasury, 28 Mar. 1860, Sen. Doc. 80, 62d Cong., 1st sess., 652–55 (hereinafter cited as Hatch Report, 1860); J.M. Potter to W.H. Seward, Montreal, 1 Aug. 1865, *Despatches from U.S. Consuls*, Montreal 1850–1906, vol. 7 (Washington, 1959).

14. Testimony of Joseph Nimmo, Sen. Sel. Com., 1890, 891–95, 903, 911–13, 1229. Nimmo, regarded as an expert on Canadian transportation policies, argued that all the public monies spent by Ottawa proved that the Canadians were aimed at "commercial supremacy on this continent." Edward P. Crapol, *America for Americans: Economic Nationalism and Anglo-phobia in the Late Nineteenth Century* (Westport, Conn., 1972), gives a comprehensive account of this fear of British imperial designs from Canada to India.

15. Sen. Sel. Com., 1890, 1234.

16. Hatch Report, 1860, 655–56; Hatch Report, 1869, 1225; statement of Senator Justin S. Morrill, 1859, 62d Cong., 1st sess., Sen. Doc. 80, 1893. Chalfont Robinson, *History of the Reciprocity Treaty with Canada*, 62d Cong., 1st sess., Sen. Doc. 17, 38. This was reprinted from Robinson's 1903 study comparing the Canadian and Hawaiian reciprocity treaties. See Robinson, *A History of Two Reciprocity Treaties* (New Haven, 1903).

17. Sen. Sel. Com., 1890, 792–93; U.S., Congress, *House Committee on Foreign Affairs Report*, 3648, 49th Cong., 2d sess., 1742. This report charged that the Canadian interpretation of the 1818 Anglo-American treaty was "preposterous in view of international laws of community and good neighborhood."

18. Message from President Grover Cleveland with reference to intercourse between the United States and Canada, 23 Aug. 1888, U.S., Congress, H. Doc. 434, 50th Cong., 1st sess., 1633.

19. Sen. Sel. Com., 1890, 891–93.

20. President Harrison Message to Congress, 2 Feb. 1893, U.S. Congress, 62d Cong., 1st sess., Sen. Doc. 80, 1688.

21. Sen. Sel. Com., 1890, 921. Nimmo and other transportation lobbyists were trying to obtain U.S. government subsidies and relaxation of Interstate Commerce Commission regulations.

22. On 3 Feb. 1893 tolls were raised on American canals such as the St.

Mary's at the Sault. The Canadians immediately altered their policy, and on 21 Feb. 1893 the American increases were rescinded. In his message on this issue, President Harrison declared that Canadian policy had been in "flagrant disregard" of U.S. rights under the Treaty of Washington. See Sen. Doc. 80, 62d Cong., 1st sess., 1688–89.

23. Sen. Sel. Com., 1890, 886.

24. Reciprocity with Canada, Pt. 2, *Report of J.N. Larned on the State of Trade with the British North American Provinces (1871)*, U.S., Congress, H. Rep., 62d Cong., 1st sess., 1293. Larned described this economic antagonism as "an unfortunate dislocation which very seriously impairs the organization and operation of the industrial energies of the American continent."

25. Sen. Sel. Com., 1890, 971.

26. Ibid., 916. Winks, in his *Canada and the United States*, 375, points out that by 1871 there was no doubt that the United States was the dominant power on the continent. But Americans retained doubts about British commercial scheming and resented Canada's unwillingness to adjust to that basic geopolitical fact.

27. Ward Report, 1876, 1362.

28. Bradford Perkins, *The Great Rapprochement: England and the United States 1895–1914* (New York, 1968); and R.G. Neale, *Great Britain and the United States Expansion 1898–1900* (East Lansing, Mich., 1966) both emphasize that Britain made concessions to improve relations with the United States. On the British naval threat in the 1930s, see John Hickerson to Secretary of State Cordell Hull, Washington, 23 Mar. 1934, *FRUS* 1934, 1:972.

29. Report on Trade Conditions in Canada by Charles M. Pepper, Special Agent of the Department of Commerce and Labor, H. Doc. 408, 59th Cong., 1st sess., 1806–7, 1808–11, 1826–27.

30. Ibid., 1828–29, 1831–33, 1835.

31. Commercial Relations of the United States and Canada by John B. Osborne, Chief of the Bureau of Trade Relations at the State Department, 61st Cong., 3d sess., Sen. Doc. 862, 47–55.

32. Ibid.

33. Joseph F. Johnson, *Report on the Canadian Banking System*, Sen. Doc. 583, 61st Cong., 2d sess., 3, 9–10, 16.

34. Special Message of President William H. Taft to Congress, 26 Jan. 1911, 61st Cong., 3d sess., Sen. Doc. 787, v–vi. Richard C. Baker, *The Tariff Under Roosevelt and Taft* (Hastings, Neb., 1941), 149–62.

35. Address of President Taft to General Assembly of Illinois, 11 Feb. 1911, 61st Cong., 3d sess., Sen. Doc. 862, 39–41.

36. *Report of British Tariff Commission on Proposed Canada-U.S. Agreement*, Sen. Doc. 66, 62d Cong., 1st sess., 4.

37. M.C. Urquhart and K.A.H. Buckley, eds., *Historical Statistics of Canada* (Toronto, 1965), 169, 182. By 1930 the United States accounted for 61 percent of foreign investment in Canada; Britain's share was 36 percent. By 1914 Canada had replaced Mexico as the largest recipient of U.S. foreign investment.

38. U.S., Congress, H. Rept. 1039, 66th Cong., 2d sess., 1–2; Sen. Rept. 108, 67th Cong., 1st sess., 1–2; Secretary of State Charles E. Hughes to U.S. Chargé

in London Post Wheeler, 16 Aug. 1921, Ambassador George Harvey to Hughes, 12 Oct. 1921. Hughes to British Ambassador in Washington A.C. Geddes, 22 Oct. 1921, Geddes to Hughes, 10 Nov. 1921, *FRUS*, 1921, 1:299–306.

39. Hughes to British Chargé H.G. Chilton, 5 July 1923. Hughes to U.S. Consul General in Ottawa John G. Foster, 7 July 1923, memorandum of conversation of Hughes with Chilton, 16 July 1923, *FRUS*, 1923, 1:495–98.

40. W.H. Herridge to Hull, Washington, 14 Nov. 1934, *FRUS*, 1934, 1:849–57. Correspondence leading up to Herridge's critique appears in *FRUS*, 1933, 2:38–42; and *FRUS*, 1934, 1:845–48.

41. Herridge to Hull, Washington, 14 Nov. 1934, *FRUS*, 1934, 1:849–57.

42. Minister in Canada Warren Robbins to Hull, Ottawa, 21 Nov. 1934, ibid., 860–70; memorandum by Undersecretary of State William Phillips, Washington, 1 Dec. 1934, ibid., 871.

43. Robbins to Hull, Ottawa, 21 Nov. 1934, ibid., 860–70.

44. U.S. Chargé in Ottawa Pierre De L. Boal to Hull, Ottawa, 14 June, 1935, *FRUS* 1935, 2:51.

45. Dean G. Acheson to Harry S. Truman, Washington, 1 Oct. 1946 and 26 Oct. 1946, *FRUS*, 1946, 5:55; 57–58 concentrated on the importance of continuing co-operation in the defence field. See too R.D. Cuff and J.L. Granatstein, *Ties that Bind: Canadian-American Relations in War-time from the Great War to the Cold War* (Toronto, 1977); C.P. Stacey, *Arms, Men, and Governments: The War Policies of Canada 1939–1945* (Ottawa, 1970); and S.W. Dzuiban, *The Military Relations Between the United States and Canada 1939–1945* (Washington, 1959). The Joint Board on Defence was the most obvious example of closer defence ties.

46. Ray Atherton to Secretary of State George C. Marshall, Ottawa, 29 Oct. 1947, *FRUS*, 1947, 3:123, 127–28.

47. Memorandum by Associate Chief of the Division of Commercial Policy Woodbury Willoughby of discussions with Hector Mackinnon and John Deutsch, *FRUS*, 1947, 3:129.

48. Memorandum by Assistant Secretary of State for Economic Affairs Willard Thorp to Undersecretary Robert Lovett, Washington, 8 Mar. 1948, *FRUS*, 1948, 9:406.

49. Ibid.

50. President Franklin D. Roosevelt to Congress, 5 June 1941, U.S., Congress, 80th Cong., 2d sess. Sen. Rep. 810, 43. An executive agreement with Canada on the seaway had been made in 1941. It then became necessary to seek enabling legislation in Congress, but this was not achieved until 1952–1953.

51. President Truman's Message to Congress on the Seaway Project, 3 Oct. 1946, ibid., 100–1.

52. Acheson to Senate Subcommittee on Seaway Project, May-June 1947, ibid., 76.

53. By December 1951 the St. Lawrence Seaway Authority Act and the International Rapids Power Development Act had been approved by the Canadian Parliament.

54. Report of the National Security Resources Board, 24 April 1950, *The St.*

Lawrence Seaway Manual: A Compilation of Documents on the Great Lakes Seaway Project, U.S., Congress, 83d Cong., 2d sess., Sen. Doc. 165, 47–49, 54–55.

55. Testimony of Frank Nash, assistant secretary of defence, before House Committee on Public Works, 11 June 1953, ibid., 60–67.

56. Ibid., 28, 77–78.

57. Ibid.

58. Ibid., 76–78.

59. Ibid., 28. President Truman, in his message to Congress, 28 Jan. 1952, ibid., 115–19, emphasized "the immediate urgency of action" to prevent the United States from being "merely a customer of Canada's for use of the seaway after it is built."

60. Ibid., 147, 166, 201–3.

61. Ibid., 201–3.

62. A chronological account of the origins and development of the seaway appears in an appendix to *The St. Lawrence Seaway Manual.* See also William R. Willoughby, *The St. Lawrence Waterway* (Madison, Wis., 1941).

63. In his August 1888 message to Congress, for example, when President Cleveland proposed retaliation against Canada, he asserted that the United States always had been actuated by a "generous and neighborly spirit." The Canadians had not reciprocated but had "imposed" upon the United States with their troublesome and ambitious imperial plans. 50th Cong., 1st sess., House Ex. Doc. 434, 1629. Thus, if Canada acted in a "neighborly" way, it should drop all these "overreaching" schemes and adjust itself to the North American context controlled by the United States.

64. Memorandum by Minister of Embassy in Canada Don Bliss to Ambassador in Canada Stanley Woodward, Ottawa, 17 Apr. 1951; memorandum by Woodward, Ottawa, 18 April 1951, *FRUS*, 1951, 2:883–85.

65. Hannigan, "Reciprocity 1911," 2–3, 18. Hannigan's model is from Immanuel Wallerstein, *The Capitalist World Economy* (Cambridge, Mass., 1979).

66. Ibid.

67. A starting point for analysis of this complex question is *Approaches to Canadian Economic History*, ed. W.T. Easterbrook and M.H. Watkins (Toronto, 1967), which presents the traditional view that Canada's economic development depended on the production and export of staples. Most monographs emphasize a standard theme, the extent to which the state took the leading role in economic development policies. R.T. Naylor, *The History of Canadian Business 1867–1914*, 2 vols. (Toronto, 1975) argues that Canada never developed an industrial-capitalist base but remained a commercial-capitalist economy.

68. On this theme, see John Dales, *the Protective Tariff in Canadian Economic Development* (Toronto, 1966); Michael Bliss, "Canadianizing American Business: The Roots of the Branch Plant," in Lumsden, ed., *Close the 49th Parallel*; and Stephen Scheinberg, "Invitation to Empire: Tariffs and American Economic Expansion in Canada," *Business History Review* 47 (1973): 218–38.

69. Geddes to Hughes, 10 Nov. 1921, *FRUS*, 1921, 1:302–11.

70. Memorandum by Armour, Ottawa, 21 Sept. 1935; Armour to Hull, 25 Oct. 1935, *FRUS*, 1935, 2:27–29.

71. Cuff and Granatstein, *Ties that Bind*, 93–112.

72. Marcus L. Hansen and John B. Brebner, *The Mingling of the Canadian and American Peoples* (New Haven, 1940).

73. John H. Redekop, "A Reinterpretation of Canadian-American Relations," *Canadian Journal of Political Science* 9 (1976): 234–40, 242–43. A basic problem with Redekop's thesis is the contention that there was no "conscious American governmental policy" behind the forces of integration. This view only can be held by ignoring the evidence that American diplomats and officials had worked, since 1906, to fashion an integrated, continental relationship. On the other hand, the underlying trends and consequences of the sub-system meant that American continental policy could be sporadic without being ineffective. Too much continentalism would have led to intensified anti-American reaction in Canada.

74. Assistant Secretary of State George Perkins to Secretary of State Acheson, 12 June 1951, *FRUS*, 1951, 2:891–92.

75. U.S. Congress, *Report of the Special Study Mission of the House Committee on Foreign Affairs to Canada*, 85th Cong., 2d sess, House Rept. 1766.

76. Address by the Honorable Mark MacGuigan to the Centre for Inter-American Relations, New York, 30 Sept. 1981, *Canada: Department of External Affairs, Statements and Speeches*, No. 81/24, 3–5, 4–7. MacGuigan gave a friendly but forthright speech, criticizing "the litany of complaints" about the Foreign Investment Review Act of 1974 and defending Canada's new energy policy, which was seen in the United States as "short sighted" and "nationalist."

77. U.S. Congress, House Report Favoring New Trade Negotiations (1880), 62d Cong, 1st sess. Sen. Doc. 80, 1375. The committee believed freer trade would prevent Canada from becoming a "producer state." This was Taft's view in 1911.

78. Taft Special Message to Congress, 61st Cong., 3d sess., Sen. Doc, 787, vi.

79. For example, Sen. Sel. Com., 1890, Glenn testimony, and Ward Report, 1876.

80. Director of Office of British Commonwealth and Northern European Affairs Henry Labouisse to Assistant Secretary for European Affairs Perkins, Washington, 8 Nov. 1949, *FRUS*, 1949, 2:404–5. This was part of a memorandum on "Seven Pending Questions" in U.S.-Canadian relations. it seems incriminating as a statement of American goals; but once again a qualification must be made, for Labouisse was complaining that Congress and the Joint Chiefs were not co-operating in efforts to increase military procurement in Canada.

CANADA'S AMERICAN ALLIANCE†

JOHN ENGLISH AND NORMAN HILLMER

Though largely unwritten and informal, two great alliances dominate the landscape of Canadian history. In the years before the Second World War, Canadian external policy was shaped by the British connection; in the years after, the United States provided most of the problems and possibilities. The alliance with Great Britain grew out of Canada's colonial dependency and found concrete form and expression in the two world wars. An alliance with the United States took root prior to 1939, and was given moral, military and economic substance in the war and the difficult peace that followed.

The Anglo-Canadian alliance had sufficient resilience and importance to survive the decline of British power after 1945. When Canada did not go to Britain's side during the Suez crisis in 1956, however, the alliance became unhinged. Nor has the American alliance lasted, even though the North Atlantic Treaty Organization and the North American Air (now Aerospace) Defence Command remain intact. These formal agreements were the products of an age when Canadians and Americans combined to ward off the threat of international Communism. During the 1960s, the two nations began to differ on how this end might best be achieved. Canada did not join the United States in fighting the Vietnam War. Eventually Canada opposed its neighbour's war. The alliance, in the sense of the "special relationship" which North American politicians so often extolled in the 1940s and 1950s, came to an end. This state of mind (for that pre-eminently was

† John English and Norman Hillmer, "Canada's Alliances," *Revue Internationale d'Histoire Militaire* LIV (1982): 31–52.

what lay at the heart of Canada's alliances), this belief in the beneficence and responsibility of American power, passed with the Cold War generation. Further tensions in the relationship — economic, diplomatic, political and bureaucratic — ensured that the alliance would not be revived.

Canada's alliances have been much more than combinations for the purposes of military security — and much less. They have been less because defence was not always the issue; more because the Anglo-Canadian and Canadian-American relationships were so intense for Canadians, so sweeping in their range and implications. They were also very difficult to define. "Alliance" is a convenient label, and it has taken on many meanings. For supporters of intimate ties with Great Britain and the United States, "alliance" conveyed the strength and potential of these relationships; for critics, sceptics or agnostics, it illustrated the dangers of getting too close to a giant. The term had the additional advantage that it could be used by both groups to stress freedom of manoeuvre and to imply equality of standing.

Equality there never was. The intensity of emotion felt by Canadians towards the mother country and towards the United States, the sheer power of these relationships in Canadian life, thought and politics, was not reciprocated in Washington, New York, London or elsewhere in the United States and Great Britain. Canadians could not boast about their population or power, so they were apt to emphasize future greatness or current goodness. One observer directed a characteristically Canadian remark to the Americans in 1932: "Our material inferiority we will balance by our moral superiority . . . you are big, but we are better; you are great but we are good."[1] This equation might be good for Canadian self-esteem, but it did little to make life in an alliance with a big power any easier.

Such problems, of course, are far from unique. They are shared by other small powers in alliance politics, formal and informal. Robert Rothstein has written:

> An alliance with a single Great Power is undesirable. An alliance of several Small Powers and one Great Power is only marginally, if at all, an improvement. An alliance with several Great Powers is desirable but difficult to achieve. The only alternative left, if an alliance policy is still to be pursued, is an equal, multilateral alliance, that is, an alliance composed entirely of Small Powers.[2]

For all the benefits, and there have been many, Canada's "alliances" have placed the country in the most difficult position of all: the adherence of one minor power to the goals and causes and leadership of a single great power. Canadians were never uncritical or unrestrained in that adherence. The United States was sometimes available to off-set British influence — and vice versa — but the options in Canadian foreign policy have always been distinctly limited.

. . .

It would be incorrect to suggest that there was a Canadian-American alliance before World War II. Mackenzie King preferred the Anglo-Canadian alliance for all its problems, and he knew that most Canadians still accepted the obligations and benefits which that relationship bestowed. There was, nevertheless, a recognition in the interwar years that Canada and the United States shared a common territory and common purposes and that they were more alike than either Canadians or Americans had previously known or admitted. The United States was a proven good neighbour, a striking contrast to the warlike Europeans and a useful counterweight to the British connection, a connection which threatened to pull them into another great war. American President Franklin Delano Roosevelt, who was extremely popular in Canada, symbolized and stimulated such feelings.

Two weeks after his victory in the 1935 election, King visited Roosevelt to negotiate a reciprocal trade agreement. King got what he wanted, the agreement between Canada and the United States that had eluded governments, negotiators and propagandists since the demise of the Reciprocity Treaty of 1854–1866. And perhaps, King hoped, the leaders derived more from the meeting than the agreement itself. King found Roosevelt "exceedingly easy to talk with," and Roosevelt assured King that "it was great just to be able to pick up the telephone and talk to each other in just a few minutes."[3] Before this encounter, American presidents and Canadian prime ministers rarely talked at all. In the next four years King and Roosevelt met regularly and became increasingly close. Each sought the other's help in preventing another European conflict and in protecting his position if war should occur. From 1937 on, military leaders tried to talk and co-operate as never before, although without notable results. In August 1938 President Roosevelt, speaking at Kingston, Ontario, announced that "the people of the United States will not stand idly by if domination of Canadian soil is threatened by any other Empire."[4] These were the seeds of an alliance which World War II germinated.

The United States remained neutral after Canada and Britain went to war in September 1939, but the Americans were clearly sympathetic to the Anglo-Canadian cause. Two agreements made between Canada and the United States before America declared war in December 1941 are of particular importance. The first was the Ogdensburg Agreement of August 1940 which, inter alia, established a Permanent Joint Board on Defence to co-ordinate Canadian-American defence planning and commitments. The Hyde Park Agreement of April 1941 was the economic equivalent of Ogdensburg. Created to deal with a dollar exchange problem, the agreement linked the economies of the United States and Canada for the purpose of defeating Hitler. In Parliament, Mackenzie King did not hesitate to assign to the agreement a "permanent" significance in the relations between Canada and the United States.[5]

Wartime rhetoric often makes the ephemeral permanent. This time, however, rhetoric did become reality. It soon became clear that the postwar world would be dominated by the United States and that for Canada this would present special opportunities and problems. Graham Towers, the Governor of the Bank of Canada, explained the consequences of American predominance in October 1942: "The economic power of the United States will be so great that we shall in any case be subject to great and probably irresistible pressure to fall in line with their wishes regarding commercial policy."[6] Towers' comments reflect the sense of inevitability and of pragmatism with which many Canadians greeted the new realities of international relations. These were not the bonds of sentiment and loyalty which lay at the core of the Anglo-Canadian alliance. Polls did show, however, that Canadians and Americans thought that they were each other's "best friend," and that both publics shared a commitment to democratic values. Accordingly, there was support in both countries when Canada sought assurance in 1945 that the special relationship of the wartime years would continue in peacetime.

When the opportunity came for a bilateral military alliance, however, the Canadians hesitated. In 1946 the Canada–United States Military Co-operation Committee proposed that the two nations sign a defence pact to counter the threat of a Russian attack on North America. Although he was genuinely fearful of the Soviets, Mackenzie King was suspicious of the Americans as well. The reluctance also appeared in the economic area. When some of King's advisers recommended a customs union with the United States in 1948, he strongly objected. While recognizing the new demands of the Cold War upon the Canadian economy, King refused to accept that either military or economic exigencies should compel Canada to enter an economic union with the United States. His opposition was steadfast:

> I [King wrote in his diary] would never cease to be a Liberal or a British citizen and if I thought there was a danger of Canada being placed at the mercy of powerful financial interests in the United States, and if that was being done by my own party, I would get out and oppose them openly.[7]

There was no need to campaign. King's successor, Louis St. Laurent, had little enthusiasm for the proposal. For that matter, neither did many Americans.[8]

In earlier times Canada had turned to Europe for protection from its enemy, the United States. In the postwar period, Canada once again employed Europe to maintain its distinctiveness from its ally, the United States. When Canada did not proceed with the customs union, the government gave as its excuse the discussions for a North Atlantic security pact. In fact, as Professor Eayrs has pointed out, a multilateral treaty was seen in Ottawa

> as a device for reducing the pressure of the Pentagon. A United States administration pledged to co-ordinate its defence policies with those of allies in Western Europe as well as those of its ally in North America would be less likely than a United States administration going it alone to lean as heavily upon its northern neighbour. Canada, allied to the United States within the North Atlantic coalition, would have more room in which to breathe and to manoeuvre than would be hers if locked into a stifling bilateral embrace.[9]

No nation worked more energetically for the North Atlantic Pact than Canada. Furthermore, to the irritation of the United States, Canada tried to expand the pact beyond the purely military. It succeeded in persuading the North Atlantic Treaty signatories to include an article calling for a broader alliance which extended to economic and cultural co-operation. Even so, the North Atlantic Treaty Organization (NATO), created in 1949, soon became for Canada little more than a North American military guarantee to Western Europe.

The Korean War spurred rearmament. In December 1950 it was announced that Canada's 1951–1952 defence budget would be three times the size of the previous year's. Despite this Asian war, in which Canada participated with the United States under the auspices of the United Nations, the focus of Canadian and American attention and defence expenditure remained upon Western Europe. J.W. Pickersgill, the influential prime ministerial confidant, counselled St. Laurent in September 1950 that "to maintain reasonably good relations with the United States and to satisfy a pretty wide section of people at home, some kind of [European] undertaking will be unavoidable."[10]

Pickersgill urged concentration on the air force, and his advice was followed. In February 1951, defence minister Brooke Claxton announced that the Canadian government would commit an air division to the defence of Western Europe. This contribution, as well as that of a ground brigade, was motivated not only by fears for European security but also by a Canadian desire to have its voice heard in NATO councils and in Washington. For Canadian political and military officials had begun to worry about the other obligations which the

United States had assumed under the guise of its NATO responsibilities. The NATO agreement had given the Americans the responsibility for strategic air operations, leading them to request the use of Canadian bases for the launching of retaliatory atomic attacks on the Soviets. The Canadians realized that this request meant the stationing of nuclear weapons and American personnel on Canadian soil. It also implied that, in times of crisis, Ottawa would not always control the operation of American men and weapons in Canada. This fact became especially troubling in 1954, when the Eisenhower administration adopted the policy of "massive retaliation": the United States would reply to its enemy by using, in secretary of state John Foster Dulles' words, "a great capacity to retaliate, instantly, by means and at places of our choosing." Canada's secretary of state for external affairs publicly expressed his concern: "From our point of view, it is important that the 'our' in this statement should mean those who have agreed, particularly in NATO, to work together and by collective action, to prevent war or, if that should fail, to win it."[11] Lester Pearson's remarks reflected his private fears about American military impetuosity and the desire to view and control the American military alliance within a broader North Atlantic framework.

Such comments were seldom made publicly. Nor were there many other Canadians who criticized American foreign and defence policy during the mid-1950s. More often journalists and analysts depicted the United States as a chivalrous giant boldly and generously bearing the burdens of free world defence. The country "was perhaps as relaxed in an alliance as it has ever been before or since."[12] In 1956, when the USSR tested an intercontinental ballistic missile and brutally crushed the Hungarian rebellion, Canadians clung ever more tightly to their neighbour and ally. Nineteen fifty-six, it is true, was also the year of a pipeline debate which aroused much concern about the American economic presence in Canada. There were some bitter words about American economic aggressiveness uttered in the House of Commons and elsewhere, but there was no repudiation of the Canadian-American alliance. James Eayrs solemnly warned Canadians that they might be forced to give up their independence in the face of compelling international danger. At such moments sovereignty would become "supremely irrelevant."[13]

In this atmosphere, Canada's willingness to permit the United States to build and man radar stations across the Canadian North is understandable. Equally understandable is the alacrity with which the new Diefenbaker government, despite some anti-American rhetoric in the election campaign, entered into the North American Air Defence Command (NORAD) in 1957. This compact made explicit the symbiotic relationship of Canadian and American air defence. It also meant much more, and Diefenbaker made commitments whose impact he did not appreciate. Perhaps he can be excused, for many aspects of the agreement and of the events which followed remain controversial today. For our purposes, NORAD's importance lies in the integration of the military command structure which it achieved and the decay of the Canadian-American alliance to which it soon contributed.

NORAD had come at a moment when Canada was at a crossroads in deciding not simply a military strategy but also a national direction. Canada's new supersonic fighter, the AVRO Arrow, represented a major technological innovation and national achievement, but it was simply too expensive for the Canadian forces alone. The government cancelled it. Aware of its large air defence responsibilities, the government decided to buy Bomarc missiles and F–101 aircraft from the United States as an alternative. The United States made such decisions easier in 1958 by entering a Defence Development and Production Sharing Agreement which in effect gave Canadian manufacturers access to the United States market. The price was considerable integration with, and dependence upon, that market.

The Bomarc presented the Canadian government with a serious problem which it seemed only dimly aware of when it first bought the missiles. To be effective Bomarcs needed nuclear warheads, and these were unacceptable to Diefenbaker's external affairs minister, Howard Green. Defence minister Douglas Harkness, on the other hand, wanted the weapons and believed that Canada was obligated to accept them because of its NATO and NORAD commitments. Compromise within the cabinet became impossible. As Diefenbaker procrastinated, the Liberal opposition contented itself with denouncing the government's division and indecision. Diefenbaker began to blame the United States for the quandary in which he found himself. President John F. Kennedy responded by showing his personal dislike for Diefenbaker all too obviously. When the Canadian prime minister refused to give automatic support to Kennedy during the Cuban Missile Crisis of October 1962, the United States could not contain its anger within normal diplomatic boundaries.

In early January 1963 the retiring NATO commander, American general Lauris Norstad, told the press at Ottawa airport that Canada was not keeping its promises to the alliance. The leader of the opposition, Lester Pearson, seized the moment, announcing that the Liberal party, if elected, would accept nuclear weapons. For Pearson's critics, it was a betrayal of a distinguished career in the search for peace. In the uproar which followed, the divisions within the Conservative party widened. The United States State Department then issued an extraordinary statement which took direct issue with the prime minister's explanation of the nature of the crisis. Diefenbaker's credibility crumbled; so did his government. The Liberals won the election which followed in April 1963. In the bitter campaign, Diefenbaker charged that the State Department and the American president were working to defeat him. The Liberals and most commentators ridiculed Diefenbaker's charges, arguing that the question was one of keeping commitments. Journalist Pierre Berton, for example, justified his support of Pearson's nuclear stand on this basis: "To earn a reputation we must stop the pretence, the indecision, the fence straddling, the welshing and the double-dealing which characterized our relations with our partners. If this election proves anything it proves that anti-Americanism is finished as a political issue. We have cast our lot with this continent for better or worse and the people know it."[14]

Pierre Berton was soon most unwilling to accept that Canada had cast its lot with such finality. Vietnam intervened, and anti-Americanism abounded in the public utterances of Canadians. In 1965 a former American ambassador to Canada, Livingston Merchant, and a former Canadian ambassador to the United States, Arnold Heeney, published a report entitled "Principles for Partnership," which declared that differences between the two countries should be settled in private. This recommendation, which described what had normally taken place in the 1940s and 1950s, provoked a strong negative reaction. Was Canada to remain silent while the United States destroyed Vietnam? Canadians increasingly thought it should not.

Canada's reservations about the United States war in South-East Asia were first expressed privately, in the time-honoured style of quiet diplomacy that Merchant and Heeney had celebrated. Prime Minister Pearson and external affairs minister Paul Martin initially questioned only the method and the scale of the American intervention. Their views were not taken seriously in Washington. In April 1965, therefore, Pearson went to Temple University in Philadelphia and publicly called upon the United States to halt the bombing of North Vietnam in order that the possibility of negotiations might be explored. This tentative move so angered president Lyndon Johnson that he summoned Pearson to his Camp David retreat and berated him in a fashion that shocked the Canadian leader. Although Pearson and Johnson both subsequently tried to mend their personal relations, they were unsuccessful. Canada's influence in Washington was much diminished, and the government's general support of American policies in South-East Asia was further weakened. In September 1967 Martin called for an unconditional halt to American bombing. The government of Pierre Elliot Trudeau, elected in 1968, sustained the criticism. In 1971 and 1972 Canada condemned the escalation of the air war. On 5 January 1973, external affairs minister Mitchell Sharp led parliament in adopting a nearly unanimous motion deploring America's Vietnam policy.

Canadians and Americans were growing apart in other ways. Canadians became more troubled about United States influence upon their economy,[15] and their governments moved cautiously to limit their reliance. Economic nationalism expressed itself in the federal budget of 1963 and in the Watkins and Gray Reports, which recommended sterner controls upon American investment. In August 1971, President

Nixon announced his "new economic policy" and imposed a ten percent import surcharge, refusing to exempt his country's major trading partner. For the leader of Canada's Conservative party, it was all too much. The old assumptions were comfortable but false: "Canada is out in the cold as far as the special privileged relationship . . . is concerned."[16] Nixon's action, in the more measured words of the Canadian foreign secretary, "threw into sharp focus the problem of Canada's vulnerability which has been a source of growing preoccupation to Canadians in recent years."[17]

It was to reduce that vulnerability that Mitchell Sharp spoke in 1972 of a "third option" in Canadian-American relations, "a comprehensive long-term strategy to develop and strengthen the Canadian economy and other aspects of its national life."[18] A Foreign Investment Review Agency (FIRA) was set up in 1974 to determine if foreign investment served the national interest; a federal government oil company, Petro-Canada, was established the next year; from 1976 the government allowed tax deductions only for advertising on Canadian radio and television stations, thus curtailing the use for that purpose of American border stations by Canadian businesses. The third option, admittedly, was honoured more in the breach than in the observance. This was hardly surprising, given the size, importance and proximity of the United States and the complexity of the relationship. The significance of the third option lay in its rhetoric and the policy direction it espoused. Both would have been unthinkable in even a demi-official foreign policy document in the heyday of the alliance — only a few years before.

In the 1980s the rhetoric grew more heated, and the policy direction more pronounced. Trudeau had fallen from power in 1979, but his return in 1980 led to stronger "Canadianization" programs, especially in the crucial area of energy. The popular National Energy Program, calling for fifty percent Canadian ownership of the petroleum industry by 1990, was directed against the United States and its massive oil companies. The strengthening of FIRA was rumoured. Washington reacted angrily. Congressmen threatened retaliation. American investors hit back by limiting the flow of new investments to Canada. American newspapers carried regular tales of a Canada no longer reasonable and neighbourly. Even that traditional champion of Canadian interests, the *New York Times*, no longer professed support for "dear Canada."[19] There were serious disagreements over the environment, fisheries, communications and wider questions of foreign policy. Hostile bureaucracies faced one another with a "philosophic self-righteousness that leaves neither side particularly inclined toward compromise."[20] The "differences that strain Canadian-American relations today," the historian H.V. Nelles argued, "are more profound than at any time in living memory."[21] Obviously Canadians agreed. In 1966 only eight percent thought Canada and the

United States were "getting further apart." In 1970 that figure was 28 percent. By 1976 it was 38 percent. In 1982 it is a whopping 49 percent.[22] Another national poll showed that the same number — 49 percent — had little or no confidence in the ability of the United States to handle current world problems.[23]

The special relationship had clearly ended. Ties with the United States would remain of necessity (in Trudeau's words) broad and deep and close,[24] but the relationship of the future would not be characterized by the regard and understanding of the past. The decline of American power relative to its allies and competitors, the winding down of the Cold War, an increasing Canadian resentment of American influence on the Canadian economy, and a renewed scepticism about the values of American society and about the good will inherent in American foreign policy aims all contributed to the fading of the alliance. Perhaps fear — of military defeat, of economic depression, of cultural immaturity — had played too large a part in creating the ties which bound the two nations.

For many Canadians a moral twilight had always surrounded the Canadian-American relationship. During the Cold War Canadians had seen mainly the light; in the 1960s the darkness came suddenly. Novelist Mordecai Richler reflected the change of atmosphere. At one time, Richler admitted in 1968, he welcomed "the day when [the frontiers] might disappear and we would join fully in the American adventure." No longer would he rejoice: "Vietnam and Ronald Reagan, among other things, have tempered my enthusiasm. Looked at another way, yes, we *are* nicer. And suddenly that's important."[25] In 1968 Ronald Reagan was governor of California; today he is, for Canadians, a controversial American president. Vietnam has taken its place (not simply for Canadians, of course) in a lengthy compendium — from Dallas through Watergate to Abscam — which has "stripped America of its essential illusion that invincible power and limitless wealth were its God-given instruments for the creation of a great society in a better world." "How strange and unfamiliar it is," the political commentator Dalton Camp concluded, "to look upon the Great Republic without awe, admiration, or envy, but with unease, dismay, and perhaps pity."[26]

As the relationship with the United States became even more difficult, the Trudeau government was bringing the Canadian constitution home from Great Britain, where it had resided since the beginning of the new nation in 1867. The constitutional issue precipitated a lively debate, at home and in Britain, that had more to do with domestic than foreign policy. Still, it was a reminder, and not always a happy one, of the once dominant British aspects of Canadian history. The ending of one of the last formal ties with the mother country was also an apt symbol for the 1980s: for good or ill, Canada and Canadians were more on their own than they had ever been.

Notes

1. Carl Berger, *The Writing of Canadian History: Aspects of English-Canadian Historical Writing* (Toronto, 1976), 139.

2. Robert Rothstein, *Alliance and Small Powers* (New York, 1968), 127.

3. W.L. Mackenzie King, Diary, 8 Nov. 1935.

4. See Robert Bothwell and Norman Hillmer, *The In-Between Time: Canadian External Policy in the 1930s* (Toronto, 1975), 145, 166–170.

5. Canada, House of Commons, *Debates*, 28 Apr. 1941.

6. "Postwar Reconstruction and Relief," *Bank of Canada Papers*, file 220–25, Graham Towers to Norman Robertson, 6 Oct. 1942.

7. J.W. Pickersgill and D.F. Forster, eds., *The Mackenzie King Record* (Toronto, 1960–1970), IV:273.

8. Recent research has shown that the Canadians exaggerated the United States' zeal for closer military and economic ties and that Professor Creighton's claim that there was an "intimate military alliance" made between the United States and Canada in 1946 and 1947 is misleading. Creighton's account is based on a misinterpretation of American motives and Canadian responses. See Joseph Jockel, "The United States and Canadian Efforts at Continental Air Defence, 1945–1947" (Ph.D. diss., Johns Hopkins University, 1978); Donald Creighton, *The Forked Road: Canada 1939-1957* (Toronto, 1976), 138–40.

9. James Eayrs, *In Defence of Canada: Growing Up Allied* (Toronto, 1980), 66.

10. Ibid., 219.

11. L.B. Pearson, "A Look at the 'New Look,'" Department of External Affairs, *Statements and Speeches* 54/16. See also John W. Holmes, *The Shaping of Peace: Canada and the Search for World Order* (Toronto, 1979–1982), II:200–1.

12. Holmes, *The Shaping of Peace*, II:221.

13. James Eayrs, *Northern Approaches: Canada and the Search for Peace* (Toronto, 1961), 15–16.

14. *Maclean's Magazine*, 6 Apr. 1963.

15. See the opinion poll evidence cited in Mitchell Sharp, "Canada-U.S. Relations: Options for the Future," *International Perspectives* (Autumn 1972): 11.

16. John Saywell, ed., *Canadian Annual Review of Politics and Public Affairs 1971* (Toronto, 1972), 245–6.

17. Sharp, "Options for the Future," 8.

18. Ibid., 1.

19. H.V. Nelles, "The Unfriendly Giant," *Saturday Night*, February 1982, 28.

20. *The Globe and Mail*, 13 Feb. 1982.

21. Nelles, "The Unfriendly Giant," 28.

22. *The Citizen*, 24 Feb. 1982. Only eighteen percent thought that the two countries were drawing closer together, half the 1966 figure.

23. *The Citizen*, 10 Apr. 1982.

24. Saywell, *Politics and Public Affairs*, 248.

25. "The North American Pattern," in *The New Romans: Candid Canadian Opinions of the U.S.*, ed. A.W. Purdy (Edmonton, 1968), 15.

26. Dalton Camp, "End of the Dream," *Saturday Night*, November 1980, 50.

A SWEET LITTLE COUNTRY†

ROBERT BOTHWELL AND JOHN KIRTON

In January 1965 the governments of the United States and Canada released a report, entitled "Principles for Partnership," designed to articulate a framework of common values, precepts and projects which the leaders and citizens of both countries could readily and equally accept as a valid expression of their past reality, present condition and future aspirations. Prepared by two-time U.S. ambassador to Canada Livingston Merchant, with the assistance of two-time Canadian ambassador to the United States A.D.P. Heeney, the report, in both its preparation and substance, highlighted a conception of the relationship founded on a trilogy of enduring mutual interests, substantive integration and procedural informality. While recognizing the divergences bred by America's predominant global power, Canada's distinctive relations with Britain, the Commonwealth and France, and America's disproportionate continental impact on Canadian society, the report stressed the overriding areas of commonality, friendship and partnership between the two countries. In order to render their unique and growing interdependence "as mutually rewarding as it is

† Robert Bothwell and John Kirton, " 'A Sweet Little Country': American Attitudes Towards Canada, 1925–1963," *Queen's Quarterly* 90, 4 (Winter 1983): 1078–1102. This study forms part of the University of Toronto's Centre for International Studies project on Canada-United States Relations. The authors gratefully extend their appreciation to the Donner Canadian Foundation for financial support, and to U.S. officials dealing with Canada who generously co-operated in a program of interviews conducted in Washington in December 1978 and at other locations on subsequent dates.

inevitable," it called for an extension of their partnership into several fields, and forwarded specific proposals for joint bodies and more integrative arrangements in a host of specific areas. And to reinforce the informal intimacy that propelled such a process, it proposed a specific regime of consultation, grounded in the principle that "wherever possible, divergent views between the two governments should be expressed and if possible resolved in private, through diplomatic channels."[1]

Over the next few years, and to the surprise of its authors, the report struck many Canadians as a profound affront. Preoccupied with the excesses of American involvement in Indochina, George Ball's declaration of the inevitability of Canada's continental absorption, and nationalist stirrings in Ontario and Quebec, these Canadians viewed "Principles for Partnership" as at best the obsolescent liturgy of a bygone era, or at worst, a somewhat insensitive declaration of long-standing, unilateral American designs. In notable contrast, knowledgeable Americans viewed this affirmation of partnership as the proud culmination of an enlightened approach that they had struggled during the previous four decades, with the aid of sympathetic Canadians and in the face of considerable internal difficulties, to enshrine as the dominant American attitude toward Canada.

It is a mark of the evolving cadence of Canadian-American relations that both perspectives were fundamentally correct. The concepts expressed under the rubric of "Principles for Partnership" represented the clearest expression, most precise codification and most self-confident assertion of a basic American attitude toward Canada that had developed within U.S. officialdom since the establishment of official bilateral diplomatic relations in the mid 1920s. During that time this attitude had continually to compete with three alternative tendencies in American foreign policy which cast Canada as a minor adjunct, respectively, of America's defiant and distrustful isolationist stance, the United States' own special relationship with the United Kingdom and the Atlantic world, and its geopolitically-grounded, yet crusading attempt to ensure international order and the predominance of American values throughout the globe. In its quest for dominance during its first two decades, the basic American concept of Canada largely succeeded, through the skill and persistence of its most committed adherents, in creatively mobilizing isolationism's stress on a unique, model North Americanness, and subsequently Atlanticism's emphasis on special relationships among Anglo-Saxon democracies, to achieve a precarious paramountcy in the period immediately after World War II. However, the intensifying preoccupations and hardening demands of America's assertive globalism during the ensuing decade and a half provided this basic attitude with a steadily diminishing scope for a convergent synthesis or independent expression. And even more fundamentally, this globalist tendency provided a powerful constraint on the ability of the basic American attitude toward Canada to absorb in full measure the belief in a more genuine partnership which Canada's own thrust toward global involvement, continental assertiveness and national confidence bred.

The basic official American attitude toward Canada, as defined and developed during the first quarter-century following the establishment mentmentof U.S. diplomatic relations in Canada, stemmed largely from the ideas and influence of a single individual.[2] Jack D. Hickerson, a Texan who entered the American consular service in 1920 with the expectation of specializing in Latin America, received orders in July 1925 to report to the American consulate general in Ottawa. Except for the climate, it was a gratifying improvement over the Brazilian backwoods, the more so because the miniature Canadian capital was on the point of launching itself on the international scene as the centre of a newly autonomous Dominion of the British Commonwealth. In defining initial American perceptions and policy toward Canada, Hickerson was heavily influenced by his very close working relationship with the American consul general, Colonel Foster, a veteran of Ottawa for twenty-four years and of Canada since the nineteenth century. Foster, a conservative Republican, liked Canadians and felt at home in Ottawa, which was, after all, just over a hundred miles from his home in the border town of Derby Line, Vermont. He became a minor expert in Canadian politics, relying on a network of friendships to maintain a political information service that was second to none.

As a good Republican, Foster had naturally seconded President Taft's 1911 reciprocity project with Canada, and was disappointed when the election of that year defeated the Laurier Liberals who had supported it. The event was thoroughly reported at the time, but, more importantly, it lived on in Foster's anecdotage and was passed on in vivid detail to his young assistant, Hickerson. The 1911 election, Hickerson learned, was a scandal in which untruth, fuelled by irrational Canadian nationalism, had prevailed. It was in the Canadians' best interest to get free trade, and it was a pity that since 1911, despite the liberal American tariff of 1913, they had done nothing to forward the cause. Foster recognized the vast disparity between the United States and Canada that had provoked Canadian uneasiness with reciprocity, and he kept abreast of the times, predicting in the mid-1920s that American radio and advertising would become bones of contention in Canadian-American relations as the smaller country sought to avoid being overwhelmed by the larger. But although Canadian restrictive actions would be understandable, Foster nevertheless believed that they too were not in Canada's longer-term interest.

Hickerson willingly absorbed Foster's reading of Canadian history and the underlying values of informality, integration and mutual interest and added to this legacy some ideas and experiences of his own.

Believing that it was out of the question that the United States would wish to dominate or absorb Canada and that it was both better and politically inevitable that both countries follow separate destinies, Hickerson was free to forge the intimate contacts that served as the primary requisite of a much more closely associated regime. As an American diplomat (or the closest thing to it in Ottawa in 1925), Hickerson found that he had access to Canada's highest political circles, where he developed knowledge of the Prime Minister, Mackenzie King, and a friendship with King's deputy, the Under Secretary of State for External Affairs, O.D. Skelton. Skelton soon felt at ease with his young American friend, lunching with him at the Château Laurier and discussing with him his plans for a professional Canadian foreign service. Hickerson obliged with information and advice, which Skelton gravely accepted, although he may not have followed it.

Before Hickerson left Ottawa in 1927 he had transferred from the consular service to the diplomatic corps, the American consulate general had become the American legation, and the first of Skelton's professional recruits had begun arriving in Ottawa. Transferring back to Washington, to serve as the State Department's first Canadian desk officer in the Bureau of European Affairs, Hickerson met more of Skelton's "boys," since the Department of External Affairs used the nearby Washington legation for seasoning its recruits, especially during Washington's abominable summers when no business was transacted and they could do no harm. Over the years, Hickerson came to know all Canadian professional counterparts until the expansion of World War II made it physically impossible, but in particular he came to know and esteem the burgeoning "stars" of the Canadian foreign service, Lester Pearson, Hume Wrong and Norman Robertson. As a result, Hickerson's range of Canadian contacts was second to none in Washington, and he was regularly employed to advise and guide American efforts on such important bilateral matters as trade negotiations and the St. Lawrence Seaway.

Nevertheless, Hickerson's work was to some extent circumscribed by three competing tendencies in American foreign policy, each of which had a specific application to Canada.[3] The first and most forceful competitor prior to 1941 was American isolationism, aimed at minimizing entangling relationships between the United States and the outside world which might embroil the republic in the perfidies of European politics and drag it back into another world war. Political intimacy with Canada was therefore precluded until, after 1935, President Roosevelt began exchanging views and confidences with Mackenzie King.[4] Even then, however, the two men did not dare reveal to the world or to public opinion how well they got on together, or how much they agreed about the nature of world politics in the pre-war decade. Hickerson, like a good professional, swallowed his private convictions on the need for a strong League of Nations and vigorous

American internationalism, as did his Canadian counterparts, circumscribed and muzzled by Mackenzie King's cautious conduct of foreign policy. Other American diplomats, slightly older, had less trouble with isolationism. A man like J.P. Moffat, American minister to Canada between 1940 and 1943 and before that consul general in Australia, had been perceived as both unsympathetic and even anti-British in the feverish pre-war climate. But for Moffat isolationism was second nature, and his rigorous professionalism would have made the expression of any other attitude almost unthinkable. For Hickerson, it meant that dreams of a better world order were something to be indulged outside office hours as he and his Canadian friends reviewed the frustration of the diplomatic life.[5]

The second competing tendency which Hickerson encountered emanated from American global preoccupations which necessarily transcended the parochial concerns dominating Canadian-American relations. The broader horizons of an ascending power bred in many quarters a lack of warmth in dealing with the Canadians, an indifference to Canadian perspectives and problems, and a tendency to devote the best and most competent of American representatives to other, more significant parts of the world. Despite Roosevelt's friendship with Mackenzie King, the American legation in Ottawa was used, during the thirties, as a dumping ground for a succession of political appointees that included the President's cousin, Warren Delano Robbins, his former secretary of commerce, Daniel Roper, and James Cromwell, husband of the richest woman in the world. It is true that for two and a half years, from 1935 to 1938, Roosevelt also sent a skilled professional, Norman Armour, to preside in Ottawa and his service coincided with the negotiation of several important trade treaties. Yet the decidedly mixed record of Roosevelt's appointees reinforced the incompetence of certain other American agencies, notably the uniquely parochial Department of Commerce, and the indifference of such personalities as Undersecretary of State Sumner Welles.[6]

Indifference, however, sowed the seeds of future influence. Although it was recognized, in Ottawa and Washington, that the Canadian minister in the United States from 1935 to 1939, Sir Herbert Marler, was a bad but politically necessary steward, the general deployment by Canada of its best resources in the American relationship and the preoccupation of U.S. officials at senior levels with other matters underscored the centrality of Hickerson as the principal continuator and formulator of American policy toward Canada. His beliefs became the foundation for action at a later time.

The third competing tendency in American foreign policy was founded on an instinct to see the republic's relationship with Canada firmly derived from the latter's membership in the British Commonwealth. Institutionally, Canada was firmly placed inside State's Bureau of European Affairs, where Hickerson adamantly believed it belonged, and, inside the bureau, in the division of British Commonwealth affairs, which Hickerson came to head. Canada's British identity usually had negative connotations: Sumner Welles resisted and eventually overcame the proposal that Canada should become a member of the Pan-American Union, a proposal which Hickerson favored because it would take some of the heat off the United States. Yet while this view of Canada as a passive agent of British influence in an American-dominated hemisphere continued to exercise much of its traditional influence, it increasingly provided America's embryonic Canadianists with concepts they could employ in their cause. To be sure, at the apex of the U.S. government little came of Roosevelt's unfounded belief that Mackenzie King might serve as a conduit for the injection of the president's ideas into the inner circles of the British Empire's policy-making. Yet the triangular Anglo-American-Canadian trade negotiations of 1937–1938 demonstrated how closely linked the destinies of the three countries really were. The relative success of the trade talks not only confirmed Hickerson's argument that Canada belonged in a North Atlantic context, but also strengthened his friendships with his Canadian counterparts and reinforced the informal procedures which he believed served both countries best.[7]

Through such techniques, Hickerson was able to maintain some elements of his favoured approach in the face of formidable obstacles, but also to forward its particular tenets and recruit internal, if somewhat unknowing, adherents to the cause. The belief of the Secretary of State, Cordell Hull, in free trade and the messianism of an assistant secretary, Adolph Berle, provided a foundation for blunting American reaction to the Ottawa trade agreements of 1932, for the tripartite agreements of 1937–1938, and for persistent attempts to work out Canadian-American grievances. In the separate work of the International Joint Commission, Secretary Kellogg's and Roosevelt's priority interest in developing a St. Lawrence Seaway and Roosevelt's frequent meetings with King, there emerged movement toward joint functional co-operation on a special, bilateral, integrated basis, common development projects on a massive scale, and a shared perspective on political events abroad. And through arrangements with Canadian diplomats, such as what was virtually a joint intelligence operation to fathom what King and Roosevelt might have said to one another privately over drinks in the president's study after dinner, Hickerson solidified his close personal relationship with Canadian figures such as Pearson and Wrong.

The advent of World War II intensified this pre-war pattern, yet added new dimensions to the original attitudes which Hickerson and Foster had established. Although east coast Americans, and particularly those in government, sympathized with the allied cause, and hence with Canada, the United States remained officially neutral and the political divergence between America and its northern neighbour became proportionately greater than before. The entry of the United States into the war in December 1941, while ending the dominance of this isolationist tendency, replaced it, with a vengeance, with a globalist focus in which Canada had little visibility. Once ensconced in his role as supreme warlord, President Roosevelt had little time and less inclination to listen to Canadian perspectives and complaints. And Prime Minister King, who understood this, kept his contacts with Roosevelt to a level of trivial joviality that placed no strains on his access to the White House, and the symbolic benefits which it brought at home.[8] Secretary of State Hull, lost in a world where free trade was temporarily an irrelevance, sank into an ill-tempered insignificance. Jack Hickerson, to whom Canadian diplomats brought their complaints about Canada's exclusion from allied strategic boards, gave a sympathetic hearing, but chose not to employ his close relationship with Hull or his contacts at the White House in the crusade for a more pronounced Canadian voice.[9]

In a global war, the Americans explained, Canada might well be a valued ally, but she could not match the contribution of the Great Powers, and "equality of sacrifice" in bilateral defence production constituted no ticket of admission into the Anglo-American Combined Boards or the Dumbarton Oaks conference which charted the future United Nations Organization. The myopia engendered by America's crusading globalism and the pervasive argument that Canadian membership would merely lead beleaguered and busy Great Power leaders to face a host of unmanageable Commonwealth and Latin American demands was reflected in, and compounded by, the renewed tendency of an undermanned U.S. diplomatic corps to send relatively innocent if not outright incompetent officers to Ottawa, below the level of minister. The American legation in the capital ambled on in a leisurely way — lively at the top, but increasingly paralyzed by a pleasant inertia in its lower limbs.[10] In negotiations Washington's delegates tended, at best, to be well briefed in only narrow areas, ready to accept what their obviously competent, well meaning and far more concerned Canadian counterparts had to say. Back in Washington Hickerson continued to serve as a knowledgeable centre of coherence but his time was now divided among several British Commonwealth nations and his power to impose himself on Canada's behalf became limited.[11] Beyond his purview there existed a widespread feeling that things were right in the relationship with Canada. Politically, Canadian diplomats were frustrated and embittered but within the broad area of economic and especially industrial co-operation, sufficient satisfaction and hence complacency prevailed.

Such American indifference to Canada initially received a powerful assist from the United States' vision of a British-dominated Commonwealth as Roosevelt, after an early effort to employ King as a channel, communicated with Churchill directly and assumed, along with his countrymen, that the British would keep the Canadians informed of globally important affairs. Yet the presumption of a special relationship between Anglo-Saxon democracies, transposed by a neutral America from a distant and belligerent Britain to a nearby Canada, provided a powerful foundation for the construction of a continental relationship embodying Hickerson's beliefs. The Ogdensburg Declaration of 1940 and the Hyde Park Agreement of 1941 led to a flourishing of intimate military and business co-operation, under the lofty rubrics of "equality of sacrifice" and "share-and-share-alike." American and Canadian diplomats, inspired by the experience and excluded from most of the high strategy of the war, began to plan for a better post-war era in which tariff reductions would sweep away the war-inspiring jealousies of economic exclusionism. And as a partner in production rather than a client in the line-up for Lend Lease Canada, it seemed, would be a full associate in such quests.

Building on these foundations, the immediate post-war period propelled the basic American attitude of partnership toward Canada into predominance. To be sure, with the demise of isolationism at the war's end, the globalism that had characterized the Roosevelt administration's conduct of high policy was left to flourish in an even more expansive form. In the American view of the world, Canada now occupied a truly paradoxical position. It was one of the few countries not obviously dependent on American handouts for its internal stability and national survival; if anything, many senior American officials overestimated Canada's capacity to contribute, alongside the U. S., to the economic recovery of Europe.[12] But however optimistically Canada's capacity and latent resources were viewed, it was still obvious that the Dominion could only have a marginal importance in solving the problems of hundreds of millions of people at a cost of many billions of dollars. At senior levels, it thus tended to be viewed as "a sweet little country" whose diplomats had somewhat simplistic views of world issues, whose problems, capable of automatic solution, were unwelcome intrusions on scarce time, and whose needs and demands would have to come a long way after the more serious and much more urgent requirements of shattered Europe or threatening Russia.

Yet despite these limitations, overall American indifference to Canada diminished markedly as Canada's productive economy, self-confident middle-power assumptions of global responsibility, and front-line position against the Soviet threat over the pole made it not just a sweet little country, but a genuinely important one as well. President Truman, although he knew Canada only slightly, had a high regard for a country that was a democracy, spoke the same language, had a good war record, and had given him several friends back in KansasCity. As a result he gave a ready and reasonable consideration to Canadian problems, although his time remained devoted to the hard global and domestic issues, and his Canadian-focused initiatives confined to efforts to have a friend appointed a consul, and to allow Canadians, along with good Americans from Missouri and Nevada, entry into West Point.

The Secretaries of State during Truman's first term, Edward Stettinius, James Byrnes of South Carolina and General George Marshall, were equally preoccupied with founding the United Nations and dealing with the demands of the oncoming Cold War. Yet at the undersecretary level, Dean Acheson and Robert Lovett, under the careful encouragement of Canadian diplomats, gave both interest and attention to Canadian-American relations. Acheson was especially close to Wrong, Pearson's successor as ambassador to Washington, as their friendship extended back over two generations to the days when their fathers studied together at the University of Toronto and when Mrs. Wrong's father, Professor Hutton, had taught them both.[13] But Acheson, like other ex-Canadians, had an explanation and justification for his own family's move from a small and relatively weak country to a large and relatively powerful one, which appeared in a letter written almost twenty years later. Canadians were, he wrote, "a tribal society, naïve, terribly serious about the wrong things and not at all aware of their real problems . . . . Their best move would be to ask us to take them over; and our best move would be to say, no."[14]

While Acheson's personal background provided him with a special sensitivity to and impatience with Canadian perspectives, it was a much more fundamental shift in the global balance of power that underscored Canada's heightened importance in Washington's geopolitical vision. The evident and increasing decline in Britain's post-war power meant that Canada was no longer a mere westward projection of British influence, and no longer was the Anglo-American special relationship of absolutely unique importance to the United States. And as America's traditional tie with the United Kingdom broadened into an Atlanticist vision, its choice of preferred partners slowly shifted from its British ally to Canada itself. During the war the U.S. had begun to move toward a trilateral relationship, in which the British and Canadians were full members and equal recipients of American information. And as Pearson's independent spirit and informal style differentiated the Canadian embassy from the British network in the post-war period, the balance began to shift further toward the Canadian pole. While the old patterns of transatlantic bilateralism and real trilateralism prevailed on the loans to Britain in 1946 and in the formation of NATO, Canada's special position began to appear in high political concerns.[15] On atomic energy, as well as in more general matters, where British security was lax and leaky, Canada showed a readiness to adopt security standards as rigorous as the Americans' own, with all the advantages and defects that came in their train. Here, as the most junior of three partners and as an unwilling middleman between the British and the Americans, the Canadians enjoyed the advantage that a moderate atomic power program coupled with an abundant uranium supply conferred. Accordingly, Canada could afford to be "remarkably modest" in tripartite atomic discussions. By refusing to assist the British in their futile assaults on American secrecy obsessions and security programs, the Canadians won the gratitude of their American opposite numbers. "We would do things for Canada without being asked," one of them recalled.[16]

On the issue of Newfoundland's status in 1948 State's Canadianists under Hickerson's leadership rapidly concluded, despite Pentagon skepticism and without public declaration, that an ailing Britain could no longer stand the hemorrhage, that an independent Newfoundland would be a nonviable proposition inviting trouble, and that Canada should take over the territory in the strategic interest of the United States and Canada itself. As a result they sought to dampen the enthusiasms of American officers stationed in Newfoundland who had sat up too late listening to the ingenious suggestions of Newfoundland patriots who would have preferred an economic union with the United States to the absorption of the island dominion into Canada. Newfoundlanders travelling to Washington were received politely but coolly at the State Department, where Hickerson gave out the word that the union of Newfoundland with Canada was in the political and strategic interests of the United States. Think, he told his subordinates, how quickly an independent Newfoundland would get into financial trouble, and how easily it could slide under someone else's influence.[17]

Taken together, America's declining isolationism, emergent globalism and modified Atlanticism transmuted the basic American attitude toward Canada into its most effective and expansive phase. As before the primary definer and defender of this attitude was Hickerson, but as he moved up to become director of the entire office of European affairs he acquired additional assets to deploy in his own right. Though no longer principally responsible for Canada, he had ready access to the principal decision-makers, retained, as the acknowledged expert, a more than active interest in Canadian affairs, and passed on his attitudinal legacy by direction and osmosis to other professionals, notably Graham Parsons, Lucius Battle, Andrew Foster, and Margaret Tibbetts, who worked the Canadian desk in the late 1940s. The American embassy in Ottawa provided adequate, but hardly outstanding support, although the friendship between the ambassador, Ray Atherton, and the Undersecretary of State, Dean Acheson, and the latter's occasional vacations in Canada helped in a minor way. More importantly, State's Canadianists continued the intimate friendships with the Canadian diplomatic stars whose intelligence, style and energy made the Canadian embassy, in their view, the most effective in Washington. Led by the triumvirate of Pearson, Wrong and Robertson, and including subordinates such as Tommy Stone and

George Magann, this group secured a companionship, respect and confidence which had discernible diplomatic effects. Pearson's independence of views and spirit, very close friendships with a full array of American officials, and highly informal, American-like modus operandi, Wrong's brilliance and unique relationship with Acheson and Stone's highly developed intelligence and informality made dealing with matters Canadian an exciting and important place for American diplomats to be.

Thus, State's Canadianists were in a strong position to insure that Canadian views were given the fullest possible senior-level consideration, especially in areas where the issues were purely bilateral and the rewards of co-operation with Canada much less obviously important.[18] They also worked hard, and largely successfully, to monitor the enormously expanded relationships, especially in defence and economics, which other departments and agencies developed with their Canadian counterparts. Under the direction of Andrew Foster, and with the aid of their DEA counterparts, they established a hard-won mechanism whereby requests for co-operative bilateral defence activities would be channeled through, and hence filtered by, the diplomatic net.

Such bureaucratic successes both reflected and reinforced the confident conviction of State's Canadianists in a conception of Canada's place in American policy that had expanded considerably beyond the wartime dimensions. Informality no longer meant simply that all Canadian-American problems were ultimately soluble, one at a time, on an ad hoc basis, through personal relationships among a small corps of diplomats. It also meant that Canadian sovereignty was to be respected, Canadian strength augmented, and minor annoyances, from the Pentagon, Commerce or even the White House, cleared off and buried in the proliferating, more institutionalized network of direct, transborder contacts among functional counterparts in all policy fields.

The American attitude toward Canada during this period was grounded in the profound conviction that now more than ever they all believed in the same thing.[19] Together they had won the war on behalf of certain ideals and in the broadest terms these ideals meant support for the new United Nations and a rigorous form of collective security, under American leadership, which the lessons of the past had demonstrated to be necessary. As the rhetoric surrounding NATO and GATT accomplishments was soon to symbolize they extended to a belief in the urgent necessity, and historical inevitability of an Atlantic community at the intergovernmental, political level, with complete freedom of passage, a common tariff and currency and, above all, a common foreign policy worked out together. And most adventurously, at the margins of political practicality the beliefs in a community of objectives, commonality of standards and lifestyles, and easy co-operation achieved their most ambitious expression in the bilateral realm. Moving beyond Acheson's vision, George Kennan, who played a part in a lengthy series of defence consultations with Canada and who reflected a broader sentiment, once plainly told Pearson that what was really "special" about the Americans' relations with Canada was that they would lead ineluctably to the union of the two countries. There would be, Kennan prophesied, an "eventual merger of Canada and the United States into one financial, economic and even political entity" after such intermediate steps as a "common breadbasket" and a "common currency at a more distant date." So strong was the appeal of such visions in Washington that Pearson, who had happily participated in negotiations looking towards a customs union with the United States the year before and who was identified by Washington's Canadianists as a covert free trader, took fright.[20]

Yet the prospects of far-reaching integration and the power of the policy tendency which legitimized it proved to be short-lived. By all the commonly accepted standards of Canadian-American relations, links between the two countries should have been especially close during the second Truman administration. An honorary Canadian, Acheson was Secretary of State. The president himself continued well-disposed toward Canada. Canada and the United States joined in the United Nations crusade in Korea and both countries rearmed in the face of the Communist menace. Canadian representatives in Washington and at the United Nations continued to enjoy a wide range of personal contacts and to enjoy a reputation for thoroughness, competence and even, in some cases, brilliance.[21]

Yet a closer examination of Canadian-American contacts during this period discloses cracks in the façade of harmony. In the field of defence production, for example, the United States had discovered that it could, if necessary, go it alone: a war industry in being had less need of Canadian supplies, except raw materials, while Canadian industry, although it benefitted from American technology and some American orders, nevertheless found the Americans less forthcoming than they had been in the greater emergency of World War II. Production relationships across the border, though still important, were therefore of less significance and enjoyed less political and diplomatic autonomy than they had between 1941 and 1945.[22]

Relations between the two capitals were not strengthened by the virtual oblivion into which the American embassy in Ottawa sank during this period. Ambassador Steinhardt (1948–50) was considered a misfit, marooned in a backwater far away from his real central European and Soviet interests. Stanley Woodward, his successor, floated amiably through his assignment, as befitted a former chief of protocol. There is no evidence that Woodward contributed to or detracted from the friendly feelings that his friend, President Truman, harboured towards Canada.

As before, therefore, the principal focus of Canadian-American dealings continued to be the Canadian embassy in Washington. The ambassador, Wrong, was admired and esteemed, as a particularly close friend of Acheson's. The closeness between the two men genuinely reflected a convergence of views, and it masked to some extent the growing distance between Ottawa's — that is Pearson's — position and Washington's. Acheson and his colleagues naturally tended to take a global perspective, one which was both narrower and more dogmatic than that of the Canadians. Rightly or wrongly, "Corporal Pearson" was less and less inclined to share Acheson's view of the shape of things, and more and more Canadian diplomats came to accept that their function was to "constrain" their overhasty southern brethren.[23] American diplomats responded with disappointment and irritation, although to some extent these feelings were limited to and personalized in Pearson. Pearson, after all, was "a politician," Hickerson later commented, a category which, to a professional diplomat, explained much.[24]

Canada's Commonwealth ties also recurred in American appraisals. The Colombo Plan was inescapable. The attempt to bridge North and South, Asia and Europe, was a noble one in theory, and getting along with the Indians, impossible though they were, was a good idea. Perhaps it was also good to have a western country that gained credibility because it lacked, even more than America, an imperialist taint. But the distancing that this entailed, as between Canada and the United States, gave public and private credence to the Canadian feeling that America's foreign policy was less than sound, and something less than wise. Increasingly, Acheson and his subordinates complained that the Canadians were choosing a romantic moral fiction over the dictates of reality and duty.

Some of the common themes of American and Canadian relations continued to hold true. Public disagreement was muted and anti-Americanism a thing unknown. Canadian and American trade policies were broadly compatible, even if free trade seemed a sentimental echo of honourable intentions. Disputes over investment and extraterritoriality of American laws served to remind Canadians that sovereignty by itself might not be an adequate guarantee of equal treatment by a more powerful neighbour. Government and public continued, in general, to believe that informal approaches, reasonable discussion and a common background would regulate the Canadian-American relationship to a rough balance.

This view was not, in this period, demonstrably misplaced on the bilateral front. A minor incident late in 1952 may serve to illustrate the prevailing attitude. It was by that point perfectly plain that the St. Lawrence Seaway Treaty of 1941 was a dead letter in the American Congress. The Canadian government, publicly and privately, urged that the old treaty be scrapped to allow Canada to get on with the project by itself. Acheson counselled delay (there were only two months left in Truman's presidency) but Truman disagreed. "[He] felt strongly," Acheson recorded, "that the Canadians had acted with great patience, that they were entitled to take this action, and that he wished to do whatever was necessary to enable them to proceed during his term as President."[25]

The Seaway issue, despite Truman's good intentions, was handed on to his successor, Dwight D. Eisenhower, to dispose of. Some members of the Eisenhower cabinet, as is well-known, heartily supported the Seaway. The president, however, was a very reluctant dragon. "I am almost sorry," he wrote to his brother, "that I ever heard the project mentioned." Since Eisenhower believed the pro-Seaway forces to be too strong, he deliberately encouraged counter-arguments from American railways whose position was, of course, strongly against. "Certain security angles" the Administration announced, made the construction of the Seaway "reasonably desirable."[26] With that ringing endorsement, another Canadian-American joint venture got underway. The special bilateral relationship was still alive — but it badly needed a transfusion and a rest in a warm climate. Yet warmth was not to come.

The return of the Republicans to power for the first time in twenty years sent a shiver of uncertainty through Canada's diplomatic establishment. Whatever Canadians' differences of emphasis were with the Democrats, during the years since 1933 the common goals and co-operative institutions of the two countries, both bilateral and international, had flourished. But the Republicans were the party of "America First," and whether that meant cherishing dreams of world supremacy or returning to pre-war isolationism it implied a blinkered, selfish and parochial way of looking at the world.

With the change of administration the urbane Stanley Woodward left Ottawa, making way for an abrasive Republican fund-raiser, Douglas Stuart. Stuart, a Chicago businessman, was a no-nonsense, commonsensical personality, who on his first day in office stood by the door of the American embassy, clocking in his effete staff with a stopwatch. Ever on the alert for signs of disrespect for the United States, Stuart listened in to the CBC and, spotting an "anti-American" play by the American humorist James Thurber, complained to a bemused Department of External Affairs. But while Stuart was no powerhouse in the field of cultural diplomacy, some Ottawa officials found his unabashed advocacy of American investment in Canada a useful tool in reminding the America-Firsters who flourished to the ambassador's right that the United States had more to gain in co-operating with Canada than in indulging in outdated flights of tariff-raising fancy. Stuart enjoyed an access to Ottawa's political circles that recalled Hickerson's; unfortunately for his staff and for the diplomatic record he preferred to keep his confidences confidential, refusing to share what the Canadians told him with his staff and with his home government.[27]

For all his limitations, Stuart qualified as a positive influence in forming Washington's perceptions of Canada. So did the Secretary of the Treasury, George Humphrey, who in civilian life had helped to form the Iron Ore Company of Canada to produce "millions of tons of iron ore that lay idle for centuries but now is being used for the benefit of civilization, not only in the United States but in Europe."[28] The Secretary of State, John Foster Dulles, had similarly enjoyed business connections with Canada; like Acheson, however, he was inclined to regard that country as afflicted with an "inferiority complex" and an "ambivalent attitude to the U.S." Nevertheless, Dulles told a group of senators, Canada was "a very important piece of real estate and should be humoured along."[29]

How far Canada could be humoured was another matter. Dulles, possibly the most globalist of all the American Secretaries of State, kept his eyes firmly fixed on the Cold War with the Soviet Union and its satellites, criss crossing the world to bolster America's allies in Europe and Asia. At home, he relied on three things: the President's support, which he usually got; compromises with right-wing, America-First Republicans on matters affecting domestic politics; and the support of the professionals of the State Department, who were expected to keep non-crucial matters out of the Secretary's hair. All three factors affected Canadian-American relations.

The America-First Republicans, as inheritors of the isolationist tradition, posed the greatest difficulty. In trade matters, Canadian officials continued apprehensive of a protectionist switch in American trade patterns. Fortunately, the switch was slow in coming, contradicted by the believers in foreign trade within the Administration. If anything, Canada was the subject of starry-eyed plans for greater free trade and economic integration by enthusiasts in the White House. Agriculture was another matter. There, Eisenhower and Dulles deferred to Ezra Taft Benson, the Agriculture Secretary: the result was a strong emphasis on domestic price supports for agricultural commodities which, in turn, fed agricultural aid programs to get rid of the resulting surplus. Complaints in private and public failed to move Benson, except to indignation, and letters to the President from Prime Minister Louis St. Laurent failed to turn Benson's flank. The defence of Canada's agricultural interests was therefore a rear-guard action, fought against heavy odds by the economics division of the State Department with the help of some briefs from the Canadian desk. The economics division did its best, and believed that under the circumstances it deserved more credit than it actually got from the Canadians for derailing some of Benson's wilder wheat aid schemes.[30]

More significantly, the State Department now took up the cudgels against the strangest idea about Canada to emanate from the Eisenhower White House — that of bilateral free trade. Canadian-American free trade was the brainchild of Clarence B. Randall, chairman of

Eisenhower's Council on Foreign Economic Policy. Randall, early in the Eisenhower Administration, did yeoman service by helping to sidetrack high tariff elements within the Republican party, thereby insuring that American trade negotiators would continue on the same relatively liberal trade route they had followed since 1933. During the mid-fifties, Randall, in keeping with standard Atlanticist precepts, became fascinated by the possibility of securing free trade with Canada, in tandem with the emergence of the European Economic Community then under negotiation. In April 1957 Randall asked the State Department to initiate a study of Canadian-American economic integration. The study was completed and handed over in mid-July, shortly after the Canadian general election that removed the Liberals from office and replaced them with John Diefenbaker and the Conservatives.

Randall was not daunted by the electoral change. The State Department study confirmed his belief that economic integration with Canada was natural, if not inevitable, and desirable in any case on general principles: "If economic integration of Europe is in the interest of the free world," he wrote, "it follows that economic integration in North American would advance the same purpose." The first step, he informed the Council on Foreign Economic Policy, should be a short one: "The United States should propose to Canada that a Joint Commission be established to study the economic integration of the two countries. It would be hard," Eisenhower's adviser added, "to see how any government in Canada could refuse to make the study." Randall noted that time had already been lost because of the State Department's reluctance to prejudice the Canadian elections. "As it turns out, nothing could have prejudiced the election in Canada," he wrote; and he would now raise the question in the early fall.[31]

State continued reluctant. Responding to a query from Eisenhower's chief of staff, Sherman Adams, Undersecretary Christian Herter reported the opinion of the "experts" who argued that "it would be inadvisable to bring up this idea as such, since they understand that even with elections out of the way the Canadians are still very sensitive on the whole question of economic relations with the United States," as discussions with the Canadian ambassador, Robertson, made plain.[32] Randall's fall discussions were mysteriously swallowed up in State's delaying tactics. Two years later, Randall was still complaining that he had been "trying to get this balloon in the air for years, and every effort was blocked by the State Department, who said that even to whisper such a thing would cause serious political repercussions within Canada and adversely affect our relationships." But Randall's attempt at resuscitating his proposal fell on ears that to him seem obdurately blocked. The next year, after one final effort had failed to get off the ground, Randall told a State Department official that in his view "the State Department has had its head in the sand on this subject and has failed to reach out and exercise creative leadership in an important matter." At the very least, Randall urged, a joint committee of prominent citizens from both sides of the border should be established to study the situation and make appropriate recommendations. For this group, he added, "Douglas Stuart, our former ambassador . . . who is loved and respected on both sides of the border, could undertake such a task to the Queen's taste." It was a lost cause, as Randall knew, and with Eisenhower's term ending and a Democratic victory impending, he uttered his "last word on the subject."[33]

However futile Randall's approach, it operated in the grand tradition of the inevitability and desirability of continental economic union, which had last sprung to life in the free trade talks of 1947–1948. At that time the State Department's reservations concerned the possible repercussions Canadian reciprocity might have in the United States; by 1957 State's economic and political advisers had come to believe that the sleeping dogs of Canadian patriotism should be allowed to dream on undisturbed by pokes with the reciprocity stick.

They had some reason. During Eisenhower's first term, only the obtuse could have missed the signs of Canadian disenchantment and resentment at the antics of Senator Joseph McCarthy and his witch-hunters; although it was definitely unfashionable to say so, State's Canada-watchers shared the Canadians' resentment. As one diplomat recalled, it took the best part of a year to keep McCarthy's witch-hunters from crossing the border and making a spectacle of themselves on Canadian soil; the other part of the year was spent answering questions from State's security officers about the reliability of colleagues.[34]

By 1956 McCarthy was on the wane, his committee an increasingly sour joke in Washington. Douglas Stuart had left Ottawa to return to private business, and his replacement, Livingston Merchant, was one of the State Department's most admired professionals. Affable and intelligent, Merchant was a symbol that professional diplomatic standards had not perished during the McCarthy purges at least for those who had operated within the comfortable confines of the Atlantic World. His influence with his colleagues was accordingly large, and his relations with Secretary Dulles were cordial, if not close. Merchant's embassy covered the years of the Canadian pipeline debate, with its anti-American overtones, opposition charges that the Liberal government was slavishly pro-American and anti-British at the time of the Suez crisis, and the eventual overturn of that government by the Conservatives in the June 1957 election. The Conservative victory surprised Merchant very much, since like other electoral prophets he had expected the usual Liberal electoral triumph. John Diefenbaker, he later reported, had won his electoral victories of 1957 and 1958 on the emotional theme song of Canadian nationalism. This was just the other side of the coin of anti-Americanism. Whereas the leaders were high-minded in their public statements, in individual ridings there were many Conservative candidates who rode into office on what was frankly and openly an anti-American attitude. "So the complaints against our actions or against apprehended actions on our part have been more emotional, higher pitched, shriller . . . than we had been accustomed to."[35]

Part of this problem, Merchant realized, might have derived from the low priority that the Eisenhower administration gave to Canadian complaints and the friendly oblivion that enveloped official appraisals of Canadian nationalism. "There is justice," he told a National War College audience, "in the Canadian complaint that they are taken for granted." The situation, though serious, was not yet desperate. "In certain areas," Merchant proposed, "a frank and avowed and open discrimination on our part in favour of Canada is warranted even at the expense of losing some goodwill with other friendly countries. I don't say that this should be our basic principle but I do say that in areas of particular importance to Canada, we should be prepared to give preferential treatment to Canada." That special treatment should include close and intimate consultation with the Canadian government which, however, should be treated at all times "as an equal and as a sovereign neighbour."

Merchant was implicitly reversing Dulles' policy of "humouring" an "important piece of real estate" that had no intrinsic importance apart from American defence. Nor was he alone in recognizing the increasing importance, coupled with diminishing reliability, which Canada in the Diefenbaker era had in the American world view. For at this time President Eisenhower's National Security Adviser decided that Canada ought to be made the subject of a "country paper" study for the National Security Council (NSC) to consider. Country papers, during the Eisenhower years, served two purposes: they pinpointed problem areas, or countries, and assessed those areas in the light of American security requirements; and they provided a Michelin guide to the principles of American policy for any bureaucrat who might require enlightenment or guidance. Because the National Security Council involved many agencies and diverse interests, the result of its policy planning was often anodyne, a consumption of time and effort for a diplomatic placebo of no special interest or value. It also sometimes encroached on the State Department's particular terrain, and as a result State tried to keep foreign policy as far removed as possible from the NSC's homogenizing machinery.[36] Although special aspects of Canadian-American relations, such as atomic energy and defence procurement, had from time to time been the subject of NSC papers and studies, this was the first time that the NSC, with CIA support, had presumed to try to put it all together.

The very suggestion violated the standard operating method that the State Department encouraged for dealing with Canada. Problems, the Canadian desk believed, should be dealt with as they arose, on an ad hoc basis, with no higher guiding principles than political feasibility and, if possible, fair treatment and equity. To bring it all together in one vast linkage was probably impossible and certainly pointless, but it might also be mischievous — and it might eventually get into the wrong hands, whether American or Canadian. State's trump in dealing with the NSC was easy enough to deploy. The Council did not have enough staff or enough information to write the first draft of a country paper: that would have to be done in State. State's aversion to the task could delay, and eventually prevent, a country paper from being compiled. As it proved, even with CIA support the NSC bureaucrats were unable to override State, and the Canadian country paper subsided. State would deal with the problem of Canadian nationalism in its own way.[37]

With the return to office in 1961 of the Democrats, whose political orientation had long been seen as compatible with Canadian interests, the traditional American attitude toward Canada was in a strong position to assert itself vis-à-vis its increasingly predominant globalist competitors, particularly after the return of a Liberal government in Canada, under Pearson, in 1963. Yet during this time a newly resurgent and far more expansive American globalism not only continued to constrain the emergence of the integrative informality of the pre-Korean era, but also engendered a major modification in basic American attitudes toward Canada itself. The United States' professional Canadianists and political leaders came slowly to realize, with considerable frustration, that a far greater measure of equality, divergence and distance had replaced the disparity, mutuality and integrative informality of the past.

To a considerable extent, this transition stemmed from the fact that America's Atlanticist orientation, which earlier had become fused in reinforcing fashion with the conventional integrationist assumptions, now began to generate disagreements, as the United States' vigorous campaigns for European integration catalyzed French resistance, and later Canadian dissent. In the conception of America's Canadianists, operating here as subjects of their committed Europeanist colleagues, U.S. support for British entry into the European Common Market, Britain's difficulties in retaining a nuclear capacity through the acquisition of the Polaris, and at the margins, the creation of a NATO multilateral nuclear force, were necessary components of the dominant quest for a more unified Europe with strong transatlantic links.[38] As a result, neither their awareness of Canada's desire for a special relationship or counterweight with the British, nor their embryonic recognition of the internal forces prompting, in some quarters, a more accommodating Canadian view of Gaullism fully offset the opposition, complications or reluctance which Canada presented to these ventures.

A somewhat similar divergence was bred by the modern manifestation of America's isolationism, particularly as these were manifest in its quest for exclusive hemispheric dominance, and tendency toward unilateral behavior, over the issue of Cuba's growing ties with the Communist bloc. Canada's willingness to continue trade with Cuba and resist potentially extraterritorial American efforts to enforce its embargo could largely be treated and contained as irritants rendered familiar by the previous disputes which divergent approaches to the People's Republic of China had spawned. Yet Canada's hesitant response to the U.S. call for firm public diplomatic support at the height of the Cuban Missile Crisis suggested a degree of political unreliability on the most vital issues, that was bred by Canada's quest for a middle-power role, as much as by Prime Minister Diefenbaker's personal indecisiveness.

Such perceptions and the divergent policy orientations which generated them presented an even greater degree of incompatibility to those American officials enamoured, under the Kennedy legacy, with propelling America's global vision into ever more distant regions. Efforts to harmonize perceptions and approaches on the difficult issue of Indochina became part of the weekly routine of American diplomats in Ottawa, who slowly became aware of Canada's genuine concern over the extent of America's increasing involvement, their superiors' impatience with the accommodating approaches of the "Ontario Hindus" on the International Control Commission, and how such divergences, along with those over nuclear weapons were grounded in Canada's general and growing desire for a more unique, independent, middle-power role in the world. Similar differences at the United Nations, where new Afro-Asian states were altering the climate, led U.S. diplomats to institute a special process of bilateral consultation, aimed at harmonizing behavior, in advance of each General Assembly session. Yet such consultations were limited to tactical planning on those issues where there was substantive consensus, required the participation not just of America's Canadianists but its first-line, United Nations team, and were premised on the fact that Canada could now deploy exclusive advantages, through a special entry into Third World middle-power circles, which U.S. diplomacy lacked.

These challenges which Canada increasingly presented to Atlanticist, isolationist and globalist tendencies extended well beyond the status of periodic interruptions to dominant U.S. thinking, to the point where they forced a cumulatively major revision of the American attitude, policymaking process and approach to Canada itself. The new American attitude, spawned by the Diefenbaker government's actions, centered on the theme of Canada's political unreliability in the context of American global diplomacy and, fuelled by Johnson's preoccupations with Vietnam and Pearson's Temple University speech, extended to a conviction that Canada was deliberately providing aid and comfort to America's opponents within the western world. This perception of unreliability spelled political problems requiring senior-level attention. Accordingly, Canadian matters increasingly became the preserve of surprised and impatient U.S. presidents and their NSC colleagues were often, as in the case of the Cuban Missile Crisis and of the State Department press release at the height of the nuclear weapons controversy, taken out of the hands of State's Canadianists corps.

In dealings with Canadians, the informality, integrative spirit and emphasis on mutual interests of earlier eras suffered a corresponding decline. For a brief period between 1963 and 1965 uninhibited personal contacts expanded to flourish at the summit levels, notably in the wide ranging discussions in 1963 at Hyannis Port, the phone calls over the 1964 Cyprus crisis and the conclusion of the automotive agreement at the LBJ ranch in 1965. Yet even during this time Pearson remained uncomfortable with Johnson's impetuous and earthy informality and especially after the Temple Speech, policy disagreements introduced a frigid chill.[39] At the lower levels personal and professional relationships continued to generate a civilized, friction-reducing discourse, and with senior-level blessing, in the case of the automobile agreement, the extension of the defence production sharing arrangements and the Colombia Power treaty, a governmentally-directed integrative trend. Yet in contrast with previous American schemes for free trade and reciprocity, such ventures were defensive American moves against unilateral, and nationalistic Canadian initiatives, circumscribed in scope and depth and increasingly dependent for their formulation and implementation on the internal Canadian debate. And the growing force of Canadian nationalism, registered in Walter Gordon's 1963 budget, the Mercantile Bank affair and internal Canadian debates over NATO and Vietnam underscored in the minds of America's Canadianists the cumulatively significant and deeply-held different interests which Canada possessed.

Notes

1. A.D.P. Heeney and Livingston Merchant, *Canada and the United States: Principles for Partnership* (Ottawa: Queen's Printer, 1965), 52, 49. See also A.D.P. Heeney, "Independence and Partnership: The Search for Principles," *International Journal* 26 (1972): 159–71; John Sloan Dickey, "The Relationship in Rhetoric and Reality: Merchant-Heeney Revisited," *International Journal* 26 (1972): 172–84; and Arnold Henney, *The Things That Are Caesar's: The Memoirs of a Canadian Public Servant* (Toronto: University of Toronto Press, 1972), 182–200. The accuracy of the report as an expression of Merchant's personal

beliefs is verified in an interview with Rufus Smith, December 1978. George Ball's projections are contained in George Ball, *The Discipline of Power* (Boston: Little Brown, 1968), 113.

2. The following paragraphs on the pre-World War II period rely heavily on an interview with J.D. Hickerson, December 1978, as confirmed by interviews with Margaret Tibbetts, August 1980, and R.G. Arneson, May 1981, and material contained in the John G. Foster Papers, Queen's University.

3. These three tendencies, labelled isolationism, globalism and Atlanticism, correspond respectively with the trilogy of Isolationism, Cold War Internationalism and Post-Cold War Internationalism that James Rosenau and Ole Holsti have argued are the central, enduring tendencies in United States foreign policy as a whole. For a summary of their work see Ole Holsti, "The Three-Headed Eagle: The United States and System Change," *International Studies Quarterly* 23 (1979): 339–59.

4. For Roosevelt's relations with Canada and King, see especially C.P. Stacey, *Canada and the Age of Conflict*, vol. 2 (Toronto: University of Toronto Press, 1981), 230–31, 307–17.

5. Hickerson and Tibbetts interviews. Moffat, as Hickerson explained, was older and more senior. As his despatches testify, Moffat, despite his views, was an able rapporteur. See *The Moffat Papers*, ed. Nancy Hooker (Cambridge, Mass., 1956).

6. Hickerson interview.

7. Ibid. See J.L. Granatstein, *A Man of Influence* (Ottawa: Deneau, 1981), chap. 3, for an evocation of the atmosphere of the 1937–38 talks.

8. See Stacey, ibid., 307–17.

9. Hickerson interview.

10. Jack Tuthill interview, Washington, December 1978. Tuthill served in the Ottawa Embassy in the latter part of the war.

11. In October 1944 Hickerson told Norman Robertson that he was disturbed by the view in high quarters that "on general political questions the views of the parts of the British Commonwealth should be co-ordinated and received through the United Kingdom." L.B. Pearson to Robertson, 30 Oct. 1944, L.B. Pearson Papers, vol. 2, Public Archives of Canada (hereinafter PAC).

12. See R.D. Cuff and J.L. Granatstein, *American Dollars, Canadian Prosperity* (Toronto, 1978), 108–17.

13. Dean Acheson, *Present at the Creation* (New York, 1969), 277.

14. David McClellan and David Acheson, eds., *Among Friends* (New York, 1980), 250.

15. Theodore Achilles interview, December 1978.

16. R.G. Arneson interview.

17. Margaret Tibbetts interview.

18. Ibid.

19. Hickerson interview; Achilles interview.

20. Julian Harrington to W.P. Snow, 12 Aug. 1949, RG 84, file 320, National Archives, Washington.

21. Lucius Battle interview, May 1980; Outerbridge Horsey interview, May 1980; Tibbetts interview.

22. See R. Bothwell and W. Kilbourn, *C.D. Howe* (Toronto: McClelland & Stewart, 1979), 249–51.

23. The argument for "constraint" is most prominent in Denis Stairs, *The Diplomacy of Constraint* (Toronto, 1972); for "Corporal Pearson" see R.D. Cuff and J.L. Granatstein, *Canadian-American Relations in Wartime* (Toronto, 1975), chap. 6.

24. Hickerson interview; see also memorandum of conversation with L.B. Pearson, 1 Oct. 1952, Dean Acheson Papers, Truman Library (Independence, Mo.).

25. Memorandum of conversation with the president, 3 Nov. 1952, Ibid.

26. D.D. Eisenhower to M. Eisenhower, 29 Apr. 1953, Whitman files, Eisenhower Library (Abilene, Kans.).

27. Willis Armstrong interview, Washington, Dec. 1979; Mitchell Sharp interview, May 1977.

28. George Humphrey to Paul Hoffman, 26 Mar. 1957, Council on Foreign Economic Policy Papers (hereinafter CFEP), Box 10, Office of the Chairman, Eisenhower Library.

29. Burt Marshall, quoted in L. Moseley, *Dulles* (New York, 1979), 358.

30. Armstrong interview.

31. Randall to Sherman Adams, 17 July 1957, CFEP Papers, chairman's file.

32. Christian Herter to Adams, 22 July 1957, ibid.

33. Randall to Edwin Martin, 31 Oct. 1960, ibid.

34. Tibbetts interview.

35. Livingston Merchant Papers, Princeton University.

36. Gordon Gray interview, Washington, December 1978; Armstrong interview. For evidence of NSC attention to Canada during this period see "Certain Aspects of U.S. Relations with Canada," NSC 5822/I, 30 Dec. 1958, National Security Council.

37. Armstrong interview; Charles Ritchie, *Diplomatic Passport* (Toronto: Macmillan, 1981), 152–53.

38. The following paragraphs are based on the interview with Rufus Smith, December 1978, the interview with Joseph Scott, December 1978 and the Armstrong interview.

39. Roger Frank Swanson, *Canadian-American Summit Diplomacy, 1923-1973: Selected Speeches and Documents* (Toronto: McClelland & Stewart, 1975), 217–66.

Freer Trade and Politics†

J.L. GRANATSTEIN

The 1911 Reciprocity Agreement and Election

. . .
The Laurier years were boom years with extraordinary increases in Canadian agriculture output and in manufacturing; indeed, manufacturing increased by six percent a year over the period 1900–1910, the sharpest growth to that time.[1]

The benefits of the great boom were not equally divided, however. While the manufacturers grew prosperous, the farmers remained dissatisfied. The prices they paid for agricultural implements were high, thanks to the protected position of the Canadian manufacturers; the prices they paid for everything were high, and the tariff was the villain with an average ad valorem rate of 28 percent.[2] In 1907 Laurier's government made some minor tariff concessions to the western farmers, but they were just a sop, not a remedy. And when the Liberal Prime Minister made a great tour of the West in 1910, he was beset with cries for free trade and for a better deal. In December, huge delegations of farmers laid siege to the Parliament Buildings, pressing their case for relief from the costs of protectionism.

† This is an excerpt from J.L. Granatstein, "Free Trade Between Canada and the United States: The Issue That Will Not Go Away" in *The Politics of Canada's Economic Relationship with the United States*, ed. Denis Stairs and Gilbert R. Winham (Toronto: University of Toronto Press, 1985), 20–54.

By that date, in fact, negotiations with the United States for a reciprocity treaty were well advanced. On 26 January, 1911, Fielding, still Laurier's Minister of Finance after fifteen years, gave the news to the House of Commons and the nation:

> ... we have arranged that there shall be a large free list. We have agreed upon a schedule containing a large number of articles which are to be reciprocally free. These are chiefly what are called natural products ...
>
> In another schedule we have provided a rather numerous list of items on which there shall be a common rate of duty in both countries ... we have had to make only moderate reductions, while they, in many cases, have had to make quite large reductions.[3]

Fielding's agreement with the United States provided free entry for live animals, poultry, wheat, corn, fresh vegetables and fruit, fish, timber and sawed boards, asbestos, brass, rolled iron, cream separators, wire, fencing wire, pulp wood and a host of other items. Most were, as Fielding had said, natural products. Other duties were lowered substantially: agricultural implements were now to have a rate of 15 percent ad valorem and tractors of 20 percent, two items of special interest to farmers.[4] Indeed, the whole reciprocity treaty seemed designed for the agricultural community. There was now virtually free access to the great American market for agricultural products and substantial concessions on farm machinery entering Canada. It was a victory for the West, a triumph for organized farmer agitation.

That was the way Fielding's announcement was seen by almost everyone. The Liberals had finally achieved what virtually every government had tried for since 1866, a renewal of reciprocity. How could this be opposed? the Conservatives asked themselves. Robert Borden, the party leader, was almost dumbstruck, a state that lasted until his caucus members went out to their constituencies and discovered that many were deeply concerned by Laurier's treaty and ready to "bust the damn thing." First off, Laurier liberalism was in difficulty generally in English and French Canada, an inevitable result of fifteen years in office. The government was seen as weak on imperial sentiment by many in English Canada, an impression that reciprocity did nothing to dispel. In Quebec, the government was viewed as being made up of vendus who had sold out to English Canada and its imperial attitudes, the presence of Laurier notwithstanding. Moreover, Ontario no longer had a lieutenant of stature at Laurier's side, the province's ministers generally being junior in status or, more seriously, in ability. It was the manufacturers, though, who were most concerned by the agreement with Washington. Their reaction was surprising because the reciprocity arrangement scarcely touched their interests. Nonetheless, reciprocity in natural products was seen as the thin edge of the wedge that would eventually see the tariff protection against manufactured products removed. By 1911, Canada had become an industrialized country with substantial manufacturing centres that had grown up behind the tariff protection of the National Policy. Now Laurier was apparently proposing to breach the walls.

The first attacks on the reciprocity agreement came from disaffected Liberals. Urged on by Clifford Sifton, Laurier's onetime minister of the interior who had left the Cabinet over the question of French-Canadian rights in the new provinces of Alberta and Saskatchewan, eighteen Toronto businessmen published a manifesto on 20 February 1911. Canada's prosperity, they argued, was owed to the National Policy and reciprocity would squander all the money invested in east-west communication lines by creating new north-south trade flows. The agreement would weaken ties with the empire. It would expose Canada to enormous difficulties if the United States withdrew at some future point, and that was a serious risk. Moreover, and this was the critical point, "to avoid such a disruption Canada would be forced to extend the scope of the agreement so as to include manufactures and other things." All in all, the Toronto Eighteen claimed, reciprocity threatened Canadian nationality "with a more serious blow than any it has heretofore met."[5]

Borden and the Conservatives were quick to take advantage of the rift in Liberal ranks. The Eighteen had included Z.A. Lash, a lawyer for the railway interests, and Lash met on March 1 with Clifford Sifton, Lloyd Harris, MP of the Massey-Harris interests, J.S. Willison, the editor of Toronto *News* and a stern critic of Laurier's imperial policies, and Robert Borden, the Tory leader. As Willison's memorandum of the meeting noted, "The four first named having fully agreed as to the course to be taken and the policy which should be pursued by a new Adminstration. . . . Their views were laid before the Leader of the Opposition by Mr. Sifton." In effect, Borden was asked to agree to a series of promises that included: Quebec and Roman Catholics should have no undue influence; American encroachments and blandishments should be resisted; in forming a Cabinet Borden should consult with Lash, Willison and Sir Edmund Walker of the Bank of Commerce to ensure that Liberals who opposed reciprocity received their due; and a number of men from outside Parliament should be brought into Cabinet. There were other points designed to take the civil service out of politics, to encourage trade abroad, and to develop a rational tariff, but the key point was that if Borden wanted the support of Liberal businessmen against reciprocity, he would have to consult Walker, Lash and Willison in setting up his Cabinet. Borden readily agreed, and the alliance between the manufacturers and financiers of central Canada and the Conservative party was sealed.[6]

From Borden's point of view, this bargain had several consequences. No longer would he have to worry about money. His party coffers would be full, and the dissident Liberals, through their specially created Canadian National League, poured vast sums more into anti-reciprocity propaganda. But many in Borden's caucus were unhappy about any arrangement with the hated Liberals and, while none knew of the full extent of Borden's deal, there were suspicions. On the verge of a political triumph, Borden had to fend off revolts within his party. Above all, the Conservative leader had made a quite unprecedented arrangement, in effect giving a form of a veto over Cabinet appointments to Walker, Lash and Willison and promising to bring in key Cabinet figures from outside the House. The Conservative party, despite its leader's earlier campaigns for clean government and progressive measures, had now been turned into the virtual handmaiden of Toronto business and finance.

The business of politics, however, was still to get elected above all else, and there was no question that the Conservatives were beginning to benefit substantially from the criticisms launched by the press, the Canadian National League, and the Canadian Manufacturers' Association's creation, the Canadian Home Market Association. The CHMA and the Canadian National League worked closely together, the League distributing the CHMA's propaganda in huge quantities — 9.5 million pieces dispatched by mid-August, 1911, and 20 000 more going out each day.

What was the thrust of the anti-reciprocity campaign? One famous pamphlet, written by journalist Arthur Hawkes, was called "An Appeal to the British-Born" and it rang all the changes, pointing out how Canada had been saved for the empire when annexation was rejected in 1849:

> It was saved not because of Britain's love for Upper Canada and Lower Canada, but because of the love of men in the Canadas for Britain. They knew, deep down in their souls, that Canada possessed Britain in a far more magnificent sense than Britain possessed Canada, and that out of their tribulation rich fruits would spring. That is even more splendidly true today.[7]

The Montreal Star, in its key election editorial, tried to draw out the differences between Canada and the United States and then urged the electors not to turn their backs on the system of government under which they had prospered:

> Shall we do it? Shall we surrender just when the battle is won?

> Shall we let the men, who deserted us in the dark days, now come
> in as full-fledged "American citizens" and take over the country
> they did not think worth living in . . .? Shall we give up, too, the
> glorious future which beckons us — the chance that we will
> become the chief state in the British empire and the most power-
> ful nation in the world? Shall we bring the sacrifices of the
> Fathers to naught?[8]

For the anti-reciprocity propagandists, the issue was not the trade
agreement so much as the possible implications of it. If ever Canada
let down her guard, the American bogeyman would swallow her whole.
What needs to be said, however, is that there were some grounds for
that belief. The United States, under President Theodore Roosevelt,
had used threats of the "big stick" against Canada during the Alaska
Boundary dispute just a few years before, and they still rankled. More
to the point, the reciprocity issue had provoked remarkably silly — if
forthright — statements from American politicians. President Taft
had sought an agreement with Canada in part because it promised to
give the newspaper publishers cheaper newsprint, something that he
hoped would get a hostile press off his back. But when his reciprocity
agreement stalled in Congress in the spring, Taft thought to ease
matters by telling the American Newspaper Publishers' Association
that Canada was "coming to the parting of the ways. . . . The forces
which are at work in England and in Canada to separate her by a
Chinese wall from the United States and to make her part of an imperial commercial band . . . by a system of preferential tariffs, will
derive an impetus from the rejection of this treaty, and if we would
have reciprocity . . . we must take it now or give it up forever . . . the
bond uniting the dominion to the mother country is light and almost
imperceptible." Taft's remarks, in context, referred to trade alone; out
of context and used in Canada by the opposition to the agreement,
they were devastating. So too were the remarks of Champ Clark, the
Speaker-designate of the House of Representatives, who said in Congress that "I hope to see the day when the American flag will float over
every square foot of the British–North American possessions clear to
the North Pole . . . ."[9]
Against this the Liberals could only say that they did not seek to tie
Canada irrevocably to the United States, that their devotion to empire
was strong, and that the economic benefits of reciprocity were worth
all risks. "Nothing more clearly shows the weakness of the case against
reciprocity," said the finance minister, W.S. Fielding, in a pamphlet
distributed in the Maritimes, "than the fact that our opponents have
to resort to the device of waving the British flag and accusing the advocates of reciprocity of disloyalty. . . . The glorious flag of the empire
was never intended to be used for so mean a purpose." The Toronto

Globe, the leading Liberal newspaper in the country, quoted a Quebec Liberal's declaration — "We are all united as one under one flag, the Union Jack" — with approval, and condemned the Conservatives, the party of loyalty in English Canada, for their alliance with Henri Bourassa and the *Nationalistes* in Quebec — "every one of them a traitor to British ideals," the *Globe* said.[10]

What happened was that in Quebec Laurier was under assault by Bourassa for his naval policy, for his too close relationship with England and English Canadians, and for his unwillingness to assist his compatriots. In English Canada, Laurier was denounced as a traitor to the empire, one who, because he was a *Canadien*, would sell Canada to the Americans. What made it worse was that the Liberal organization was enfeebled, the Conservatives well financed and eager. Indeed, some historians have suggested that in Ontario, at least, the Conservatives were so well prepared that they could have won an election on virtually any pretext.[11] That suggested that reciprocity was perhaps less of an issue than might have been thought.

In some ways the results confirmed that. Reciprocity had been put in place for the western farmer — but in Manitoba the Conservatives took eight out of ten seats, and cynics attributed that to the great influence of the Canadian Pacific which was vehemently opposed to the agreement. In Alberta and Saskatchewan, however, the Liberals won fifteen of seventeen seats. But elections in 1911 (as ever after) were won in Ontario and Quebec: in Ontario, Laurier took only thirteen of eighty-six seats; in Quebec, the Tories and *Nationalistes* took twenty-seven of sixty-five. The overall result was that the Conservatives had one hundred and thirty-four seats to eighty-seven for Laurier. Reciprocity had been defeated, and J.W. Dafoe, the pro-reciprocity editor of the *Manitoba Free Press*, was convinced that he knew why: Laurier had held office by placating various powerful interests at the expense of the general public, but "the moment he showed signs of putting real Liberal doctrine into effect, the interests combined and crushed him."[12] There was more than a little truth in that assessment.

On the other hand, it was also true that reciprocity had run up against nascent Canadian nationalism. The anti-reciprocity forces had draped themselves in the bloody shirt of loyalty to Crown and Empire, appealing to the Britishness of the electorate, but they had also talked Canada, Canada, Canada. They knew their audience well, and their appeals to anti-Americanism, then as always a corollary of Canadianism, struck a great wellspring of sentiment. Canadians, although still more fervent in their loyalty to the empire than the king, were beginning to think in nationalistic terms a half century after confederation, beginning to consider that their country had a chance to become something special. In effect, they voted, as a Canadian writing in the *Yale Review* after the election put it, to "let well enough alone!"[13]

One more point is worth nothing. The Prairie farmers who had pressed so hard for free trade did not forget their defeat at the hands of the Conservatives and the Canadian Manufacturers Association. The 1911 election shook the old party system thoroughly, and the 1917 election that followed, with its Union Government and conscription issue, shook it further still. The result was that by the end of the war, the new Progressive party was in formation on the Prairies and in rural Ontario. The Progressives' issue was the tariff first and foremost, and the defeat of reciprocity in 1911 was the spur for its formation. Before long, provincial governments were tumbling, and the farmers' party was forming the second largest bloc in Ottawa. In this instance, if in no other, the reciprocity issue had major political consequences after the fact.

. . .

The Trade Agreements of 1935 and 1938

. . . Although the Progressive party was calling for a new National Policy that recognized the benefits that could accrue to agriculturalists through low tariffs, the Borden government and its successor, the Meighen government, remained wedded to the old National Policy of protection. That attitude cost Arthur Meighen the election of 1921, and it brought Mackenzie King to power. King's inclinations were toward lower tariffs, but many of his Ontario and Quebec supporters took a different view, and with the Progressives sitting as a third party in the minority House of Commons he could do little.

The Americans did not help. In May 1921 the Administration of President Harding, very responsive to protectionist pressures, pushed through an Emergency Tariff Act, and the next year the Fordney-McCumber tariff raised the protective wall around the United States.[14] That weakened any desire in Canada to hold out tariff concessions to the United States.

What was striking in the circumstances was that Canadian exports to the United States remained as high as they did in the face of the Fordney–McCumber wall. In 1920, exports were $581.4 million, the highest level ever. Over the course of the 1920s, exports dropped, but in every year they were substantially higher than in the prewar and war years, the lowest point being $334.9 million in 1921 and the highest being $515.3 million in 1929. Imports from the United States followed a roughly similar pattern, the peak being $921.2 million in 1920 and the low point being $509.0 million in 1922.[15]

But there were more American tariffs to come even before the Depression began in the fall of 1929. The Smoot-Hawley tariff erected the highest protective barriers ever, and Congressman Willis Hawley said bluntly that "we alone have a right to say what shall happen in this market and the conditions on which outsiders may enter in trade."[16] So the Americans did, and the result was entirely predictable. Trade plunged, the effect of the tariff adding to the impact of the slowdown in economic activity. Writing in *The Nation* in 1931, Alex Skelton, later a senior civil servant in Ottawa, tabulated the effect. "There are," Skelton wrote, "few more striking examples of the time-worn fallacies of protectionist argument."[17]

In the circumstances, the Canadian response was inevitable. Although there were "feelers" from President Hoover and some indication that he would exempt Canada from the harshest of the agricultural tariffs in return for a pledge to develop the St. Lawrence seaway, the Mackenzie King government, with an election in the near future, could not accept that type of near-blackmail. The Canadian minister in Washington, Vincent Massey, told the Prime Minister that the Hoover proposal would be "interpreted in Canada as an effort . . . to force us into active co-operation on the St. Lawrence plan . . . and would lead to a serious revulsion of feeling against the United States." King agreed, and he told Parliament that he could "conceive of no greater misfortune" than the linking of the two issues. Soon afterwards, the King government increased tariffs on a large number of items imported from the United States and, to make the retaliatory nature of that action all the more obvious, lowered duties on 270 items imported from the empire and 98 items imported from nations to which Canada had accorded most-favoured-nation status. Overall, the average ad valorem ration was 26 percent as compared to 37 percent in the United States. The new result, as the American legation estimated, was to penalize "American trade totalling $175 000 000 the iron and steel industry along with fruit and vegetable farmers to be hurt the most."[18] In effect, King was trying to divert trade from the United States to Britain.

But if Liberals expected the tariff changes to help their re-election, they had misjudged. The Conservatives under Richard B. Bennett swept into power in October 1930, their ultra-protectionist rhetoric and their promises to blast their way into markets sounding better to the voters than Mackenzie King's more platitudinous and milder verbiage.

Bennett inherited the Depression at its nadir. Trade plummeted. At the worst, exports to the United States were below the prewar figures; so too were imports. The fall-off was very substantial. Imports of $893.5 million in 1929 were reduced to $393.7 million in 1931, $217.2 million in 1933; exports fell from $515.3 million in 1929 to $249.8 million in 1931 and $172.9 million in 1933.[19] Those collapsing figures represented thousands of Canadians — and Americans — out of work.

Bennett's answer was to raise tariffs — to 30 percent on the average in 1933 — and to seek to widen the benefits from imperial preferences.

At the Ottawa Conference of 1932, a number of trade arrangements were thrashed out. The results were mixed. Canadian exports to the United Kingdom rose from $179 million in 1932 to $304 million in 1935 while imports from Britain increased from $93.5 million in 1932 to $116.6 million.[20] There was no doubt that Canada was the chief beneficiary of the Ottawa pacts, but the increases in trade scarcely made up for the American losses. Worse yet, the imperial system put in place at Ottawa seemed to the Americans to be a deliberate challenge.

But there were changes in store in the United States. The Roosevelt Administration, in office since 1933, and particularly its secretary of state, Cordell Hull, looked on low tariffs as a positive good and on increased trade as a way to world peace. When Bennett and Roosevelt met in 1933 they agreed "to begin a search for means to increase the exchange of commodities between our two countries. . . ." The search had begun but the process was slow, the delays all being on the American side. By early 1935, W.D. Herridge, the minister in Washington, was reporting that the American negotiators were hard at work laying out their position. None doubted that the Americans wanted to get most-favoured-nation status for their exports to Canada; but the two countries' teams did not meet until late August 1935 to begin detailed bargaining.[21]

By this time, Canada had a group of tariff specialists. Dana Wilgress, the head of the Department of Trade and Commerce's commercial intelligence service, Hector McKinnon, the commissioner of tariff, and Norman Robertson, a counsellor in the Department of External Affairs, were all experts, well versed in the tariff schedule, knowledgeable about Canadian industry and agriculture, and skilled at negotiation. These men would dominate Canadian trade policy into the 1950s and beyond.

The Americans, as expected, pressed for most-favoured-nation status and for reduction below that level on a number of items. In return, they offered Canada most-favoured-nation status, guarantees that newsprint, wood pulp and a few other items would stay on the free list, and substantial reductions in duty on such items as whisky, cattle, cheese and apples. They refused concessions on codfish, milk or cream and potatoes, all items of great import to the Canadians. The negotiations stalled by the end of August, and they were not started again until after the election of 1935 had returned Mackenzie King to power.

King was eager to resume negotiations, so eager in fact that a few days after the election he called on the American minister at home. "He made it plain," the minister reported to Washington, "that there were two roads open to Canada, but that he wanted to choose 'the American road' if we made it possible for him to do so." King then met with the trade experts and with his ministers concerned with the subject and, as he wrote, "I got the impression that it was going to be possible for us to effect an agreement."[22] The experts were sent back to Washington at the beginning of November, did their work at a "terrific pace," and by November 8 the draft agreement was on President Roosevelt's desk. Mackenzie King was there soon after, and in his discussions with the President, he secured additional concessions on lumber, cattle, cream and potatoes. The agreement, the first trade pact between the two countries since 1854, was signed on November 15.

The two nations exchanged most-favoured-nation status, and the Americans reduced their rates by 20 to 50 percent on 63 items, including lumber, cattle, fish, cheese, cream and apples, and they undertook to keep 21 items on the free list. The Canadians extended their entire intermediate tariff to American products, a reduction of 2.5 to 5 percent on most items. In sum, the agreement rolled the situation almost back to where it had been in 1920, before the Fordney-McCumber tariff and before King's retaliatory measures.[23] It was a major achievement for the Canadian trade experts and for Mackenzie King, who had pushed the pace of negotiation in a most uncharacteristic way. The results showed fairly quickly. Imports from the United States rose to $490.5 million in 1937 from $312.4 million in 1935; exports to the United States rose to $372.2 million from $273.1 million two years earlier.[24]

Neither the United States nor Canada was satisfied that the 1935 agreement went as far as it could. Robertson noted that the preamble declared the agreement to be "a *first step* toward the lowering of barriers impeding trade between the countries." Its scope had been limited by the margins of preference bound in favour of empire countries and by the fact that the President could only cut tariffs by a maximum of 50 percent, thanks to the U.S. Trade Agreement Act. Moreover, Robertson said, political conditions had prevented any concession on grains and fresh codfish.

It was the imperial preferences that complicated matters. As Robertson put it, "Our own tariff on American cheese is seven cents a pound and we are obligated to maintain a margin of preference in favour of Australia of six cents a pound over foreign cheese so that we could only reduce the duty on American cheese to six cents a pound, and then on condition that Australian and New Zealand cheese entered free."[25] Thus the process was interlocked, complex, and very political. If Canada wanted to encourage trade with the United States, it had to negotiate with Britain and other empire countries at the same time. And always there was the fact that to allow the importation of American steel, for example, caused difficulties in the Maritimes and in Hamilton. There was also the danger that when Britain and the United States met to talk trade, they might try to ease their differences by asking Canada to make concessions. That in fact came to pass.

It took substantial efforts to get the United States to the table with

Canada again. The British-American negotiations of 1937 had produced a request that Canada abandon some of its preferences in the British market, but the Canadians simply refused to agree unless there were simultaneous Canadian-American talks. The Americans were reluctant, but in the end they agreed. And Norman Robertson of the Department of External Affairs set out the basic outline of Canadian commercial policy in a memorandum. The aim "is a determination to liberalize the system of imperial preference by insisting that freer trade within the Empire shall be a stride toward and not a flight from freer trade with the world. Our stake in world trade and the peculiar degree of dependence of our industries on export markets have identified Canada's real national interest with the revival and liberation of international trade. At this particular juncture of affairs," he continued, "the most effective single agency operating in the direction in which we want to go is the United States Trade Agreement policy. . . . We have, therefore, every interest in the maintenance of what are now the main lines of American commercial policy. . . . "[26] Robertson was saying in effect that Canada and the United States had the same interests in trade questions, that both wanted more trade and lower tariffs, and that imperial preferences were an impediment for both countries. That was an important memorandum because it made those points crystal clear and because it was written by a man whose influence on trade policy extended into the mid-1960s.

Canada's negotiations with the United States, conducted in parallel with the British-American talks, began in October 1937 and lasted for more than a year. Each and every commodity required a separate negotiation with the Americans and the British and often the Australians, South Africans or New Zealanders. The process was infuriatingly slow and complicated. For example, Canada had told the Americans that it was willing to give up the preference Canadian wheat enjoyed in Britain if satisfactory concessions were made for its wheat entering the United States. The difficulty was that although the United States was usually a large exporter of wheat and in ordinary years there were no or small imports of wheat from Canada, nonetheless there were political considerations at play. The Canadians rejoined by threatening to insist that the preference in the United Kingdom stand, a move that led the Americans to offer reductions on bran and other feeds. That suggestion was good but not good enough, and the wheat question remained undecided while other items were negotiated.

The Americans were easier to deal with than the empire countries. As Robertson wrote a friend, "Triangular trade negotiations — with Australia, South Africa and the Colonial Empire each off at its own peculiar tangent are dreadfully difficult & rather discouraging. I was the last Imperialist in the Dept. of External Affairs — and now I've gone too. You may never have had the 'language difficulty' but I can get on with the Americans a damn sight more easily than with the English & the Australians. . . . Our direct negotiations with the U.S. are the least of our worries right now," he said. "We can cope with them but not with God's Englishmen and the inescapable moral ascendancy over us lesser breeds."[27]

Nonetheless the agreement was finally ready for signature on November 17. For Canada, the agreement required the abandonment of preferences in Britain on wheat, pears, honey, salmon and other items; the British in turn gave up preferences in Canada on a range of manufactured goods. In its pact with the United States, Canada gained easier access to the American market for 129 of its products; and where there had been quotas in the 1935 agreement, the 1938 pact either removed or substantially increased them. The Americans for their part won easier entry into Canada for a variety of manufactured products, so much so in fact that the retired Conservative leader R.B. Bennett denounced the agreement and the Canadian Manufacturers' Association objected vehemently as did every other interest that had lost protection. Even so, the press and public response was highly favourable. Greater trade was a good thing in the Depression years, and the public could see, even if the CMA could not, that tariffs inhibited trade.

Moreover the Depression trade agreements had one virtue that the 1911 agreement had not. They were not "free trade" agreements, but merely agreements to adjust tariffs, and as such they did not carry the emotional baggage that accompanied the 1911 reciprocity pact. It was not selling out Canada to the Americans to lower tariffs; it was simply an attempt to get trade moving again and to create jobs. As such, the critics were disarmed; their complaints sounded like the special pleading it was.

The impact of the agreements, particularly in the 1938 pact, is difficult to measure precisely. The average Canadian ad valorem ration was now 24 percent, roughly at the level in force from 1912 to 1921.[28] However, the war that began in September 1939, less than a year after the pact's signature in Washington, altered the normal trade flows substantially. What the treaty of 1938 did accomplish was to create much trust between Canadian and American politicians and officials. Both sides already knew that their ultimate trade goals were similar; when the war began, those shared perceptions would prove very helpful.

. . .

The Free Trade Negotiations of 1947–1948

What form would postwar trade take? The Canadian politicians and officials knew what they wanted. In 1943, for example, Norman

Robertson, the Undersecretary of State for External Affairs since 1941, wrote to the prime minister to suggest Canada support a British initiative for early discussions. "Their approach, on the basis of multilateral Convention of Commerce providing for tariff reductions and removal of other barriers to the exchange of goods, is the only really sound and comprehensive method of securing satisfactory conditions of trade and perhaps, in the long run, of political security."[29] The future, Robertson said, lay in multilateralism as the way for Canada to gain access to United States and world markets. What that meant was that each nation subscribing to the Convention of Commerce would agree to a progressive reduction in all tariffs or in certain categories of tariffs to a maximum of say, 70 percent. That step could be supplemented by bilateral arrangements, but the sticking point for Robertson was that the Americans had to lower their tariffs. The imperial preferences could be abandoned.

These high hopes were fated to go a-glimmering. There were discussions through the remainder of the war and into the peace, but the pace was very slow. Robertson was discouraged: "My feeling," he told Mackenzie King, "has been that we had a real opportunity immediately after the end of the war and during the first phase of reconversion for drastic and relatively painless tariff revision. The longer this operation is postponed the more difficult it will be to carry out."[30] Even so, by late 1947, the General Agreement on Tariffs and Trade, a multilateral convention, was in place, and the GATT did lower tariffs generally, although not nearly as much as Robertson and the Canadians had hoped.

By the time the GATT was on the scene, Canada was enmeshed in new economic difficulties. After the war, the Canadian government had embarked on a bold and generous plan to help its allies and to cushion the shock of peacetime reconversion at home. Huge loans were made to Britain, France and the Low Countries in a deliberate attempt to rebuild prewar markets, to help the devastated countries of Europe to restore their economies, and to keep Canadians working. In all, about $2 billion were devoted to this, with $1.25 billion going to Britain, a sum fully one-third the size of that loaned by the United States. There were some grumblings about the British loan in Quebec, but most Canadians seemed to agree with the Leader of the Opposition, John Bracken, that it was "essential to the preservation of the Canadian economy as we see it today. Ours is an export economy; we are more than any other country dependent upon foreign nations for a market for our products."[31]

There were, however, some difficulties. Britain had not made sterling convertible at war's end and, exactly as during the war, Canada's trade surplus with Britain was not sufficient to cover the trade deficit with the United States. The foreign loans compounded the problem. So too did the great rush by Canadians to buy luxury goods from the

United States. During 1946 the Canadian deficit with the United States was $603 million all told, with $430 million as the deficit on merchandise trade. That deficit quickly ate into the Canadian holdings of American exchange. In other words Canada, like the rest of the postwar world, was running short of American dollars, the scarcest commodity of all.

The Marshall Plan, proposed by Secretary of State George Marshall in a Harvard convocation address on 5 June 1947, seemed one way the United States could help ease this difficulty. If America could give the European countries the goods they needed to rebuild, the dollar shortage in Europe might be overcome and reconstruction speeded. But how could this scheme help Canada? During the war Roosevelt had thought it was going too far for Canadian goods to be sent to Britain under lend-lease and to be paid for by the United States. But in 1947 that was precisely what the Canadians wanted under the Marshall Plan. Their wishes seemed no more likely to be realized than in 1941, for Congress was, as always and properly so, concerned with the needs of American farmers and producers.

By the fall of 1947 the Canadian problem had become critical. The exchange fund was running dry and drastic measures were required. At a meeting between Canadian and American officials in Washington from October 28 to 31, the Canadians laid out two alternative solutions to their exchange difficulties. The need, as Clifford Clark, the deputy minister of finance, said, was "to save between $400 and 500 million in exchange." To do this Canada had two plans. Plan A was drastic, discriminatory, and long term:

Plan A

1. A loan from the Export-Import Bank of $350 million;
2. Rationing of pleasure travel which might save $30 to $40 million;
3. Import restrictions which might save a gross of about $446 million and a net of about $300 million. Every identifiable consumer item from the United States would be completely banned, except that citrus fruits, prunes, cabbages, carrots and textiles would be put under quotas and reduced by one-third to one-half. Capital goods would also be stringently restricted. The reason for the difference between the gross and net savings is of course that Canadian industry would have to import additional capital goods in order to manufacture the consumer goods in Canada;
4. Diversion of exports which might net $50 million. . . .

Plan A simply appalled the Americans; it would be "difficult to get out from under and far more difficult for us to defend in the U.S.," they said.

Plan B was marginally more palatable:

Plan B

1. A loan of $500 million from the Export-Import Bank.
2. Rationing of pleasure travel which might save $30 to $40 million.
3. Non-discriminatory import restrictions which might save a net of $175 million. These restrictions would apply to the commodities of all countries, although by selection the restrictions would hit chiefly goods from the United States. . . . Every country would have its quota. . . .
4. Long-term measures. These measures would include diversion of Canadian exports perhaps under a trade treaty whereby the U.S. tariff was reduced, and participation of Canada in the Marshall Plan. In the latter connection, Canada hopes that the U.S. may be able to place some of the procurement for the Plan in Canada or make U.S. dollars available in the U.K. or Western Europe for the purchase of commodities in Canada.[32]

Plan B did not please the Americans, but they indicated that they expected to be able to give Canada a positive answer on Marshall Plan purchases by November 15. They said they were "very receptive" to discussing a new trade treaty that would go beyond the GATT, although Congress was certain to be difficult. But the loan from the Export-Import Bank was troublesome, and the Americans refused to budge from opposition for two weeks. Only with great difficulty did Canada secure a standby credit of $300 million from the Bank and a promise of assistance in borrowing up to $200 million more on the private New York money market.

The cabinet accepted that package on November 13 and announced the dollar-saving restrictions on November 17. Ironically, the package was made public the same day that Canada accepted the GATT agreement with its promise to lower tariffs and trade expansion.[33]

The package worked. With substantial difficulty, Canada secured a place in the Marshall Plan. Offshore purchases were permitted by Congress, and Canada benefitted to the tune of a billion dollars by 1950. That measure went a long distance toward easing the dollar shortage and to keeping up trade. And the restrictions worked so well that they were lifted far faster than any had expected.

Only the trade discussions led nowhere, although for a time they promised a new reciprocity arrangement of the widest possible scope. The Canadian intention, as John Deutsch, director of the international economic relations division of the department of finance, wrote to a friend, "is to try to work out further tariff cuts, particularly in the manufactured goods field, which would make possible a better balance in the enormous one-way trade associated with our branch plants."[34] Deutsch and Hector McKinnon, chairman of the Canadian Tariff Board, initially met with representatives from the State Department in late October 1947 to raise the idea. McKinnon had said that he and Deutsch were authorized "to explore the possibility of concluding a comprehensive agreement involving, wherever possible, the complete elimination of duties." According to the American summary of the meeting, McKinnon had said that:

> ... the Canadian Government would be willing to enter into an agreement even if it necessitated a major readjustment and reorientation of Canada's international economic relations. They feel that Canada must either integrate her economy more closely with that of the United States or be forced into discriminatory restrictive policies involving greater self sufficiency, bilateral trade bargaining and an orientation toward Europe with corresponding danger of friction with the United States, if not economic warfare.[35]

That was frank enough, even if the idea of a Canadian tilt toward a virtually prostrate Europe was not entirely believable in 1947.

How far were the Canadians prepared to go, the Americans asked. A customs union was out of the question, Deutsch and McKinnon replied. That "would be politically impossible in Canada because it would be interpreted as abandoning the empire and constituting a long step in the direction of political absorption by the United States."[36] Moreover, both parties realized that a customs union meant that Canada would be an unequal partner and would have to adjust her tariff to that of the United States. Deutsch privately told friends that "the price of a customs union with the U.S. is a loss of political independence in the sense that we would no longer be in effective control of our national policies.... Policy would be shaped in Washington. A customs union ... may be a fine thing.... But let us not blink the price."[37]

Nonetheless the Americans were considering just such a proposal. A trade agreement would not get through Congress but, as Paul Nitze of the State Department's Office of International Trade Policy, wrote, "some plan sufficiently bold and striking to fire the imagination of the people and force favorable action by Congress" might. His idea was "a special form of customs union under which there would be substantially free trade between the two countries but each would retain its separate tariff vis-à-vis third countries." Nitze thought there would have to be some exceptions to free entry, but even so this solution could meet the Canadian concerns about the orthodox type of customs union.[38]

This idea was presented to Deutsch at a Washington dinner party on 31 December 1947. Deutsch thought the idea would be "political dynamite" and promised to sound out his masters in Ottawa.[39] Deutsch personally liked the idea. The son of a Saskatchewan farmer, he was a free-trader by inheritance and conviction, and such a scheme would force inefficient central Canadian manufacturers to adapt or die. It would also increase the overall competitiveness of Canadian business and offer a promising opportunity to switch exports from the collapsing British market to the dynamic and growing American one.

In Ottawa, Deutsch found some skepticism at the Bank of Canada and in some quarters at the Department of Trade and Commerce. But C.D. Howe, the minister of trade and commerce, was enthusiastic, and so was Douglas Abbott, the minister of finance. Clifford Clark and Lester Pearson, the senior officials in finance and external affairs, were also supportive, and so too, much to Deutsch's surprise, was Mackenzie King. "It is clear to me," King noted in his diary, that "the Americans are losing no opportunity to make their relations as close as possible with our country."[40] Deutsch had the green light, and the staffs in Ottawa and Washington went to work on the plan in deep secrecy.

The Americans, it seems clear, saw this as an opportunity. Woodbury Willoughby of the commercial policy division of the State Department wrote that Canada and Britain were at the parting of the ways, unconsciously sounding much like President Taft thirty-seven years earlier. What was more, there was little cost to the United States in the plan. "Taken as a whole," Willoughby wrote, "imports from Canada would offer little threat to American producers. Nearly three-fourths by value of our present imports from Canada are already on the free list and in most other cases the duties do not offer a serious barrier." The only areas where there were problems, he argued, did not pose insuperable difficulties — wheat, flour, fish fillets, potatoes, cattle, aluminum, zinc, cheese, frozen blueberries, and silver fox furs.

The Canadians, Willoughby thought, had more difficulties. The Americans had a great advantage in manufacturing because of the size of their market, but "a transition period during which duties were progressively reduced would greatly ease problems of readjustment in Canadian industries." He added that the Canadians believed "that there are many products that could be manufactured as cheaply in Canada as in the United States and that the effect of duty elimination would be to encourage specialization." In other words, some products might be made in Canada to serve the whole North American market.[41]

The overall plan, ready by the beginning of March, involved seven main points:

a) Immediate removal of all duties by both countries.
b) Prohibition of all quantitative restrictions on imports after five years except that (1) the United States would retain right to impose

absolute quotas on imports of wheat and flour, and (2) Canada would retain right to impose absolute quotas on imports of certain fresh fruits and vegetables during Canadian growing season.

c) The United States would retain right to impose absolute transitional (five-year-period) quotas on certain products now subject to tariff quotas . . . with provision for progressive increase in quotas during five-year period.

d) Canada would retain right to impose absolute transitional quotas on certain products during five-year period, with provision for progressive increase in quotas during period.

e) Provision would be made for joint consultation, particularly for working out joint marketing agreements for agricultural products.

f) Any controls imposed on exports of short-supply items would be made subject to principle of equal sacrifice and equal benefit, and advance consultation would be required before imposition of such controls.

g) Consideration is being given to a clause ensuring, in the event that one country is subject to military attack, continued free access to the products of the other.[42]

There were great advantages to this plan. It was simple and easy to operate. It would effectively eliminate all imperial preferences granted by Canada, a long-sought U.S. goal. And Canada, the Americans thought, could even offer the same proposal to the British. For Canada, the scheme gave virtually free access to the American market on most Canadian goods immediately, and it allowed Canadian manufacturers five years to prepare for free trade. It would also mean greater integration of the continent, although as Deutsch argued, the chaos in the world economy was forcing this in any case. The only question was whether Canada negotiated now as an equal or later as a supplicant.[43]

The plan found its way to the prime minister by mid-March. His initial reaction again was good, or so Deutsch told Willoughby. But in fact, by that time King had begun to reverse direction. On March 6, the prime minister liked the idea; ten days later, he had some doubts. These were increased when *Life* magazine came out — quite coincidentally, it seems — with an editorial calling for a customs union. That article frightened King. A week later he wrote in his diary that the customs union was "almost the largest proposal short of war any leader of a government has been looked to to undertake. Its possibilities are so far-reaching for good on one hand, but possible disaster if project were defeated that I find it necessary to reflect a good deal before attempting final decision."[44]

Two days later on March 24, King reached his decision. He picked up a book, Sir Richard Jebb's *Studies in Colonial Nationalism* (published in London in 1905) and was struck by a chapter "The Soul of Empire." Would free trade not destroy the unity of the empire and, worse, destroy the regard in which Canadians held King? Would it not allow the Tories to portray him as selling out Canada to the Yankees? That did it. "I would no more think of at my time of life and at this stage of my career attempting any movement of the kind than I would of flying to the South Pole," King wrote.[45] The customs union was dead, bar the shouting.

There was some. Pearson tried to persuade King to go ahead, as did Hume Wrong, the Ambassador in Washington. But it was no use. Even though he was seventy-three years old and only months away from retirement, King so dominated his government that he could get his way. The best the officials could get was a suggestion in the official note to the Americans suspending the talks that "it is thought that trade discussions might begin again if and when a satisfactory North Atlantic Security Pact is signed. It would be natural for the trade discussions to be related to the pact, since they are concerned with measures for economic defence against aggression." The talks that eventually led to the North Atlantic Treaty had been underway for some time in complete secrecy, but they eventually dragged out so long that it was clear that it would be 1949 before the customs union talks would resume, if ever. And once King was gone in the fall of 1948, his successor, Louis St. Laurent, was more than a little cool to the resumption of negotiations. He was concerned about his province's attitude and concerned too that if he, a French-Canadian, did away with imperial preferences and linked Canada to the United States, the reaction in English Canada might resemble that of 1911.[46]

Thus the customs union died on the drawing boards. To some, it was the chance of a lifetime to link Canada on favourable terms with the American economy. To others, and particularly to Mackenzie King, it was yet another attempt to see Canada swallowed up by the giant to the south. It was also political dynamite, just as Deutsch had said in December, but the explosion might have been powerful enough to destroy the government. The idea was gone, not to return in a powerful form until the 1980s.

Toward Free Trade Again?

Throughout the 1950s, Canada's trade generally boomed. But there were potentially disquieting signs. Despite valiant efforts, embodied in the loans to Britain and Western Europe, trade with overseas countries tended to fall as a percentage of total Canadian trade, while trade with the United States mounted annually. In 1955, 60 percent of Canadian exports and 73 percent of her imports came from the United States. In addition, the United States was the source of 76 percent of foreign capital invested in Canada.[47] More and more, Canada was becoming a country with one market only.

That condition worried many. When John Diefenbaker came to power in 1957 one of his post-election promises was a pledge to shift 15 percent of Canada's trade from the United States to Britain. This was, the new prime minister said, "a direct challenge to British industry and initiative." The officials in Ottawa, who had known nothing of this promise before it was delivered, were flabbergasted. A diversion of trade on that scope was impossible to achieve for it meant an increase in imports from Britain of $625 million. How could such growth be achieved when the British share of the Canadian market was continuing its decline — from 56.1 percent in 1870 to 16.8 percent in 1921–1931, and down to 8.5 percent in 1956? Moreover, for more than half of the Canadian import market, Britain had no chance as a supplier, either for lack of goods or because of design problems. What that meant in effect was that 35 percent of the trade in suitable areas would have to be switched from American to British suppliers. Such a move was impossible and the Diefenbaker initiative died quickly. So too did a British ministerial proposal for Canada-U.K. free trade in September 1957, an idea that Diefenbaker dismissed on the grounds that he "could not see what advantage there would be in it for Canada."[48]

On the other hand, the Diefenbaker government actively sought a larger share of the American market in defence-related materials. After a long diplomatic campaign, Canada secured American agreement in 1958 to a defence production-sharing agreement that was intended to give Canadian firms a crack at the American market, thereby offsetting the heavy purchases made by the Canadian forces in the United States. The next year, in fact, the Eisenhower government agreed to exempt Canada from the provisions of its Buy American act, that restricted government purchasing to American firms. As a result, Canadian suppliers were freed from the 6 to 12 percent premiums which the act ordinarily added to foreign bids for defence contracts, and tariffs were treated lightly. In effect, the exemption created a kind of sectoral free trade arrangement in defence production, a logical continuation of the Hyde Park Agreement of 1941. The results, however, never quite lived up to expectations, although during the Vietnam War, for example, Canadian sales to the U.S. Department of Defense were substantial.

Even though it had sought the defence production agreement with Washington, the Diefenbaker government continued to fear for its overseas markets. This was most evident in the government's opposition to the proposal that Britain enter the European Common Market. What concerned Ottawa was the extent to which European trading arrangements would shrink Canadian markets overseas while increasing Canadian dependence on the United States. Despite official studies that demonstrated that British entry would have only a relatively minor impact on Canadian trade to the United Kingdom — only 10 percent of Canadian-British trade would be affected, Gordon Churchill, the former minister of trade and commerce wrote to Diefenbaker — the government resisted strongly. At the Ghana meetings of Commonwealth finance and trade ministers, Donald Fleming and George Hees created a ruckus with their assaults on British desertion of the Commonwealth. John Diefenbaker did the same at the Commonwealth prime ministers' meeting in 1962, and charges of a betrayal of the empire-Commonwealth were in the air. In the end, the Canadian Conservatives were saved by President deGaulle of France who blocked Britain's entry into Europe in January 1963.[49]

Still, the Common Market had serious implications for Canada. It implied that Europe was on the way to becoming an economic unit of great power. At the same time, the emergence of Japan as an economic giant was also well underway. What did all this mean? To Simon Reisman of the department of finance, a free trader then and later, it meant that Canada should move toward free trade with the United States. Speaking in confidence to Grant Dexter of the *Winnipeg Free Press* in October 1961, Reisman's reasoning was clear. The pressure to unite Europe was exerting similar pressure on North America, and in self-defence Canada and the United States should move closer together. "He does not believe our nationhood would be menaced. There might be some loss of sovereignty. But so there is in Europe." The historical processes could not be checked. "Our relationship to the U.S. has been getting closer and closer over the decades. . . . Integration need never be political. He did not see why it must be. But the economic integration — defence and all that — must go on apace. This was inevitable and, he thought, desirable."[50]

Perhaps it was, but the idea was not pursued. What was sought instead was a special place for Canada at the Kennedy Round trade negotiations in Geneva. There were difficulties. The Liberals had returned to power in the elections of April 1963, and there were serious differences between the generally free-trading Mitchell Sharp and his department of trade and commerce and the more protectionist Walter Gordon and his department of finance. The Canadian position was that linear tariff cuts, proposed by the Americans who wanted all the GATT countries to reduce tariffs by half over five years, were not equitable for Canada, which was dependent on raw material exports and the imports of manufactured goods. As one trade official said,

> Since we import about ten times more manufactured goods than we export, a linear cut in the Canadian tariffs to match a linear cut in the tariffs of our major trading partners would clearly be

out of balance in terms of compensating benefits received and
given by Canada, as well as being out of all proportion in terms
of the degree of adjustment that would be required in Canadian
industry as compared with the mass production industries of the
U.S. and Europe.[51]

That position was reluctantly accepted by the Geneva participants.

To work out the detailed Canadian position, the Canadian Tariffs
and Trade Committee, chaired by Norman Robertson and with
Hector McKinnon as vice chairman, began hearings at the beginning
of 1964. These two veterans of trade negotiations in the 1930s might
have reflected on the changes in the way trade policy was formed in
Canada. In 1911, Fielding had dealt with the Secretary of State; in
1935, three officials had talked with a similar number from Washington; by 1964, hearings were held to which industry presented four
hundred and fifty separate briefs and the government negotiating team
for Geneva had representatives from Trade and Commerce, Finance,
External Affairs, Mines and Technical Surveys, Agriculture, National
Revenue and Industry, and a cabinet committee chaired by the Prime
Minister kept watch. Policy now was carefully detailed, not made up
as the negotiators went along.

The result at Geneva, after long negotiations and cabinet wavering,
was that Canada made concessions on $2.5 billion worth of imports,
almost $2 billion of which came from the United States. In return, the
Americans offered concessions on a similar amount of Canadian
exports, eliminating duties on lumber and paper and on some classes
of fish and agricultural products. Other U.S. tariffs were substantially
reduced.[52] It was not quite free trade, but to a substantial extent tariffs
were now becoming almost inconsequential.

In some areas of production, in fact, Canada was interested in free
trade. The idea had emerged in the auto industry and there had been
suggestions for sectoral free trade made as early as 1964 by Norman
Robertson. But it was the auto sector that was critical. On 1 November 1963 the Canadian government extended to imports of motor
vehicles and parts a duty rebate plan which had been put in place a year
earlier for auto transmissions and engines. Under the plan, Canadian
manufacturers could earn duty rebates on imported parts and vehicles
by increasing exports from Canada. To the United States, this was an
indirect subsidy to Canadian exports and thus subject to the American
countervailing duty statute. For the next eighteen months, there were
negotiations and American threats of action, but all this culminated in
June 1964 with broad negotiations on the whole North American auto
market. The Americans and Canadians both had decided that free
trade in vehicles and parts was in their joint interest, and an agreement
to that effect was signed in January 1965.[53] The basic concept was that
if the U.S. parent companies made room in their domestic markets

and operations for the products of their Canadian subsidiaries, then the branch plants could specialize and become more efficient. The Auto Pact eliminated duties on Canadian cars, trucks, buses, parts and accessories for assembly admitted to the United States; Canada did the same, but in recognition of the fact that costs and prices of cars in Canada were higher and would remain so for a time, only manufacturers who met specified criteria could import duty free into Canada. Congress accepted the Auto Pact — after much hesitation and a major White House and Treasury-Commerce Department lobbying effort — in October 1965.[54] By June 1967, according to American figures, trade in auto parts had expanded rapidly to become the largest single item in Canadian-American trade. U.S. exports to Canada rose from $660 million to $1.3 billion and U.S. imports from $75 million to $900 million between 1964 and 1966. Investment in the Canadian auto industry as a result of the Auto Pact was estimated at $500 million, Canadian vehicle production was up 35 percent and employment in the auto industry up 27 percent. Half the cars and trucks produced in Canada were being sold in the United States.[55]

So favourable to the Canadian interest was the Auto Pact that President Johnson (angry at Canada's Vietnam policy and at Pearson's Temple University speech calling for a bombing halt) actually snapped at the Canadian Ambassador that "You screwed us on the auto pact!"[56] Before too many years had passed, however, Canadians were beginning to feel that they had been screwed when the balance in trade of auto parts turned sharply in favour of the United States after 1973 and reached $3 billion in 1979. Sectoral free trade, in other words, had its advantages and disadvantages.[57] On the other hand, the auto industry in Canada had grown and developed markedly. Without the Auto Pact, it might have withered.

The limited success of the Auto Pact has encouraged Canadians and Americans to look to additional sectors of the economy where free trade might be beneficial. For Canada, suffering in 1980 from a trade deficit of $17.8 billion in manufactured end products,[58] there were only a few sectors where Canadian goods might be able to compete. Not surprisingly those sectors were included in the list. Textiles, data services, steel, agricultural implements, petrochemicals and government procurement were all mentioned in the exchanges between the two governments, and in early 1984 the pace of discussion and preliminary negotiation between officials of both countries was accelerating. The climate seemed right. Already some 80 percent of Canada's exports to the United States enter free of duty, while 66 percent of American exports to Canada are duty free; the total trade between the two countries amounts to $110 billion a year. Foreign competition is increasing and while tariffs have fallen substantially, thanks to the rounds of multilateral trade negotiations since 1946, various new non-tariff barriers have been put in place. Thus, to some there again seemed to be advantages in tying Canada and the United States together in the face of an increasingly hostile trading environment throughout the world. As the Canadian ambassador in Washington put it, "More than ever, Canadian industry must be competitive to survive, both within Canada and in export markets. More than ever Canadian industry must have open and secure access to U.S. markets to achieve economies of scale and effective rationalization of products lines needed to remain competitive."[59] The Americans could say much the same things.

If there were pressures for free trade, there were countervailing forces too. In the United States, the trade deficit for 1984 was expected to reach $100 billion dollars, and protectionist sentiment for what the *New York Times* called "fortress America" was mounting. Industries had turned to the government for help in stemming the flow of imports, and the Reagan Administration had responded to the increasing number of requests by cutting imports of Japanese autos, specialty steels, motorcycles, textiles and apparel. Democratic presidential candidates, not to be outdone, called for "domestic content" regulations.[60]

In Canada, by contrast, there has been generally strong support for the government's efforts to move into negotiations with the United States. The Progressive Conservative party appears to have shed its history and, according to Michael Wilson, formerly the Opposition critic on international trade and later minister of finance, Canada has to move quickly to free trade before protectionist sentiment in the United States makes agreements impossible. There are also critics. Senator Michael Pitfield has bemoaned the absence of discussion in Canada on the implications of free trade and feared that the government was pressing ahead so fast that the country would be committed to the scheme before the people realized it. Abraham Rotstein of the University of Toronto noted that Canadians think free trade is fine so long as it comes in the sectors where Canada gets the advantages. "But no one asks: what does the U.S. want in return? Just as there's no free lunch, there's no free trade."[61]

What of the political implications for Canada? Sylvia Ostry, deputy minister of international trade, argues that although Canada's economic links with the United States have increased in recent years, Canada remains very much a nation with a sense of itself. Mitchell Sharp, a former politician and as such probably more sensitive than Sylvia Ostry to public moods, disagrees. He told a Washington conference that "to enter into a free trade area arrangement with the United States is to alter fundamentally the direction of Canadian policy, not so much in economic terms as in political terms, and I do not think Canadians are prepared to do so."[62]

No one should expect a historian to attempt to forecast the future or to try to guess what the outcome of this debate will be; that is something best left to the futurologist political scientists and politicians. But historians can indicate the causes of debate in the past and can show how questions were resolved. They can also highlight the trends in long-lasting issues.

The first thing that must be said is that reciprocity has always been contentious. There has never been a period when everyone cheered as one in favour of it. There were always the businessmen and farmers whose special interests would be hurt by unimpeded access to the Canadian market for American products. There were always those who feared the United States — for its republicanism, for its bellicosity, for its polyglot and violent society. And there were always those who wanted Canada to remain a British country, part of the empire-Commonwealth, and who feared that reciprocity inevitably would pull Canada into the American union as another state or states. Against the critics were those Canadians, very often those with their own special interests, who wanted reciprocity. At various times this has included the businessmen of Montreal who feared that their markets in England were gone or the farmers of the Prairies who wanted cheap farm implements and less expensive consumer goods. There were also those, like Laurier, who believed that reciprocity made simple economic sense, that prosperity was good for Canadian unity and that reciprocity meant prosperity, and that the super-imperialists were draping themselves in the bloody shirt of loyalty only to protect their wealth. The British connection, in other words, was a powerful factor in every discussion of reciprocity in our history, a disincentive for those who sought closer trade links with the Americans. It is fair to say that this factor no longer matters.

Canadian nationalism still matters, however. The first time that nationalism was raised as a counter to reciprocity was in 1911 (to be sure, along with imperialism), and it was also a factor in the trade discussions of the 1930s and in the decision to abort the customs union talks of 1947–48. In some respects, this economic nationalism has been little more than a reaction by central Canadian businessmen to protect their manufacturing interests against American competition. Overall it has always been something more. There has been, and remains, a strong feeling among Canadians that there are differences between their society and that of the United States and a fear that an open border for trade might somehow weaken the fragile flower of Canadian nationalism. Vincent Massey once wrote a book called *The Price of Being Canadian*, which sketched out the higher costs and somewhat shrunken opportunities that Canadians had to bear to retain their separateness. To many that price has historically been too much to bear, one explanation for the large numbers of Canadians who live in the United States. But Canadians have been generally prepared to pay the price of being Canadian, and the strong, if ill-defined, fear of the United States and its economic power has helped them to that decision.

There can also be no doubt that reciprocity discussions between Canada and the United States historically have intensified when times were bad. The interest in the idea in the 1850s fits the pattern, as does that in the 1880s. In 1911 the economy was just reaching the end of a long boom, and in the 1930s the trade discussion took place in the gloom of the Depression. The customs union negotiations of 1947–1948 occurred in a period of great postwar dislocation, a time when the growth of the Canadian economy seemed seriously in jeopardy because of a lack of American exchange. And, of course, the current interest in sectoral free trade in Canada has its roots in a very shaky economy. When times are difficult, in other words, Canadians and Americans think about bringing their economies together; when the economy is booming, there is a lessening of interest in reciprocity.

There is also a foreign dimension to reciprocity. In the 1930s, the two countries came closer together economically because the United States was interested in cracking the British preferential system and was prepared to make some concessions to Canada to achieve this. In 1947–48, with the European economies in ruins because of the war and with the Soviet armies standing at the Elbe, there was a clear understanding in Washington, and in Ottawa, that the two North American nations had interests in common. The 1947–48 talks discussed the possibility of a defence clause as part of the customs union package, a significant inclusion, and the discussions then underway for the North Atlantic Treaty also had, at Canadian insistence, an economic component. In the threatening world of the 1980s, is it not possible that free trade talks similarly might have a defence dimension? Or has the strong reaction against the testing of the cruise missile in Canada and the calls for a nuclear freeze that occasionally enlivened the 1984 election campaign made the possibility of closer military links between Canada and the United States less likely?

There is another aspect to the history of Canadian-American reciprocity discussions that needs mention, and that is the bureaucratic element. To 1935, the trade discussions were almost entirely one-man shows on each side. The prime minister would send an emissary to Washington who would negotiate in secret with his American counterpart. In 1935, for the first time, small teams of trade experts negotiated on behalf of their countries, a similar pattern occurred in 1947–48. But that process could not take place again. The Kennedy Round negotiations of the early 1960s set the pattern for the current era — public hearings across the country to receive industry briefs, a very large officials' committee with representation from ten or more departments in Ottawa, each with its own special interests to advance or protect, and a cabinet committee of powerful ministers to haggle over the policy and agree on the concessions. There seems no reason to believe that any new government could alter that bureaucratic-political structure; if anything, the increasing complexities of the trade issues between Canada and the United States make such a structure inevitable. Can radical changes in Canadian trade result from such a structure? Or does the increased bureaucratization of the process mean that only incremental change can ever result?

Finally, it is a truism to say that every trade agreement benefits some and hurts others. The western farmers in 1911 thought they had made gains in the draft reciprocity treaty of that year, but the central Canadian manufacturers feared its implications. The 1947–48 negotiations posed a threat to Canadian manufacturing, as John Deutsch and Hector McKinnon knew, but they believed (even if Prime Minister Mackenzie King did not) that the protections they had negotiated would certainly allow the strong industries to adapt, to survive and to have clear benefits for Canadian consumers. In that particular case, the political leadership weighed the bargain and found it wanting. In terms of his political calculus, Mackenzie King was probably right to have acted as he did in scuppering the customs union. To King, the politics and emotions of the issue took precedence over the economic implications, in substantial part because he remembered what had happened to Laurier in 1911 when the economic implications had been allowed to outweigh the political. There is a lesson there. Reciprocity or customs union or sectoral free trade, whatever its name, is very much an emotional political issue, and there seems little reason to believe that the 1980s have altered this fundamental fact. There are not very many lessons in history that stand out clearly; one that does, however, is that free trade between Canada and the United States has major political implications in Canada. Any political leader who forgets that does so at his peril.

Notes

1. G.W. Bertram, "Economic Growth in Canadian Industry, 1870–1915," *Canadian Journal of Economics and Political Science* 29 (May 1963): 170.

2. W.A. Mackintosh and K.W. Taylor, "Canadian Tariff Policy," *Canadian Papers 1938*, prepared for the British Commonwealth Relations Conference, Canadian Institute of International Affairs, 97.

3. Paul Stevens, ed., *The 1911 General Election: A Study in Canadian Politics* (Toronto: Copp Clark, 1970), 9.

4. Ibid.

5. Ibid., 66–67. See also R.C. Brown and R. Cook, *Canada 1986–1921* (Toronto: McClelland and Stewart, 1974), 181–82.

6. Stevens, *The 1911 General Election*, 69–70; R.C. Brown, *Robert Laird*

Borden (Toronto: Macmillan, 1975), 1: 178–80 takes a less dark view of this agreement.

7. Stevens, *The 1911 General Election*, 81.

8. Ibid., 113ff.

9. L.E. Ellis, "Canada's Rejection of Reciprocity in 1911," *Canadian Historical Association Report 1939*, 99ff and L.E. Ellis, *Reciprocity 1911* (Toronto: Ryerson, 1939), esp. chap. 8.

10. Stevens, *The 1911 General Election*, 174, 179.

11. See for example, Robert Cuff, "The Conservative Party Machine and the Election of 1911 in Ontario," *Ontario History* 57 (September 1965).

12. Stevens, *The 1911 General Election*, 220.

13. A Canadian, "Why Canada Rejected Reciprocity," *Yale Review* (January 1912): 184.

14. M.B. Cohen, "The Opening of Canadian Diplomatic Relations: The Economic Impetus," Canadian Historical Association Paper (1975), 9.

15. M. Urquhart and K. Buckley, eds. *The Historical Statistics of Canada* (Toronto: Macmillan, 1965), 183.

16. R.N. Kottman, "Herbert Hoover and the Smoot-Hawley Tariff: Canada, A Case Study," *Journal of American History* 62 (December 1975): 609ff.; and R.N. Kottman, *Reciprocity and the North Atlantic Triangle, 1932–1938* (Ithaca: Cornell University Press, 1968), chap. 2.

17. Alex Skelton, "A North American Customs Union," *The Nation* (4 Nov. 1931).

18. Kottman, "Herbert Hoover," 630; Mackintosh and Taylor, "Canadian Tariff Policy," 97, 100.

19. Urquhart and Buckley, *Historical Statistics of Canada*, 183.

20. Ibid.

21. J.L. Granatstein, *A Man of Influence: Norman A. Robertson and Canadian Statecraft, 1929–68* (Ottawa: Deneau, 1981), 48ff.

22. *Foreign Relations of the United States 1935* (Washington, 1952) 2:29.

23. Granatstein, *A Man of Influence*, 48ff.

24. Urquhart and Buckley, *Historical Statistics of Canada*, 183.

25. Granatstein, *A Man of Influence*, 59.

26. Ibid., 66.

27. Ibid., 74.

28. Mackintosh and Taylor, "Canadian Tariff Policy," 97.

29. Granatstein, *A Man of Influence*, 123.

30. Ibid., 128.

31. R. Cuff and J.L. Granatstein, *American Dollars — Canadian Prosperity: Canadian-American Economic Relations 1945–50* (Toronto: Samuel Stevens, 1978), 29.

32. U.S. National Archives, State Department Records, file 842.5151/11-147, "Canadian Dollar Problem: Discussions" (28–31 Oct. 1947); Department of External Affairs, Records, file TS 265(s), "Summary of U.S.-Canadian Financial Discussions, 28–31 October 1947," att. Wrong to Clark, 1 Nov. 1947.

33. Cuff and Granatstein, *American Dollars*, chap. 3.

34. Queen's University Archives, J.J. Deutsch Papers, file 5, Deutsch to

Wilgress, 23 Dec. 1947.

35. "U.S.-Canadian Trade Relations," State Department Records, file FW611.422/10–2649, 29 Oct. 1947.

36. Ibid.

37. Queen's University Archives, Grant Dexter papers, memo of conversations, 4 Dec. 1948 and 31 Jan. 1950.

38. Nitze to Wilcox, 18 Dec. 1947, State Department Records, file 842.5151/10–2649.

39. Cuff and Granatstein, *American Dollars*, 70.

40. J.W. Pickersgill and D. Forster, *The Mackenzie King Record 1947–48* (Toronto: University of Toronto Press, 1970), 4, 261.

41. "Proposed Tariff Reciprocity Arrangement with Canada," 22 Jan. 1948, State Department Records, FW611.422/10-2649.

42. Ibid., "Suggested Time-Table," 16 Feb. 1948.

43. Memo, no date, Deutsch Papers, file 560.

44. W.L.M. King Papers, Diary, March 6, 16, 22, 26, 1948, Public Archives of Canada; *Life*, 15 Mar. 1948.

45. King Diary, 24 Mar. 1948.

46. Cuff and Granatstein, *American Dollars*, 79ff.

47. P.K. Kresl, "Before the Deluge: Canadians on Foreign Ownership 1920–1955," *American Review of Canadian Studies* 6 (Spring 1976): 100. On free trade sentiment in the U.S. in the 1950s, see R. Bothwell and J. Kirton, "A Sweet Little Country," *Queen's Quarterly* 90 (Winter 1983): 1093ff.

48. J.L. Granatstein, draft chapter "Conservative Economics" for book on "Canada 1957–67."

49. Ibid.

50. Dexter Papers, Memorandum, 12 Oct. 1961.

51. Granatstein, *A Man of Influence*, 365ff.

52. Ibid.

53. Documents on Public Archives of Canada, Department of Finance Records, v.3905, file 8705–01; on J.F. Kennedy Library, Boston, Herter Papers, vols. 7, 14.

54. L.B. Johnson Library, Austin, M. Manatos Papers, Box 6, memos on Canadian Auto Parts file.

55. Position paper in Joint U.S.-Canada Committee on Trade and Economic Affairs file, m.f. 44, Council of Economic Advisors Records, Johnson Library.

56. Lawrence Martin, *The Presidents and the Prime Ministers* (Toronto: Doubleday, 1982), p. 219.

57. J.F. Keeley, "Cast in Concrete for all Time? The Negotiations of the Auto Pact," *Canadian Journal of Political Science* 16 (June 1983): 281ff; *Globe and Mail*, 29 Mar. 1980; 27 Feb. 1982; Stephen Clarkson, *Canada and the Reagan Challenge* (Toronto: James Lorimer, 1982), 126ff.

58. Ibid., 125.

59. Allan Gotlieb, in *The Roundtable Report*, 1 (February-March, 1984); A.S. Cartwright, address to Canadian General Electric Shareholders, 25 Apr. 1984. See also M.M. Hart, "Reviewing Canada's Trade Policies," a paper prepared for the Institute for Research on Public Policy, Ottawa, 1984.

60. *New York Times*, 4 Mar. and 5 Aug. 1984. See also M.M. Hart, "Canada–United States Sectoral Free Trade," a paper prepared for the Institute for Research on Public Policy, Ottawa, 1984 for an analysis of private and governmental responses to sectoral free trade.

61. *Globe and Mail*, 16 Mar. 1984.

62. Ibid., 13 Apr. and 11 May, 1984. Also A. Rotstein's *Rebuilding from Within* (Ottawa: Canadian Institute for Economic Policy, 1984), 32ff.

SECTION 2
GOVERNMENT POLICY

For much of Canada's short history the absence of foreign policy seemed the very essence, if not of statesmanship, then of political wisdom. Statements that were concrete and substantial were also by definition a target, a focus for divisions and opposition. More recently, the word "policy" has taken on a magic ring; Ottawa abounds in "policy analysts"; announcements of the new and dramatically different are frequently, even frivolously, made. In so complicated and multi-faceted a business as contemporary Canadian-American relations, however, even the most agile politician or bureaucrat would be hard pressed to state Canadian "policy" with precision and in detail. Perhaps that is just as well.

The following section provides snapshots of official Canadian attitudes and policies over a fifty-year period. None, with the possible exception of Mitchell Sharp's Third Option paper, attempts to embrace all the parts of a complex Canadian-American connection. Each, however, is a reflection of the far-reaching scope of the relationship, and of the importance the government has attributed to the United States since the outbreak of the Second World War.

The origins of the modern Canadian-American relationship lie in the Ogdensburg Agreement of 1940 and the Hyde Park Declaration of 1941. They were the tersely-written, informal products of crisis, greased by an extraordinarily close relationship between President Roosevelt and Prime Minister King. Although they had limited purposes, the two declarations laid the foundation for the much broader co-operation that was to come during and after the Second World War.

Ten years on from Ogdensburg and Hyde Park, Canada was again fighting at America's side, this time in Korea under the auspices of the United Nations. Canadians still thought of themselves as saviours, perhaps because it is part of their makeup. The mission of Canadian foreign policy was not only to rescue the world from international Communism, but also to restrain the use of American power and save the United States from itself. In the spring of 1951, External Affairs Minister L.B. Pearson made it clear, in a way Washington certainly did not like, that the days of "easy and automatic" relations were over. Canada, with its new importance in U.S. and free world planning for defence and development, planned to use what leverage it had to ask hard questions about how the Americans were discharging their international responsibilities "and how the rest of us will be involved." Pearson wanted the Korean conflict to remain manageable and to be done with quickly, so that no further threats to the peace of the area would result.

In the final analysis, Canada would always be on the American side. Formal and informal connections between the two countries increased apace, none more than in the military sphere. The Permanent Joint Board on Defence had been created by the Ogdensburg Agreement and, even though it diminished in importance after the United States entered the war in December 1941, it continued on into the postwar years as an umbrella organization for functional military co-operation and a forum for ensuring that matters of common concern could at least be aired. The most significant postwar military ties, however, were on a service-to-service basis. The most tangible and public product of these linkages was the 1957 agreement creating an integrated North American Air Defence Command, the recommendation for which came from the air staffs of the two countries. Newly-minted Prime Minister John Diefenbaker, though elected to some extent on an anti-American platform, quickly approved the agreement, but the Department of External Affairs held out for firmer arrangements ensuring consultation between the two governments. A formal exchange of notes in 1958 was the result.

The Vietnam War of the 1960s and early 1970s raised questions not simply about U.S. judgement but also about Canada's involvement in American alliances and arms-sharing agreements. Such arrangements now carried the odour of collusion in a bad war. In 1967, University of Toronto professors approached Pearson, now prime minister, with the suggestion that weapons not be sold to the Americans until the intervention in Vietnam ceased. Pearson explained that Canadian-American defence co-operation was a seamless web necessary to the Atlantic alliance and very beneficial to Canadians. He also reiterated the government's support of a negotiated settlement of the conflict reached through quiet, not public, diplomacy.

It was not only university professors who were disillusioned by the war in Vietnam. Canadians grew increasingly wary of American methods and leadership, while Washington was inclined all the more to raw assertions of its national interest in a world where friends were harder than ever to find. The Trudeau government's Third Option paper, written after Canada felt the force of President Nixon's 1971 New Economic Policy, was a deliberate effort to insulate Canadians from American cultural and economic strength. Canada looked now — in vain, as it happened — to Europe and Japan for diversification of its trade. It adopted a series of measures restricting foreign investment, regulating television and cablevision programming originating in the U.S., and instituting cultural non-tariff barriers. In 1981, Secretary of State for External Affairs Mark MacGuigan went to New York to explain to Americans that the much-despised Foreign Investment Review Agency and the National Energy Program should be viewed as "the firm wish of the people of Canada" and the product of the drive for more national independence.

The Mulroney government's free trade initiative represented the clear rejection of third option thinking. Canada's economic future, the prime minister argued, lay firmly with the United States. And that made Canada's political future more, not less, secure.

THE OGDENSBURG AGREEMENT, 1940†

W.L.M. KING

... In the matter of time and significance, the conversations between President Roosevelt and myself on matters pertaining to the common interest of our two countries in the defence of their coasts, divide themselves naturally into two groups: the conversations which took place prior to the commencement of the war, and those which have taken place since.

The first conversation was on the occasion of a visit I paid the president at the White House, as long ago as March 1937. At that time the discussion had reference to the position on the Pacific as well as on the Atlantic coasts. It was then agreed that, at some time in the future, meetings might be arranged between the staff officers of both countries to discuss problems of common defence.

On September 30 of that year, the president paid a visit to Victoria, British Columbia, crossing on a United States destroyer from Seattle. This visit led to arrangements for talks between staff officers regarding Pacific coast problems, which took place in Washington in January 1938.

I think I may say that on every occasion on which I have visited the president in the United States, or on which I have met the president on his visits to Canada, matters pertaining to the defence of this continent have been a subject of conversation between us.

The defences on the Atlantic were referred to particularly in our

† Canada, House of Commons, *Debates*, 12 November 1940, 55–58.

conversations in August 1938, in the course of the president's visit to Kingston, and the opening of the Thousand Islands bridge at Ivy Lea. At that time, it will be recalled, the president made the open declaration that the people of the United States would not stand idly by if domination of Canadian soil were threatened by any other empire. To this declaration I replied at Woodbridge, Ontario, two days later, that we too had our obligations as a good, friendly neighbour.

Our common problems of defence were discussed at length and in a more concrete and definite way when I visited Washington in November 1938, to sign the new Canadian-United States trade agreement.

In the summer of 1939, the president paid a visit to Canadian waters off the Atlantic coast. He subsequently told me that this visit, like his similar visit to Victoria two years earlier, had been occasioned by his concern with the problem of coastal defence.

With the outbreak of war, the question of coast defences became of vital importance. At the same time, the fact that Canada was a belligerent and the United States a neutral complicated the problem of pursuing the discussions. In the face of the European menace it was obviously desirable to give expression to the needs of joint defence. To the means, however, of effecting this end, the most careful consideration had to be given in order that there might be no grounds for the belief that there was any attempt on Canada's part to influence the policies or to interfere in the domestic affairs of a neutral country. Had there not been, between the president and myself, complete confidence in each other's purpose and motives, I question if the situation could have been met without occasioning genuine embarrassment to one side or the other, if not indeed to both. Fortunately, in the light of our previous conversations, there was no danger of the position being misunderstood, and my visit with the president at Warm Springs, in April of the present year, afforded an exceptional opportunity for a careful review of the whole situation.

This is perhaps an appropriate place for me to say that, from the beginning, and at the time of each conversation, the president made it perfectly clear that his primary interest in the subject was the defence of the United States. I was equally frank in making it clear that my concern was the effective defence of Canada, and the defence of the British commonwealth of nations as a whole.

If one thing above another became increasingly evident in the course of our conversations, it was that our respective countries had a common interest in the matter of the defence of this continent. Since this was the case, everything pointed to the wisdom of planning carefully in advance for whatever contingency might arise.

The conversations begun between the president and myself before the war, in the direct manner I have described, and at Warm Springs taken up anew after Canada had entered the war, were supplemented as the weeks went by, by conversations conducted through diplomatic channels. Staff conversations followed in due course.

I should perhaps say that I gave to my colleagues who were members of the war committee of the cabinet my entire confidence with respect to the conversations I had had with the president, and subsequent steps were taken with their knowledge and full approval. I should also like to say that the British government was kept duly informed of what was taking place. The Canadian government likewise was kept informed of the defence matters directly discussed between the British government and the United States. The discussions naturally included questions pertaining to the leasing of air and naval bases on the Atlantic.

As I have already mentioned, the president had announced the day before our meeting at Ogdensburg that conversations had been taking place between the two governments. The Ogdensburg agreement formally confirmed what the previous conversations and planning had initiated. It made known to the world that plans of joint defence were being studied and worked out between the two countries. It did one thing more: it made clear that the board which was being established to make studies and recommendations was not being formed for a single occasion to meet a particular situation, but was intended to deal with a continuing problem. The board on joint defence was, therefore, declared to be permanent.

By a minute of council approved by His Excellency the Governor General on August 21, the establishment of the Permanent Joint Board on Defence was formally ratified and confirmed.

With the permission of the house, I should like to insert in Hansard a copy of the complete minute:

> The committee of the privy council have had before them a report, dated 20 August, 1940, from the Right Honourable W.L. Mackenzie King, Prime Minister and Secretary of State for External Affairs, representing:
>
> That on 17 August, 1940, at the invitation of the President of the United States, he proceeded to the United States to Ogdensburg in the state of New York, to meet Mr. Roosevelt for the purpose of discussing mutual problems of defence in relation to the safety of Canada and the United States;
>
> That conversations on this subject between the Prime Minister and the President of the United States, accompanied by the Secretary of State for War of the United States (Mr. Stimson), took place on August 17, and the following joint statement with respect to agreement which had been reached was, on August 18, released for publication by the Prime Minister and the President:

"The Prime Minister and the President have discussed the mutual problems of defence in relation to the safety of Canada and the United States.

It has been agreed that a Permanent Joint Board on Defence shall be set up at once by the two countries.

This Permanent Joint Board on Defence shall commence immediate studies relating to sea, land and air problems including personnel and material.

It will consider in the broad sense the defence of the north half of the western hemisphere.

The Permanent Joint Board on Defence will consist of four or five members from each country, most of them from the services. It will meet shortly."

That the actions of the Prime Minister in conducting the said conversations and in agreeing, on the part of Canada, to the establishment of a Permanent Joint Board on Defence for the consideration of the defence of the north half of the western hemisphere, are in accord with the policy of the government as approved on many occasions by the war committee of the cabinet and the cabinet itself.

The Prime Minister, therefore, recommends that his actions in conducting the said conversations and in agreeing to the establishment of the said Permanent Joint Board on Defence be ratified and confirmed.

The committee concur in the foregoing recommendation and submit the same for approval.

THE HYDE PARK DECLARATION, 1941†

W.L.M. KING

… On March 12, I described the United States lease-lend act as one of the milestones of freedom, pointing the way to ultimate and certain victory. The lease-lend act settled the principle of United States assistance to Britain and the other democracies. It did not, however, solve all of the complex economic problems involved in the mobilization of the resources of the United States and Canada in order to render to Britain, in the speediest manner, the most effective assistance and support.

One of the reasons for my recent visit to the United States and my conferences with the president, was the urgent need for Canada to find an immediate solution of some of the problems involved in our wartime economic relations with the United States and with the United Kingdom. Before indicating the extent to which a solution has been found in the Hyde Park declaration, I shall outline briefly the problems themselves.

It will be readily recognized that we, in Canada, could not possibly have embarked upon our existing program of war production if we had not lived side by side with the greatest industrial nation in the world. Without ready access to the industrial production of the United States, and particularly the machine tools and other specialized equipment so necessary in producing the complex instruments of modern war, Canada's war effort would have been seriously retarded. We would

† Canada, House of Commons, *Debates*, 28 April 1941, 2286–2289.

have been forced to embark upon the production of many articles which, because of limited demand, could only have been produced at high cost, and over a considerable period of time. Canada also lacks certain essential raw materials which must be procured from the United States. Since the outbreak of war, we have steadily expanded our purchases in the United States of these essential tools, machines and materials which were required both for our own Canadian war effort, and in the production of war supplies for Britain.

Even in normal times Canada purchases much more from the United States than we sell to our neighbours. In peace time we were able to make up the deficit by converting into United States dollars the surplus sterling we received as a result of the sale of goods to Britain. But from the outset of war, this has been impossible. The government realized at once that Canada would be faced with a growing shortage of United States dollars to pay for our essential war purchases. To conserve the necessary exchange the foreign exchange control board was established on 15 September, 1939. As the need has grown, increasingly stringent measures have been adapted to reduce the unessential demands for United States dollars in order to conserve sufficient funds to make our payments for essential weapons and supplies of war. These war purchases could not be reduced without a corresponding, or perhaps an even more serious, reduction in our war effort. Despite the drastic measures taken to conserve exchange, the lack of United States dollars was becoming, as one writer expressed it, one of the most serious "bottlenecks" in Canada's war effort.

The problem of exchange was the most urgent problem we faced in our economic relations with the United States. But we also realized a growing danger of possible unnecessary duplication of production facilities on the North American continent, with consequent undue pressure on scarce labour and materials if Canada and the United States each tried to make itself wholly self-sufficient in the field of war supplies. We felt it imperative to avoid such waste, which might well have had the most serious consequences. The experience of the Department of Munitions and Supply, and the studies of the permanent joint board on defence, both suggested the same solution. That solution was the co-ordination of the production of war materials of Canada and the United States. This was in reality a simple and logical extension, to the economic sphere, of the Ogdensburg agreement.

The practical experience of a year and a half of organizing and developing war production in Canada revealed that many of the essentials of war could be made in the comparatively small quantities required by Canada only at a prohibitive cost. They could, however, be produced economically in the United States where the demand was large enough to result in the economies of large-scale production. On the other hand, the production of other weapons and materials had been developed in Canada to the point where output could be expanded more quickly, and probably more economically, than new productions facilities could be organized in the United States. It was, therefore, only common sense to extend to the production of war materials the same reciprocity in which, at Ogdensburg in August last, our two countries had permanently placed their defence.

During my Easter visit, I had the opportunity of preliminary discussions with the Secretary of State, Mr. Cordell Hull, and the Secretary of the Treasury, Mr. Morgenthau, at Washington. I also, later, had an opportunity of conferring with Mr. Harry Hopkins, who has been entrusted with immediate direction and supervision of the measures to be taken under the lease-lend act. On Sunday April 20, I spent the day with the president at Hyde Park. At the close of the visit, I gave to the press a statement of the understanding which the president and I had reached regarding the problems I have mentioned. That statement it is proposed to call the Hyde Park declaration. The declaration reads:

Among other important matters, the President and the Prime Minister discussed measures by which the most prompt and effective utilization might be made of the productive facilities of North America for the purposes both of local and hemisphere defence, and of the assistance which in addition to their own programme both Canada and the United States are rendering to Great Britain and the other democracies.

It was agreed as a general principle that in mobilizing the resources of this continent each country should provide the other with the defence articles which it is best able to produce, and, above all, produce quickly, and that production programmes should be co-ordinated to this end.

While Canada has expanded its productive capacity manifold since the beginning of the war, there are still numerous defence articles which it must obtain in the United States, and purchases of this character by Canada will be even greater in the coming year than in the past. On the other hand, there is existing and potential capacity in Canada for the speedy production of certain kinds of munitions, strategic materials, aluminum and ships, which are urgently required by the United States for its own purposes.

While exact estimates cannot yet be made, it is hoped that during the next twelve months Canada can supply the United States with between $200 000 000 and $300 000 000 worth of such defence articles. This sum is a small fraction of the total defence programme of the United States, but many of the articles to be provided are of vital importance. In addition, it is of great importance to the economic and financial relations between the two countries that payment by the United States for these supplies will materially assist Canada in meeting part of the cost of Canadian defence purchases in the United States.

In so far as Canada's defence purchases in the United States consist of component parts to be used in equipment and munitions which Canada is producing for Great Britain, it was also agreed that Great Britain will obtain these parts under the lease-lend act and forward them to Canada for inclusion in the finished articles.

The technical and financial details will be worked out as soon as possible in accordance with the general principles which have been agreed upon between the President and the Prime Minister.

The immediate purpose of the joint declaration is set out in its first paragraph, which might be described as the preamble. It states that the president and I discussed measures by which the most prompt and effective utilization might be made of the productive facilities of North America. Let me emphasize the two words: prompt and effective. They indicate that while recognizing the short-run necessity of speed, the vital importance of the time factor, we have not lost sight of the long-run necessity of the utmost efficiency in the organization of our war production.

The preamble goes on to recognize a twofold object in ensuring this prompt and effective utilization of the productive facilities of both countries. Not only does it envisage the extension of the scope of our joint defence arrangements to the economic sphere, but it recognizes the advantages of co-ordinating the use of the resources of both countries as a means of speeding up and increasing the volume of aid to Britain from this continent.

Let me state this in another way. The Hyde Park declaration is more than an extension of the Ogdensburg agreement for hemispheric defence. It is also a joint agreement between Canada and the United States for aid to Britain.

. . .

Honourable members will, I am sure, be more interested in the broad significance of the Hyde Park declaration than in its technical aspects.

Its most immediate significance is that, through the co-ordination of war production in both countries, it will result in the speeding up of aid to Britain by the United States and Canada. As a result of the better integration of North American industry, the proposed arrangement will, through increasing total production, have the further effect of increasing the total volume of aid to Britain. It will have a corresponding effect upon Canada's war effort. Full utilization of the production facilities we have built up, and specialization on those things which we are best fitted to produce, will increase both our national income and our own armed strength, as well as increasing our capacity to aid Britain.

As I have already said, the agreement will go a long way towards the solution of the exchange problem and, in this way, will remove one of the financial obstacles to the maximum war production programme of Canada and the United States. We, in Canada, have reason to be gratified at the understanding shown by the president and by the secretary of the treasury, of Canada's difficult exchange problem. We may, I am sure, feel an equal confidence that in the working out of the detailed technical and financial arrangements, Canadian officials will find the same generous measure of understanding and the same spirit of co-operation.

I have spoken thus far of the immediate significance of the declaration, of the effect it will have in speeding up aid to Britain in the critical months ahead, and of its importance in assisting us to meet our exchange problem. But beyond its immediate significance the Hyde Park declaration will have a permanent significance in the relations between Canada and the United States. It involves nothing less than a common plan of the economic defence of the western hemisphere. When we pause to reflect upon the consequences, in Europe, of the failure of the peace-loving nations to plan in concert their common defence, while yet there was time, we gain a new appreciation of the significance for the future of both Canada and the United States of the Ogdensburg agreement and of this new declaration which might well be called the economic corollary of Ogdensburg.

For Canada, the significance of the Hyde Park declaration may be summarized briefly as follows. First, it will help both Canada and the United States to provide maximum aid to Britain and to all the defenders of democracy. Second, it will increase the effectiveness of Canada's direct war effort. And finally, through the increased industrial efficiency which will result, it will increase our own security and the security of North America.

CANADA, THE UNITED STATES, AND KOREA, 1951†

L.B. PEARSON

. . . One of the cardinal facts in the world today is the emergence of the United States to a position of unquestioned leadership in the free world. A great shift of power and influence has occurred within the last few years, with the result that the United States now stands pre-eminent. By any test it is not only the most powerful of the free states of the world; it is immensely the most powerful. We in Canada know the United States so well that we can view this great and historic development without apprehension, and feel indeed relief and satis-faction that power is in the hands of a nation which has such a deeply rooted democratic tradition, whose people have no desire to dominate other countries, and which has shown its good will towards less fortunate peoples on so many occasions by acts of magnanimity and generosity.

This feeling, I think, is increased by a consideration of what our position would be today if the United States had not decided to assume the responsibilities throughout the world which its new posi-tion has thrust upon it. We have good reason to believe that it will discharge those responsibilities with conscience, courage, and respect for the interests of others. The predominance of the United States, however, is bound to raise new problems for all those countries which share its values, and which are associated with it, and proud to be associated with it, in the defence of freedom. These new problems

† L.B. Pearson, Canada, House of Commons, *Debates*, 7 May 1951, 2751–2756.

must be understood and must be solved if friction is to be kept to a minimum and the forces of freedom are to be strong and united.

In considering, for instance, Canada's relations with the United States it is not enough to take refuge in thought or in words, as I see it, in the usual clichés of 135 years of peace or the unguarded boundary. Certainly in my view any spokesman for the Canadian government or the Canadian people on external affairs has a duty to go deeper than this in the examination of this important question. Such an examination can also lead to a clarification of issues only if it is made within the wider framework of the position of the United States as the leader of our free alliance against the dangers which threaten us. The maintenance, let alone the strengthening, of an alliance of free nations is never easy, and requires tolerance, patience and great understanding. It is not easy in war; it is not easy in times of normal peace. It is especially difficult, I think, in a period such as the present of part war and part peace, with all its frustrations, tensions and anxieties.

Therefore I am sure we all agree that this imposes on the peoples of all free states a special obligation to face the problems of their mutual relationships with candour and frankness, but also with a firm resolve to understand each other's points of view. It seems to me that the unity of the free world would be in real jeopardy if there were no free discussion of our common objectives and of the possibly different means by which they can best be reached. Much of that discussion will and should be carried on confidentially between governments, but the people have a right to be kept informed of the problems involved and the principles of action which the government may think to be necessary for their solution. Therefore honest discussion of the issues before us, so long as it is conducted in cool and reasonable terms, will not weaken the free world. I am convinced on the contrary that it is an indispensable part of the process of developing our united strength, although of course in this kind of discussion one always runs the risk of misinterpretation and the placing of a wrong emphasis on what may have been said.

In all these relations between the governments in our alliance of free countries, no single government can of course surrender its judgement into the keeping of any other government, however close and friendly that government may be. It may at times, however — and I have said this before, although it is sometimes forgotten — have to yield to the collective judgment of the group reached after discussion and consultation. That is the only way that democracy can be carried on within our own country. It is the only way that democracy can be carried on internationally. The decision when to hold out and when to yield is often a terribly difficult one to make. Yet it is on that decision that the unity and close co-operation among members of our alliance will so often depend; and on that so much else depends. Oversensitiveness and obstinacy, on the one hand, over the maintenance of national rights and national sovereignty, and arrogance or carelessness, on the other, in overriding them, might in either case produce serious and even dangerous division among the countries of the world.

That division, which would lead possibly to disunity and even disruption, gives the foe that threatens us his greatest comfort and his greatest opportunity. Particularly during these times — I am sure we all agree with this — must the United Kingdom, the United States and Canada maintain and strengthen their special ties of friendship within the larger group. It would be folly to think that any one of us can go it alone. It would also be a fatal error, made previously by two dictators, for any potential enemy to think that we intend to take that course, folly also for him to draw wrong conclusions from that mistaken interpretation of our democratic differences of opinion. On the big issues we stand together within our countries as well as between our countries, even though we may sometimes seem verbally separated. It is, I think, as much the responsibility of public and press opinion as of governments to keep these differing voices from resulting in different policies. Policy for the free world must be forged not on a shifting basis of emotion but on the hard anvil of facts. Only in that way can it be well-tempered and strong.

One of the most important of these facts is that of persistent Soviet communist hostility. Another is, as I have said, the new position of power and responsibility of the United States as the leader of the free world. This latter fact, as I see it, means that our own relations with the United States have entered upon a new phase within the last few years. It does not mean that they should not be or cannot be as close and friendly as they have been in the past. Canadians, with very few exceptions, indeed — and those exceptions mostly of the communist persuasion — all hope this will be the case and want to do what they can to make it possible and even easy. Certainly that is the policy of this government, as it has been throughout the years.

Well, what is the nature of this change I have been talking about, and not only inside the house? Hitherto questions which from time to time we have had to discuss and decide with the United States were largely bilateral matters between neighbours. They arose from such things as border disputes, differences over the diversion of water and so on, or had to do with commerce back and forth across the boundary. Of course they were often complicated and difficult enough. Now, however, we are not only neighbours but allies. I think perhaps that is the simplest way to indicate the change that has come over the nature of our relations with the United States. We have always been good neighbours, accustomed to settling our differences in a neighbourly spirit. Now we are good allies, and as allies we must do our best to settle, in our customary friendly way, such differences as may exist between us from time to time. But the questions we shall have to discuss in this way will often be of a new character arising from our senior and junior partnership in a common association. They will often deal with the policies to be followed by that association in the North Atlantic pact or within the United Nations, very often indeed within the United Nations.

It is perhaps not unnatural that many people in Canada and the United States have not yet realized this change. It has come about rather suddenly, and I doubt if in either country we have yet completely adjusted ourselves to it. On Tuesday of last week, I believe, the Prime Minister (Mr. St. Laurent) gave an illustration of one of the new categories of subjects under discussion between Canada and the United States when he announced in this house the recommendations of the permanent joint board on defence, which had been accepted by both governments, for the revision of the lease under which the United States holds certain bases in Newfoundland. The discussions on this subject between Canada and the United States were carried on in a friendly and co-operative spirit, as is our habit, and they have resulted in a compromise which I think will commend itself to the house as reasonable in the circumstances. The problem itself arises out of the defence requirements of the United States on Canadian soil, requirements not merely for its own security but for the security of the free world. It also arises, however, out of the necessity of the United States meeting these legitimate requirements in a way which recognizes Canadian jurisdiction and, even more important, Canadian self-respect.

In an age of atomic weapons and long-range bombers Canada is obviously now of far greater importance to the defence of North America and the north Atlantic area than ever before. For that reason, and because we are now joined as allies in the North Atlantic treaty, inevitably from time to time there will be other defence questions of very great importance to both countries which must be discussed. I have no doubt that we shall be able to find satisfactory solutions to those questions as well, but it will be easier to find them if we in Canada continue to remember the very heavy responsibility the United States has shouldered for the common defence, and if the United States continue to appreciate that the alliance in which we are joined with them will not be as strong as it should be unless the various defence arrangements which may be necessary on our soil are worked out in such a way that they will commend themselves wholeheartedly to Canadian public opinion.

Another — and I suppose at the moment the most pressing — problem we face with the United States, because it is indeed a phase of United States–Canadian relations though it is also of far wider and deeper significance, involving as it does the whole question of global war or global peace, is the policy to be adopted at the present time in Korea. For the time being I think the role of diplomacy in Korea is secondary, because the scene there is now dominated by the heavy fighting which has been going on for the past few weeks. The first wave of the new Chinese attack has been checked and broken by United Nations forces, but the attack is not yet spent — far from it. This is probably just a lull before another storm. So it seems to me that for some time to come, while this heavy fighting is going on, the task of upholding the purpose and will of the United Nations in Korea must rest upon the fighting men who have withstood so courageously the attacks made upon them by much more numerous enemy forces. One Canadian battalion, as we know, has had an important part in the recent fighting. Additional Canadian troops have now arrived in Korea, and before many more days have passed a full Canadian brigade group will be in action. These men, along with those of the other United Nations forces, and particularly the forces of the United States, will have more effect upon the course of events in Korea over the next few weeks than any diplomatic moves; and I know the thoughts of every one of us will be with them, and perhaps especially with those of our own men who are going into action for the first time.

In those circumstances perhaps it would not be appropriate for me to say too much about the actual situation in Korea, but there are a few things I should like to say. The present Chinese attack must be broken before we can again begin to entertain any hope of a peaceful and honourable settlement there. When it has been broken, as we hope it will be, and with heavy losses to the enemy, the Chinese communists may be in a mood to negotiate an honourable settlement — the only kind of settlement we have ever contemplated — or at least to desist from further attacks. While I think it would be quite unrealistic to hold out hope of an early settlement in Korea, or even of an early end to the fighting, nevertheless we should always remember that the United Nations stands ready to negotiate, though not to betray its trust or yield to blackmail. The statement of principles adopted by the general assembly by an overwhelming majority on January 13 last, which would provide for a cease-fire to be followed by a Korean settlement and by the negotiation of a wide range of Far Eastern problems, still represents the considered opinion of the United Nations. If the Chinese government and the North Korean government wish to take advantage of the offer contained in that statement, it is open to them to do so. Of their willingness to do so, however, there is no sign whatever. The approaches made to Peking by the good offices committee established by the United Nations assembly have all been rebuffed. The North Korean government, in a broadcast message as late as April 18, has repeated its determination to drive the United Nations forces from the peninsula. We can only hope that the heavy losses which the aggressors are now suffering and will suffer in Korea may produce a more accommodating frame of mind.

In the meantime, the United Nations forces are heroically and skilfully fulfilling the task which has been given to them, which is the defeat of armed aggression in Korea. This is — and it should not be forgotten — the sole military objective of the forces of the United Nations in Korea, the defeat of aggression so that a free, democratic and united Korea can be established. . . .

. . .

Furthermore, Mr. Speaker, I suggest it is not an aim or objective of the United Nations in its Korean policy to interfere in the internal affairs of any Asian country, to replace one regime by another. Its aim, as I said, is to defeat aggression and so prevent other acts of aggression by proving that aggression does not pay. To some that may seem to be too limited an objective. . . .

. . .

It is also sometimes loosely said that the United Nations forces are fighting in Korea to defeat communism. There is perhaps some colour for this mistake, since the aggression perpetrated is by communist states, and has its roots in the totalitarian communist nature of those states. Free men everywhere must be determined to resist communism. But it is a confusion, I think, of categories to think that communism as a doctrine or form of government must be fought by armed forces, or that such is the purpose of the United Nations military action in Korea. When communism, or indeed fascism, results in acts of military aggression, that aggression should be met by any form of collective action, including military collective action, which can be made effective. But the purpose of such action is to defeat aggression. Communism itself, as a reactionary and debasing doctrine, must be fought on other planes and in different ways; by the use of economic, social, political and moral weapons. . . .

. . .

Since the United Nations objective in Korea, then, is to defeat aggression, it follows, I think, that the methods used should be designed to limit and localize the conflict and not to spread it. As long ago as 31 August 1950, I said in this house that it was not the purpose of this government to support any course of policy which would extend the scope of the present conflict in Korea, a conflict which should be confined and localized if it is in our power to do that; also that United Nations policy should be to avoid giving anyone else an excuse for extending the conflict. Mr. Speaker, that is still our view.

One way by which the conflict could be spread would be by authorizing the United Nations commander in Korea to conduct aerial bombing in China. As I said on April 26 last in the house, it is possible to visualize a situation in which immediate retaliatory action without prior consultation might be unavoidable in pursuing enemy bombers back to, and in attempting to destroy, the Manchurian air bases from which they came. It is our view, however, that the bombing, as well as the blockading, of China should, if at all possible, be avoided, since such action would involve grave risk of extending the fighting without, as we see it, any corresponding assurance that such extension would end the war. The history, the position, the social and economic organization, and the political situation in China would not seem to give much hope for any such decisive result from such limited action. Indeed, it may be felt, on the contrary, that this limited action which has been suggested would inevitably develop into unlimited action against China, about the possible result of which the Japanese perhaps are best fitted to give testimony. One result we can, however, expect with some certainty, and that is great satisfaction in Moscow over such a development. It may be that the Chinese communists, by indulging in massive air activity over Korea, will make some kind of retaliation necessary. They have, however, not yet taken such action, and in that sense have not yet conducted an all-out war against the United Nations forces in Korea. . . .

If the Chinese communists change that situation, the responsibility for the consequence would rest entirely with them and not with the United Nations forces.

I am, of course, Mr. Speaker, aware that this policy of restraint in which all the governments who have forces in Korea concur to the best of my knowledge, may complicate the problems facing the United Nations commanders in Korea. These problems, however, in the opinion of many, would be immensely more complicated if the fighting were extended to China.

The question, I think, above all other questions at the moment, is, in short, whether aerial bombardment of points in China, together with a naval blockade and the removal of all restrictions from Chinese forces in Formosa, would be sufficient to bring China's participation in the war in Korea to an end without bringing about intervention by the forces of the Soviet union. It was felt by many last November that if United Nations forces advanced to the very borders of Manchuria and cleared North Korea of the enemy, the war would then end; that there would be little risk of communist China intervening, or, that, if it did, the intervention could be contained and defeated. As we know, and as I said last February in the house, it did not work out that way, for one reason or another. In the light of that experience, we should, I think, before we take any new decisions which will extend the war, be reasonably sure that this extension will have compensating military and political advantages. Let us not forget we would be playing for the highest stakes in history.

Another way in which the conflict could be extended, in the hope that it would be ended sooner, would be by facilitating and assisting the return to the mainland of China of the forces at present in Formosa under the command of Generalissimo Chiang Kaishek. We should remember, of course, that these forces, or forces under the same command, have been driven from China by their own countrymen. The question to be answered, therefore, is this: Is there any reason to believe that these Chinese nationalist forces now in Formosa would have greater success in China than they had previously, unless they were supported by troops and equipment from other countries which could ill be spared for such a hazardous venture, with all its possible long-drawn-out consequences?

The desire to localize the conflict and prevent it from spreading remains, then, our policy, though we must recognize that while it takes only one to start a fight, it takes two to limit, as well as two to settle, a fight.

. . .

These are two questions which I know are uppermost in our minds these days. What is going on in the Far East? What is the policy of the alliance which has been built up, and which is getting stronger every day, to meet the dangers ahead, and within that alliance what is the relationship of a junior partner like Canada to its neighbour and its very senior partner in this association, the United States of America? It is not easy these days to be too optimistic about the course of events; but time is going on, and while time is going on we are getting stronger. In that sense, but only in that sense, time may be said to be on our side if we take advantage of it. If we do take advantage of it, and if we grow stronger militarily, economically and in every other way, then I think, as I have said before, that we have no reason to regard the future with panic or despair. But the remedy, Mr. Speaker, rests with us.

THE NORAD AGREEMENT, 1958†

Agreement Between the Government of Canada and the Government of the United States of America Concerning the Organization and Operation of the North American Air Defence Command (NORAD).

The Ambassador of Canada to the United States of America to the Secretary of State of the United States of America

CANADIAN EMBASSY, WASHINGTON, D.C.

12 May 1958.

No. 263

Sir,

I have the honour to refer to discussions which have taken place between the Canadian and the United States authorities concerning the necessity for integration of operational control of Canadian and United States Air Defences and, in particular, to the study and recommendations of the Canada-United States Military Study Group. These studies led to the joint announcement of 1 August 1957, by the Minister of National Defence of Canada and the Secretary of Defense of the United States, indicating that our two Governments had agreed to the setting up of a system of integrated operational control for the air defences in the continental United States, Canada and Alaska under an integrated command responsible to the Chiefs of Staff of both

† Canada, *Treaty Series*, 1958, no. 9, Ottawa, 1959.

countries. Pursuant to the announcement of 1 August 1957, an integrated headquarters known as the North American Air Defence Command (NORAD) has been established on an interim basis at Colorado Springs, Colorado.

For some years prior to the establishment of NORAD, it had been recognized that the air defence of Canada and the United States must be considered as a single problem. However, arrangements which existed between Canada and the United States provided only for the co-ordination of separate Canadian and United States air defence plans, but did not provide for the authoritative control of all air defence weapons which must be employed against an attacker.

The advent of nuclear weapons, the great improvements in the means of effecting their delivery, and the requirements of the air defence control systems demand rapid decisions to keep pace with the speed and tempo of technological developments. To counter the threat and to achieve maximum effectiveness of the air defence system, defensive operations must commence as early as possible and enemy forces must be kept constantly engaged. Arrangements for the co-ordination of national plans requiring consultation between national commanders before implementation had become inadequate in the face of a possible sudden attack, with little or no warning. It was essential, therefore, to have in existence in peacetime an organization, including the weapons, facilities and command structure which could operate at the outset of hostilities in accordance with a single air defence plan approved in advance by national authorities.

Studies made by representatives of our two Governments led to the conclusion that the problem of the air defence of our two countries could best be met by delegating to an integrated headquarters, the task of exercising operational control over combat units of the national forces made available for the air defence of the two countries. Furthermore, the principle of an integrated headquarters exercising operational control over assigned forces has been well established in various parts of the North Atlantic Treaty area. The Canada-United States region is an integral part of the NATO area. In support of the strategic objectives established in NATO for the Canada-United States region and in accordance with the provisions of the North Atlantic Treaty, our two Governments have, by establishing the North American Air Defence Command recognized the desirability of integrating headquarters exercising operational control over assigned air defence forces. The agreed integration is intended to assist the two Governments to develop and maintain their individual and collective capacity to resist air attack on their territories in North America in mutual self-defence.

The two Governments consider that the establishment of integrated air defence arrangements of the nature described increases the importance of the fullest possible consultation between the two

Governments on all matters affecting the joint defence of North America, and that defence co-operation between them can be worked out on a mutually satisfactory basis only if such consultation is regularly and consistently undertaken.

In view of the foregoing considerations and on the basis of the experience gained in the operation on an interim basis of the North American Air Defence Command, my Government proposes that the following principles should govern the future organization and operations of the North American Air Defence Command.

1) The Commander-in-Chief NORAD (CINCNORAD) will be responsible to the Chiefs of Staff Committee of Canada and the Joint Chiefs of Staff of the United States, who in turn are responsible to their respective Governments. He will operate within a concept of air defence approved by the appropriate authorities of our two Governments, who will bear in mind their objectives in the defence of the Canada-United States region of the NATO area.

2) The North American Air Defence Command will include such combat units and individuals as are specifically allocated to it by the two Governments. The jurisdiction of the Commander-in-Chief, NORAD, over those units and individuals is limited to operational control as hereinafter defined.

3) "Operational Control" is the power to direct, co-ordinate, and control the operational activities of forces assigned, attached or otherwise made available. No permanent changes of station would be made without approval of the higher national authority concerned. Temporary reinforcement from one area to another, including the crossing of the international boundary, to meet operational requirements will be within the authority of commanders having operational control. The basic command organization for the air defence forces of the two countries, including administration, discipline, internal organization and unit training, shall be exercised by national commanders responsible to their national authorities.

4) The appointment of CINCNORAD and his Deputy must be approved by the Canadian and United States Governments. They will not be from the same country, and CINCNORAD staff shall be an integrated joint staff composed of officers of both countries. During the absence of CINCNORAD, command will pass to the Deputy Commander.

5) The North Atlantic Treaty Organization will continue to be kept informed through the Canada-United States Regional Planning Group of arrangements for the air defence of North America.

6) The plans and procedures to be followed by NORAD in wartime shall be formulated and approved in peacetime by appropriate national authorities and shall be capable of rapid implementation in an emergency. Any plans or procedures recommended by NORAD

which bear on the responsibilities of civilian departments or agencies of the two Governments shall be referred for decision by the appropriate military authorities to those agencies and departments and may be the subject of intergovernmental co-ordination.

7) Terms of reference for CINCNORAD and his Deputy will be consistent with the foregoing principles. Changes in these terms of reference may be made by agreement between the Canadian Chiefs of Staff Committee and the United States Joint Chiefs of Staff, with approval of higher authority as appropriate, provided that these changes are in consonance with the principles set out in this Note.

8) The question of the financing of expenditures connected with the operation of the integrated headquarters of the North American Air Defence Command will be settled by mutual agreement between appropriate agencies of the two Governments.

9) The North American Air Defence Command shall be maintained in operation for a period of ten years or such shorter period as shall be agreed by both countries in the light of their mutual defence interests, and their objectives under the terms of the North Atlantic Treaty. The terms of this Agreement may be reviewed upon request of either country at any time.

10) The agreement between parties to the North Atlantic Treaty regarding the status of their forces signed in London on 19 June 1951, shall apply.

11) The release to the public of information by CINCNORAD on matters of interest to Canada and the United States of America will in all cases be the subject of prior consultation and agreement between appropriate agencies of the two Governments.

If the United States Government concurs in the principles set out above, I propose that this Note and your reply should constitute an agreement between our two Governments effective from the date of your reply.

Accept, Sir, the renewed assurances of my highest consideration.

N.A. Robertson,
Ambassador of Canada

The Department of State of the United States of America to the Ambassador of Canada to the United States of America

DEPARTMENT OF STATE, WASHINGTON, D.C.

12 May 1958

Excellency,

I have the honour to refer to Your Excellency's Note No. 263 of 12 May 1958, proposing on behalf of the Canadian Government certain principles to govern the future organization and operation of the North American Air Defence Command (NORAD).

I am pleased to inform you that my Government concurs in the principles set forth in your Note. My Government further agrees with your proposal that your Note and this reply shall constitute an agreement between the two Governments, effective today.

Accept, Excellency, the renewed assurances of my highest consideration.

Christian A. Herter,
for the Secretary of State

CANADA, THE UNITED STATES, AND VIETNAM†

L.B. PEARSON

I need hardly tell you that the situation in Vietnam is one to which the Government attaches great importance in the formulation of Canadian foreign policy. That importance reflects not only the implications of the problem for world peace and the international processes of change by peaceful means, but also the concern which the Government shares with responsible citizens at the toll the hostilities are taking in terms of human suffering as well as of wasted resources and lost opportunities for human betterment. On these points, I think there can be few differences of opinion.

The real problem, of course, for governments no less than for individuals, is in translating hopes and convictions into constructive action. Constructive action, in turn, depends on a realistic assessment of the nature of the situation which it is desired to change and of the likely consequences of any given action, whether public or private, in relation to the problem. Therefore, at every stage, we must ask whether any particular step is likely to advance the issue any distance towards a solution — or even towards a more satisfactory state of affairs. Any answer to this question becomes doubly difficult in the

† "Text of the reply by the Prime Minister, the Right Honourable L.B. Pearson, to representatives from a group of university professors, including the Faculty Committee on Vietnam at Victoria College, University of Toronto, 10 March 1967," Department of External Affairs, *Statements and Speeches*, 67/8.

context of problems where the direct involvement and the direct responsibility for action rest essentially with others.

Let me be more specific. I realize, as the public debate over Vietnam here and elsewhere over the past few years has shown, that it is possible to arrive at different assessments of the rights and wrongs of the various positions represented in the conflict. This is inevitable, and, in the long run, useful, in a free society, always provided, of course, that the differences of opinion are genuine and based on the fullest possible range of facts. But, whatever the view one might hold about the origins and development of a situation such as we face in Vietnam today, I believe that the right and proper course for the Canadian policy-maker is to seek to establish that element of common ground on which any approach to a solution must ultimately rest.

This is precisely the direction in which we have attempted to bring Canadian influence to bear — the search for common ground as a base for a solution to the Vietnam crisis by means other than the use of force. We have spoken publicly about our belief that a military solution is neither practicable nor desirable and we have encouraged the two sides to enter into direct contact to prepare the ground for formal negotiations at the earliest practicable time.

In what might be called a process of public diplomacy, the parties themselves have gone some distance over the past year or so in defining their positions. This open exchange of propositions is, of course, useful in settling international problems, but it must, I think, be accompanied by other, less conspicuous, efforts, since public positions are generally formulated in maximum terms. One aspect of these quiet efforts could be an attempt to develop a dialogue with the parties, stressing to them the urgency of seeking more acceptable alternatives to the means being used to pursue their objectives; another might be an attempt to find channels by which the parties could, in quite confidential ways, move out beyond their established positions, abandoning where necessary, tacitly or explicitly, those aspects of their positions where compromises must be made in the interests of a broader accommodation.

As I have said, I am convinced that the Vietnam conflict will ultimately have to be resolved by way of negotiation. But I do not think that a Geneva-type conference (or, indeed, any other conference) will come about simply because the Canadian Government declares publicly that this would be a good idea. It will come about only when those who are at this time opposed to such a conference can be convinced that it would be in their best interests to attend and negotiate in a genuine desire to achieve results. And, in the process, confidential and quiet arguments by a responsible government are usually more effective than public ones.

Similarly, when it comes to making channels, or "good offices," available to the parties to enable them to make contact with each other,

I think that too many public declarations and disclosures run the risk of complicating matters for those concerned.

In short, the more complex and dangerous the problem, the greater is the need for calm and deliberate diplomacy. That may sound like an expression of timidity to some of the proponents of political activism at Canadian universities and elsewhere today. I can only assure them, with all the personal conviction I can command, that in my view it is the only way in which results can be achieved. Statements and declarations by governments obviously have their place and their use in the international concert, but my own experience leads me to believe that their true significance is generally to be found not in initiating a given course of events but lies rather towards the end of the process, when they have been made possible by certain fundamental understandings or agreements reached by other means.

As far as the bombing of North Vietnam is concerned, there is not the slightest doubt in my mind that this is one of the key elements, if not the key element, in the situation at the present time. You may recall that I was one of the first to suggest publicly that a pause in these activities might provide openings for negotiations. Subsequently, I have repeatedly stressed that I would be glad to see the bombing stopped, Northern infiltration into the South stopped, and unconditional peace talks begin. This has been and will remain, in broad outline, the Canadian government's position — a position which we have adopted not in a spirit of timidity but in a sense of reality, because we believe it corresponds to the facts and because we believe that a negotiation involves reciprocal commitments. Any other position taken by the government, I am convinced, would be unhelpful.

In your letter you also called upon the Government to reveal all military production contracts related in any way to the Vietnam war, and to consider refusing to sell arms to the U.S.A. until the intervention in Vietnam ceases. While I can appreciate the sense of concern reflected in your suggestions, I think it might be helpful if I were to try to put this question in a somewhat broader perspective than the problem of the Vietnam war alone.

Relations between Canada and the U.S.A. in this field are currently covered by the Defence Production Sharing Agreements of 1959 and 1963, but in fact they go back much farther and find their origins in the Hyde Park Declaration of 1941. During this extended period of co-operation between the two countries, a very close relationship has grown up not only between the Canadian defence industrial base and its U.S. counterpart but also between the Canadian and U.S. defence equipment procurement agencies. This relationship is both necessary and logical not only as part of collective defence but also in order to meet our own national defence commitments effectively and economically. Equipments required by modern defence forces to meet even limited roles such as peace keeping are both technically sophisticated and very costly to develop and, because Canada's quantitative needs are generally very small, it is not economical for us to meet our total requirements solely from our own resources. Thus we must take advantage of large-scale production in allied countries. As the U.S.A. is the world leader in the advanced technologies involved, and because real advantages can be gained by following common North American design and production standards, the U.S.A. becomes a natural source for much of our defence equipment. The U.S.-Canadian production-sharing arrangements enable the Canadian government to acquire from the U.S.A. a great deal of the nation's essential defence equipment at the lowest possible cost, while at the same time permitting us to offset the resulting drain on the economy by reciprocal sales to the U.S.A. Under these agreements, by reason of longer production runs, Canadian industry is able to participate competitively in U.S. research, development, and production programs, and is exempted from the "Buy American" Act for these purposes. From a long-term point of view, another major benefit to Canada is the large contribution which these agreements have made and are continuing to make to Canadian industrial research and development capabilities, which, in turn, are fundamental to the maintenance of an advanced technology in Canada.

In this connection, I should perhaps point out that the greater part of U.S. military procurement in Canada consists not of weapons in the conventional sense but rather of electronic equipment, transport aircraft, and various kinds of components and sub-systems. In many cases, the Canadian industries which have developed such products to meet U.S. and continental defence requirements have, at the same time, been able to develop related products with a civil application or have been able to use the technology so acquired to advance their general capabilities. For a broad range of reasons, therefore, it is clear that the imposition of an embargo on the export of military equipment to the U.S.A., and concomitant termination of the Production Sharing Agreements, would have far-reaching consequences which no Canadian Government could contemplate with equanimity. It would be interpreted as a notice of withdrawal on our part from continental defence and even from the collective defence arrangements of the Atlantic alliance.

With regard to your specific request that we reveal all military production contracts related in any way to the Vietnam war, there is so far as I am aware no way in which the Canadian Government — and perhaps even the U.S. government — could ascertain the present whereabouts of all items of military equipment purchased in Canada by the U.S.A. Such equipment goes into the general inventory of the U.S. armed forces and may be used for such purposes and in such parts of the world as the U.S. Government may see fit. The converse is true of equipment which is purchased in the U.S.A. by the Canadian government. This long-standing arrangement — which is sometimes known as the "open border" — reflects the collective defence relation-ship of Canada and the U.S.A. and is an important element in the broadly based co-operation of the two countries in the defence field. It would not, in my judgement, be consistent with that relationship for the Canadian Government to seek to impose the sort of restrictions which you suggest, nor am I convinced that, by taking such a step, we should be contributing in any practical way to achieving a political solution to the Vietnam problem.

The Third Option, 1972†

MITCHELL SHARP

. . .

In the review of Canadian foreign policy which the Canadian Government published in 1970 under the title *Foreign Policy for Canadians*, the challenge of "living distinct from, but in harmony with, the world's most powerful and dynamic nation, the United States" was described as one of two "inescapable realities, both crucial to Canada's continuing existence" in the context of which Canadian policy needs — domestic and external — must be assessed. The other was the "multi-faceted problem of maintaining national unity."

If the importance of this unique relationship is such as to affect the whole of Canada's foreign policy, it is in turn influenced by the nature of the world environment, and of the relations the United States and Canada have with other countries. As was recognized in the foreign policy review, and has been dramatically illustrated by more recent developments, the postwar international order is giving way to a new pattern of power relations. The preponderant position of the two super-powers, the United States and the U.S.S.R., is being reduced by the emergence of other major power centres. China, with its vast population and immense potential, has emerged from its long isolation, achieved the status of an important nuclear power, and taken its place in the community of nations. Western Europe is making historic strides towards unity through the enlargement and development of the

† Mitchell Sharp, "Canada-U.S. Relations: Options for the Future," *International Perspectives*, special issue (Autumn 1972), 1–24.

European Economic Community. Japan has developed as a modern, industrial giant in Asia. Confrontation is giving way to negotiation and accommodation in East-West relations and major progress has been achieved on the road toward a political settlement in Europe.

In this evolving new world situation, enlarged opportunities are opening up for Canada and the United States to extend and broaden their relations with Communist countries and with the developing world, while continuing to develop their ties with their more traditional political and trading partners. These major changes will undoubtedly have a bearing on Canada-U.S. relations in the years ahead and on the option that may be open to Canada in particular.

The Canada-U.S. relationship, as it has evolved since the end of the Second World War, is in many respects a unique phenomenon. It is by far our most important external relationship, but it is more than an external relationship. It impinges on virtually every aspect of the Canadian national interest, and thus of Canadian domestic concerns.

Because of the vast disparity in power and population, it is also inevitably a relationship of profoundly unequal dependence; the impact of the United States on Canada is far greater than Canada's impact on the United States.

Some two decades ago, Lester B. Pearson warned that, as the two countries became more interdependent, relations between them would become more, not less, difficult. As interactions increased, conflicts of interest and differences of views were also bound to increase. Preserving harmony in the relationship would require careful and sensitive management.

In recent years, however, the occasional strains and difficulties that have affected relations between the two countries have also had a more basic and deep-seated source. In a Canada undergoing profound and rapid changes associated with industrialization, urbanization, improved education, cultural development, and a major reassessment of values, there has been a growing and widely felt concern about the extent of economic, military and cultural dependence on the United States, and the implications for Canadian independence.

Apart from the relationship itself, which has become more complex, public attitudes in Canada have also changed. In the past, Canadians have generally supported an easy-going, pragmatic approach to our relations with the United States in the belief that Canada's separate national existence and development were fully compatible with an unfolding, increasingly close economic, cultural and military relationship between the two countries. Many Canadians no longer accept this view, or at least do not regard it as self-evident. It is widely believed that the continental pull, especially economic and cultural, has gained momentum. In this on-going national debate, the fundamental question for Canada is whether and to what extent interdependence with the United States impairs the reality of Canada's independence. How strong has the continental pull become? Can it be resisted and controlled and, if so, at what price?

. . .

Perhaps more than ever before, the Canada-U.S. relationship is becoming an absorbing focus of much Canadian thinking about the Canadian condition. This is nowhere more evident than in the foreign policy review, which attributes its own genesis in part to "frustration . . . about having to live in the shadow of the United States and its foreign policy, about the heavy dependence of Canada's economy on continuing American prosperity, and about the marked influence of that large and dynamic society on Canadian life in general."

This is a relatively new set of perceptions. In fact, one of the most dramatic aspects of such evidence as is provided by the public opinion polls has been the change in Canadian attitudes over the past two decades. In the 1950s and early 1960s, most Canadians were firm in their support for U.S. policies and certainly gave no evidence of perceiving a U.S. threat to Canada. In 1956 as many as 68 percent of those polled supported the idea of free trade with the United States. On the more general issue of dependence, the polls taken between 1948 and 1963 indicated that at least half of those polled did not think Canadian life was being unduly influenced by the United States. Indeed, a 1963 poll recorded 50 percent as believing that dependence on the United States was beneficial to Canada. All in all, attitudes during that period appeared to be much more congenial to close Canadian involvement with the United States than is the case today.

The evidence suggests that the overriding issue to emerge from the Canada-U.S. relationship for most Canadians today is that of economic independence. For example, a cross-section of various polls indicates that 88.5 percent of Canadians think it important for Canada to have more control over its own economy; that two of every three Canadians view the current level of American investment in Canada as being too high; that, while seven out of every ten Canadians are prepared to acknowledge that American investment has given them a higher standard of living than they might otherwise have had, almost half of them would be willing to accept a lower living standard if that were the price to be paid for controlling or reducing the level of American investment. These are admittedly national averages. They do not necessarily do justice to pronounced regional variations.

If the national mood is to be comprehended in one sentence, it would appear that Canadians remain aware of the benefits of the American connection but that, today more than at any other time since the Second World War they are concerned about the trend of the relationship and seem willing to contemplate and support reasonable measures to assure greater Canadian independence.

It is a matter of more than passing interest that the movement of people between Canada and the United States runs in remarkable parallel with the attitudes reflected in the public opinion polls. The 1950s, for example, saw an average of some thirty thousand Canadians a year moving to the United States, against a reverse flow of only about eleven thousand. These were the years of the "brain drain," when doctors, engineers, teachers, artists, writers and musicians comprised the largest group of Canadian emigrants. By the 1960s, the net flow of Canadians moving across the border started to level off dramatically until, in 1969, for the first time in the postwar period, the movement of Americans to Canada actually exceeded that of Canadians to the United States by a small margin.

The trend may prove temporary. It probably reflects, to some extent at least, U.S. restrictions on Canadian immigration and the impact of the Vietnam war. Nevertheless, the trend is not without significance. It cannot easily be explained by the normal quantitative factors. The difference in per capita gross national product between the two countries has not varied widely on either side of the 25 percent mark and the gap in real per capita income has stayed about the same since the war. The skilled Canadian can still command a significantly higher salary in the United States.The sunny climates of California and Florida as places of retirement have also not changed. Indeed, the eighteen thousand Canadians who emigrated to the United States in 1969 obviously felt all the old pulls. But something evidently had changed.

Canada had matured. The outlines of a more distinct national profile were emerging. An increasingly industrial economy had taken shape. The revolution in communications gave promise of knitting the country more closely together. A quieter revolution had transformed the face of French Canada. The flow of immigrants from Europe and elsewhere was adding new dimensions to Canadian life. The foundations of Canada's cultural personality were being strengthened.

Inevitably, Canadians became more aware of themselves, of the kind of society they were intent on shaping, of the particular problems that lay ahead for them. They were concerned about maintaining national unity; about equalizing economic opportunities as between the different regions of the country; about the best ways of meeting the challenges of a bilingual and multicultural society. They were concerned about their future prosperity; about the problem of providing employment for the most rapidly expanding labour force of any industrialized country; about the management of the resources with which their country had been so richly endowed. They were concerned about the quality of their life; about the risks of blight brought about by unplanned urban growth; about the threat to the environment represented by industrial and technological growth; about the fragile balance of nature in the Arctic and the quality of the waters off Canada's coasts.

If these concerns can be brought within a single focus, it is that of Canada's distinctness. And for Canada distinctness could, in recent years, have only one meaning: distinctness from the United States. What more and more Canadians were brought to realize was that, with all the affinities and all the similarities they shared with the United States, Canada was a distinct country with distinct problems that demanded Canadian solutions. It was not and is not that Canadians underrate the tremendous achievements of American society or its unbounded capacity for self-renewal. It is simply that more and more Canadians have come to conclude that the American model does not, when all is said and done, fit the Canadian condition. Such a conclusion has led, not unnaturally, to the assertion of the right of Canadians to fashion their national environment according to their own perceptions.

In this changing context, what is to be done about the continental pull and the internal momentum with which it is thought by many to be endowed? It is probably useful to start out by acknowledging that there are immutable factors that cannot be changed. Our history, our geography, our demographic structure have imposed and will continue to impose limitations on Canada's freedom of action. Whether we defend it or not, there will be three thousand miles of common frontier with the United States. Chinese Walls, Maginot Lines or Iron Curtains have never lived up to the claims of impermeability that were made for them. We could conceivably keep out American products but not American ideas, tastes or life styles. We could theoretically have one hundred percent Canadian content in our broadcasting but could hardly ban the airwaves to American stations. We could prohibit the migration of people but not eliminate the strong interpersonal relationships on each side of the border. Canadian independence can be realistic only within some measure of interdependence in the world. Canadian energies should not be wasted or efforts misspent on policies that give little promise of being achievable.

In examining the options before us, therefore, we must necessarily focus on those areas of the Canada-U.S. relationship where movement is not foreclosed by factors about which nothing can be done.

This is not the first time Canadians have asked themselves which way they should go. The factor of geography remains a constant element in the equation. The disproportion between Canada and the United States in terms of power has not changed all that much. The continental pull itself has historical antecedents. The pursuit of a distinctive identity runs through the process of Canadian nation-building.

But if the signposts are familiar, the landscape is undoubtedly different. Many of the old countervailing forces have disappeared. The links across the common border have increased in number, impact and complexity. New dimensions are being added to the Canada-U.S. relationship all the time. On both sides, there is now difficulty in looking upon the relationship as being wholly external in character.

The world trend is not helpful to Canada in resolving this dilemma. For the trend is discernibly in the direction of interdependence. In the economic realm, in science, in technology, that is the direction in which the logic of events is pointing. In Canada's case, inevitably, interdependence is likely to mean interdependence mainly with the United States. This is a simple statement of the facts. It does not pretend to be a value judgment. In point of fact, the balance of benefits of such a trend for Canada may well be substantial.

But this evades the real question that looms ahead for Canada. And that is whether interdependence with a big, powerful, dynamic country like the United States is not bound, beyond a certain level of tolerance, to impose an unmanageable strain on the concept of a separate Canadian identity, if not on the elements of Canadian independence.

To pose these questions is simple enough. To propound answers to them is more difficult because any answer is likely to touch on the central ambiguity of our relationship with the United States. The temper of the times, nevertheless, suggests that Canadians are looking for answers. It is also apparent that many of the answers are in Canadian hands. This is because few of the problems engendered by the relationship are, in fact, problems of deliberate creation on the U.S. side. They are problems arising out of contiguity and disparity in wealth and power and, not least, out of the many affinities that make it more difficult for Canadians to stake out an identity of their own.

The real question facing Canadians is one of direction. In practice, three broad options are open to us:

a) We can seek to maintain more or less our present relationship with the United States with a minimum of policy adjustments;
b) We can move deliberately toward closer integration with the United States;
c) We can pursue a comprehensive, long-term strategy to develop and strengthen the Canadian economy and other aspects of our national life and in the process to reduce the present Canadian vulnerability.

Such a statement of options may err on the side of oversimplification. The options are intended merely to delineate general directions of policy. Each option clearly covers a spectrum of possibilities and could be supported by a varied assortment of policy instruments. Nevertheless, the importance of the options notion is not to be discounted. For, in adopting one of the options, Canadians would be making a conscious choice of the continental environment that, in their view, was most likely to be responsive to their interests and aspirations over the next decade or two. Conversely, no single option is likely to prove tenable unless it commands a broad national consensus.

The first option would be to aim at maintaining more or less the present pattern of our economic and political relationship with the

United States with a minimum of policy change either generally or in the Canada-United States context.

The formulation notwithstanding, this is not an option meaning no change. In the present climate, any option that did not provide for change would clearly be unrealistic. The realities of power in the world are changing. Some of the international systems that have provided the context for our monetary and trading relations in the postwar period are in the process of reshaping. The United States is embarked on a basic reappraisal of its position and policies. The Canadian situation is itself changing and new perceptions are being brought to bear on the Canada-U.S. relationship. All this suggests that some adjustments in Canadian policy are unavoidable.

The first option would neither discount the fact of change nor deny the need to accommodate to it. But it would imply a judgment that, at least on the present evidence, the changes that have occurred or are foreseeable are not of a nature or magnitude to call for a basic reorientation of Canadian policies, particularly as they relate to the United States.

In practical terms, this would mean maintaining the general thrust of our trade and industrial policies, including a large degree of laissez faire in economic policy, a multilateral, most-favoured-nation approach as the guiding principle of our trade policy, emphasis on securing improved access to the U.S. market, the vigorous export of commodities and semi-processed goods, and continuing efforts to industrialize domestically by rationalizing production, in large part for export. Presumably, little or no change would be made in the present way of handling matters at issue with the United States, which is one of dealing with each problem as it arises and seeking to maintain something of a "special relationship."

But there is another side to the coin. The changes that are taking place on both sides of the border point to new opportunities and new constraints emerging for Canada. We would aim at seizing the opportunities and managing the constraints to the best of our ability. In the process we would be concerned about the balance of benefits for Canada, but we would be less concerned about how any given transaction or act of policy fitted into some overall conception of our relationship with the United States.

Nevertheless, other things being equal, we would seek to avoid any further significant increase in our dependence on the United States and our vulnerability to the vicissitudes of the U.S. market and to changes in U.S. economic policy. An effort to diversify our export markets would not be incompatible with the first option; nor would a policy to take advantage of accelerating demand for our mineral and energy resources to secure more processing and employment in Canada and, generally, to reap greater benefits from this major national asset; nor would some further moderate Canadian action to achieve greater control over the domestic economic and cultural environment.

In sum, this is essentially a pragmatic option. It would not, by definition, involve radical policy departures. It would deal with issues as they arose on the basis of judgments made in relation to each issue. It is not a static option because it would address itself to the solution of problems generated by an environment which is itself dynamic. One of its main attractions is that, we trust, it would not foreclose other options.

The precise implications and costs of this option are difficult to predict because they would vary significantly depending on developments over the short and medium term. Accommodation of current U.S. preoccupations, however limited, would entail some costs and could involve an increase in our dependence on the United States. If U.S. difficulties proved more durable, and if significant improvements in access to other markets did not materialize, pressures might develop in the United States and in Canada for further special bilateral arrangements. Alternatively, if protectionist attitudes in the United States were to find reflection in official policy, we might be forced to seek other markets on whatever terms we could and perhaps to make painful adjustments in order to reorient our industry to serve mainly the domestic market.

On more optimistic assumptions about the course of U.S. policy and the future of the international trading system, the first option might be followed for some time with ostensible success. The real question is whether it comes fully to grips with the basic Canadian situation or with the underlying continental pull. There is a risk that, in pursuing a purely pragmatic course, we may find ourselves drawn more closely into the U.S. orbit. At the end of the day, therefore, it may be difficult for the present position to be maintained, let alone improved, without more fundamental shifts in Canadian policy.

The second option is to accept that, in a world where economies of scale are dictating an increasing polarization of trade and in the face of intensified integrating pressures within North America, the continuation of the existing relationship, based on the economic separation of Canada and the United States, does not make good sense, and to proceed from that conclusion deliberately to prepare the ground for an arrangement with the United States involving closer economic ties.

The option spans a considerable range of possibilities. At the lower end of the scale, it might involve no more than the pursuit of sectoral or other limited arrangements with the United States based on an assessment of mutual interest. In effect, this would represent an extension of past practices except to the extent that such arrangements would be pursued more as a matter of deliberate policy. We might seek, for example, to adapt to other industries the approach reflected in the Automotive Products Agreement. The chemical industry is one such industry that could lend itself to rationalization on a North-South basis. The aerospace industry might well be another. We might also endeavour to negotiate a continental arrangement with the United States covering energy resources. Under such an arrangement, U.S. access to Canadian energy supplies might be traded in exchange for unimpeded access to the U.S. market for Canadian uranium, petroleum, and petrochemical products (to be produced by a much expanded and developed industry within Canada).

This more limited form of integration has a certain logic to it and, indeed, warrants careful examination. It may be expected, however, to generate pressures for more and more continental arrangements of this kind that would be increasingly difficult to resist. Experience with the Automotive Products Agreement suggests that, in any such sectoral arrangements, there may be difficulty in maintaining an equal voice with the United States over time. Nor could we be sure that the concept of formal symmetry, on which the United States has lately insisted, is one that can easily be built into a sectoral arrangement without impairing the interests of the economically weaker partner. In the energy field, by dealing continentally with the United States, we would almost certainly limit our capacity to come to an arrangement with other potential purchasers, in Europe or Japan, quite apart from possibly impinging upon future Canadian needs. In sum, we might well be driven to the conclusion that partial or sectoral arrangements are less likely to afford us the protection we seek than a more comprehensive regime of free trade.

A free trade area or a customs union arrangement with the United States would, to all intents and purposes, be irreversible for Canada once embarked upon. It would, theoretically, protect us against future changes in U.S. trade policy towards the rest of the world, though not against changes in U.S. domestic economic policy. This option has been rejected in the past because it was judged to be inconsistent with Canada's desire to preserve a maximum degree of independence, not because it lacked economic sense in terms of Canadian living standards and the stability of the Canadian economy.

A free trade area permits greater freedom than a customs or economic union, which calls for a unified external tariff and considerable harmonization of fiscal and other domestic economic policies. It might enable us, for example, to continue to protect our energy resources by limiting exports to the surpluses available after meeting present and prospective Canadian requirements and to ensure against harmful pricing practices. It would not debar us from continuing to bargain with third countries for improved access to their markets or from protecting ourselves against low-cost imports. Yet it must be accepted that the integration of the Canadian and U.S. economies would proceed apace and we should be bound to be more affected than ever by decisions taken in Washington with only limited and indirect means of influencing them.

Internationally, there is a real risk that the conclusion of a free trade arrangement between Canada and the United States would be taken as setting the seal upon the polarization of world trade. To the extent that it was, our room for bargaining with third countries would inevitably be reduced and our economic fortunes become more closely linked with those of the United States.

The experience of free trade areas (such as the European Free Trade Association) suggests, in any case, that they tend to evolve toward more organic arrangements and the harmonization of internal economic policies. More specifically, they tend towards a full customs and economic union as a matter of internal logic. A Canada-U.S. free trade area would be almost certain to do likewise. Indeed, such a course could be argued to be in the Canadian interest because, to compete, we would probably require some harmonization of social and economic costs.

If a free trade area or customs union is a well nigh irreversible option for Canada, this cannot necessarily be assumed to be the case for the United States. A situation could easily be imagined in which difficulties arose in certain economic sectors or regions of the United States when the Congress might feel constrained to seek to halt or reverse the process. The central problem, here as elsewhere, is the enormous disparity in power between the United States and Canada.

It is arguable, therefore, that in the end the only really safe way to guard against reversal and to obtain essential safeguards for Canadian industry and other Canadian economic interests might be to move to some form of political union at the same time. The object would be to obtain for Canadians a genuine and usable voice in decisions affecting our integrated economies.

At first glance this might look like pursuing the argument to an unwarranted conclusion. The Europeans, it could be argued, have, after all, found it possible to operate a customs union without substantial derogations from their sovereignty. Even if this changes to some extent as they progress towards economic and monetary union, the prospects for full political union or confederation continue to look relatively remote.

But the configuration of power in Europe is different. The European countries are more recognizably different from one another; their identities are older and more deeply anchored; and they are much more nearly equal in resources and power. There is a certain balance in the decision-making system of the European Economic Community that would not be conceivable in a bilateral Canada-U.S. arrangement. For the Europeans, moreover, the problem has been one of transcending historical conflicts. For Canada, on the contrary, the problem has been one of asserting its separate identity and developing its character distinctive from that of the United States in the face of similarities, affinities and a whole host of common denominators.

Throughout this discussion it has been assumed that proposals for free trade or a customs union with Canada would be welcomed in the United States. This is not an unreasonable assumption, taking account of the substantial interpenetration that already exists between the two economies and the vested interests that have been created in the process on the part of U.S. business and labour. It is, nevertheless, an assumption that remains to be tested against changing attitudes in the United States and the implications for U.S. trade and other policies that, like Canada's, have been global rather than regional in their general thrust. Congressional reaction, in particular, would be a matter of conjecture until the issue was on the table. Political union would presumably raise issues of a different order of complexity, although it has from time to time had respectable support in some circles in the United States.

If we were to opt for integration, deliberate and coherent policies and programs would be required, both before and after an arrangement was achieved, to cope with the difficult adjustments that would be entailed for Canada. An adequate transitional period would be essential. Some safeguards for production and continued industrial growth in Canada would have to be negotiated. Agriculture might emerge as another problem sector. In practice, any safeguards would probably be limited largely to a transitional period and could not be expected to cushion the impact of integration for an indefinite future. A tendency for the centres of production — and population — to move south might, in the long run, be difficult to stem. But the more relaxed environment Canada has to offer and the lesser prominence of pressures in Canadian society might also, over time, exert a countervailing influence on any purely economic trend.

The probable economic costs and benefits of this option would require careful calculation. The more fundamental issues, however, are clearly political. In fact, it is a moot question whether this option, or any part of it, is politically tenable in the present or any foreseeable climate of Canadian public opinion.

Reactions and attitudes would no doubt differ across the country. The cleavage of interest between the central, industrialized region and the Western provinces on this issue has become apparent in recent years. Attitudes rooted in historical tradition could be expected to play their part in the Atlantic Provinces. The reaction in the French-speaking areas is more difficult to predict. On the one hand, they tend not to draw a very sharp distinction between the impact of economic control of local enterprise whether exercised from the United States or from elsewhere in Canada. But it is not unlikely that among many French-speaking Canadians the prospect of union with the United States would be viewed as risking their eventual submergence in a sea of some two hundred million English-speaking North Americans and as a reversal of the efforts made in Canada over the last ten years to create a favourable climate for the survival and development of the

French language and culture in North America.

There is a real question, therefore, whether the whole of Canada could be brought into union with the United States. Of course, full-fledged political union is not the basic intent of this option. But, to the extent that the logic of events may impel us in that direction, almost any form of closer integration with the United States may be expected to generate opposition in Canada. If it is true, moreover, as appears to be the case, that a more vigorous sense of identity has been taking root among Canadians in recent years, it is unlikely that opposition to this option would be confined to particular parts of the country.

The basic aim of the third option would be, over time, to lessen the vulnerability of the Canadian economy to external factors, including, in particular, the impact of the United States and, in the process, to strengthen our capacity to advance basic Canadian goals and develop a more confident sense of national identity. If it is to be successfully pursued, the approach implicit in this option would clearly have to be carried over into other areas of national endeavour and supported by appropriate policies. But the main thrust of the option would be towards the development of a balanced and efficient economy to be achieved by means of a deliberate, comprehensive and long-term strategy.

The accent of the option is on Canada. It tries to come to grips with one of the unanswered questions that runs through so much of the Canada-U.S. relationship, and which is what kind of Canada it is that Canadians actually want. It is thus in no sense an anti-American option. On the contrary, it is the one option of all those presented that recognizes that, in the final analysis, it may be for the Canadian physician to heal himself.

The option is subject to two qualifications. "Over time" recognizes that the full benefits will take time to materialize, but that a conscious and deliberate effort will be required to put and maintain the Canadian economy on such a course. "To lessen" acknowledges that there are limits to the process because it is unrealistic to think that any economy, however structured, let alone Canada's, can be made substantially immune to developments in the world around us in an era of growing interdependence.

The option is one that can have validity on most assumptions about the external environment. A basically multilateral environment, of course, in which trade is governed by the most-favoured-nation principle, would enhance its chances of success. But it would not be invalidated by other premises. That is because the option relates basically to the Canadian economy. Its purpose is to recast that economy in such a way as to make it more rational and more efficient as a basis for Canada's trade abroad.

The present may be an auspicious time for embarking on this option. Our trading position is strong. We are regarded as a stable and affluent country with a significant market and much to offer to our global customers in the way of resources and other products. Our balance of payments has been improving in relative terms. We are no longer as dependent on large capital inflows as we once were. A new round of comprehensive trade negotiations is in prospect during 1973. Above all, there is a greater sense of urgency within Canada and greater recognition abroad of Canada's right to chart its own economic course.

The option assumes that the basic nature of our economy will continue unchanged. That is to say that, given the existing ratio of resources to population, Canada will continue to have to depend for a large proportion of its national wealth on the ability to export goods and services to external markets on secure terms of access. The object is essentially to create a sounder, less vulnerable economic base for competing in the domestic and world markets and deliberately to broaden the spectrum of markets in which Canadians can and will compete.

In terms of policy, it would be necessary to encourage the specialization and rationalization of production and the emergence of strong Canadian-controlled firms. It is sometimes argued that a market of the size of Canada's may not provide an adequate base for the economies of scale that are a basic ingredient of international efficiency. The argument is valid only up to a point. The scale of efficiency is different for different industries and there is no reason why a market of twenty-two million people with relatively high incomes should prove inadequate for many industries which are not the most complex or capital-intensive.

The close co-operation of government, business and labour would be essential through all phases of the implementation of such an industrial strategy. So would government efforts to provide a climate conducive to the expansion of Canadian entrepreneurial activity. It may be desirable, and possible, in the process to foster the development of large, efficient multinationally-operating Canadian firms that could effectively compete in world markets. It may also be possible, as a consequence of greater efficiencies, for Canadian firms to meet a higher proportion of the domestic requirement for goods and services. But that would be a natural result of the enhanced level of competitiveness which the option is designed to promote; it is not in the spirit of the option to foster import substitution as an end in itself with all the risks that would entail of carrying us beyond the margins of efficiency.

The option has been variously described as involving a deliberate, comprehensive, and long-term strategy. It is bound to be long-term because some substantial recasting of economic structures may be involved. It is comprehensive in the sense that it will entail the mutually-reinforcing use and adaptation of a wide variety of policy instruments. Fiscal policy, monetary policy, the tariff, the rules or competition, government procurement, foreign investment regulations, and science policy may all have to be brought to bear on the objectives associated with this option. The choice and combination of policy instruments will depend on the precise goals to be attained. The implications, costs, and benefits of the option will vary accordingly.

In saying that the strategy must be deliberate, it is accepted that it must involve some degree of planning, indicative or otherwise, and that there must be at least a modicum of consistency in applying it. One implication of the conception of deliberateness is that the strategy may have to entail a somewhat greater measure of government involvement than has been the case in the past. The whole issue of government involvement, however, needs to be kept in proper perspective. The Government is now and will continue to be involved in the operation of the economy in a substantial way. This is a function of the responsibility which the Canadian Government shares with other sovereign governments for ensuring the well-being and prosperity of its citizens in a context of social justice. A wide variety of policy instruments and incentives is already being deployed to that end, largely with the support and often at the insistence of those who are more directly concerned with the running of different segments of the economy. It is not expected that the pursuit of this particular option will radically alter the relation between Government and the business community, even if the Government were to concern itself more closely with the direction in which the economy was evolving.

Much the same considerations apply to the relationship between the federal and provincial jurisdictions. It is true that, in the diverse circumstances that are bound to prevail in a country like Canada, the task of aggregating the national interest is not always easy. There may be a problem, therefore, in achieving the kind of broad consensus on objectives, priorities and instrumentalities on which the successful pursuit of anything on the lines of the present option is likely to hinge. Part of the problem may derive from a divergent assessment of short-term interests. In terms of longer-range goals, it is much less apparent why federal and provincial interests should not be largely compatible or why the elaboration of this option should not enhance and enlarge the opportunities for co-operation with the provinces. Indeed, there are many areas, such as the upgrading of Canada's natural resource exports, where the implications of this option are likely to coincide closely with provincial objectives.

What of the impact on the United States, which could be critical to the success of the option? There again, it is necessary to keep matters in perspective. There is no basic change envisaged in Canada's multilateral trade policy. On the contrary, we could expect to be working closely with the United States in promoting a more liberal world-trading environment. Nor does the option imply any intention artificially to distort our traditional trading patterns. The United States would almost certainly remain Canada's most important market and source of supply by a very considerable margin.

The fact remains, nevertheless, that the option is directed towards reducing Canada's vulnerability, particularly in relation to the United States. A good deal of this vulnerability derives from an underlying continental pull, which is inadvertent. To that extent, the risk of friction at the governmental level is lessened, although it would be unrealistic to discount it altogether. Much would depend on what policy instruments were selected in support of this option and how we deployed them. The state of the U.S. economy could be another factor determining U.S. reactions at any given time. On any reasonable assumptions, however, such impact as the option may unavoidably have on U.S. interests would be cushioned by the time-frame over which it is being projected and should be relatively easy to absorb in a period of general growth and prosperity. When all is said and done, the option aims at a relative decline in our dependence on the United States, not at a drastic change in our bilateral relationship. As such, it is not incompatible with the view, recently advanced by President Nixon in his address to the House of Commons, that "no self-respecting nation can or should accept the proposition that it should always be economically dependent upon any other nation."

The continental pull appears to be operating most strongly in the economic and cultural sectors. There are those who, like Professor John Kenneth Galbraith, argue that U.S. economic influence can be disregarded so long as Canada manages to maintain a distinct culture of its own. Many Canadians would disagree with him. Nevertheless, no prescription for Canada is likely to be complete that did not attempt to cover the cultural sector.

There are differences between the economic and the cultural forces that are at work in the Canada-U.S. relationship. In the first place, culture has more than one dimension; it means different things to different Canadians. Second, the cultural interaction between Canada and the United States is, if anything, even less a matter of governmental policy than the interaction between the two economies. Third, it is much harder to influence the movement of ideas than it is to influence the movement of goods. Finally, it is evidently not a threat about which the public at large feels anything like the concern that, according to the opinion polls, it feels about the threat to Canadian control of the domestic economic environment.

This is one reason why the cultural scene requires separate discussion. But there is another. In the economic sector, it is clear, Canadians do face difficult choices. It is a moot question whether this is really true when it comes to the cultural sector. This is not to discount the importance of a healthy cultural environment to the Canadian sense of identity and national confidence. It is merely to suggest that in this sector the essential choices may, in fact, already have been made.

Domestically, two prescriptions have, by and large, been applied. The first is regulatory. It recognizes that some of the means of cultural expression are subject to the competition of the marketplace in the same way as the offer of other services. The purpose of regulation in these instances is simply to ensure that, where the standards of the product are equal, the Canadian offering is not ruled out by terms of competition that are unequal. This is the general philosophy that has guided the efforts of the Canadian Radio and Television Commission. It is probably applicable in other areas where the Canadian product — whether film, record, or publication — is held back because the requisite measure of control of the distribution system is not in Canadian hands.

The other prescription has been to give direct support to cultural activity in Canada. This role has, on the whole, fallen to government. Support has taken the form of financial assistance, but also of institutions that have been established to encourage the expression of Canadian creative talent. The Massey Commission judged in 1951 that money spent on cultural defences was, in the end, no less important than money spent on defence so-called. In the eyes of most Canadians, this remains a valid judgment.

As in the economic sector, any policy aimed at lessening the impact of U.S. influences on the Canadian cultural scene should presumably have an external dimension. This is not simply a matter of diversification for its own sake. Canada's cultural roots are, after all, widely ramified. International projection will enable Canada to reaffirm its distinctive linguistic and cultural complexion. But it will also give Canadians the opportunity to test their product in a wider market and to draw, in turn, on the currents of cross-fertilization.

In sum, Canadians will not be able to take their cultural environment for granted. It is on the cultural front, as on the economic front, that the impact on Canada of the dynamic society to the south finds its strongest expression. The impact has no doubt been magnified by the development of the mass media and their counterpart: the mass market. French-speaking Canadians may be less exposed to it for reasons of language, but they are not immune. Canadians generally appear to find it more difficult to focus on it than on the U.S. impact on the Canadian economy, perhaps because the many affinities between Canadians and Americans tend to make any concept of a threat unreal. On the whole, the general directions of Canadian policy in the cultural sector have been set and they have been pursued with reasonable success. Perhaps we have already turned the corner. But it remains for these policies to be extended to other vulnerable areas and to take account of the further impetus that the new technologies may give to the cultural thrust of the United States as it affects Canada.

This is, fortunately, an area in which there is broad convergence between the perceptions and goals of the federal and provincial governments. It would not be unrealistic, therefore, to look to a high degree of co-operation between the two levels of government in creating the kind of climate we shall need over the next decade or two if Canadian themes are to find their distinctive expression.

It is also one of the areas in which Canadians can act with the least risk of external repercussion. It has been said that culture is imported rather than exported. This is not wholly true. But to the extent that cultural influences are brought in willingly, they can be shaped domestically without affront to the exporter.

. . .

The foreign policy review speaks of living distinct from but in harmony with the United States. There is no anomaly in this proposition. The concept of distinctness is taken for granted as the natural context for international relations and no qualitative inferences should be drawn from it one way or the other. There are many countries in the world that certainly regard themselves as being distinct and have no difficulty in living in the closest harmony of purpose and endeavour with other countries. There is no intrinsic reason, therefore, why Canadian distinctness should in any way inhibit the continued existence of a fundamentally harmonious relationship between Canada and the United States.

It is fair to assume that, in the 1970s and 1980s, Canadian-American relations may become more complex than they have been in the past. It is part of the trend toward increasing complexity in the relationship that a larger number of issues may arise between us that engage the national interest on each side. It is also to be assumed that, if the national interest were interpreted in a new and possibly narrower focus, the issues arising between us would, on occasion, be judged to bear more critically on it than when the relationship was more relaxed. Finally, as governments on both sides of the border are more and more being drawn by their various domestic constituencies into areas of social and economic activity that involve the shaping of national goals, the nature of the issues between us and the means of resolving them may change.

There is nothing in all this that should be thought to imply a scenario for greater contention. Far from it. There will, of course, be issues, such as Canada's policies on foreign ownership and perhaps in relation to energy and other resources — and in many other areas — where perceptions will differ. The same will almost certainly be true of United States policies as that country continues to grapple with secular and structural problems of economic adjustment. On occasion, as [U.S.] Secretary of State Rogers recently put it, each government "may be required to take hard decisions in which the other cannot readily concur." In the main, however, we should expect both countries to manage change in a spirit of harmony and without doing unnecessary damage to interests on the other side. Above all, it is in Canada's interest to work closely with a dynamic and outward-looking United States whose influence and the leverage it can bring into play will continue to be critical to the achievement of some of Canada's principal objectives in the international environment.

In the final analysis, harmony is not an extraneous factor in the Canada-United States relationship because it is based on a broad array of shared interests, perceptions and goals. It also reflects the many affinities that have linked Canadians and Americans traditionally and that continue to link them as members of changing but still broadly compatible societies. What is at issue at the moment is, as someone has aptly defined it, "the optimum range of interdependence" between Canada and the United States. All the evidence suggests that the issue is being reviewed on both sides of the border. But, understandably, it is of immensely greater significance for Canada. If the outcome is a Canada more confident in its identity, stronger in its capacity to satisfy the aspirations of Canadians and better equipped to play its part in the world, it is an outcome that is bound to make Canada a better neighbour and partner of the United States. Above all, it is an outcome that should buttress the continuation of a harmonious relationship between the two countries.

FOREIGN INVESTMENT AND CANADIAN ENERGY, 1981†

MARK MACGUIGAN

. . . We all know that Canadian-U.S. relations are vast and complex. Today we often hear that Canadian policies are vexing the relationship. Tonight, I will give you the background to some of those policies.

My reason for wanting to provide this context or framework is a belief that unless and until Americans, both inside and outside government, appreciate more fully the rationale for Canadian economic policies, the goal of managing the relationship effectively will prove elusive. We have to understand each other, or we risk talking right past each other.

Let me begin with several political facts of Canadian life. First, all Canadians think of themselves as self-appointed experts about the United States. Second, all Canadians believe they know just what needs to be done to straighten out Canada-U.S. relations. Third, while Canada-U.S. relations tend to get buried on page forty-eight of the *New York Times*, it is big box-office in Canada. So, we have a usual situation of perceived general omniscience on one side and relative disinterest (albeit usually benign) on the other. These are aspects of

† Mark MacGuigan, "The Canadian Perspective on Foreign Investment and Energy Questions," Bureau of Information, Department of External Affairs, *Statements and Speeches* 24, 1981. The text is taken from a speech by MacGuigan, then Secretary of State for External Affairs, to the Centre for Inter-American Relations, New York, 30 September 1981.

the political environment which affect the way politicians in Canada have to deal with the topic.

Precisely because it is a potentially volatile topic, a succession of Canadian governments have placed great store in conducting relations with the U.S. on a business-like and case-by-case basis. The emphasis has been on dealing with most bilateral difficulties in a direct and low-key manner, and not through negotiations in the press. Over the years, the United States has welcomed this rational, problem-solving approach, and the state of the relationship reflected this. Beyond the obvious utility of these methods, the genuine respect and warmth existing between the two peoples made such a way of doing business natural. There have been difficulties. I think of 1971 when the U.S. took a number of national economic policy decisions directed toward trade, the so-called "Nixon shock," which were nothing short of traumatic for Canadian policy-makers at the time, and which subsequently reinforced Canadian determination to strengthen national control over our economy.

But it is with a general history of co-operation in mind that I turn to a set of American concerns, some of which have recently prompted U.S. officials to express public surprise at what they call Canada's nationalist and short-sighted policies. Perhaps in the next few minutes, I can help to alleviate this apparent state of shock.

Clearly, important elements of the U.S. private sector, Congress, and administration see a disturbing change in Canadian economic policies. In addition to the words "nationalist" and "short-sighted," the terms most often used to characterize this supposedly sudden shift in direction are "interventionist," "restrictive," and "discriminatory." In the view of some prominent Americans, at least, it is no longer possible to look northward and recognize the Canada they thought they knew.

Accompanying this generalized concern in some quarters is a more specific complaint, voiced mostly by corporate spokesmen, that the "rules of the game" have been abruptly changed in Canada, and that this amounts to unfair treatment. The companies involved have not hesitated to act on their convictions and seek support in this country, often from their friends in Congress.

This level of alarm is unjustified, but to a degree it is understandable, since the commercial and economic stakes are high. Over 21 percent of U.S. foreign direct investment world-wide is in Canada; according to the latest available figures, this amounted to more than $38 billion. So there is a strong degree of exposure involved. But be reassured that it is two way. In 1980, two-way trade between the two countries totalled some $90 billion, the largest trading relationship in the world between any two countries. The point is that neither side wishes to jeopardize economic links of such importance.

A key to ensuring that damage is not done is knowledge. I would like

Americans to know more about Canadian realities. They would then recognize that these realities are not threatening to U.S. interests but reveal a country in the process of strengthening itself, not at the expense of others, and in a way which will in fact result in a more capable neighbour and ally for this country.

What is happening in Canada is for us an exciting process — the enhancement of our nationhood. Our domestic debates over the form of our government are well known to you and have their roots in the original bargaining which led to Confederation over one hundred years ago. Perhaps less well known is the on-going debate over economic development policy which has paralleled the political discussion.

These two strands are now coming together as the constitutional issue nears a decisive stage and as the overall direction of economic development policy is clarified. The combined effect of this "coming of age" will be noticeable to a near neighbour, but if our lines of communication are kept open, one hopes not too unsettling.

Our Prime Minister summed it up as he introduced President Reagan in the House of Commons on March 11 this year. "In the years to come the United States will be looking at a dynamic neighbour to the north. By putting its own house in order, Canada will grow confident in itself. We will establish more clearly where our interests lie and we will pursue them with renewed vigour. One thing will remain unchanged, however: our deep friendship for the United States."

What we hope our American friends will realize is that, in economic terms, this clarifying of national interest is based on political traditions and economic structures different from their own. More than two hundred years ago our paths diverged, although our goals remained much the same. The parting of the ways led to different political institutions and when compared with different geographic circumstances as well, even a different attitude towards the role of government.

A good example is the degree to which Canadian governments have historically felt the need to intervene in national life to knit together and develop a huge, under-populated and, in some cases, forbidding land. Among the results are national television and radio networks, national airlines, the Canadian National Railway family of companies, and a host of other government undertakings, meant to mobilize capital, technological, and human resources on a scale of effort and risk which some of the challenges of our national development call for. The need for and familiarity with government intervention in the Canadian economy remain to this day.

I should point out that government involvement of this sort represents a pragmatic Canadian response to a particular set of circumstances, and by no means reflects any philosophical discomfort with the role of private enterprise. The private sector has been and will remain the driving force behind Canada's economic development. We share with you the perception that one of the best guarantors of a free society is a free economy. But Canadian economic development needs to be as coherent as possible and as forward looking as possible in terms of overall benefits to Canadian society. And for those reasons, Canadian governments, at the provincial as well as federal levels, are at ease with their responsibilities for judicious intervention in the development process.

In part, this is directly due to a second fundamental difference between the two countries, the structure of the two economies. Canada's economy is a tenth the size of yours, and is more heavily dependent on primary resource industries. The manufacturing base in Canada is narrower and is significantly foreign-controlled. Although in many respects general Canadian and U.S. economic interests are parallel, in some important specific ways they diverge. In the past twenty years, the public debate on the degree to which such a divergence was desirable or possible has centred on the question of foreign ownership.

While Canadians acknowledge the benefits which foreign investment has brought them, it became clear by the beginning of the 1970s, after a decade of study, of the very high degree of foreign ownership and control and that there were very significant costs involved as well. These are well known; they relate to the negative effects on the performance of the economy of locating so many of its command centres outside Canada, on the social development of Canada, which needs more research and development for our engineers and scientists; or the effects of the branch-plant phenomenon on the Canadian potential for developing interesting trade prospects. And so on. And the events of 1971 left us feeling suddenly vulnerable.

Accordingly, in 1974, the government established a foreign investment review process whose task is to screen foreign investment for significant benefit to Canada. You will notice that I used the word "screen," not "block." As of August 1981, the Canadian government had an approval rate for applications by American investors of 90.5 percent, hardly grounds for suggesting that they have been subjected to harsh treatment.

In view of the litany of complaints about the Foreign Investment Review Agency (FIRA), I would like to point out a few facts. Even now, after seven years of the FIRA regime, foreign ownership figures in Canada are at a level which I am sure you will agree would simply not be tolerated in the U.S. For example, according to the latest available figures (1978), foreign investment in the United States accounted for 5 percent of the mining industry and 3 percent of the manufacturing sector. The comparable Canadian levels are 37 percent and 47 percent. The contrast is stark.

Furthermore, in 1978, non-residents controlled about 30 percent of all non-financial industries in Canada; the comparable U.S. figure was about 2 percent. Finally, while only two of the fifty largest firms in the

United States are foreign-controlled, nineteen of the fifty largest firms in Canada are foreign-controlled.

I regret bombarding you with these statistics, but I believe that the reason for Canadian action on foreign investment must be clearly understood. No country could allow these levels of foreign involvement to continue indefinitely. No country ever has. I do not have to remind this audience of the more recent reaction in this country to a degree of foreign penetration much, much lower than that occurring in Canada.

The essential point is that, having determined that the amount of foreign ownership and control was a concern, Canada chose to deal with the problem totally in accordance with our intentional undertakings. There has been no question of nationalization, confiscation or forced sale. Foreign investors have simply been told the conditions under which they would be welcome.

And I should emphasize the notion of welcome. Canada needs and wants foreign investment which will benefit all parties concerned. Foreign companies and individuals will continue to do business profitably in Canada. I do not believe that those who are complaining about our policies are in fact arguing that they have lost money on their investments. Certainly not. And by comparison with other countries, there are very few more secure places to invest money than Canada.

Let me now turn to the vexed question of energy. In the energy field, the cause of much recent anxiety has been Canada's National Energy Program (NEP). Within the context of the obviously special significance the energy sector has for Canadian economic development, that program is founded on three basic principles — security of supply and ultimate independence from the world oil market; opportunity for all Canadians to participate in the energy industry, particularly oil and gas, and to share in the benefits of its expansion; and fairness, with a pricing and revenue-sharing regime which recognizes the needs and rights of all Canadians, with respect to the development of all of Canada's regions.

From where I sit, one aspect of the NEP which has been much misunderstood is "Canadianization." The Canadianization objective is really very simple: it is to increase the share of the oil and gas industry owned and controlled by Canadians — to 50 percent of the industry a decade from now. In the strategy adopted to achieve this utterly legitimate objective, the emphasis is on making room for Canadian oil and gas companies in the industry in Canada, not on forcing out foreign companies. There is no question that we intend to give Canadian companies the opportunity to grow more quickly. What we have not intended or done is to make the operations of large international oil firms unprofitable. For example, the net cost to U.S. firms exploring in Canada will remain lower than in the United States.

But we are dealing with an extraordinary situation. Throughout the

1950s and 1960s, non-residents owned nearly 80 percent and controlled over 90 percent of Canadian oil and gas assets. They also controlled nearly 100 percent of the assets employed in refining and marketing operations. Canada did not have a single Canadian multinational oil company, not even a small one. We did not have a vertically integrated domestic company, until Petro-Canada acquired Pacific Petroleum in 1978.

Before the NEP, an unintended by-product of government policies was increased foreign ownership. New windfall profits due to increases in oil and gas prices favoured the firms already in the business with the largest production. Most of these were foreign-owned. These same foreign-owned firms were also the main beneficiaries of the earned depletion allowance, since this deduction from taxable resource income was available only to firms whose principal business was resources and who had existing resource income. The pre-NEP policy framework virtually guaranteed that the big (and the foreign-owned) would get bigger.

No other developed country faced this predicament. Indeed, as I look around, it is a predicament tolerated by no country, period. By 1980, the 74.0 percent foreign-owned and 81.5 percent foreign-controlled Canadian oil and gas industry generated almost a third of all the non-financial sector profits in Canada. Without changes, enormous power and influence in Canada was destined to fall into a few foreign hands. We simply decided that we had to act and had to act now.

But, unlike some other countries, Canada has preferred the carrot to the stick. The operations of foreign firms in Canada are still very profitable and, to the extent that they increase Canadian ownership, they can now be even more so.

I want to dispel any impression that the NEP has suddenly made the role of foreign firms in the Canadian hydrocarbon industry uncertain and unpredictable. Certainly the rules of the game have changed from ten, twenty or thirty years ago. Perceptions change; needs change; situations change. Where do they not change? But the changed rules are clear. They can be ignored to the detriment of future balance sheets. Or they can be used advantageously by foreign-owned corporate citizens of Canada who are sensitive to the Canadian environment and to the opportunities there for profitable investment.

I should add that the NEP gives foreign companies an incentive to acquire Canadian shareholders and partners. To the extent that they do, they can benefit from higher exploration grants just like firms which are already more than 50 percent Canadian-owned. Let's not forget the many foreign-controlled companies who are quietly rearranging their affairs in Canada to take advantage of the NEP, and in so doing, to continue to grow and prosper in Canada.

Before leaving the subject of Canadian energy policy, let me deal with an assertion often made about another aspect of the NEP's impact. I have seen it claimed that the recent takeovers of foreign-controlled Canadian oil and gas subsidiaries by Canadians have been at "fire-sale" prices caused by the NEP.

In fact, the biggest single takeover since the NEP, the purchase of Hudson's Bay Oil and Gas from Conoco, was at a price that Conoco itself has termed fair and reasonable. The price included a premium of 52 percent above the pre-NEP stock market price. The highest premium of all, 67 percent, was won by St. Joe's Minerals for the alleged "forced" sale of Candel Oil Limited, in order to ward off a takeover attempt on St. Joe's itself. Not bad business for an alleged shotgun wedding. In comparison, the average premium in over sixty takeovers in Canada since 1978 was 35 percent. Indeed, the government in Canada has consistently been criticized for Petro-Can purchases on the grounds that the premiums paid have been too high.

One last note — the takeover fever in Canada began long before the NEP. It has had involved Canadian as well as foreign firms and sectors beyond energy. I suggest that some recently interested observers of Canada step back a bit for a little perspective.

I have taken some time tonight to discuss Canadian investment and energy policies. I did so because these are areas of concern to many in the United States, and this seemed a good opportunity to explain the Canadian position before a largely American audience. I would not like to leave the impression, however, that these American concerns and our responses define the state of relations between us. The United States' own record on trade and investment is not unblemished. Measures have been taken, for example, to assist industrial sectors having difficulty meeting international competition. Buy-American preferences abound. There are sectors of the U.S. economy from which foreign investors are excluded. We are still awaiting action on shared environmental and fisheries issues. Raising these problems gives me no pleasure. It does, however, help to put the bilateral situation into better perspective.

Let me conclude these remarks by returning to a point I made earlier. For Canada, the state of relations with the United States is a crucial matter, full of political sensitivity. Energy and investment questions lie at the heart of the relationship between our two countries. The Canadian government has developed policies in these areas which command broad national support. The government has sought to take American concerns into account (we amended provisions of the NEP, for example), but the main lines of our policies are set. They are set because they correspond to the firm wish of the people of Canada. They are in the political mainstream, and also in the mainstream of a larger, wider current of Canadian economic and political history.

Let us be clear about this. Contrary to a recent Atlantic Council report on the subject, the Canadian policies in investment and energy are not the product of short-term political expediency. The genesis of these policies can be traced back through at least two decades of spirited and intensive national debate. It would be a mistake to suppose that a Canadian government would be able or willing to resist the historical momentum of our country's growing determination to have the necessary amount of control over its own destiny.

Recriminatory rhetoric will get us nowhere — except into a more excited and more nationalistic home environment.

It is the reality of the Canada-U.S. relationship that two different countries can grow separately in their own ways, yet retain bonds of friendship and respect through a common heritage of basic values — the sort we have protected together in two world wars, in Korea, in Iran, in the North Atlantic Treaty Organization (NATO), and the North American Aerospace Defence Command (NORAD). Those values find their ultimate expression in the countless personal links which are the fabric of our relations. In the long run, those values and those personal links define the quality of our relationship.

Canada and the United States have followed distinct paths from the beginning. Our challenge has always been to contain and channel our disagreements so that they did not impede the steady flow of friendship. We must continue to accept this responsibility.

But we must do more. We must visualize our relationship, including our problems, in a world perspective, in a world of general turbulence in which like-minded countries are few enough that we cannot afford to be distracted from achieving together our common goals of freedom, justice, democracy, and friendship among all peoples.

FREE TRADE, 1988†

BRIAN MULRONEY

Right Hon. Brian Mulroney (Prime Minister): . . . Mr. Speaker, it is with pride that I rise to support this bill which will give Canada a new, more certain and more beneficial trade relationship with the United States of America.

I believe it is a good agreement for Canada. It is an idea older than Confederation itself whose time has finally come. It will stand the test of honest scrutiny. It is I believe genuinely in the national interest. The free trade agreement is necessary to secure access to our most vital market and is consistent with policies which are already strengthening our economy and improving the well-being of Canadians.

We on this side of the House support the free trade agreement because we believe it will bring prosperity and economic benefits to Canadians from coast to coast.

Some Hon. Members: Hear, hear!

Mr. Mulroney: Free trade will mean lower prices for Canadian consumers, better jobs, and greater individual opportunities. Free trade will help the regions of this country. It will do so by creating a broader and deeper pool of national wealth, not just by redistributing existing resources.

[*Translation*]

Mr. Speaker, free trade will help us to sustain our social security

† Canada, House of Commons, *Debates*, 30 August 1988, 19049–19058.

programs. Nothing endangers them more than economic decline. Nothing guarantees them better than an expanding economy. The values we have as Canadians and the distinctive quality of life we bring to North America will be enriched by free trade. By strengthening our economy, free trade will help us support cultural programs that enhance the capability of our artists, writers, and performers to express themselves to Canadians and to the world. Free trade will also improve our capacity to strengthen our national programs ranging from the environment to regional development to child care.

Free trade will strengthen our foreign policy. It will be welcomed globally as a beacon of hope for the forces of more open trade, particularly, Mr. Speaker, among developing nations and as a bulwark against protectionism.

My purpose today is to outline the rationale for this initiative, measure the results against our objectives, separate myth from fact, and assert the reasons why I believe this agreement deserves the support of all Canadians.

[*English*]

Almost four years ago the Government received an overwhelming mandate for change from the people of Canada. It is a mandate that we are doing our very best to honour with vigour and determination. Several years ago, before I entered the House of Commons, I set out an agenda for Canada.

First, I said that the new Government must establish that special relationship of trust at all levels with our allies, including our greatest friend and ally, the United States of America. Second, we have to send signals around the world that investment capital is welcome here and that this is a good, an honourable, and a decent place to do business. We have to state clearly that the private sector is the only motor whereby new wealth, new jobs and new opportunity can be created for Canadians. I also said that we must energetically stand and press for the lowering of barriers to trade because trade is our life blood. In that direction lies our future prosperity.

Government in Canada must see its role as creating, with the private sector, a greater and freer access to world markets and higher levels of trade. That was true when I made that statement over five years ago and it is very much true today.

Some Hon. Members: Hear, hear!

Mr. Mulroney: That is precisely what we have delivered during our mandate. More Canadians are working today at rewarding and satisfying jobs than ever before. Inflation is low, the dollar is strong, business is expanding, and consumers are confident. The Canadian economy has out-performed all other OECD economies over the past four years. Relations with the United States have improved substantially. The sour mood and the petulance of the seventies and early eighties is gone. When neighbours quarrel, everybody suffers. When neighbours co-operate, everyone benefits.

Some Hon. Members: Hear, hear!

Mr. Mulroney: We on this side of the House prefer the advantages of co-operation to the futility of confrontation. We are proving, as best we can, that co-operation works. The biggest challenge for government today is to manage the forces of change, and that is what we are trying to do.

In the information age ideas are the new currency of power. High-tech industries and universities have become the arsenals in the nation's influence. In the nuclear age economic strength is becoming as much an alternative to military power as a basis for it. The proportion of world income generated from the sale of natural resources is declining. Capital has become more mobile, moving literally at the speed of light. Investment funds, the motor of growth, flow where there is political stability and profitable economic opportunities.

For all countries, especially the already industrialized countries like Canada, prosperity depends on the quality and skills of our people in harnessing technology, fostering innovation, and establishing an environment for stable growth. We have in this country world-class industries and world-class financial institutions. Our economy is diversified and strong. In the last four years we have recaptured much of the road lost. We are well equipped to prosper and to manage change if we make the right policy decisions now.

We know from painful experience what happens when we make the wrong choices, when we try to swim against the tide, for example, on energy policy or investment policy, or to resist the global trend toward more open trade. One has only to walk through western Canada from the late seventies to the early eighties to see the devastation inflicted on western Canada by a wrong policy choice in energy. That will not happen again.

Some Hon. Members: Hear, hear!

Mr. Mulroney: We must master change, not run from it. We must meet competition, not hide from it. There is no sanctuary from the difficult realities of the unfolding decades. If properly grasped, Canada's future holds the promise of ongoing economic renewal. If rejected, Canada's prospects can be thwarted and our horizons diminished. Canada's youth has understood this challenge. Our young people are saying no to the attitudes of the 1930s and yes to the opportunities of the 1990s.

Some Hon. Members: Hear, hear!

Mr. Mulroney: The newly industrializing countries are not going to decide that their new prosperity has been a mistake. The Europeans are not going to revert to a pastoral life. Far from it, by 1992 the Europeans will have the largest, most powerful trading bloc that the world has ever known. Australia and New Zealand recognize where their interest lies and are rapidly accelerating their free trade association. So, Mr. Speaker, what is the best prescription for Canada?

[*Translation*]

For anyone ready to listen, to study events and trends and to learn from them, the message has emerged in a persuasive way, with the authority of genuine scholarship and the benefit of real life experience. New challenges demand objective analyses and fresh approaches.

[*English*]

The answers of a generation ago, a decade ago, must be reviewed in light of a rapidly changing world and Canada's role in it. Trade is the lifeline of Canada's prosperity. Trade with the United States, our most valued commercial partner, is the key to a secure economic future for this nation in the next century. Trade abroad means jobs at home here in Canada.

How best do we ensure this reality with the United States? In recent years independent analysis has sharpened the focus and I believe has helped to point the way for all of us. The Senate report on free trade with United States issued in 1982, under the chairmanship of Senator George Van Roggen, said that "the desired restructuring, growth and competitiveness of Canadian industry can best be achieved by the negotiation of a bilateral free trade agreement with the United States."

Some Hon. Members: Hear, hear!

Mr. Mulroney: The report pointed out that it is precisely at the strengthening of the national fabric, both political and economic, that a Canada-U.S. free trade agreement is aimed.

In August of 1985, at a meeting of the U.S. National Governors Association, seven of Canada's ten Premiers called for comprehensive free trade negotiations with the United States and two of the three absent Premiers soon thereafter conveyed their support.

The report of a special joint parliamentary committee on Canadian trade relations in 1986 urged "immediate trade discussions with the United States."

Then there was the powerful contribution to our national debate, which I think everyone would acknowledge, by the Macdonald Royal Commission on the Economic Union and Development Prospects for Canada. Over a three-year period, from 1982 to 1985, the Macdonald Commission analysed options for Canada's economic future. It heard from hundreds of Canadians, individuals and institutions, held public hearings in thirty-two cities, in all ten provinces, and sponsored three-day debates in major centres across Canada. Its research alone fills seventy-two volumes.

In 1985 the Macdonald Royal Commission concluded that free trade for Canada with the United States would be "a prudent course which will help make us richer and, by making us richer, strengthen the fabric of our country and increase our self confidence."

Some Hon. Members: Hear, hear!

Mr. Mulroney: No analysis was more thorough, no body of research more impressive, and no conclusion more compelling to my colleagues and myself than that of the Macdonald Royal Commission calling for a comprehensive free trade agreement with the United States of America.

This Government chose to act on that strong analysis and on that recommendation. This was not just the view of the Hon. Donald Macdonald, a distinguished former Minister of Finance in the Government of Canada. It was also endorsed by other commissioners such as Tommy Shoyama, a widely respected former Deputy Minister of Finance; by Laurent Picard, former President of the CBC, by Albert Breton and Clarence Barber, both prominent economists; by Jean Wadds, a former High Commissioner to London; and by Michel Robert, a distinguished Québec lawyer soon thereafter elected President of the Liberal Party of Canada.

Meanwhile, the Government had been pursuing studies and consultations on the same topic. In 1985, we issued a major discussion paper setting out the options for Canada. We appointed the late Tom Burns, a veteran trade policy expert and former President of the Canadian Exporters Association, to consult with Canadian business and labour leaders.

We established an international trade advisory committee, involving prominent Canadians from all regions of Canada. We appointed fifteen sectoral advisory groups. And we invited the Public Service to review options and explore prospects with the Americans and bring forward plans for a clear and realistic course of action.

In all of these consultations, in all of the studies and analyses there was one overwhelming and singular conclusion: Canada had to act quickly and decisively to confront the new reality of the future.

We are a nation of only twenty-five million people, heavily dependent on trade and living next door to the largest and richest market on earth. Almost 75 percent of our exports, worth $108 billion, will go to the United States.

Millions of jobs are dependent on the success of this economic relationship, which is the largest between two nations anywhere in the world. That rich market, on which so many Canadian jobs depend, was turning inward and protectionist.

. . .

Indeed, as the Macdonald Commission noted, Canada's economic growth is critically dependent on secure access to foreign markets. More, better, and more secure access to the U.S. market represents a basic requirement, while denial of that access is an ever-present threat.

Access to our most important market was indeed being threatened. About 40 percent of our exports to the United States were subject to quotas, "voluntary" restraint and other restrictions.

[*English*]

At that time, by way of illustration of the mood and atmosphere that existed in the United States, the Ottinger Bill, passed three successive years by the United States House of Representatives, sought to destroy the Auto Pact. That was the object of that exercise. The Americans demanded punitive action against Canadian steel, uranium, cement, subway cars, fish, lumber — in fact virtually all of our exports. There was a crisis a month for one Canadian exporter after another, as new trade barriers were erected against Canadian products and new legal interpretations were advanced to inhibit Canadian access to the U.S. market.

That is the challenge that we faced at that time and the negotiation of a bold new trade agreement offered the most realistic solution on behalf of the people of Canada.

I doubt that any other initiative taken by any Canadian Government has been the subject of as much thought and consultation with Canadians as the launching of the free trade negotiations.

. . .

What are the results? In a phrase, security of access and opportunity for economic growth. It is a good deal for Canada, one that serves our national interest, one that fulfils the objectives — not perfectly. Perfection is a rare commodity in our society and in our lives — but it is one that largely fulfilled the objectives that we had set for ourselves and for the government of Canada.

Most of all, it is a fair deal for both countries, for Canada and the United States. Most obviously, Canadians will pay less for American products. All tariffs on U.S. imports will be removed over the next ten years. There will be no more U.S. quotas on Canadian uranium exports. There will be no more U.S. import tax on Canadian oil exports. There will be no more U.S. customs user fees on any Canadian exports.

Most fundamentally and most importantly, the agreement will replace the politics of trade with the rule of law, a feature which is of particular value to the smaller of the two trading partners. From now on, any U.S. trade legislation affecting Canada will have to be consistent with the free trade agreement. From now on, all actions by the United States within the scope of the agreement, whether by the executive branch, the Congress or independent regulatory agencies, will be subject to notification beforehand, to consultation and, if necessary, to dispute settlement. From now on, final decisions on disputes regarding access to that vital market will be taken, not just by the Americans as they have been all too often in the past, but by Americans and Canadians acting together.

Canadian exporters will have a solid defence against harassment by their American competitors. This is good news, for example, to the fish and potato exporters of the Maritimes who have endured six vexatious but expensive investigations launched by their American competitors. Canadian industry will at last escape being sideswiped as the Americans pursue safeguard actions against other foreign exporters, but hit us on the rebound. This is good news for industrialized Ontario particularly.

Canadian exporters of lumber, shakes and shingles, and other goods will at last be able to challenge unilateral decisions imposing duties on their exports to the United States of America. Bi-national review will assure greater fairness, greater objectivity and, I believe, greater caution by U.S. regulators in the first instance. This is particularly good news for British Columbia, Ontario, Québec, New Brunswick, Nova Scotia and, indeed, for all exporting provinces.

This agreement builds on fifty years of bilateral and multilateral negotiations with the United States. The agreement takes a hodge-podge of existing agreements and ad hoc arrangements and translates them into a coherent and binding framework of rules tailored to the trade and investment realities of the twenty-first century. The agreement establishes a new blueprint for almost $200 billion a year in two-way trade. There will be new opportunities for duty free and more secure access by Canadian exporters. That is why our pork and beef industries and manufacturers in all regions are expressing solid support for the free trade agreement. Its provisions regarding services, business travel, investment, government procurement, trade remedy law and dispute settlement, establish trade rules for the future for Canada and the United States and I believe, as others have said in this House and elsewhere, offer a model to the world.

. . .

But the agreement's main achievement lies not so much in the removal of tariffs or in new rules as in its ability to change attitudes, increase confidence and inspire innovation. The combination of new and better rules and improved dispute settlement procedures will ensure that trade and investment between Canada and the United States become more secure and more predictable. The success will be measured by the confidence of investors, Canadians, Americans and others, to establish new plants in Canada and to modernize existing facilities.

. . .

If there is a link between increased trade with the United States and our quintessential Canadianness, it is that free trade enhances Canadian vitality and ensures the expression of our nationhood. The weight of history and experience, I believe, confirms that basic truth.

. . .

From time to time the Opposition contends that Canadians have not been exempted from U.S. trade laws. I have not, by the way, heard any of them advocating that Canada should give the United States an exemption from Canadian trade laws, which is the mirror image of what they purport to seek for Canada.

This Canadian Government has no intention of allowing Americans, or anyone else, to dump their products in our market, or to take advantage of subsidies to undercut Canadian companies in their own market. Until our laws are replaced by a system of new disciplines, and Canada and the United States have given each other a pledge to work together for five to seven years to create those new disciplines, our laws, the laws of Canada, remain in place to protect our industries and our workers from unfair trading practices.

Some Hon. Members: Hear, hear!

Mr. Mulroney: Some people in this House and elsewhere profess concern about the energy provisions of the agreement. Interestingly, those concerns do not come from the Canadians who produce the energy nor the Canadians who invest in energy. These concerns do not come from the Canadians who work in the oil fields, nor the provinces that own the resource.

Some Hon. Members: Hear, hear!

Mr. Mulroney: Let me deal directly with the pricing argument: under the free trade agreement, Canadians will be able to sell their energy for whatever price the market determines, at home or in the United States. In this regard, the northeastern states represent a particularly lucrative market for our electricity and natural gas exports. For example, Quebec has recently signed a twenty-one-year contract with New York to export electricity for more than double the price that Quebecers pay. This is possible because the market alternatives for our energy in New York are more expensive oil-fired generation using imported oil from offshore sources.

Similarly, Alberta natural gas stands to make promising inroads in the New England and mid-Atlantic U.S. markets. For decade after decade western Canada has only asked for the same opportunities as other provinces. Now it has an opportunity to grow and to prosper, and all members should be supporting it.

Some Hon. Members: Hear, hear!

Mr. Mulroney: The argument that we can be forced under the agreement to share our energy resources deserves but a brief comment.

What we have agreed to do in times of significant oil shortages, and what the previous Liberal Government undertook to do for all of the western industrialized countries under the International Energy Agency in 1974, is to reduce our consumption and to supply our foreign customers, including the United States, with a proportion of our supply at commercial terms. While the critics have been inventing problems on the energy issue, they have completely overlooked one huge advantage. We have achieved for the producing provinces, and for all Canadians, guaranteed access to the United States market.

Some Hon. Members: Hear, hear!

Mr. Mulroney: Billions of dollars of energy exports formerly subject to the winds and whims of U.S. protectionism will now enter that vast market free and unencumbered. Think of what this means for investment and job creation here in Canada. Think of the beneficial impact that this will have upon our regions of Canada that have been asking for fair access to that tremendous market. Think of what it means to the hopes and aspirations of young people from western Canada, British Columbia, to Newfoundland and Labrador whose resources are so vital in the development of their regions.

[*Translation*]

Small wonder that Premiers such as Robert Bourassa, Don Getty and Grant Devine so strongly support this agreement. The producing provinces have been seeking precisely such a trading instrument for decades. It gives their regions an historic opportunity for durable prosperity.

[*English*]

But guaranteed access to the huge American market also means more investment and more exploration in Canada. It enhances our security of supply and benefits consumers as well as producers. To suggest that Canadians have given up control of our energy resources is nonsense. Decisions about how we develop our resources and what we do with them — even in times of shortage — are decisions that only Canadians will make, in the national interest of Canada.

As for water, Canada's rivers and lakes are not for sale. Geography is not a commercial commodity under the GATT, the free trade agreement, or any other agreement. No specious argumentation nor any distorted interpretation from the Opposition will ever alter that plain fact. Listen to what —

An Hon. Member: Who wrote this?

Mr. Mulroney: A member asks, "Who wrote it." Listen to what Senator Van Roggen says. He wrote it. I want to thank my honourable friend for triggering my memory. Senator Van Roggen says: "Many of the attacks on the free trade agreements are mischievous, and motivated by partisan politics. The nonsense about water diversions is a good example. Water diversions," says Senator Van Roggen, "never entered into the negotiations."

[*Translation*]

In fact, Mr. Speaker, there is nothing in this agreement which obliges anyone in either country to sell anything they do not wish to sell! The Leader of the Opposition is fond of saying that this agreement puts Canada "up for sale." Ultimately, silly slogans and blind jingoism will crumble when hit with the truth, when confronted with the facts. The Agreement in essence adopts current Canadian investment policies — policies that have manifestly won broad support in Canada and around the world and which helped rescue our economy from the blight of previous regimes. Traditionally sensitive sectors such as transportation, communications, culture, and energy continue to be subject to special restrictions. Major direct takeovers will still be subject to review, i.e. about two thirds of all corporate assets in Canada.

What is often neglected, Mr. Speaker, is what Canada has gained in terms of investments namely that our investments in the United States which, per capita, are three times greater than American investments here will not suffer discrimination, and that is a tremendous advantage for Canadian investors.

. . .

[*English*]

Under the free trade agreement, Mr. Speaker, the Auto Pact, so vital to the national interest and so important to Ontario's economy, will be more secure as part of a broader accord. The President of Chrysler Canada, Moe Closs, has said, and I quote:

> The Canada/U.S. F.T.A. will save the Auto Pact . . . As we see it, the F.T.A. will permit the Canadian auto industry to continue to grow and prosper by ensuring that our access to the vast U.S. vehicle market will not be hindered by tariff barriers and the threat of trade irritants.

Clearly, the Auto Pact, which is subject to cancellation by either party on twelve months' notice, will be significantly less vulnerable to abrogation as part of this comprehensive free trade agreement than if it stood alone against the winds of protectionist action in the United States Congress.

Some Hon. Members: Hear, hear!

Mr. Mulroney: Moreover, the Auto Pact's safeguards are retained and the content rules strengthened, to the advantage of North American producers.

What about the most vital aspect of all, jobs? The overwhelming consensus among private, non-governmental research institutions and economists in Canada is that there will be a net gain in jobs for Canada.

I know that some parties and some groups in Canada do not view jobs with the same priority that the government does. It is a most important consideration in the conclusion of this kind of arrangement, and all of the independent analysis, mostly all that can be obtained, indicates that the gains in job creation will be substantial.

Mr. Axworthy: Minuscule.

Mr. Mulroney: In April of this year, the Economic Council of Canada concluded an extensive impact analysis of the free trade agreement and determined that the agreement will generate some 250 000 new jobs as the agreement takes effect. The logic is straightforward. Improved access to the U.S. market will lead to more investment, larger and more specialized enterprises, less protection, less harassment, lower consumer prices and higher wages and incomes. This logic is already at work in Canada.

. . .

We have the ability to manage change. With this agreement we now have the instrument to ensure that we can manage change in Canada's national interest. There will be greater opportunity and more certainty in the future of our exporters, our investors and our workers. The decision we make on the free trade agreement is the key step in redeeming the promise of this great country. With this agreement, with sound economic management and with stronger scientific, technological, educational and literacy programs, we can build a much better Canada. We have a clear choice.

The twenty-first century can be one of enormous accomplishment for all Canadians. We have the brain power, the resources and we have the national will. Canada is young and Canadians can still dream of a destiny unattainable by most of the world. The free trade agreement, most of all, is about our most precious asset — our youth. The young people of Canada had been uppermost in my mind as prime minister throughout this long and challenging negotiation. They shall be the principal beneficiaries of this new trading agreement. They shall become the new leaders of Canada in a new world in a new century.

James Joyce, one of the favourite Irish poets of the Leader of the Opposition and myself, once observed that "the past is consumed in the present and the present is alive only because it gives rise to the future."

The free trade agreement is about Canada's future — one Canada, united, prosperous and strong with guarantees of prosperity and economic growth for the future.

Some Hon. Members: Hear, hear!

Mr. Mulroney: We cannot compete in the world by withdrawing from it. We cannot gain freer access to the world's markets by limiting access to our own. We cannot grow and prosper by shrinking from opportunity and turning our back on reality.

[*Translation*]

We chose to negotiate not because it was easy, not because it was without political risk, but because it was in the national interest. We are proud of our distinctiveness as Canadians. We are proud of the values that mark us clearly as Canadians. We are determined to preserve and enrich those qualities which ensure a uniquely Canadian way of life. Our future will be built by Canadians doing their very best, providing world class results in a genuine national commitment to excellence.

SECTION 3

POLITICAL AND MILITARY RELATIONS

In the aftermath of the 1903 Alaska boundary decision, a Canadian public servant wrote to the prime minister that Canada would always be treated unjustly in international diplomacy so long as its interests were represented by Great Britain. Simply get rid of John Bull, and the U.S. would realize that they must play the game fairly. Where was the prestige in pushing a little guy around, especially one who was bound to fight back?

Once the British were removed from the equation, however, American strength and Canadian vulnerability became all the more readily apparent. The disparities in the relationship make it inevitable that students of Canadian-American affairs will be preoccupied by the question of influence — the undoubted influence of the U.S. on Canada and the attempts, much less likely to succeed, of Canada to bring influence to bear on the United States. Canada was not able to have its way with the U.S., commentators agree, except in certain relatively unimportant cases. But neither was it an easily-manipulated pawn of the United States.

In the first reading in this section, Dalhousie University's Danford Middlemiss outlines the smooth functioning of the relationship through agreed procedures, shared institutions, and collegial, disciplined bureaucracies. Middlemiss points out that the decision to seek the closest possible Canadian-American economic defence collaboration was Canada's too, a decision made so that the junior partner could maintain "a credible defence effort on an economically sound basis." The U.S. had different but complementary concerns, shared interests which help to account for the successful operation of joint institutions. Not everyone, however, is in agreement on the salutary, equalizing, neutralizing effect of such arrangements. More and more it is said that they restrict the freedom of movement of both partners, are open to undue influence by American members, and add yet further bureaucracy to the myriad levels and channels of the relationship. Interdependence, therefore, can breed problems of its own; the more the contact, the more potential for conflict.

Kenneth Curtis, a former U.S. ambassador to Canada, and environmental expert John Carroll clearly believe both in the inevitability of interdependence and the utility of contact. Their view of the International Joint Commission, the best-known of the joint organizations of the United States and Canada, is balanced: effective, yes, but too narrowly-conceived and specialized to have a far-reaching impact. Having a wide experience of Canada, the authors are alive to Canadian worries about transboundary environment and resource questions. They understand, however, that such sensitivity is not widespread in the United States. Issues vital for Canadians are often merely local or regional ones in the United States. Americans wonder what all the shouting is about; Canadians' image of the U.S. as an "inconsiderate, uncaring, even bullying country with no regard for the consequences of its actions on a neighbouring people" is reinforced.

Two York University academics, Canadian specialist J.L. Granatstein and United States historian Robert Cuff, present a decidedly more jaundiced interpretation of Canadian foreign policy and Canadian-American relations. American leaders, they state, sought to advance national aims by exaggerating the post-Second World War Communist menace to Congress and the people — and also to Canada. Ottawa policy makers were "actors in a charade, a charade in which the players themselves were often deceived." The deceived then did their own deceiving, whipping up anti-Communism in Canada in order to provide a cover for an activist foreign policy grounded in economic advantage.

After the publication of the Granatstein-Cuff article in 1972, the critics lined up. The determination not to retreat once again into isolationism was in substantial measure interpreted as the result of home-grown insecurities generated by the failures of the 1930s and the horrors of the Second World War. Canadian diplomats had a North Atlantic rather than simply North American perspective; Great Britain in particular remained crucial in Canadian thinking. There were few illusions about the United States, but a real fear that, if not handled carefully, Americans would again run away from the world or use their undeniable clout unwisely. It is this thesis — that Ottawa's main foreign policy goal was to influence and indeed constrain American power — which lies at the heart of Halifax political scientist Denis Stairs' study of Canada's diplomatic role in the Korean War.

Victor Levant, a Montreal professor, takes the opposite view of Canada's Vietnam experience. Advertised as impartial and objective because of a peacekeeping role on various commissions there over two decades, he says, our participation was anything but. Instead Ottawa tilted disgracefully towards America, our policy a deliberate, cynical one driven by a mixture of economic self-interest, fear of Communism, and dependence on the United States.

DEFENCE CO-OPERATION†

DANFORD W. MIDDLEMISS

> It now seems evident that in the larger weapon systems now required for air forces, Canadian work in the design, development and production of defence equipment will have to be closely integrated with the major programs of the U.S.A. The U.S.A. Government recognizes this and they are now prepared to work out production sharing arrangements with us. To accomplish effective integration of defence production resources of Canada and the U.S.A. will require time and continuing efforts in co-operation.
>
> — John Diefenbaker

Prime Minister John Diefenbaker's statement of 23 September 1958,[1] which presaged his government's formal cancellation of A.V. Roe's CF–105 Arrow fighter aircraft program on 20 February 1959, signalled the abandonment of Canada's experiment in defence production self-sufficiency. In effect, the Canadian government was acknowledging that the research, development, and production of complete weapons systems tailored to the quantitatively limited, yet qualitatively demanding, requirements of the Canadian armed forces was, for the most part, simply too expensive for the country to bear on its own. At the same time, however, Ottawa was confronted with a fundamental,

† Danford W. Middlemiss, "Economic Defence Co-operation with the United States 1940–63," in *An Acceptance of Paradox: Essays in Honour of John W. Holmes,* ed. Kim Richard Nossal (Toronto: Canadian Institute of International Affairs, 1982), 86–109.

yet in many respects familiar, policy dilemma; how to reconcile Canada's expanding defence commitments with its decreasing capacity to procure the military hardware necessary to fulfil these obligations in an economically viable manner.

That the Diefenbaker government sought to resolve this policy dilemma through the medium of defence production sharing arrangements with the United States is by now an established fact.[2] What is less well-known is that these arrangements — whose essential core, under the rubric of the Defence Production and Development Sharing Agreements, remains intact more than twenty years later — exemplify a pattern of co-operative, bilateral policy-making which students of Canadian-American affairs have tended to overlook or downplay in the past.

Tempting as it is to explore the reasons underlying the persistent neglect of such an important aspect of the continental relationship, I will focus instead on the perceptions, motivations, and behaviour of the key persons responsible for the formulation and implementation of the policies, regulations, and procedures which together constitute the essence of the Canada-United States economic defence relationship. In so doing, I will attempt to penetrate the often obscuring veil of traditional "black box" explanations to identify and analyse the conditions and factors which gave rise to and sustained this continental relationship, one which is remarkable from the standpoint of its longevity and the high degree of co-operation it has engendered over the years.

The Setting: Prelude to Production Sharing

Beginning in World War II, geographic proximity and perceptions of a common external military threat fostered a mutual awareness in Canada and the United States of the need for closer governmental collaboration on matters relating to North American defence. This growing sense of shared interests was soon translated into a policy of joint continental defence co-operation in the Ogdensburg Declaration (18 August 1940). At the same time, pressures arose to extend the policy beyond the purely military sphere and into the realm of defence economics.

As the war intensified in Europe, Britain found it increasingly difficult to supply Canada with badly needed weapons or to pay for war materials obtained in Canada. Caught unprepared by the war with only rudimentary defence production facilities, and cut off from its traditional source of military equipment, the Canadian government turned to the United States for the weapons, components, and tooling necessary to satisfy its own, as well as Britain's, defence requirements. The war also disrupted the triangular pattern of trade which had enabled Canada to pay for its imports of United States supplies with foreign exchange gained from British purchases of Canadian products. Reluctant to accept the short- and long-term economic sacrifices entailed in the Anglo-American lend-lease approach to wartime problems,[3] and sensitive to the political advantages of an independent Canadian contribution to the allied war effort,[4] the prime minister of the day, Mackenzie King, approached the United States government with a novel solution to Canada's exchange problem.

Taking the initiative personally, King obtained President Roosevelt's agreement — enshrined in the seminal Hyde Park Declaration (20 April 1940) — to "a sort of barter" in war materials between Canada and the United States.[5] By providing an official rationale both for United States procurement in Canada to offset the foreign exchange impact of Canadian defence purchases in the United States and for the removal of administrative and legislative barriers — most notably the protectionist provisions of the 1933 "Buy American" Act — which hampered the access of Canadian firms to the United States defence procurement system, this declaration and the various arrangements later devised to implement it enabled the Canadian government to build the nucleus of a thriving defence industry on a sound financial foundation.

Whether or not the climate of co-operation engendered by the Hyde Park Declaration would be carried over into the postwar period remained unsettled, although the initial indications were favourable. Mackenzie King's grandiose conception of Hyde Park "laying the enduring foundations of a new world order"[6] received support in principle from a Canada-United States agreement (30 November 1942) "that post-war settlements must be such as to promote mutually advantageous economic relations between them and the betterment of world-wide economic relations."[7] Moreover, as the war in Europe drew to a close, the Canadian government, fully aware that the processes of decontrol and demobilization would require careful co-ordination if Canadian firms dependent on supplies from the United States were not to suffer, agreed to a proposal from the United States in May 1945 to continue the Hyde Park "spirit of co-operation" in reconverting North American industry to a peacetime footing.[8]

With the war's end, these agreements became largely stillborn symbols of both governments' belief in the efficacy of a co-ordinated approach to economic defence matters. Lacking both the status of a formal agreement and the machinery for its own implementation, the Hyde Park Declaration had depended for its successful operation on the co-operation and administrative ingenuity of bureaucrats on both sides of the border.[9] Once hostilities ended, however, the political will to co-operate evaporated as the former sense of urgency gave way to a general feeling of war-weariness and, more importantly, as the joint agencies were dismantled and the key personnel responsible for implementing the wartime transborder economic defence arrangements dispersed.

The emergence of Cold War strategic perceptions shortly thereafter, however, focussed attention on the need for Canada-United States collaboration in postwar defence planning to counter the Soviet bomber threat to North America via the exposed polar route. President Truman's 1946 "oral message" to Prime Minister King, in acknowledging that "the two Governments should negotiate some equitable means of sharing the financial burden of any defences agreed to be necessary around the northern perimeter of the continent,"[10] contained the germinal elements of future cost sharing arrangements for the construction of joint defence projects on Canadian soil. Agreement on the principles of continental defence collaboration in 1947[11] brought with it a concomitant requirement for consultation and co-operation to deal with certain economic defence issues, chief among which were rearmament, military equipment standardization, and industrial preparedness.

Several factors reinforced this military impetus toward bilateral economic defence interdependence. For Canada, few realistic options to bilateralism existed. War-ravaged Europe lacked both the political will and the economic resources necessary for effective collaboration with Canada, and, in any case, the wartime experience had left Canadian military planners determined to avoid the production and supply problems associated with an overseas economic defence partnership. Moreover, the painfully slow progress toward equipment standardization had demonstrated that a multilateral approach offered no panacea for Canada's immediate postwar economic defence problems.[12] Finally, by 1947 Canada was again confronted with a serious balance-of-payments problem with the United States, one that would be exacerbated by the rearmament programs which the Pentagon was advocating both to rectify the vulnerability of the Canadian north and to bolster European defences against the growing Soviet threat.[13]

To balance its own economic concerns against United States military interests, the Canadian government mounted a broad-based and energetic "educational" campaign to persuade the United States government and business communities of the merits of extending the Hyde Park principle of reciprocal defence procurement into the postwar era. The appeal to pragmatism, simplicity, and, above all, mutual self-interest which characterized this campaign were well illustrated in an address which Prime Minister Louis St. Laurent made some time later to the Rensselaer Polytechnic Institute in Troy, New York, on 14 October 1949. He said, in part

... the only way in which we in Canada can hope to carry out plans for standardization is to reach an understanding with the authorities of your country on procurement.

We cannot undertake to manufacture all the many and complicated and costly items of arms and equipment for modern military forces: many of these things we must obtain from your manufacturers. But, in order to pay for them, we must be in a position to provide you with certain other items for your forces which we can produce efficiently in Canada. That is how we co-operated, under the Hyde Park arrangement, during the war. And both countries benefited.

It seems to us only common sense to apply the same policy in peacetime; but that is not possible under your present ["buy American"] legislation. Such a policy would, however, not mean any loss of business for your manufacturers or of employment for your labour. All it would mean is that you would sell arms and equipment for our forces and we would reciprocate by supplying some of the needs of your forces.

. . . Without some arrangement for reciprocal defence purchasings with the United States, Canada cannot make the most effective contribution to the security of this continent and the North Atlantic area. And our aim in Canada is the greatest possible co-operation for our common security consistent with the maintenance of our independence as a nation.[14]

Some important steps toward closer bilateral economic defence collaboration had already been taken. On 12 April 1949 the Joint Industrial Mobilization Committee was created to arrange for exchange of information on industrial planning and to make recommendations to the two governments concerning co-operation in these matters between the two countries.[15] An even more important development was the 12 October 1949 decision of the Canada-United States Permanent Joint Board on Defence (PJBD) "to initiate a new program for reciprocal military procurement, based upon objectives similar to those of the Hyde Park Declaration."[16] These objectives — the dispersal of North American industrial capacity to minimize the effects of a Soviet surprise attack; the establishment of specialized sources of supply in Canada to supplement United States sources; the implementation of the shared goal of standardization by providing foreign exchange (through United States purchases of Canadian defence products) to allow Canada to procure American-type military equipment; and the maintenance of a balance of trade in arms between the two countries — coincided exactly with the arguments that Canadian PJBD members, most notably General A.G.L. McNaughton, had been impressing upon their United States counterparts for some time.[17]

The final, tangible expression of the success of McNaughton's efforts came with the May 1950 announcement of a reciprocal defence procurement agreement whereby each nation would purchase from the other fifteen to twenty-five million dollars of military equipment over the year commencing 1 July 1950.[18] Although this agreement was heralded as "a major step in the integration of military production in the two countries," in fact it was a very limited measure requiring no changes in the restrictive "buy American" legislation and promising no significant change from the average annual level of United States military expenditure in Canada throughout the 1946–1950 period.[19] In any case, this tentative step in the direction of closer continental economic defence ties was soon overtaken by events.

The outbreak of hostilities in Korea in June 1950 transformed Western perceptions of the scope, immediacy, and intensity of the Soviet threat to Western Europe and North America and generated a mutual appreciation among Canadian and American policy-makers of the need to accelerate and consolidate the hitherto slow and piecemeal process of continental economic defence collaboration. Thus, in acting as the catalyst for large-scale rearmament programs in both countries, the Korean War greatly accentuated the bilateral significance of economic defence issues for the two governments.

To provide a policy framework for gearing the economies of both countries to a maximum state of preparedness, the two governments agreed to a "Statement of Principles for Economic Co-operation" in an exchange of notes on 26 October 1950. The notes reaffirmed the general concepts of the Hyde Park Declaration and proposed that the two governments "co-operate in all respects practicable, and to the extent of their respective executive powers, to the end that the economic efforts of the two countries be co-ordinated for the common defence and that the production and resources of both countries be used for the best combined results."[20]

The 1950 agreement paved the way for a transformation of the nascent pre-Korean War linkages between the supply, production, and procurement agencies in each government into effective mechanisms of joint economic defence collaboration. Drawing on the hard-won lessons of World War II, C.D. Howe, as minister of the new Department of Defence Production (DDP) created in 1951, quickly gathered a group of knowledgeable, capable, and highly motivated businessmen into his department to direct Canada's postwar rearmament program. They, along with Howe himself, could readily grasp and deal with the myriad technical and administrative aspects of defence production and procurement. Moreover, they shared with their counterparts south of the border a common sense of mission and a pragmatic approach to continental industrial mobilization.

Relations between lower-level bureaucratic officials in both governments exhibited such a high degree of informality, easy access, and close personal rapport that most bilateral economic defence problems were resolved through special, often improvised, administrative arrangements rather than by formal legal agreements worked out at the more senior diplomatic and political levels of government. When substantive policy differences did arise, however, Howe preferred to deal with his United States counterparts in his own characteristic "horse-trading" fashion. Howe excelled at employing this person-to-person bargaining technique and firmly believed in the efficacy of a direct, business-like approach to resolving intergovernmental issues, one which he called "quiet economic diplomacy."[21]

This approach to bilateral affairs proved to be remarkably successful, especially for Canada. Not only did United States procurement agencies become more aware of Canadian industry's capacity to supplement indigenous sources of supply, once restrictions on the flow of defence goods between the two countries had been removed, but Canada's Department of National Defence (DND) was also increasingly able to rely on Canadian suppliers to meet its equipment requirements. Moreover, United States military spending in Canada rose steadily, so that by the end of the Korean War defence trade between the two countries was approximately balanced.[22]

Confronted with recessionary tendencies in their economies because of reductions in post-Korea defence spending, however, both the Canadian and United States governments returned to their former protectionist military procurement practices. Thus, despite a high-level October 1953 agreement reaffirming the 1950 Statement of Principles and assuring Canada of preferred treatment from the United States on defence production and trade issues,[23] the steady downward trend in reciprocal military procurement following Korea indicated that the political will necessary to sustain the process of close continental defence collaboration was receding as both governments turned inward to deal with their own pressing peacetime economic and political problems.[24]

Nevertheless, following the Soviet detonation of a hydrogen bomb in 1953, renewed emphasis on the subject of North American anti-bomber defences prevented the spirit of Hyde Park from dissipating altogether. For example, Canadian officials were able to gain some economic concessions for Canadian manufacturers in return for allowing the United States to construct an early warning radar line across the Canadian Arctic. The formal 1955 agreement for the "Establishment of a Distant Early Warning System" (the DEW line) reaffirmed the 1951 Pine Tree line principle "that electronic equipment at installations on Canadian territory should, *as far as practicable*, be manufactured in Canada," stipulated that Canadian defence contractors were to be granted "equal consideration" with their American counterparts in bidding on DEW line contracts, and indicated that this consideration would be based on clearly defined economic criteria — that is, product availability, cost, and performance.[25]

While its reference to the "equal consideration" principle set an important precedent for later defence production sharing arrangements, the DEW line agreement also revealed the practical limitations of Canada-United States economic defence collaboration after the Korean War. First, the agreement was very restricted in its intended scope. It applied only to this single case of a United States defence project being constructed on Canadian soil and made no provision for extending the principle of Canadian industrial participation to other joint defence projects wherever located. In addition, it dealt only with a narrow range of defence products (electronics equipment) and emphasized preference to "qualified Canadian labour" rather than to Canadian electronics manufacturers. In short, the agreement was oriented to construction, not to technology.

Secondly, the agreement was ad hoc in nature. The crucial issue of the "practicability" of Canadian bids had to be negotiated separately on a case-by-case basis. Furthermore, the United States contracting agency was provided with a discretionary loophole for disallowing Canadian bids because the agreement stipulated that the economic criteria noted above need only be included in the "factors to be taken into account" regarding Canadian participation. Finally, the agreement produced very limited benefits for Canada. Canadian defence contractors found themselves at a distinct disadvantage when competing directly with their established counterparts in the United States and the "practicability" clauses effectively precluded significant Canadian participation in the DEW line project. As the DDP's annual report for 1955 soberly recorded: "Owing to very strict delivery deadlines and the experiences of American industry in this field, only a limited number of contractors were placed in Canada for the manufacture of electronic equipment for the DEW line."[26]

The DEW line example illustrates the nature of the dilemma facing the Canadian defence industry after the Korean War: the industry had developed in a substantial capacity to produce military equipment; yet the largest prospective market for this equipment, the United States, was for the most part inaccessible — despite formal agreements providing for reciprocal arrangements to facilitate transborder defence procurement.[27] Confronted with the urgent need to preserve what was perceived to be a valuable production capacity, the DDP's response was as simple as it was obvious: if Canadian industry could not compete effectively in the lucrative United States defence market, new markets would have to be found elsewhere. The most logical and convenient place to begin was at home.

Put simply, as an outgrowth of its Korean-inspired "industrial preparedness" program,[28] the DDP embarked after 1953 on a policy of developing a Canadian industrial base capable of producing a limited variety of specialized defence products for the Canadian armed forces. The novel element in this policy was the decision to rely primarily on Canadian suppliers to fill the major equipment needs of the Canadian military. To implement this policy, the DDP instituted extensive programs of government assistance to certain manufacturing sectors (aircraft, electronics, and shipbuilding) that were to constitute the backbone of what C.D. Howe hoped would be a specialized and highly sophisticated Canadian defence industry.[29]

Situated on the leading edge of developments in modern weapons technology, the Canadian aircraft industry became the chief beneficiary of the new policy.[30] By virtue of its enormous and increasing capital investment in this sector, however, Ottawa became, to a large extent, the captive of its previous policies. Having nurtured the aircraft industry through its birth and infancy, the government felt compelled to take an active role in guiding the industry through adolescence into adulthood. Indeed, the government's involvement in the aircraft industry in the 1950s reflected the changing emphasis of federal policies toward the defence industry as a whole, with the original military rationale for this support being supplanted by economic and political considerations.[31] This involvement played a key role in propelling the Canadian government into the production sharing arrangements with the United States.

The Process of Co-operation: Production Sharing, 1958–63

At the same time as the Arrow project was encountering increasing severe economic and political difficulties, DDP officials were actively seeking United States acceptance of the principle of Canadian industrial participation in several other air defence projects then under consideration by both governments. In the latter half of 1958, joint discussions were underway regarding cost/development/production sharing with respect to the Bomarc anti-aircraft guided missile, the Semi-Automatic Ground Environment (SAGE) control system, northern radar improvements, and ballistic missile early warning systems.

During a visit to Ottawa by President Dwight Eisenhower (8–11 July 1958), Prime Minister Diefenbaker raised the question of the integration of the defence production capacities of the two countries.[32] At separate meetings, several DDP officials, most notably David Mundy, then director of the department's Electronics Branch, discussed with John Foster Dulles, Eisenhower's secretary of state, the possibility of infusing greater Canadian content into the major United States air defence production programs. Mundy sought to convince Dulles that it was in American interests to have some form of joint production sharing with Canada, especially if Canada was to make a significant contribution to the North American Air Defence (NORAD) Command which had been established the year before. Dulles received these arguments with only polite attention, and the real value of these discussions lay elsewhere. Above all, they exposed officials of the United States Department of Defence (DOD) who were present at the talks to the Canadian production sharing proposals, and, in so doing, they established a useful point of reference for bilateral departmental discussions in the latter part of 1958.[33]

One outgrowth of the Eisenhower-Diefenbaker meeting was the creation of a Canada-United States Ministerial Committee on Joint Defence. The formal agreement establishing the committee noted that the NORAD arrangements "increased the importance of regular consultation" "between the two governments, required supplementary channels of communication, and advocated periodic ministerial review of matters which "would include not only military questions but also the political and economic aspects of joint defence problems."[34] Soon afterwards, this committee set up a Senior Policy Committee on Joint Canada-United States Production Sharing, a body which was to play an important role in the production sharing negotiations which immediately followed.[35]

In August 1958, Defense Secretary Neil McElroy and Defence Minister George Pearkes headed delegations which met to discuss Canadian participation in a continental air defence improvement plan. This proposal was approved by the United States administration and by the Canadian Chiefs of Staff Committee and was forwarded to the Diefenbaker cabinet for consideration in September 1958.[36] On 23 September, Diefenbaker announced his government's decision: production of the CF–105 interceptor was postponed pending a review six months later; the Astra flight and fire control system and the Sparrow air-to-air missile system was cancelled; and the Bomarc-SAGE radar package was approved for introduction into Canada. Diefenbaker also noted that discussions were to be held regarding Canadian industrial sharing in these air defence programs.[37]

The Senior Policy Committee met twice in the fall of 1958 (9 October and 18 November) and by the second meeting had approved the following two objectives of Canada-United States production sharing:

> The immediate objective is to increase the participation of Canadian industry in the production and support of North American defence weapons and equipments. The continuing long-term objective is to co-ordinate the defence requirements, development, production and procurement of the two countries in order to achieve the best use of their respective production

resources for their common defence, in line with the concept of interdependence and the integration of military arrangements.[38]

Several factors accounted for the rapid agreement on the principle and main objectives of production sharing. First, the earlier bilateral talks had prepared the basic foundations for joint acceptance of the sharing concept. Secondly, no outside government agencies or pressure groups were brought directly into these discussions; indeed, Canadian industry was presented with a fait accompli by the DDP. Thirdly, DDP officials were able to make persuasive arguments on behalf of the production sharing concept, arguments which for the most part were well received by United States defence officials anxious to preserve Canadian "goodwill" with respect to the completion of North American air defences.[39]

Once the basic policy framework was established, detailed discussions began on the specific means to implement these goals.[40] A number of ad hoc working groups were created to work out the "nuts and bolts" of production sharing. These technical groups sought to review United States defence equipment requirements to identify promising items for Canadian industry to bid on, and to devise procedures and arrangements to facilitate Canadian participation in specific projects of mutual interest. A steering group was established to coordinate all activities related to production sharing.

Some success resulted from these early efforts. A cost-sharing program — one-third Canadian, two-thirds American — was agreed upon for four specifically designated joint air defence projects (the Bomarc missile, the SAGE control system, and the heavy and gap-filler radars for the Pine Tree line), and on 30 December 1958 President Eisenhower approved the basic cost and production sharing policies as set out in NSC 5822 (dated 12 December 1958).[41]

While a promising start had been made, this initial limited approach to production sharing soon proved to be unsatisfactory from the Canadian standpoint. One reason for this related to the government's decision to cancel the CF–105 Arrow program. Having burgeoned rapidly from a relatively modest venture in advanced jet fighter development into the most expensive defence procurement program underwritten by Ottawa to that time, the Arrow program had run counter to the Diefenbaker administration's commitment to fiscal restraint and was ingloriously terminated in February 1959 amidst highly emotional recrimination on all sides.[42]

The demise of Canada's showcase of defence production self-sufficiency increased the pressures on the new government to make good its promises that production sharing would provide Canadian industry with "greater opportunities" than before to gain "a reasonable and fair share" of work in defence programs of interest to both countries.[43] Unfortunately, sharing on the four substitute projects amounted to too little, too late for Canadian defence suppliers. For example, Canadian content on the Bomarc project came to only $5.7 million because most of the contracts had already been let to United States firms by the time the production sharing program had been instituted.[44] This same pattern was repeated for the other joint projects.

In response to the DDP's dissatisfaction with the results of these early measures, the Senior Policy Committee agreed in mid-1959 that "an intensified effort" was required to familiarize United States defence procurement officers and contractors with the objectives and procedures of production sharing.[45] The DDP launched a major educational effort in the United States in an attempt to "massage" the United States procurement system intensively at all levels. It increased the size of its staff at its main office in Washington and stationed officers at key DOD procurement centres and with major United States defence contractors. In effect operating as military trade commissioners, these DDP officials supplied United States agencies with detailed, continuously updated reports of Canadian defence production facilities and commodities and encouraged direct contacts between defence buyers and sellers on both sides of the border. In addition, the DDP's minister remained in constant communication with the defence secretary, DDP deputy ministers held continuous discussions with the assistant secretaries of the United States military departments in order to devise and implement procedures to facilitate greater Canadian industrial participation in United States defence projects, and lower level DDP production branch officials took part in frequent technical work group meetings to resolve specific administrative problems relating to production sharing.[46]

The combination of Canadian persistence and United States cooperation resulted in several remedial steps to overcome many of the early difficulties encountered in the operation of the bilateral sharing program during 1959 and 1960. The United States military departments revised their Armed Services Procurement Regulations to exempt an expanded list of designated Canadian products from the provisions of the "Buy American" Act and the application of United States customs duties. Informal procedures were developed to allow DDP officials to assist in the administration of United States defence contracts let in Canada and to permit Canadian quality control inspection under these contracts. Some headway was also made toward the relaxation of United States security regulations with respect to production sharing projects.

Despite these encouraging signs, Canadian officials were still far from satisfied. Exemptions to the "Buy American" Act continued to be granted on a case-by-case basis and, as the DDP's minister, Raymond O'Hurley, warned in 1959: "There is no document which my department can issue to a potential Canadian bidder guaranteeing that the statute will not be applied."[47] To overcome this problem, the DDP wanted to place the entire Canadian-American economic defence relationship on a more permanent and stable foundation. In general terms, this would involve the incorporation of the principle of freer access for Canadian firms wishing to participate in United States defence projects into the Department of Defense procurement regulations. Specifically, this meant having the informal measures already negotiated with the United States armed services — exemptions from customs duties, tariffs, and the "Buy American" Act — clearly spelled out in these regulations. DDP officials believed that, in practice, United States defence procurement officials, lacking high-level policy direction regarding production sharing, sometimes ignored, misunderstood, or applied these existing arrangements in a discriminatory and arbitrary manner. The DDP was confident that a formal "blanket exemption" for Canadian manufacturers would help to eliminate many of these problems by giving the production sharing principle a more authoritative status within the complex United States defence procurement system.

Moreover, the DDP regarded the waiver of the "Buy American" Act restrictions as only a minimum concession by the United States government. Its attitude was that, with or without these exemptions, United States suppliers would continue to receive a sizeable share of Canadian defence contracts because of competitive advantages favouring United States firms.[48] Thus, regardless of any formal concessions granted by the Department of Defense, the previous imbalance in defence trade would likely continue to Canada's disadvantage.

Therefore, in addition to the formalization of the production sharing principle in the United States procurement regulations, the DDP wanted the DOD to agree to make a "special effort" to buy Canadian defence products to help rectify this historical imbalance. Furthermore, anxious to promote sales of advanced technology Canadian products, the DDP sought to exclude raw material sales, "bricks and mortar" construction contracts, and "metal-bashing" products with limited engineering content from the ambit of production sharing.[49] In return, while the DDP believed no reciprocal concessions were required from Canada in view of existing United States defence trade advantages, it was tacitly understood that Canada would continue to purchase its major weapons systems from United States sources where this was "sensible" or "necessary."[50]

Between 1960 and 1962 the efforts of Canadian civil servants to improve the production sharing arrangements were crowned with considerable success. Agreements were reached regarding product qualification and industrial security procedures,[51] and Canadian defence firms were exempted from a 1960 United States executive directive designed to reduce the growing American balance-of-payments deficit.[52] However, by far the most important development for Canada was the firm statement of the United States commitment to production sharing issued by the secretary of defence, Thomas Gates, on 28 July 1960.

Citing several precedents of economic defence co-operation with Canada, the "unsettled world situation," and a geographically derived "mutual interest" in North American defence, a departmental directive, "Defence Economic Cooperation with Canada," stipulated a "policy of maximum production and development program integration in support of closely integrated military planning between the United States and Canada" and decreed that "United States defense economic cooperation with Canada must not only continue, but be expanded." Additionally, the Department of Defense would seek "the best possible co-ordination of the material programs" of the two countries, "including actual integration insofar as practicable" of their industrial mobilization efforts, and would assure Canada of "a fair opportunity to share" in research, development, and production programs "of mutual interest" to both countries. To achieve these objectives, Gates specified which existing United States regulations and procedures were to apply to Canadian defence contractors and directed the military departments to comply with the policies and objectives of production sharing outlined in the directive and to collaborate in developing additional regulations to facilitate the implementation of the program.[53]

Despite the progress made, the program was not immune to continuing stresses and strains. Problems arose in part from dissatisfaction with the operation of the program itself and in part from the general deterioration of Canadian-American political relations in the early 1960s. Pentagon officials criticized Canadian contractors for their frequent inattentiveness to United States defence procurement procedures and practices[54] while Canadian manufacturers, suspecting a lingering tendency among United States procurement officers to favour domestic over Canadian sources of supply, pressed for guaranteed percentage shares of United States defence contracts.[55]

An apparent diminution of Canadian support for United States foreign and defence policies in the early 1960s generated political reverberations which threatened to engulf the production sharing program. Two issues were of particular significance in this respect: Diefenbaker's hesitant endorsement of President Kennedy's handling of the 1962 Cuban missile crisis, and Canada's delay in acquiring nuclear warheads for several weapons systems.[56]

Canada's belated and somewhat ambiguous support for its chief ally during the missile crisis raised the question of the degree of Canadian support for NORAD to which the production sharing program had been intimately linked by the DDP since 1958. As one reporter noted, the Canadian Government's refusal to allow the full dispersal of North American Air Defence Command forces during the Cuban crisis has led to grave difficulties with some elements of the U.S. government which are at just sub-crisis levels ... There are genuine fears for the future of the North American defence partnership, the defence production arrangements ... and for American support for a wide variety of Canadian interests.[57]

While some of these assertions were exaggerated, the goodwill on which production sharing was founded was undoubtedly shaken by the Canadian government's performance during the 1962 crisis.[58]

However, the more serious United States concern about Canadian policy both predated and succeeded the missile crisis. The issue of Ottawa's acceptance of nuclear warheads for its armed forces was highlighted by both the missile crisis itself and the passing of the 1 November 1962 deadline for Canada's agreement to equip its CF–104G squadrons in the North Atlantic Treaty Organization with nuclear weapons. The adverse implications for production sharing of the Canadian government's reluctance to enunciate a clear policy statement on the nuclear issue were nowhere stated more clearly than by David Golden, a former chief architect of the defence sharing concept. Golden warned:

It will be a disaster if defence production sharing is ended. We cannot go on expecting Washington to take politically difficult decisions like allowing us an equal break in their defence market and yet refuse to take the politically difficult decisions that face us. If we won't take nuclear arms we must be prepared to face the consequences. This year [1962] we will have sold $200 million worth of items and equipment to the U.S. under the deal. It is this business that forms the solid base on which our most advanced technology has grown. With this under our belts we have been able to go on to win substantial export orders in other parts of the world. But if we lose the U.S. market we are finished. The Canadian demand cannot support an advanced industry by itself.[59]

By 1963, therefore, growing Canadian and United States dissatisfaction with the operation of the production sharing program and a general deterioration of bilateral relations which showed signs of spilling over into the economic defence area prompted DDP officials once again to approach their Department of Defense for modifications to the program. Their motivation was twofold: first, to insulate the program from the changing climate of intergovernmental relations which, in the DDP's view, made it increasingly difficult to reconcile the divergent economic and military rationales underlying the sharing arrangements; and secondly, to dampen domestic criticisms of the program.

The specific catalyst for Canadian action was provided by the announcement by the defence secretary, Robert McNamara, on 7 July 1962 of a multi-billion dollar "cost reduction program" to help alleviate worsening United States balance-of-payments problems through reductions and greater efficiency in defence spending.[60] Because the majority of United States defence purchases in Canada were made on a "sole source" basis (that is, let without competitive tenders), and because Canada enjoyed a surplus of trade under the production sharing program, there were fears that Canadian participation in production sharing might be adversely affected by the DOD's new regulations.[61] Indeed, during 1963, United States defence procurement in Canada showed a marked decline, the first such reduction since 1959.[62]

However, while Canadian officials monitored the United States cost reduction program very closely, it was only after a new Liberal government headed by Lester Pearson had been elected in April 1963 that the DDP decided to approach the DOD about exemptions from the balance-of-payments measures. Because the new administration had come to power pledged to honour existing Canadian defence commitments, DDP officials believed that Canadian production sharing grievances would now be accorded a more favourable reception in the Pentagon.[63]

Having previously acknowledged that the production sharing program was "in difficulty" as a result of a possible "misunderstanding" between the two governments concerning the application of the American currency arrangements,[64] on 6 June 1963 the newly appointed DDP minister, C.M. Drury, led a Canadian delegation to meet with Mr. McNamara in Washington. The Canadians wanted clarification of two important issues: Canada's status with respect to the 1962 United States defence gold-flow directives; and the DOD's understanding of the relative production sharing trade balance between the two countries.

On the first issue, McNamara was quick to reassure Drury that the production sharing program would "not be limited by the so-called balance of payments directives . . . and that full consideration [would] be given to all qualified Canadian sources." Drury reported that:

> Our meeting was held in a spirit of great cordiality and [it] reaffirmed positively the intention of both our countries to continue to support a defence production sharing program. Assurances

were given that the difficulties experienced by both countries in respect of balance of payments problems should not be allowed to interfere with the continuation and enlargement of this program.

Drury also alluded to a new factor that had arisen out of this meeting:

> It was recognized that both countries have balance of payments problems. However, it was agreed that such problems must not interfere with our joint production sharing objectives. *The maintenance of a general balance in our cross-border procurement of equipment* seems the best answer to concern at the drain on foreign exchange reserves through such procurement [emphasis added].[65]

The addition of this "general balance" rider to original defence sharing principles resulted from a compromise on the second issue discussed at this meeting — the state of the cumulative balance of military trade under the sharing program.

Before 1963, neither government had officially advocated some form of equilibrium in production sharing trade.[66] McNamara, however, raised this issue at the June meeting on the grounds that the military trade balance was substantially in Canada's favour. The Canadians, on the other hand, maintained that McNamara had overestimated the extent of Canada's surplus because of confusion about what items should be included in the statistics. DDP officials were surprised to learn, for example, that the Pentagon included Canadian sales of uranium to the United States Atomic Energy Commission as well as DEW line construction contracts placed in Canada in its production sharing figures — items which the DDP had never considered to be defence purchases under the terms of the program.[67] As always, the Canadians believed that only high technology products should be counted in the figures. To eliminate future misunderstandings, DDP officials argued for a stricter definition of those items which should qualify for inclusion in the crossborder defence trade statistics. The Canadians also contended that for comparison purposes, the sharing figures should be kept separate from those relating to the overall bilateral trade balance.[68] In the end, McNamara acceded to the DDP's criteria in return for Canadian acceptance of the condition that a "general balance" would be maintained in reciprocal procurement under the defence production sharing program. In addition, McNamara — partly with a view to avoiding closer congressional scrutiny of the program via the involvement of the General Accounting Office — agreed to allow Canada to keep the statistical records for the program.[69]

It also became apparent that during the June meeting the two delegations had reaffirmed an earlier informal "understanding" regarding the rationalization of production sharing effort. Drury noted that:

> For the future, as in the past, Canada expects to procure from United States defence industry those items which it does not make economic sense to try to produce in Canada. In return we look to continuing opportunities for Canadian industry to supply United States defence requirements where Canadian companies can compete on the basis of price, quality and delivery.[70]

Later, in outlining his government's plans to purchase the American-made Hercules rather than a more costly Canadian military cargo aircraft (the Canadair CL–44), Drury explained the reasoning behind Ottawa's acceptance of this understanding: "If the position of the Canadian government should be that we are going to produce all our own military equipment, even on an uneconomic basis, then the willingness of the United States to have us share in the production of their military equipment . . . I think would be seriously prejudiced."[71]

Thus, it was evident that the Canadian government recognized that production sharing was a two-way proposition and believed that a tacit division of labour between Canadian and United States industry was indeed both "sensible" and "necessary" from the political standpoint of maintaining amiable relations between the two governments. This was especially true because, despite the purported supremacy of strictly economic criteria in the operation of the program, Canadian industrial participation was largely predicated upon political factors, not the least of which was the continued goodwill of the United States Defense Department.[72]

The reaffirmation of the commitment of both governments to the principle of production sharing, as modified by the June 1963 understandings, paved the way for a major expansion of the original 1958 concept. Despite the broadened base of access provided by the production sharing arrangements, Canadian manufacturers were encountering serious problems in participating in the early stages of United States military procurement programs. For example, Canadian defence contractors and DDP officials complained that protectionist NIH ("Not Invented Here") attitudes prevented Canadian manufacturers from acquiring a fair share of the all-important research and development contracts of the Department of Defense.[73] Beginning in 1959, therefore, DDP officials had sought DOD approval of the concept of research and development sharing as an essential complementary element of the production sharing program.

Progress in this direction had been facilitated by several bilateral interservice agreements and informal understanding.[74] While these arrangements provided opportunities for Canadian firms not only to compete for research and development contracts but also to acquire United States financing for certain development projects, a number of shortcomings remained. For example, Canadian products developed under these contracts were not automatically excluded from the provisions of the "Buy American" Act or the United States small business and labour surplus area "set asides." Nor were there uniform agreements regarding Canadian access to military specifications and other classified technical data. Furthermore, the United States practice of conducting military research and development under a service "design authority" to meet specific Department of Defense requirements had the unfortunate effect of placing in United States hands the initiative for selecting projects for Canadian participation; beleaguered United States project officers, however, seldom had adequate time to solicit Canadian proposals.[75] Finally, because the Canadian share of the funding for joint development projects frequently approached 100 percent, the United States service representatives who monitored the projects had little or no incentive to curtail costs and often demanded such high standards that "prices rose to unacceptable levels."[76]

DDP and DOD officials sought to resolve these difficulties in discussions held in the summer of 1963, and in November a "Memorandum of Understanding in the Field of Cooperative Development Between the United States Department of Defense and the Canadian Department of Defence Production" was signed by McNamara and Drury.[77]

The agreement outlining the terms and procedures for administering the "Defence Development Sharing Program" was very satisfactory from the DDP's standpoint. First, it set out a common policy for the three United States service departments to follow. Secondly, it was intended to remain in force "indefinitely." Thirdly, in requiring a minimum 25-percent funding contribution by the DOD, it would help to reduce Canadian research and development costs by giving the service departments a vested interest in the success of joint development projects. Fourthly, by stipulating that projects would be chosen "by mutual agreement," it removed the onus from United States officers for selecting appropriate projects for Canadian industry participation. Fifthly, it exempted Canadian-developed products from restrictive United States procurement regulations. Sixthly, it established procedures similar to those applicable to the original production sharing program regarding security matters and the disclosure and transmission of classified information. Finally, it reaffirmed the earlier division-of-labour principle by stipulating that the DOD would not duplicate Canadian research and development efforts unless it was clearly in the United States national interest to do so.

By the end of 1963, DDP and DOD officials had managed to overcome the most serious problems relating to bilateral economic defence collaboration. Canadian defence sales in the United States had increased steadily from $96.3 million in 1959 to a high of $254.3 million in 1962. Perhaps of even more significance, Canada had recorded defence trade surpluses of $48.3 million and $126.9 million in 1961 and 1962 respectively, leaving a cumulative production sharing balance of $69.7 million in Canada's favour by the end of 1963.[78]

Thus, for the short term at least, the program had ensured the economic survival of the Canadian defence industry and had relieved the pressure on the government's balance-of-payments position vis-à-vis the United States. Insofar as they could compete freely for virtually all United States defence contracts and could be assured that their bids would be evaluated on exactly the same basis as those of their United States counterparts, Canadian firms were accorded a unique status in the United States defence procurement system. From an American perspective, the arrangements had enabled Canada to upgrade its military contributions to NORAD and NATO by procuring Bomarc missiles, F–101B and F–104G aircraft, and by assuming operational and financial responsibilities for sixteen Pine Tree radar stations.[79]

Conclusions

By the end of 1963 the Canadian and United States governments had established effective policies and procedures for achieving their respective defence sharing objectives with a minimum of political conflict. What were the main features of the transborder political processes which permitted the fashioning of this successful economic defence relationship?[80]

In the first place, the defence sharing arrangements evolved out of more than two decades of continuous economic defence interaction between the two governments. Arising out of a shared perception of the growing military and economic interdependence between the two countries, the basic principle of bilateral economic defence collaboration agreed to early in World War II was reaffirmed and elaborated upon in response to a succession of external military crises and domestic economic exigencies after the war.

The *overriding consensus* regarding the long-term goals of this collaborative process remained essentially intact over the years and provided a solid foundation on which new procedures and arrangements could be built to suit the requirements of changing circumstances. In 1958, of several reasonably attractive options open to Ottawa in the wake of its short-lived, "go-it-alone" defence industrial strategy (ranging, for example, from "off-the-shelf" procurement on the world market, to development, production, licensing, and offset purchasing arrangements with one or more other countries), *only* the Canada-United States production sharing option was even considered by the Canadian government. This demonstrates the powerful influence exerted by the principles, procedures, and techniques of the earlier pattern of bilateral economic defence interaction.

Secondly, while neither Ottawa nor Washington seriously questioned the basic principle of collaboration established as early as 1941, each government adhered to it for quite different reasons. For Canada, the motivation was primarily economic: to maintain a credible defence effort on an economically sound basis. For the United States, the incentive was mainly military: to preserve Canada's commitment and contribution to European and especially North American defence. Thus, while the specific Canadian and United States interests in economic defence collaboration were by no means perceived as identical, neither were they seen to be mutually exclusive.

It was the recognition of the fundamental *complementarity* of these interests that enabled Canadian officials to convince the Americans that a mutually advantageous "bargain" could be struck in the form of production sharing. In other words, the DDP was able to persuade the DOD that each party would gain reciprocal, but different, benefits from these arrangements, and these benefits would be equitably distributed between the two countries. This implicit "trade off" or balancing of compatible long-run objectives and different, but coincidental, short-run interests of the main national bureaucratic actors, encouraged the development of a stable and co-operative (non-zero-sum) process of interaction between the two governments after 1958.

Once this bargain had been struck and the basic policy framework of bilateral defence production sharing agreed upon, the trans-governmental "bureaucratization" of relations between Canada and the United States in this issue-area was accelerated.[81] The relationship between, and the behaviour of the small group of civil servants in each government responsible for formulating and implementing the specific production sharing arrangements constituted a third important factor encouraging the growth and expansion of this co-operative and, by and large, successful transborder policy process. Indeed, it was this human element — so often neglected by academics — that imbued production sharing with its fundamentally pragmatic nature.

Through their shared commitment to the goal of economic defence co-operation and their appreciation that the attainment of this end was essentially a technical and administrative matter, these civil servants adopted a "problem-solving" approach to production sharing. Their conviction that immediate, concrete results were what really mattered was rooted in the sense of collegial identification which historically had developed primarily along *functional* (that is, professional and administrative) rather than purely national lines. Thus, the regular use of informal, person-to-person channels of communication, in which the telephone rather than the diplomatic pouch became the accepted (and most convenient) link between individuals sharing similar outlooks and experiences on each side of the border, helped to foster an atmosphere of mutual respect and goodwill among those bureaucrats charged with the formidable task of overcoming legal and administrative obstacles to the effective operation of the vaguely defined concept of production sharing.

These Canada and American bureaucrats worked hard to preserve this climate of co-operation by preventing the politicization of the production sharing policy process. They did this in two ways. First, they tightly controlled *access* to the process: day-to-day involvement was limited to a very few DDP and DOD officials while non-governmental groups, such as Canadians and United States defence firms and their respective industrial lobbies, were excluded from direct participation in policy-making. Moreover, outside government and defence industry circles, the production sharing program was deliberately accorded a very low profile by both the DDP and the DOD.[82] Even within these two departments, lower level bureaucrats attempted to defuse potentially contentious issues, such as the waiver of the "Buy American" Act restrictions against Canadian firms, by devising informal, often ad hoc, administrative procedures and tacit "understandings" among themselves *before* such matters could be brought to the attention of senior departmental officials and cabinet members in either government.[83] In this manner, the production sharing policy process was kept insulated, in both a horizontal and a vertical sense, from outside interference.

Secondly, these bureaucrats eschewed actions which might violate the long-standing "rules of the game" pertaining to economic defence collaboration between the two governments. For example, both sides assiduously avoided making overt public threats to reinforce their particular points of view on difficult issues. Furthermore, they sought to eliminate explicit linkages between production sharing and other Canada-United States policy areas. Adherence to these behavioural norms was very much in evidence in the restraint exhibited by both DDP and DOD production sharing officials during the period of strained Canadian-American relations in 1962 and 1963, a period during which quite significant advances occurred in the defence sharing program itself.

The emergence over time of this particular "style" of Canadian-American diplomacy — one which I have labelled, perhaps inadequately, as transgovernmental bureaucratic relations — provided an effective method for handling most of the recurring bilateral economic defence issues. The main objectives of both governments were attained, problems were solved, conflict was minimized and for the most part avoided, and a stable, responsive policy process was established.

However, before too many unwarranted "lessons" are drawn from this brief study, it is well to remember that this diplomatic approach evolved as much through the fortuitous interplay of history and circumstance as through the deliberate contrivance of individuals, agencies, and governments. This caveat aside, the Canadian-American defence production sharing arrangements provide a fertile ground for those wishing to explore the intimate connection between the external and internal "environments" of public policy-making.

Notes

1. Cited in Jon B. McLin, *Canada's Changing Defense Policy, 1957–1963* (Baltimore 1967), 227.

2. See Danford W. Middlemiss, "A Pattern of Co-operation: The Case of the Canadian-American Defence Production and Development Sharing Arrangements, 1958–1963" (Ph.D. diss., University of Toronto, 1976).

3. R.D. Cuff and J.L. Granatstein, "The Hyde Park Declaration, 1941: Origins and Significance," *Canadian-American Relations in Wartime* (Toronto 1975), 81.

4. J.W. Pickersgill, ed., *The Mackenzie King Record* (Toronto 1960), vol. 1, *1939–1944*, 187–9.

5. Ibid, 191. For the declaration see Canada, *Treaty Series*, 1941, no. 14.

6. Canada, Parliament, House of Commons, *Debates*, 28 Apr. 1941, 2289.

7. Canada, *Treaty Series*, 1942, no. 17.

8. Canada, *Treaty Series*, 1948, no. 1.

9. Middlemiss, "Pattern of Co-operation," 40–58.

10. United States, Department of State, *The British Commonwealth; Western and Central Europe*, vol. 5 of *Foreign Relations of the United States, 1946* (Washington 1969), 60 (hereinafter *FRUS 1946*).

11. Canada, *Treaty Series*, 1947, no. 43. This was an outgrowth of the terms of the 35th recommendation of the Permanent Joint Board on Defence: see "Canada: Discussions Relating to Joint Defence Measures," *FRUS 1946*, vol. 5, 65–7.

12. Middlemiss, "Pattern of Co-operation," 77–8.

13. This "problem" stemmed from the high United States dollar content in any Canadian-made military equipment that would constitute part of Ottawa's contribution to the rearmament effort. In addition, the postwar reimposition of the "Buy American" Act's provisions militated against offsetting United States defence purchases in Canada.

14. Prime Minister L. St. Laurent, *Statements and Speeches*, 49/34.

15. Canada, *Treaty Series*, 1949, no. 8.

16. McLin, *Canada's Changing Defense Policy*, 174.

17. John Swettenham, *McNaughton* (Toronto 1969), vol. 3, *1944–1966*, 196–8.

18. *Debates*, 19 May 1950, 2653.

19. Ibid. United States expenditures had averaged abut $21 million annually: Middlemiss, "Pattern of Co-operation," 82.

20. Canada, *Treaty Series*, 1950, no. 15. The notes outlined six broad "principles" of developing a co-ordinated program of requirements, production, and procurement.

21. "Canadian industrial development," address at Northeastern University, Boston, 4 Oct. 1954, C.D. Howe Papers, 89–2, folder 48, Public Archives of Canada.

22. While Canadian defence expenditures in the United States remained relatively constant at $130 million annually, United States defence spending in Canada rose from $27.7 million for the last nine months of 1951, to $103 million in 1952, and finally to $127 million in 1953: Department of Defence Production (hereinafter DDP), annual reports for the years cited.

23. *External Affairs* V (Nov. 1953), 326, and Howe to Bateman, 10 Oct. 1953, Howe Papers, S–14–9.

24. As C.D. Howe noted: "When defence contracts are let these days, both of our Governments are inclined to turn first to their domestic production facilities and only because they have to, or for some very special reason, do they look across the border. This may be regrettable but it is one of the facts of life and must be accepted as such." "Address to the Canadian Club of Boston," 4 Oct. 1954, Howe Papers, 89–2, folder 48, Public Archives of Canada.

25. Canada, *Treaty Series*, 1955, no. 8 (emphasis added).

26. Canada, DDP, *Report, 1955*, 18. Between 1955 and 1957 Canadian firms received approximately $8.8 million in DEW line subcontracts: Canada, Parliament, House of Commons, *Debates*, 9 Feb. 1960, 916. See also *Debates*, 2 Mar. 1959, 1529.

27. For details of these arrangements, see Middlemiss, "Pattern of Co-operation," 243.

28. According to Howe, the objectives of this policy were "to provide our forces with the best of modern equipment; to build up our mobilization reserves; to provide facilities capable of all-out production should an emergency develop. The program is designed to strengthen the economic fabric of our country." "Address to 65th annual meeting of the Vancouver Board of Trade," 29 Jan. 1952, Howe Papers, 89–2, folder 60.

29. Assistance took the form of capital grants and loans to industry as well as accelerated depreciation allowances: see Middlemiss, "Pattern of Co-operation," 174–5.

30. Ibid., 174–6.

31. Whereas in 1951 the DDP's main objective had been to encourage the rapid growth and expansion of aircraft production to meet Canadian and United States rearmament demands, by the mid-1950s it was attempting to "stabilize work loads and employment to the greatest extent possible," C.D. Howe, *Debates*, 27 June 1956, 5456–7.

32. *Debates*, 8 July 1959, 56–9.

33. Confidential interviews with former senior DDP officials (hereinafter confidential interviews).

34. United States, *Department of State Bulletin* XXXIX (4 Aug. 1958), 208–9, and United Nations, *Treaty Series*, no. 4792, CCCXXV (1959), 250.

35. DDP, *Report, 1958*, 26. The Canadian members of the Senior Policy Committee were: the deputy minister, DDP; the deputy minister, Department of National Defence; the assistant under-secretary of state for external affairs; the assistant secretary of the Treasury Board. The American members were: the assistant secretary (material) of the air force, chairman; the assistant secretary (logistics) of the army; the assistant secretary (material) of the navy: *Debates*, 2 Mar. 1959, 1527. The different organizational composition of this committee helps to explain the different Canada-United States interests and goals in production sharing.

36. McLin, *Canada's Changing Defense Policy*, 87, and cited in "U.S.-Canada Defence Production and Development Sharing Program," a background paper received from LeRoy J. Haugh, director, Procurement Analysis and Planning, Office of the Assistant Secretary of Defense (Installations and Logistics), 6 (hereinafter Haugh Document).

37. McLin, *Canada's Changing Defense Policy*, 225.

38. DDP, *Report, 1958*, 26.

39. For a detailed discussion of these negotiations, see Middlemiss, "Pattern of Co-operation," 221–32.

40. This paragraph is based on confidential interviews with former senior DDP officials and "Canada-U.S. defence sharing," notes prepared (12 Apr. 1966) by the DDP for Ambassador Ritchie's address in Washington, D.C., 31 Jan. 1967; also, DDP, *Report, 1959*, 16, 25.

41. Haugh Document, 6. In April 1959, the United States armed services exempted these four projects from the "Buy American" Act and certain United States customs duties: DDP, *Report, 1959*, 25.

42. For the best available account of the rise and fall of the CF–105 program, see James Dow, *The Arrow* (Toronto 1979). See also Middlemiss, "Pattern of Co-operation," 176–96.

43. *Debates*, 20 Feb. 1959, 1222–3.

44. Ibid., 2 Mar. 1959, 1519, 1528.

45. DDP, *Report, 1959*, 26.

46. Confidential interviews and *Debates*, 2 Mar. 1959, 1528, and 8 July 1959, 5659.

47. *Canadian Aviation* XXXII (Apr. 1959), 129.

48. For example, well-established United States defence firms often had written off their development, pre-production, and tooling costs on previous defence contracts: *Canadian Aviation* XXXII (Apr. 1959), 28.

49. This was the reaction of certain DDP officials who deplored the "accountant's mentality" which had led to Canada's acceptance of the one-third, labour-intensive construction portion of the air defence package in the early months of production sharing: confidential interviews and *Debates*, 2 July 1959, 5354, 8 July 1959, 5658, and 28 Jan. 1960, 456.

50. Of course, what was to be considered "sensible" or "necessary" by either

government was a moot point. Canadian officials regarded this
"understanding" as only a "cosmetic" reciprocation on Canada's part, one
designed to provide the United States negotiators with something to assuage
their industry's concerns regarding the apparently one-sided nature of
production sharing: confidential interviews with former senior DDP officials.

51. Middlemiss, "Pattern of Co-operation," 254–5, 257, 262–5.

52. United States, "Directive by the President concerning steps to be taken
with respect to the United States balance of payments," 16 Nov. 1960, *Code of
Federal Regulations*, Title 3, 1959–1963 Compilation (Washington 1964),
809–11.

53. The Department of Defense directive, 2035.1, is reproduced in DDP,
Production Sharing Handbook (4th ed; Ottawa 1967), appendix A.

54. For examples of these criticisms, see Middlemiss, "Pattern of
Co-operation," 289–90.

55. Ibid., 241.

56. These two issues are discussed in P.V. Lyon, *Canada in World Affairs*,
vol. 12, *1961–1963* (Toronto 1968), at 27–64 and 76–222 and R.W. Reford,
Canada and Three Crises (Toronto 1968), 149–215.

57. Quoted in Lyon, *Canada in World Affairs 1961–1963*, 56.

58. Reford, *Three Crises*, 214; also, "The big stick the Pentagon holds over
Canada's defence industry," *Maclean's* (23 Mar. 1963), 3.

59. Cited by Clive Baxter, "Now we pay the piper for our defence tune,"
Financial Post, 1 Dec. 1962.

60. "McNamara plans $3 billion a year in arms savings," *New York Times*
(8 July 1962), 1.

61. "U.S. $queeze will crimp defence orders in Canada," *Financial Post*, 25
May 1963, 1, and *Canadian Aviation* XXXV (Dec. 1962): 21.

62. United States defence procurement in Canada declined from a
production sharing high of $254.3 million in 1962 to $142.0 million in 1963:
see Middlemiss, "Pattern of Co-operation," appendix A, table 1, 496.

63. Confidential interviews.

64. *Debates*, 24 May 1963, 243.

65. Drury's account of his discussions with McNamara can be found in
Debates, 7 June 1963, 769–70.

66. However, the Canadian government itself had already sown the seed of
this "equilibrium" idea when DDP Minister O'Hurley had stated that he
thought Canada-United States defence purchases should be "equalized."
O'Hurley's statement had been prompted by his lack of enthusiasm for the
early results of production sharing: see *Debates*, 28 July 1960, 7115–16.

67. "Snag in new defence deal must match U.S. orders," *Financial Times*, 10
June 1963.

68. Ibid., and confidential interviews.

69. Confidential interviews.

70. *Debates*, 7 June 1963, 770.

71. Ibid., 3 Apr. 1964, 1761.

72. McLin, *Canada's Changing Defense Policy*, 181–2, 190.

73. For examples, see Middlemiss, "Pattern of Co-operation," 300–1.

74. Ibid., 284–7.
75. Foster Lee Smith, "Canadian-United States scientific collaboration for defense," *Public Policy*, XXX (1963), 331–2.
76. McLin, *Canada's Changing Defense Policy*, 187.
77. This memorandum is reproduced in *Production Sharing Handbook*, appendix B, B–45 to B–48.
78. Middlemiss, "Pattern of Co-operation," appendix A, table 1, 496.
79. See, for example, Canada, *Treaty Series*, 1961, no. 5.
80. In arguing that this economic defence relationship was "successful," I am referring only to the operation of the transborder policy process during the period 1940–63. At the same time, however, I am aware that some commentators contend that the production sharing arrangements have had a detrimental impact on Canada's political, economic, and military interests over the past fifteen years. Because a comprehensive analysis of these consequences would take me well beyond the intended scope of this article, those wishing to pursue this issue should consult: "A Pattern of Co-operation: The Case of the Canadian-American Defence Production and Development Sharing Arrangements, 1958–1963," Danford W. Middlemiss (Ph.D. diss., University of Toronto, 1976), 449–66; John J. Kirton, "The consequences of integration: the case of the Defence Production Sharing Agreements," in W.A. Axline et al., eds., *Continental Community? Independence and Integration in North America* (Toronto 1974); Canada, Parliament, Standing Senate Committee on Foreign Affairs, *Canada-United States Relations*. II: *Canada's Trade Relations with the United States* (Ottawa 1978), 89–94; and ibid., House of Commons, Standing Committee on External Affairs and National Defence, *Minutes of Proceedings and Evidence*, 32nd Parl., 1st sess., no. 22, 13 Nov. 1980, testimony of Ernie Regehr.
81. The theoretical underpinnings of this concept of "transgovernmental bureaucratic relations" can be found in the works of R.O. Keohane and J.S. Nye Jr., "Transgovernmental relations and international organizations," *World Politics* (Oct. 1974), and Graham T. Allison, *Essence of Decision: Explaining the Cuban Missile Crisis* (Boston 1971), especially Allison's "Model II" and "Model III."
82. For example, during the May 1959 United States congressional discussions regarding possible amendments to the "Buy American" Act, not a single reference was made to the recent DOD exemptions to Canadian firms: Middlemiss, "Pattern of Co-operation," 271 (note 33).
83. A prime example was the fact that the United States Defense Department effected a major policy change in the "Buy American" Act by simply amending the Armed Services Procurement Regulations; Congress apparently was not even aware of this change at the time.

Transboundary Environ-
mental and Resource Issues†

KENNETH M. CURTIS AND JOHN E. CARROLL

At any given time, the top ten items on the list of irritants on the U.S.-Canadian diplomatic agenda includes a number of transboundary environmental issues.[1] The list also invariably contains one or more fishery disputes, water resource questions of one sort or another, and occasionally conflict over disputed maritime boundary claims. All of these issues have one thing in common: they are invariably perceived as local or regional, and thereby inconsequential, by Americans, and they are often treated as national issues involving great national pride and honour (and often national values) by Canadians. This difference in approach alone is sufficient to exacerbate the bilateral seriousness of these issues and insure a place for them on the diplomatic agenda. All of these issues stem from the necessity . . . of sharing the continental commons, the common watersheds and drainage basins, the common air masses, and the common seas and all that is in them.

Transboundary Environmental Problems

Bilateral disputes over the allocation of boundary and near-boundary

† Kenneth M. Curtis and John E. Carroll, *Canadian-American Relations: The Promise and the Challenge* (Toronto: Heath, 1984), 27–37.

water resources and air masses are not new phenomena on the U.S.-Canadian scene, as the long record of debates over the Great Lakes levels and pollution concerns and the competition for scarce water resources on the prairies indicate. Indeed, it was precisely these two areas of concern that led to the late nineteenth-century formation of the International Waterway Commission and by 1911 its successor, the International Joint Commission. As near-border economic development intensified, the foundation was laid for escalating conflict, culminating in the extensive scope of environmental conflict we witness today.

The Boundary Waters Treaty of 1909 and the treaty's vehicle for implementation, the International Joint Commission (IJC), have built a foundation that has underlain bilateral environmental relations between Canada and the United States for nearly three-quarters of a century. Touted worldwide as a unique model of what can be accomplished by two nations with sufficient will, the treaty and the commission have long been respected for their unusual spirit of collegiality; for their long record of sound scientific and technical findings; for the unique nature of their organization and approaches; and, perhaps most significantly, for their success in conflict avoidance. Recognition on all of these grounds is justified, though a caveat is in order: the commission's task under the treaty has been narrow and specialized; its work has been relegated to noncontroversial areas where there was already diplomatic recognition that agreement could be achieved; and most of its efforts, especially in recent years, have led to nonbinding recommendations that the two governments can (and often do) ignore. Hence the work of this in many respects admirable treaty and vehicle is confined and its impact limited.

The Boundary Waters Treaty established the rules and procedures by which boundary waters (including waters flowing across as well as those forming the boundary) would be allocated in relation to upstream and downstream interests and among various categories of users. The IJC's decisions in this area are binding. The treaty also provided a vehicle whereby the two federal governments could refer matters (in theory any matters, but in practice mainly air and water pollution matters) to the IJC for nonbinding recommendations and advice. This aspect of its mandate has occupied most of the commission's time in recent years.

The treaty governs U.S.-Canadian interaction over the Great Lakes, ranging from lake level matters of great consequence to hydroelectric power, navigation, and shoreline impacts to water pollution questions in the lakes (all except Lake Michigan, which is not considered international and therefore is not under the purview of the treaty) and their connecting channels (St. Mary's, St. Clair, Detroit, and Niagara rivers and the St. Lawrence). In fact, the 1909 treaty even uses the word pollution, which was unusual at that early date but a reflection of the early pollution concerns in portions of the lakes and connecting channels, particularly in the Detroit and St. Clair rivers. Since its earliest origins, the IJC has devoted a major portion of its work to water quality in the lakes; it was, for example, involved in an intense period of pollution investigation, analysis, and surveillance, especially in Lakes Erie and Ontario (the "lower lakes"), culminating in the Great Lakes Water Quality Agreements of 1972 and 1978.

The commission was given principal responsibility for implementing the conditions of these two agreements and established a Great Lakes Regional Office at Windsor, Ontario, to carry out this task. Pollution in Lakes Erie and Ontario peaked in the early 1970s and reductions in overall pollution have been recorded in recent years. However, the nature of the lakes' pollution has changed from the more conventional municipal sewerage and industrial effluent to much more unconventional and difficult to manage toxic substances. These substances, especially in the Niagara River, are now emerging as a particularly difficult bilateral dispute — one which is certainly exacerbated by the dramatic Reagan administration budget cuts for the U.S. Environmental Protection Agency, the lead federal agency in water quality and through the 1970s a major presence on the lakes.

The true impact of the Boundary Waters Treaty and the IJC on water quality in the Great Lakes is yet to be assessed. Clearly, the lakes would not be cleaner without this bilateral involvement. Whether they would be dirtier without that involvement is not as certain. There is no doubt, however, that the efforts of the IJC under the treaty have informed millions of people in both countries of the lakes' problems; that there are serious threats to the water quality of the upper lakes (Huron and Superior) which were thought to be safe; and that scientists from both governments can work well together in generating data and presenting findings acceptable to both sides. The blame for continuing deterioration of the lakes may well, therefore, be placed at the feet of those in government and elsewhere in the two societies who have the responsibility of receiving this data and acting on it. One thing is certain: serious pollution in the Great Lakes does not result from the sharing of the lakes by two countries. This pollution would exist, at the very least at present levels, even if the lakes were wholly contained within one nation. It cannot be said that the lakes suffer from being an international "no man's land." Indeed, they have received increased attention because of their international status and may be the better for that attention today.

The scarcity of water and particularly potable water in the U.S.-Canadian international prairie region has also provided a setting for transboundary environmental disputes. On the dry prairies the countless small rivers and streams take on an image larger than life, at least by the standards of those living in well-watered areas. Hence, those used to water abundance wonder at the seriousness of disputes, highlighted by diplomatic headlines, over such water sources as the Poplar River (site of a Saskatchewan coal-fired power plant), the Souris River (embroiled in the great Garrison irrigation dispute), the Red River (with its chronic pollution and flooding problems), and such tiny prairie streams as the Pembina and the St. Mary. Greatest among the prairie disputes are the Poplar and Garrison issues, both of which have caused political earthquakes in Ottawa and much consternation in Washington.

The government of Saskatchewan's construction of a large (up to 1 200 MW) coal-fired power plant and associated coal mines on the Poplar River just a few miles north of the U.S. border offers many benefits to that province, while nothing but costs to adjacent Montana. The Poplar issue is particularly noteworthy in that it is the only transboundary environmental problem to contain all three of these distinct elements: water quantity or apportionment, water quality, and air quality. The operation of the plant presents costs to Montana in all three areas (albeit the extent of those costs are much debated). Water-scarce northeastern Montana begrudges any loss of water rights (even though the Poplar water apportionment settlement increases Montana's water entitlement on other streams). This agricultural region is also concerned about impacts on the quality of its irrigation water and about the effect of air pollutants (from a plant without sulfur pollution controls) on its crops and livestock. Its fears have been heard loudly and clearly in Washington, bringing strong pressure there to resist Canadian plans. The IJC has been actively involved, mitigating the water apportionment and quality aspects of this dispute. There is no question, however, that Montana suffers opportunity costs because of Canada's ability to exercise the western "first in time, first in right" philosophy (which derives from western prior appropriation water-rights doctrine, but which could apply to pollution as well).

In contrast, the Garrison irrigation dispute[2] is well known in Canada but seldom discussed in the United States. In the late 1940s ambitious plans were laid to carry out substantial federal manipulation of the waters of the dry Missouri Basin. Part of this plan included the large-scale diversion of the Missouri River into the northward-flowing Souris-Red River-Hudson Bay drainage, thereby irrigating (and substantially revolutionizing the future of) central and eastern North Dakota. The great Garrison debate, very much a U.S. domestic environmental issue aside from its bilateral ramifications, was the result.

Along with providing much additional water to the farms, municipalities, and (hopefully) industries of North Dakota, this diversion from a Gulf of Mexico to an Arctic drainage basin, according to the findings of many scientists and of the IJC, will result in pollution of the Canadian Souris and other rivers north of the border (from agricultural run-off and soil leaching) such that a number of Manitoba communities would be deprived of their only source of water. Perhaps more important, the transfer of Missouri River fish parasites and disease biota into Canada's Lakes Winnipeg and Manitoba would take place, thereby threatening (or even destroying) a well-established commercial fishery and the social fabric of the societies dependent upon that fishery.

Manitoban and Canadian objections to Garrison did not begin as early as they could have; but when they started, they reverberated with great force all across the land, as they still do today. The province of Manitoba, with strong Ottawa backing, has protested loudly and consistently to Washington and to any American audience that would listen. All segments of the Canadian society, including peoples as far removed from Manitoba as Halifax and Vancouver, are well versed on Garrison. The media (and particularly editorial writers) have kept this issue in the forefront nation-wide: almost every week the current events surrounding Garrison are debated in the Canadian House of Commons.

Garrison is a classic example of the type of U.S.-Canadian issue that quickly becomes associated with the national interests of Canada but is viewed south of the border (by the few who are even aware of it) as strictly a local or regional issue. Garrison is, of course, a major issue in North Dakota and commands some minor interest in South Dakota and Minnesota; but it is unknown or viewed as of little consequence elsewhere. The true bilateral danger of Garrison is not in water pollution or biota transfer, although those problems are real enough, but rather in the great foreign relations costs of the issue. A whole generation of Canadians is growing up with the Garrison symbol, a symbol in which the United States plays the role of an inconsiderate, uncaring, even bullying country with no regard for the consequences of its actions on a neighboring people, even when the cost of rectifying the problem and avoiding those consequences is small. It is doubtful whether the American people consciously want to assume this image before the Canadian people, but this is what is happening.

Seriously compounding the Garrison issue is the fact that the highly respected and truly bilateral International Joint Commission, after extensive study, has found that to proceed with the project as planned would indeed bring the harm to Canada that that country fears, thereby violating the Boundary Waters Treaty of 1909. To the extent Americans support (or permit) Garrison to go forward, they are helping to maintain their image in Canada as not only an uncaring people but one clearly willing to discard the treaty and all that it represents. In all likelihood Americans would not be so disposed if they realized the consequences of their action. Danger to both peoples thus lies in the ignorance of too many Americans about Canada and its concerns. Until such time as the U.S. Congress and administration agree to significant modification of the project or its repeal, Canadians will ensure that it remains a serious bilateral issue and a continuing thorn in the side of the diplomatic relationship.

Serious bilateral environmental problems have also arisen in the coastal marine environment. The Eastport oil refinery controversy on the Atlantic coast has continued for a decade, as Canadian opposition to the siting of a large, proposed oil refinery (one hundred thousand barrels per day) at Eastport, Maine, has intensified over the years. Access to the refinery site involves the transiting of oil-carrying super-tankers through Canada's narrow Head Harbour Passage, a navigationally challenging task intensified by severe currents and high fog regimes. At risk in the event of an accident is not only the local marine ecosystem and shorelines but — of great importance to Canada — an increasingly valuable commercial fishery throughout the Bay of Fundy. This dispute is heightened by the U.S. claim of the right of "innocent passage" through these Canadian waters and the Canadian counterclaim that passage of so much oil at such high risk is not "innocent." The debate continues unresolved as the American proponent of the project, the Pittson Company, after gradually obtaining its various permits to begin construction, could not resolve all legal requirements. In Canada the issue, though not as well known nationally as Garrison, is as intensely opposed. The political stakes are high, even though the passage of time may have resolved the debate itself. Foreign relations costs are still being incurred.

On the West Coast there is the issue of U.S. oil tanker transport between Alaska (and perhaps eventually Asia) to Washington State refineries, and the passage of this oil in supertankers through the dangerous and ecologically sensitive waters of the Strait of Juan de Fuca in the vicinity of both Victoria and Vancouver. Although boundary claims are not an issue here, the need for a mandatory vessel traffic management system with bilateral implications has been a part of this dispute. Such a system has been achieved by bilateral agreement; but British Columbians still perceive a significant threat of damage and have kept Ottawa under some pressure.

Air quality disputes have a shorter history than do water-related disputes, being highlighted by the early Trail Smelter controversy in British Columbia-Washington, which is the only bilateral environmental dispute ever to be settled by binding arbitration. Other air quality differences, such as the Michigan-Ontario (Detroit-Windsor and Sarnia-Port Huron) urban-industrial air pollution problems, the Cornwall Island smelter problem (Ontario-New York), and the air quality aspects of the Poplar River power plant (Saskatchewan-Montana), have not ended so decisively. What is clear, however, is that the acid rain issue has emerged into so dominant an issue in the bilateral relationship that all other air quality issues are now being subsumed by these negotiations, discussions that are gradually leading toward a new international air quality treaty or agreement.[3]

The acid rain issue is a giant among all U.S.-Canadian environmental problems and will likely have a long-term impact on the relationship and on how it is conducted in the future. The stage is set for a bilateral problem, given that so much of Canada is geologically highly vulnerable to acid deposition; that a high percentage of all deposition in Canada (at least 50 percent) derives from U.S. sources; and that Canada's forest productivity, a critical factor in the nation's future, may be endangered. The fact that the United States is much less concerned over the seriousness of the issue (as well as significantly less aware); that U.S. vulnerability is probably much less; and that Canada contributes only a small portion (about 15 percent to 20 percent) of U.S. acid deposition creates further imbalance and thus exacerbates the bilateral dispute. The stakes involved in the acid rain debate are economically (and therefore politically) and also quite possibly ecologically much higher than those associated with other bilateral environmental issues. The populations affected, many millions in both countries, include many who live far removed from the international border — people who are experiencing bilateral problems for the first time. The real cost of the acid rain dispute may well be, however, in foreign relations: this is the first environmental issue of a magnitude and consequence sufficient to pose a direct threat to the long-term health of the U.S.-Canadian relationship.

Other such transboundary environmental disputes that have received their share of attention over the years, particularly in the Canadian media, include the Skagit-High Ross Dam issue in Washington-British Columbia; the Atikokan power plant issue in Ontario-Minnesota; the Cabin Creek coal mine issue in British Columbia-Montana; and the Champlain-Richelieu issue in Quebec-Vermont.[4] All of these issues have one characteristic in common: all the benefits accrue on one side of the border, while all the costs accrue on the other. And, because issues cannot in practice be linked or traded off against each other, there is little basis to establish a give and take compromise; resolution of such issues calls for a willingness by the polluter to increase costs so as to protect persons across the border.

The vast majority of U.S.-Canadian transboundary environmental issues are directly energy related, whether derived from power plants or coal mines near the border, hydroelectric dams on transboundary rivers, or oil transport at sea. Many of them have resulted historically from significantly higher levels of both population and industrial development south of the border. In recent years an increasing number have resulted from Canadian plans (and, for the first time, ability) to develop near-border resources with transborder impacts, in what has been called Canada's near-border "development corridor." Some result from a U.S. tendency to designate national parks, wilderness, and wild and scenic rivers in equally near-border locations where they are in the path of pollution crossing the border. Others result from

Canada's need to maintain its position in relation to world competition for its resource exports. Still others result from the U.S. drive for energy independence.

For these and other reasons, transboundary environmental conflicts are increasing in number and complexity, are long lasting, and are not even susceptible to management and containment, much less resolution. Through the Boundary Waters Treaty of 1909 and its Harmon Doctrine (which gives the upstream nation superior water rights), an attempt was made to establish rule and order. Neither nation readily applies the treaty nor uses it to its maximum potential, however; this failure, combined with their inability to act decisively on an international air-quality agreement, has created chaos in the area of transboundary issues. Both peoples will suffer the erosion of their relationship and the loss of future opportunities until they choose to use the means available to resolve these questions and introduce order.

Fishery and Boundary Questions

The Canadian society is in many respects fish oriented. Canada's heritage and culture place a high premium on commercial fishing, fish consumption, and fish export to the world market; and they are thus based upon the allied industries and way of life that such a major national commitment entails. This involvement is characteristic not only of the ocean coasts but also of the provinces with interior waters. Six of Canada's ten provinces have an important interest in commercial marine fishing and two others are committed to inland freshwater commercial fisheries. Furthermore, given this priority scale and Canada's present and future export prospects, Ottawa has begun heavy subsidization and investment in this national fishery, giving all Canadians a much more direct stake in it.

In almost every way, the U.S. society is opposite (even though the total value of the U.S. catch, given greater access to the warm Pacific, Gulf of Mexico, and south Atlantic waters, is higher). Although the fishery was part of New England's heritage, virtually no region of the United States is as oriented toward a fishery heritage and lifestyle or as economically dependent on fish as is so much of Canada. In the United States there is little interest in fish export, a low per capita fish consumption, and limited political support for a national fishery constituency. (New England is an exception, accounting for the unyielding U.S. fishery position regarding negotiation with Canada on a fishing treaty in recent years. Senate opposition to the ratification of that treaty was led by Senators Edward Kennedy of Massachusetts and Claiborne Pell of Rhode Island.) Further, there is very little federal investment in the fishery and little subsidy available. Americans are not about to substitute the sacred cow symbolic of their beef-eating preferences for the once sacred (at least in Boston!) cod.

Hence, fundamental differences in approaches to fish exist within the two countries; and Canada is infinitely more sensitive to threats to its fisheries than the United States, a point not readily understood by Americans. This greater Canadian fishery concern has emerged in the Eastport oil refinery issue, the West Coast oil tanker issue, and even in the inland Garrison Diversion issue. It is in the area of head-to-head conflict over the allocation of fish stocks, however, that the most serious differences have arisen. This situation has been exacerbated by the strong resentment harboured by American fishermen toward their much larger, better equipped, government-subsidized Canadian competitors, a resentment fueled by the ability of those competitors to sell large quantities of their catch to the U.S. market at low prices (benefiting the U.S. consumer but at a cost to U.S. fishermen).

Bilateral fishery disputes have been a continuing feature of U.S.-Canadian relations and have occurred inshore and offshore on both the Atlantic and Pacific coasts, including along both Pacific coast boundary areas, for many years. Arguments over valuable salmon resources on the Washington-British Columbia and British Columbia-Alaska borders have been long-lasting and difficult of resolution; they are aggravated not only by competition for the stock but also through the high level of government investment by both nations in hatchery and fish-ladder facilities. As long as salmon are valuable, as long as they continue to fail to recognize international boundaries, and as long as there continues to be some question as to precisely where those boundaries fall and whose fish belong to whom, these sharp and emotional disputes will continue without resolution. Other Pacific fisheries questions, including those surrounding tuna and groundfish, lend themselves much more readily to resolution — either bilaterally or in the broader multilateral sphere.

The East Coast situation has been less sanguine, in spite of there being only one border. Simmering differences between Canadian and American commercial fishing interests in the Bay of Fundy-Gulf of Maine, and especially on Georges Bank, a very fertile fishing ground, burst into loud and acrimonious debate in 1977; at that time both nations unilaterally extended their seaward boundaries two hundred miles, creating a new boundary dispute with an overlapping claim on the critical Georges Bank. This simultaneous unilateral extension had other repercussions: it raised the hopes of New England as well as eastern Canadian fishermen, and these groups (along with the Canadian government) began to significantly increase their level of investment in the Georges Bank fishery, thus raising the future stakes in this dispute and making resolution much more difficult. A reasonably good prospect of achieving joint management of the fishery stocks in question, a condition extant prior to 1977, deteriorated with these rising stakes, the boundary dispute, a hardened political attitude of key New England politicians, and the inability of the weakened Carter administration to achieve necessary treaty ratification in the U.S. Senate. All of these factors coalesced to create what developed into one of the most serious U.S.-Canadian disputes in the late 1970s and early 1980s, ending in a crisis of Canadian confidence in the American people that will persist for some time to come.

The question that Americans must ask is to what extent and how accurately have they calculated the foreign relations costs of this dispute. The issue is much broader than fish; and once again Americans, through ignorance, have failed to recognize the issues of critical importance to Canada. Instead of assessing the whole situation and making a decision, U.S. politicians often seem to act out of ignorance in order to protect a narrow regional interest, thereby damaging their credibility in Canadian eyes. The East Coast fisheries dispute, a dispute that remains unresolved and threatens the economic viability and ecological integrity of one of the finest of North American fisheries, has left a residue of sour relations that will colour the ultimate settlement and allocation of the stocks for a long time.

Related to these fisheries issues is the matter of the maritime boundary disputes — sovereignty questions that have arisen largely through the unilateral extension of the offshore two-hundred-mile economic zones. Few Americans are aware of the fact that all four U.S.-Canadian maritime boundaries (Maine-New Brunswick, Washington-British Columbia, Alaska-British Columbia, Alaska-Yukon) are in dispute. These disagreements are most directly concerned with hydrocarbon exploitation: all four areas are thought to have oil and gas reserves. For the present, the Atlantic and Arctic disputes are the most consequential, although the two Pacific disputes involve latent problems. The Atlantic (Georges Bank) dispute did not inherently affect the fishery, for a joint stock management plan could have been achieved without boundary resolution; nevertheless, the U.S. refusal to work toward this end caused a linkage of fish both to hydrocarbons and the sovereignty question. It also caused an historic referral of this sovereignty dispute to the International Court of Justice (the World Court) at the Hague, a signal to the world that these two nations are unable to achieve resolution alone. It remains to be seen whether the U.S. claim to Georges Bank, based on the location of a deep channel separating the bank from the Nova Scotia mainland, or the Canadian claim, based on equidistance between Nova Scotia and New England, will be granted recognition. At stake are both hydrocarbons and the fishery, for the bitter fishery dispute may preclude access to one nation's portion of the bank by citizens of the other nation.

The Beaufort Sea dispute encompasses a substantial overlapping claim to a sea bottom that is undoubtedly rich in natural gas. The area of disputed territory is wide farther offshore, and relates to differing interpretations of the direction of the international boundary from the mainland to the North Pole. This and the Pacific boundary disputes all result from differing interpretations of early treaties involving the United States, the United Kingdom, and Russia (once sovereign over Alaska). It is possible that these three boundary disputes will take precedence from and ultimately be settled by the findings of the World Court on the Georges Bank dispute. All these disputed boundaries have natural-resource ramifications and, so long as they remain unsettled, preclude resource development.

Water as a Continental Resource

Water sources flowing near the U.S.-Canadian boundary and as resources capable of destruction by pollution have already been discussed. The topic of water as a continental resource still remains. During the 1960s considerable debate concerned the disposition of the continental water resource, in the context of significant American demand and enormous Canadian supply. This dichotomy of demand and supply created opportunity and political controversy, especially in Canada, which often views itself as in the greedy line-of-sight of American "resource-grabbers." Early Canadian discussion of possibly providing water for a thirsty and perhaps well-paying U.S. market suddenly ended with the crafting of the extremely ambitious, controversial, and almost certainly unworkable North American Water and Power Alliance (NAWAPA), a megascale plan (referred to in Canada as a "diabolical plot") to move large quantities of freshwater out of northern Canadian and Alaskan river basins southward through the Rocky Mountain Trench to the arid American Southwest and Mexico. This and other plans for largescale interbasin transfer southward created an intense fear in a Canadian society that felt that water was inextricably linked to Canada's heritage and future independence. These plans were perceived not as opportunities but as tangible threats to the Canadian nation. Such thinking became so implanted in the Canadian psyche that politically such matters are not discussable. Canada does indeed have considerable quantities of unused freshwater in the north (although to term this water wasted is erroneous as it fulfills ecological purposes). The U.S. demand for that water increases yearly. An emerging issue is the "mining" of deep groundwater and the consequent drawdown of aquifers and their pollution, one example being the depletion of the Great Plains groundwater aquifers and the various proposals for coal slurry pipelines, both of which look to the Great Lakes for a necessary water source.

Whether great interbasin transfers are, in real terms, desirable is an open question. Whether Canadian anathema to this question will ever disappear, however, may be a question of equal import. Water was the issue dominant in the 1960s and has been replaced by energy in the years since. Yet there are many observers who say that by the advent of the 1990s, water will again take its place as *the* primary resource question in North America. There is no question that continental demand for water in the coming years of water shortage, especially in the energy-rich West, will keep this issue high on the U.S.-Canadian agenda. It is the responsibility of both peoples to prepare to meet this challenge.

Notes

1. For the definitive work on U.S.-Canadian environmental relations, see John E. Carroll, *Environmental Diplomacy: An Examination and Prospective of Canadian-United States Transboundary Environmental Relations* (University of Michigan Press [U.S.] and John Wiley and Sons, Ltd. [Canada], 1983).

2. An in-depth treatment of the Garrison issue as a bilateral issue can be found in John E. Carroll and Rod Logan, *The Garrison Diversion Unit: A Case Study in Canadian-U.S. Environmental Relations* (Montreal: C.D. Howe Institute, 1980).

3. For an in-depth analysis of acid rain as a bilateral issue, see John E. Carroll, *Acid Rain: An Issue in Canadian-American Relations* (Washington: Canadian-American Committee, National Planning Association, 1982). See also John E. Carroll, "Acid Rain Diplomacy," *Alternatives*, 11, no. 2 (1983).

4. For a description of these and other disputes, see John E. Carroll, "When Pollution Knows No Boundaries," *National Parks and Conservation Magazine* 52, no. 3 (1978), 19–24; and "Shadows on the Border," *The Living Wilderness Magazine*, 45, no. 156 (Spring, 1982) 18–22. See also Carroll, *Environmental Diplomacy*.

ANOTHER LOOK AT THE COLD WAR†

J.L. GRANATSTEIN AND R.D. CUFF

American foreign policy since the early 1960s has come under increasing academic attack. W.A. Williams, Lloyd Gardner and Gar Alperovitz, among others, have helped to revise our understanding of the motives and consequences of American policy. The trail of upset applecarts littering the roadways after this critique is impressive indeed. Among the best of this work is that of Gabriel Kolko who had already contributed greatly to revisionist history with his early works. These analyzed American economic structure and the nature of the state in the Progressive era and radically altered the standard textbook views. *The Politics of War: The World and United States Foreign Policy, 1943–45* was his first major work in the area of foreign policy, and it was followed early in 1972 by *The Limits of Power: The World and United States Foreign Policy, 1945–1954*, co-authored with Joyce Kolko.

There are substantial differences in Kolko's approach and analysis compared with those of the other revisionist critics of American foreign policy. These are important, but it is the general outline of his work that concerns us here.

The picture Kolko's two books present of American foreign policy is very different from the usual ordered landscapes. No brief summary can do justice to Kolko's detailed, brilliant argumentation, but what is instantly clear is that Kolko has seen all the sources that are available.

† J.L. Granatstein and R.D. Cuff, "Looking Back at the Cold War: 1945–54," *Canadian Forum* LII (July 1972): 8–11.

The scholarship is formidable and, as Kolko himself notes, he has no patience with the premise that "ideological correctness on contemporary foreign relations is an adequate substitute for accuracy and depth."[1] Ideological correctness there may be in Kolko's books, but there is also accuracy and depth, and this is easily the most important aspect of his work.

What is Kolko telling us? In his two books on foreign policy, the United States is not the selfless white knight pouring its treasures out in lend-lease and the Marshall Plan for the general good. Nor is it a nation obsessed with fears of Communism and acting irrationally in the face of the bogeyman. Not at all. The United States in Kolko's view and that of his revisionist colleagues is a nation like the others, interested above all in the advancement of its own interests. American policy makers, convinced and certain of the correctness of their analysis, knew full well what they were doing as they tried to restructure the world to advance their country's economic interests. And they knew, too, that they could use the fear of Communism as a useful tool both abroad in securing concessions and at home in persuading a sometimes balky Congress. As Kolko argues:

> It was often politically convenient for America's leaders to fix the blame for capitalism's failures on the cautious men in the Kremlin. . . . If, in the end, all of Washington's postwar leaders superficially attribute to one cause — Russia — the justification for everything they wish to do, it is only because such a style of explanation becomes critical to the very conduct and future of an American foreign policy for which these men have yet to find domestic legitimation and enthusiasm.[2]

In this typical brief Kolko quotation a series of still contentious theses are advanced in a matter of fact way, including the idea that the Communists were cautious, that the United States used the Communist scare for its own purposes, and that the American public was at first less than enthusiastic about the direction its leaders were going.

Kolko presents substantial evidence to suggest that the United States administration after 1945 created phony war scares and on several occasions rejected out of hand peace overtures from the Soviet Union. He argues, too, that American military expenditures remained relatively low until after the Korean War began, and even businessmen who might have been expected to welcome large expenditures were unenthusiastic. The United States "spent about what it could afford on the military establishment . . . and as much as it thought the real, as opposed to publicized, threat of Soviet power and polices warranted to maintain its decisive military supremacy."[3]

This assessment of Soviet weakness is basic to the argument. The Soviet Union was on the defensive, in Kolko's view, desperate to keep a buffer between Germany and itself, desperate to keep the aggressive, capitalist West at bay. Virtually all Soviet actions in the immediate postwar period were of this character, Kolko argues, including the seizure of power in Czechoslovakia, an event that Kolko attributes more to the incompetent, inept manoeuvres of Czech conservative politicians than to a world-wide conspiracy of militant Communism. Even the Korean War appears here in a different light. Syngman Rhee is the villain of the piece, and if this is by now almost conventional wisdom, few will fail to be surprised by Kolko's variations on the theme. The South Koreans fell back before inferior North Korean forces, Kolko contends in a particularly provocative section, in a deliberate attempt to commit deeply the Americans. Their goal, of course, was the eventual forcible unification of the peninsula under Southern control.

The overall argument of Kolko's two foreign policy books at base rests on economic foundations. Here the main enemy of the United States is London, and the chief American goal is the destruction of the sterling bloc and of Commonwealth trade preferences. When lend-lease was offered during the war, for example, one of the conditions demanded by American negotiators was an end to Empire preferences, and this theme persisted into the postwar period. When an American loan was finally offered to the desperate British in 1947 it was less than London had expected, the terms were substantially stiffer, and the intentions were based on self-interest: lend the British money so they can buy American goods. The same story recurs when the Marshall Plan is discussed, although in 1948 the Americans also aimed to prop up Western Europe against the threat of Communism. Not against a Soviet invasion, however; rather, the threat as perceived in Washington was from internal subversion or, worse, a democratic Communist victory at the polls. The formation of NATO was similarly based, Kolko claims, and was not primarily directed at the Russians. It was

> much more the outcome of Europe's desire to prevent a resurgent Germany from yet again disturbing the peace, to which the United States added its desire to strengthen Western Europe's ability to cope with internal revolt as well as to sustain a psychological mood of anti-Soviet tension that the Administration thought functional. . . . [The] real Communist danger in Western Europe was internal.[4]

The differences between the received version of postwar foreign policy and Kolko's analysis are striking indeed. But if American policy can be perceived so differently what could similar critical questioning tell us about Canadian foreign policy in the same period? The range of public and private papers to which Kolko has access unfortunately is simply not available in Canada — if it even exists — but some of the questions that he and the revisionists ask of the United States might be usefully asked of Canada. How did calculations of global influence vs. idealism affect Canadian decision-makers? Did they manipulate Canadian public opinion to serve their own interests? Did they employ anti-Communism as a tool for this end? How did economic considerations figure in this process?

The accepted version of Canadian foreign policy after 1945 goes something like this: Despite the obstructions thrown up by the near-senile Mackenzie King, Canadian policy makers soon realized that the United Nations was not going to function as the collective security guarantor of world peace. The cause of the collapse of wartime hopes clearly lay in Soviet policy, and as early as summer, 1947 Canadian diplomats began calling for a western alliance. Planning was spurred by the rape of Czechoslovakia in February 1948 and in 1949 NATO was formed, in large part a tribute to the skill of Canadian diplomacy. When war broke out in Korea in June 1950 Canada participated loyally despite some misgivings over American tactics, and in the new situation caused by the war and its revelations about the Soviet willingness to use force the government despatched substantial numbers of troops to Europe. In addition to military measures, Canada contributed heavily to the recovery of Western Europe with mutual aid and with loans. All in all, the authorized version goes, Canadian policy is at one with virtue. The old isolationism was dead. The new era of involvement was begun. A revisionist critique might portray Canadian policy makers as actors in a charade, a charade in which the players themselves were often deceived. Not only were American leaders like President Truman and Secretary of State Acheson exaggerating the Communist threat to Congress, but to Canada, too. That such deception could be practised so easily and so successfully should not be completely surprising given the Canadian dependence on American intelligence sources, given the omnipresence of American news sources and wire services, and given the shared value system of Canada and the United States. The fear of Communism seemed as real to some Canadians as it did to many Americans, perhaps after the revelations of the Gouzenko spy trials even more so.

The rumblings from Britain (with its ever so slightly suspect Labour government) seemed confirmatory of much of the American information, and Britain was in no condition to serve as a makeweight to American policy and presence even if Canadians had wanted such a thing. Confronted with a strong United States, a United States that bargained aggressively for trade concessions, and a United States on which our economic future seemed to be dependent, our policy-makers accepted the information and perceptions — deceptions, too, Kolko would add — that prevailed in Washington. It all squared with Canadian opportunities and needs so well.

For clearly, if Canada did its part, Canada would get a share in decision-making. This was the argument advanced by the nationalist-imperialists at the turn of the century; it was similarly the expectation of men like Louis St. Laurent and Lester Pearson after 1945. If we did our part loyally, then we would be listened to at the heart of the new Empire. First responsibility, then influence. And such influence might be of extraordinary value in benefitting Canada economically — or at least in ensuring that American actions would not hurt us. Such at least was the rationale.

There were other pressures that tended toward acceptance of the American view. In the prewar era when the policies of Mackenzie King held sway, there was scant scope for a man of ambition and talent in the area of foreign policy. King himself, O.D. Skelton, Loring Christie, and one or two others held such power as there was and most of the remaining members of the Department of External Affairs were functionaries, political appointees, or too junior to exercise much influence. The war and its quantum jump in Canadian power had seemingly altered all that, and the department attracted some of the ablest men in Canada. If Canada retreated to prewar somnolence once again, these people would either leave External or wither. It is no slur whatsoever to say that men such as Pearson, Norman Robertson, Hume Wrong, and indeed Louis St. Laurent himself wanted Canada to play a role that fitted their talents. The largest possible role in the world for Canada meant the largest possible role for them, a role that they believed themselves completely capable of carrying out. It was, of course, quite honourable and proper for these men to feel this way, especially since a larger Canadian role was what they believed fitting and proper. Their needs and desires squared precisely with their perception of Canada's. The problem was that the only game in town was run by Washington. Neutrality seemed unthinkable and unworkable. The Empire-Commonwealth was weak and Britain was financially if not yet spiritually bankrupt. The aims and needs of Washington, therefore, were those of the strong, and it seemed to be the best of sense to be attached to them.

Equally, too, the policy of involvement was an explicit rejection of the past policies of delay, evasion, quasi-neutrality and "Parliament will decide." To press vigorously for a policy, almost for any policy, was a positive good simply because it was so different from what had prevailed in the past. The era of Mackenzie King was an embarrassment that had to be lived down, and the way to do this was to take positions. Of course, King was still present, at least to 1948. But he was old and terribly tired, worn down by the strain of the war and terribly dependent on his already chosen successor, Louis St. Laurent. And when King made the Quebec lawyer his Secretary of State for External Affairs in 1946 the die was cast. King's hesitations, his fears of the Americans, his querulousness about the world-wide ambitions of External Affairs, all could be overridden now. And they were.

What is striking is the extent to which King did fear the Americans. For a man who all his life had been accused by his opponents of continentalist predispositions, King was surprisingly firm in his beliefs. It was not that he was anti-American. Some of his best friends, after all, were Americans. It was simply that he was convinced the United States had designs on Canada, that it would seek enormous influence in Canada even if only because it feared the prospect of an eventual attack over the Pole. It was simply that he was a genuine Canadian nationalist in the Laurier mould. It was simply that he believed the best policy was for Canada to be left alone and to leave alone. Involvement meant trouble, and trouble meant strain on the fabric of national unity. King's policy was consistent — he had argued exactly the same when the British were the world leaders — and it was not necessarily wrong.

To St. Laurent and his supporters, King's obsession with national unity was not misplaced. It was, after all, vital in this divided country, and no politician who had survived the war years could question its necessity. But to these new policy makers the problem was capable of more than one solution. It could be handled, for example, by finding an external policy that unified the country. As a philosophy, Communism was as hated in Quebec as in English Canada. The church had condemned it repeatedly and the Soviet repression of Catholicism in Eastern Europe had not been calculated to win approval in the province of Quebec. The government, clearly interested in whipping up sentiment against the Soviet Union, did its best to help the process of opinion formation along. In a speech to a Richelieu Club meeting shortly after he had become Prime Minister, for example, Mr. St. Laurent had turned to a bishop at the head table and said pointedly, "Your excellency, we would not like to see you stand the type of trial which Cardinal Mindszenty had to undergo." Such arguments must have been persuasive because, although there were grumbles from the traditional isolationists, there was no major outburst in Quebec against the Canadian commitments to NATO or Korea. Nor was there any serious objection from English Canadians, and even the CCF supported government policy after the Czech coup persuaded most socialist critics of American capitalism that the Soviets were infinitely worse. The new policy *was* the policy of national unity, and as Brooke Claxton, the Minister of National Defence, remarked to a friend in a slightly-different context, "With this Prime Minister . . . we can do anything." It seemed so.

The reasons discussed thus far were important, of course, in shaping Canadian responses to the postwar world and they seem very much like those Kolko attributes to American policy and opinion makers. But this is not all. The economic reasons that Kolko presents as the genuine American motives for supporting Western European recovery and NATO also have their Canadian parallels.

In the first place Canadian trade before the war and during it had been extraordinarily dependent on the British market. Our agricultural products in particular desperately needed British sales, and if this market should be lost or should the British be so insolvent as to not be able to pay for orders, the effect on Canada would be calamitous. The answer seemed to be a loan to Britain that could be used to finance British purchases in Canada, and $1.25 billion was advanced for this purpose in 1946. This was a staggering sum of money, equal to more than twice the whole federal budget in 1939 and fully one-third of the sum eventually loaned by the United States in 1947. In addition, almost $500 million more was loaned to our other European trading partners.

Canada then had — and recognized this — an enormous stake in maintaining Europe as a free market for its goods. Our trade was tiny with Eastern Europe and very extensive with the North Atlantic states, and our self interest was clear. Canadian motives for supporting Western European recovery were as fully founded on economic motives as were those of the United States. And if the Americans were prepared to negotiate toughly with their desperate friends, so too were we. In December, 1947, for example, the British tried to back out of some foodstuff contracts with Canada and were sharply rebuffed by Mackenzie King and the Canadian negotiators. There was no gratitude among nations, King harrumphed in his diary, and if the British went back on their contracts "we will have to cancel all and let our farmers and others sell wherever they wish, to whatever countries they wish."

Unfortunately Canada was soon to find itself in much the same position vis-à-vis the United States. The government decision to put the Canadian dollar at par with the U.S. dollar had reduced American capital inflows at a time when imports were rising and loans to Europe were increasing. The resulting dollar exchange crisis necessitated a series of temporary measures to cut imports, reduce tourist spending, and to right the balance. Ironically, on the same day that the restrictions were announced Canada signed the General Agreement on Tariffs and Trade. GATT, among other things, reduced Canadian tariffs on 70 percent of American imports and similarly lowered U.S. barriers to Canadian products. The effect was to spur resource industries in Canada and to weaken manufacturing. GATT also struck a heavy blow at Commonwealth preferences. The short term measures against American imports then were far exceeded in importance by the long term.

In this situation, the Americans could afford to be generous when the Canadians tried to win some benefits under the Marshall Plan. It was not aid we were after, but the right to have Marshall Plan dollars spent by Europeans for Canadian goods. By April 1949, fully $706 million had been spent in Canada, a large enough sum to go some distance to rectifying the exchange problem. Soon the barriers to American imports would be down, soon American capital would be flowing north once more, soon the Korean War would spur the rearmament of the West and prosperity would return.

Simply put, the questions Kolko and the revisionists direct to American aims can be usefully asked to Canada. Our policy to Europe seems to have been motivated by self-interest. Our politicians seem to have mobilized the fear of Russia to win support for their economic-based policies. Our leaders accepted the American view. But what must also be said is that the Americans clearly pursued a policy of self-interest in their relations with Canada, too. Concessions were offered, but concessions were demanded in return. Now, however, we can better see the implications of these few crucial years. We could win special treatment from Washington, but some day the price would have to be paid. And paid. And paid again.

Notes

1. Gabriel Kolko and Joyce Kolko, *The Limits of Power: The World and United States Foreign Policy, 1945–1954* (New York: Harper and Row, 1972), 7.
2. Ibid., 5.
3. Ibid., 479.
4. Ibid., 498–9.

THE DIPLOMACY OF
CONSTRAINT†

DENIS STAIRS

Canadian security policies are prone to quick births and slow deaths. Born in times of urgent peril and crisis, when there are premiums on haste, they die in periods of tranquility, the victims of indifference, neglect and the infirmities of old age. In their middle years, they are sustained as much by inertia as by purpose — creatures partly of genuine perceptions of external menace, but partly too of static habits of decision-making and unchallenged habits of mind.

The most recent crisis to generate spurts of major innovation in Canada's external affairs was not, as some are wont to suppose, the coming to power of Pierre Elliott Trudeau as Prime Minister in 1968, or even the appointment in 1963 of Paul Hellyer as Minister of National Defence. Nor was it the Cuban missile crisis of 1962; nor any of the peacekeeping episodes of the late 1950s and early 1960s. It was instead the outbreak of the Korean War, which in Ottawa and other capitals in the West served to confirm and entrench, where it did not actually create, alarming perceptions of the Soviet Union and its "satellites" as aggressively hostile powers, ominous and threatening, not only politically but militarily as well. The members of the North Atlantic pact, hitherto an alliance in support more of morale than of military capabilities, looked accordingly to the expansion of their armies, and Canada's was among them.

† Denis Stairs, "Canada and the Korean War: The Boundaries of Diplomacy," *International Perspectives* (Nov.–Dec. 1972), 25–32.

In the winter of 1950–51, the Federal Government embarked upon a program of military expenditures that was to cost five billion dollars over three years. On its completion, the Canadian defence establishment had assumed dimensions that it was to maintain without major change for nearly two decades. This, taken together with the range and intensity of the policy community's rapidly-expanding linkages with other members of the alliance (notably the United States) and the strength and persistence of its perceptions of hostile Soviet intent, set parameters to the conduct of Canada's external relations which have begun only recently to display the symptoms of senility, weakening and giving way under the pressure of changing conditions abroad.

Of these latter transformations, the current advances in negotiations between the governments of North and South Korea are both a symbol and a part. But they are a reminder, too, of the only occasion since 1945 on which Canadian armed forces have been dispatched abroad for the explicit purpose of combat. Canada's role in the diplomacy of the Korean War may thus warrant brief review.

In the spring of 1950, the Korean peninsula was divided into two parts along the 38th Parallel, a politically convenient but economically and topographically meaningless boundary that had been established as the demarcation line between the American and Soviet zones of occupation at the end of the war with Japan. The failure of the occupation authorities to agree on procedures for the creation of a unified and independent Korean state, and the differences in their respective policies of occupation, had resulted (as in Germany) in a hardening of the division between the two sectors.

In the autumn of 1947 the Americans, as a last resort, had raised the matter in the United Nations General Assembly, and at their request, a Temporary Commission on Korea had been charged with the task of supervising an election throughout the peninsula as a prelude to unification and independence. The Commission, of which Canada was a member, was denied effective access to the Soviet zone and, much to the disgust of Prime Minister Mackenzie King (whose opposition to Canada's involvement in the Commission's proceedings had generated for a time a major crisis within the Canadian Cabinet), it had ultimately decided to accede to an American proposal that it proceed with elections in the South alone. There duly emerged an administration under the leadership of Dr. Syngman Rhee, and it was followed in August 1948 by the transfer of governmental functions from the American occupation authorities to what was now described as the "Republic of Korea." Shortly thereafter the Soviets had administered elections of their own, constructing in the area north of the 38th Parallel a "People's Democratic Republic." In December the United Nations General Assembly passed a resolution declaring:

that there has been established a lawful government (the Government of the Republic of Korea), having effective control and jurisdiction over that part of Korea where the Temporary Commission was able to observe and consult and in which the great majority of the people of all Korea reside; that this Government is based on elections which were a valid expression of the free will of the electorate of that part of Korea and which were observed by the Temporary Commission; and that this is the only such Government in Korea.

The resolution also created a new United Nations Commission on Korea, of which Canada was not this time a member. It was directed to continue the work of its predecessor by observing the withdrawal of occupation forces and by generally facilitating the process of political transition and eventual (it was hoped) unification.

During the ensuing months, relations between the two Korean regimes, supported by their respective great-power patrons, were hostile and uneasy, with indications on both sides of acquisitive intent. In the first half of 1950, military and para-military skirmishes of ambiguous origin erupted along the border areas with such frequency that when John W. Holmes, the Acting Permanent Representative of Canada to the United Nations, first heard of the North Korean invasion June 25, he assumed that nothing unusual was afoot.

Revisionist historians now dispute the claims of American policy-makers to innocence in the events leading up to the North Korean attack, assigning them at least partial responsibility for the developing conditions of conflict. In some of the more extreme versions they are accused of connivance and conspiracy too. Of these two classes of argument, the first is far more convincing than the second, but in either event they have little bearing on the Canadian case. For whatever one believes of Washington, there can be little doubt that in Ottawa the outbreak of major hostilities in Korea came as a complete surprise.

So did the American response. Policy-makers in Washington had been making it clear for some time that they considered the Korean (and Formosan) theatres to be outside their strategic defence perimeter in the Pacific and, as recently as February 1950, General Douglas MacArthur had advised the Canadian Secretary of State for External Affairs during a visit to Tokyo that Korea was strategically unimportant to the United States, and therefore did not fall within the American protective umbrella. In consequence, External Affairs Minister Lester Pearson assumed that the U.S. Government would respond with little more than verbal protests, a view which was shared by John Holmes in New York and by Hume Wrong, the Canadian Ambassador in Washington.

In the absence from the Security Council of the Soviet Union (which since January had been boycotting the proceedings on the matter of Chinese representation), the United States secured the passage of a resolution on the afternoon of Sunday June 25, calling for an immediate cessation of hostilities and the withdrawal of North Korean forces. The resolution also requested reports on developments in the theatre from the United Nations Commission on Korea, and asked "all members to render every assistance to the United Nations in the execution of this resolution and to refrain from giving assistance to the North Korean authorities." This initiative received Mr. Pearson's support in the House of Commons on June 26, when he expressed the hope "that as a result of the intervention of the United Nations some effective action may be possible to restore peace." But in an off-the-record press conference some hours later, he told reporters that he did not anticipate that military measures would be taken by either the Americans alone or the United Nations as a whole.

As early as Sunday evening, however, President Truman had authorized General MacArthur to evacuate American nationals from Korea, under the protection south of the Parallel, if necessary, of the United States Air Force. He was authorized also to offer logistical support to the South Korean forces, and to assume operational command of the Seventh Fleet. Late the following day he was ordered in addition to give combat air and naval support to the South Koreans in Republic of Korea territory, and to dispatch the Seventh Fleet to patrol the Formosa Strait. These measures were to be made legitimate in the name of the United Nations, from which an authorizing resolution would be pursued at a meeting of the Security Council scheduled for Tuesday afternoon.

Throughout the early phase of the war, the principal concern of the Canadian authorities was that the American response (upon which depended the postures of all the other Western allies, Canada included) be conducted under United Nations auspices. This was partly because it was felt that the strength of the organization as an agent for the maintenance of collective security depended on its being used, or at least on its being *seen* to be used, as the primary vehicle for countering aggression. If actions in constraint of "aggressor" powers were taken unilaterally, such promise as the United Nations still held out for international methods of security enforcement would be lost. More immediately, however, it was also because the Canadians realized that, if the Americans acted unilaterally, there would be little opportunity for constraining their behaviour, whereas if they responded through the United Nations, their policies would be exposed (within limits) to inhibiting multilateral influences, of which Canada's was one.

This was regarded as particularly important in the Korean context because it was possible, in the absence of such constraints, that the Americans, by a mixture of distorted perceptions of self-interest and inflexibly ideological conceptions of their opponents, would be drawn into a major Asian war, thereby involving the Soviet Union and/or the Communist Chinese. This would be a disaster in itself. In addition, it would mean that American attentions and resources would be diverted away from Western Europe, which in the Canadian view — as in that of the other Western allies — was a far more vital theatre.

When, on Tuesday morning, Mr. Pearson was informed by the U.S. Ambassador of the President's decisions, therefore, he telephoned Hume Wrong in Washington to stress the importance of urging the Americans to bring their action under United Nations auspices, and to withhold public announcements of their initiative until the Security Council's authorization had actually been obtained. When Mr. Wrong raised the matter at a late morning meeting of State Department officials with the Washington ambassadors of the NATO powers, however, he was advised that the American view was that the June 25 resolution had provided them with all the authority required. On the apparent assumption that the Soviet Union would continue to boycott the Security Council, they believed in any case that the matter of timing was not serious since their informal discussions with other Council members had revealed that their proposal for a more explicit resolution would pass that afternoon without great difficulty — as indeed it did. In it, the Council recommended "that the members of the United Nations furnish such assistance to the Republic of Korea as may be necessary to repel the armed attack and to restore international peace and security in the area concerned." Later in the week, on June 30, President Truman ordered General MacArthur to impose a naval blockade on the Korean coast and to make full use of the ground forces under his command in responding to the North Korean assault.

Had the Americans decided to intervene against the North Koreans entirely without the blessing of the United Nations (as the State Department's George Kennan would have liked them to do), Canadians would have had as little to do with the war in Korea as they had subsequently had to do with the war in Vietnam — perhaps less, given that Canada was not a member of the U.N. Commission on Korea whereas it was, and is, a member of the International Control Commission. With the passage of the resolutions of June 25 and 27, however, the Canadian Government acquired on the one hand a battery of pressures, from constituents at home and abroad alike, to contribute to the conduct of the hostilities themselves (an outcome of which the Americans heartily approved), and on the other a licence to intervene in the making of decisions (a consequence with which the Americans were naturally displeased).

To the extent that payment of dues buys access to the club, the second of these acquisitions was contingent on the first and, like buyers in every market, the Canadians sought to maximize their marginal utilities. Their military expenditures came, therefore, in dribs and drabs, constrained in part by the poverty of their resources (early in

July the Director of Military Operations and Plans was to advise the Minister of National Defence that, if all the units of the Active Force Brigade Group were brought up to strength and allowed to concentrate on training, they would be reasonably efficient after a period of six months), in part by the fear — soon dispelled — that such dabblings in overseas wars would not go down well in Quebec, in part by a reluctance to divert Canada's meagre defences away from the North Atlantic area, and in part by the simple sluggishness of the mechanics of collective military effort.

The first instalment, as it happened, came easily. Three Canadian destroyers sailed for the Western Pacific on July 5 and were ultimately assigned to General MacArthur's Unified Command on July 12. But in Korea, armies, not navies, were in the greatest jeopardy and hence in greatest need. On July 14, therefore, U.N. Secretary-General Trygve Lie dispatched a message to fifty-three member governments asking them to examine their "capacity to provide an increased volume of combat forces, particularly ground forces," and his multilateral plea was supported by American bilateral pressure. On July 19 the Canadian cabinet accordingly deliberated again. And again it settled on equipment, not men.

A squadron of RCAF long-range transport aircraft was assigned to service in the Pacific airlift (its efforts were later augmented by civilian flights chartered from Canadian Pacific Airlines). But of ground forces there were none. Not until August 7, under steadily-increasing pressure at home and abroad, did the Government finally announce its intention of recruiting a brigade-size Special Force of volunteers "for use in carrying out Canada's obligations under the United Nations Charter or the North Atlantic Pact." The full deployment of the brigade in the Korean theatre was even then not finally determined until late in February 1951.

But, if the Canadians paid their dues with reluctance, they exercised their privileges with enthusiasm. Their principal concern throughout the diplomacy of the war was to constrain and to modify American behaviour (since they could not hope themselves to modify the behaviour of America's opponents) with a view ultimately to containing the scope and duration of the hostilities. Their principal dilemma was to find a way of doing so without alienating the Americans entirely from their practice of acting in concert with their allies in the United Nations. For Mr. Pearson in particular, therefore, the exercise of diplomatic judgment involved not merely decisions with regard to the timing and tactics of diplomatic manoeuvre but also calculations with respect to the limits of American patience.

On what issues did the maintenance of allied pressure on Washington offer some possibility of success? On what issues did it not? And precisely when in particular cases was it "better" to give in to American resistance and fight again another day than to persist in one's opposition? Such preoccupations reflect a utilitarian morality upon which it is possible for good men to differ, but their importance for the conduct of Canada's diplomacy in the Korean War was so central as to warrant illustration.

The pattern of Canadian behaviour became very evident, for example, in the first few days after the passage of the resolutions of June 25 and 27, when State Department officials turned their attention to drafting yet a third Security Council proposal — this one authorizing the United States to establish a United Nations Command. Hume Wrong was deluged with instructions from Ottawa.

To emphasize the "United Nations" character of the commitment in Korea, he was to recommend to the Americans that they reduce in their draft the number of references to the "United States." To diminish the possibility of U.N. forces becoming involved in issues other than the purely Korean, he was to suggest that they improve upon the precision of such casual phrases as "in the area," which were used in their resolution to define the scope of U.N. objectives. To secure the explicit exclusion of Formosa from the sphere of U.N. Command operations, he was to propose that they include in the draft a geographically-defined boundary around Korea within which General MacArthur would be acting on U.N. authority, and beyond which he would not.

On receiving the last of these directives, Mr. Wrong gave vent to his exasperation. In a reply which accorded well with the opinion of Mr. Holmes in New York, he advised Ottawa that so complex an amendment might seriously delay the progress of proceedings at the United Nations. The Americans, in any case, had made it clear that their "neutralization" of Formosa was an ingredient of their own policy, which was quite independent of the U.N. They would not react favourably to a suggestion that implied scepticism about the reliability of their guarantees, and which was redundant besides. There was, moreover, a limit to the number of "treks" he could undertake with dignity to an already harassed Department of State.

In consequence of Mr. Wrong's complaints, this particular "trek" appears not to have been taken at all, while the ones that were proved ultimately to have been in vain. But the episode nonetheless exemplifies not only the substance of the Government's intent but also the tactical calculations to which the pursuit of its intent was constantly subject.

To provide another example, if late June and early July, when Canada had still to announce a significant contribution to the conduct of the war, was an inappropriate time to influence the course of American policy, then an appropriate time was when the Government was in the process of paying its dues. Hence, when Mr. Pearson flew on July 29 to Washington to inform the Americans of plans then being developed for the recruitment of a Canadian Army Special Force and to discuss the conditions under which it might be made available, he used the occasion to insist on two requirements. The first was that the troops would not be ordered into combat before they had been trained to the satisfaction of their Canadian officers. The second was that under no circumstances would they be involved in the defence of Formosa. To these, the Americans readily agreed (although in connection with China their inability later to control effectively the public utterances of General MacArthur subsequently led, on more than one occasion, to additional Canadian protests).

Once MacArthur had reversed the fortunes of the war after his amphibious attack through Inchon in mid-September, there ensued a new series of policy questions which, until then, had not been explicitly considered. These related in particular to the definition of the U.N.'s general objectives in the theatre. The resolution of June 27, devised while the North Koreans were still hurtling down the peninsula, had made vague reference only to the need "to repel the armed attack and to restore international peace and security in the area." On the face of it, this suggested that the U.N.'s task would be completed once the security of South Korea had been re-established at the 38th Parallel. At the same time, however, the United Nations had been committed since the winter of 1947–48 to the ultimate objective of Korean unification, and it did not officially recognize the government in the North as a legally-constituted regime. Now that the North Korean army was in total disarray, therefore, the temptation to occupy the northern zone and settle the matter once and for all was difficult to resist. The danger was that an advance into North Korean territory would escalate the conflict beyond manageable proportions by inciting the intervention of the Communist Chinese.

General MacArthur had advised the American Army Chief of Staff, General J. Lawton Collins, as early as July 13 that his intention was to destroy the North Korean forces entirely, and not merely to drive them out of South Korea, and he was not long in persuading his colleagues to a similar view. On September 7 the American Joint Chiefs of Staff recommended that ground operations be carried "beyond the 38th Parallel as necessary" to ensure the destruction of the North Korean forces. President Truman, after discussions with his National Security Council, agreed on September 11 that MacArthur should be authorized to proceed into North Korean territory, subject to there being "no indication or threat of entry of Soviet or Chinese Communist elements in force." In the more detailed directives which the General received later in the month, he was instructed also to ensure that "no non-Korean ground forces" would be used in areas of North Korea bordering on Soviet or Chinese territory.

There remained the question of the involvement in these decisions, post hoc, of the United Nations. At first, the Americans argued that a formal resolution would not be necessary because the security council had already authorized the restoration of "international peace and security *in the area*," an ambiguity to which the Canadians had objected from the beginning, and to which they — among others — were not now disposed to fall victim. Fearful of a Soviet or Chinese intervention, they at first strongly opposed any crossing of the Parallel, and when after several days of informal discussions the Americans succeeded in having Britain and seven other countries sponsor a resolution recommending, among other things, that "all appropriate steps be taken to ensure conditions of stability throughout Korea," Mr. Pearson was urged by his senior staff not to support their initiative. Assured privately by the Americans, however, that the advance would not be allowed to proceed beyond the narrow waist of the Korean peninsula (roughly half-way between the 38th Parallel and the Manchurian border), and anxious to support the implementation of other features of the new resolution (which recommended procedures under United Nations auspices "for the establishment of a unified, independent and democratic government in the sovereign state of Korea"), Mr. Pearson ultimately decided to support it.

An informally-expressed Canadian suggestion that the passage of the resolution be postponed until there had been diplomatic contact with the North Korean regime was rejected by the American secretary of state, and Canadian plans for proposing modifications in the draft in order to win the support of the Indians had to be abandoned because of the swiftness of events. On October 7 the resolution carried by a vote of forty-seven (Canada reluctantly included) to five (Soviet bloc) with seven abstentions (India's among them). Within hours, American units in Korea had followed their earlier example of their South Korean counterparts and had crossed the 38th Parallel.

Their sojourn in North Korea was to be short-lived. By the end of the month, General MacArthur's headquarters were receiving sporadic reports of contacts with Chinese forces. On November 5 he filed a special report to the United Nations advising the members that his troops "in certain areas of Korea" were "meeting a new foe." Three days later President Truman authorized him to bomb bridges linking North Korea and Manchuria across the Yalu River.

Throughout the preceding weeks there had been repeated attempts by the British, French and Canadians at the United Nations and elsewhere to obtain explicit agreement from the Americans to establish an unoccupied "buffer zone" in Korea's northernmost provinces, but to no avail. General MacArthur was in any case unreceptive to such restrictions, and his superiors in Washington were not disposed to insist. When on November 14 the Truman administration requested allied approval of the "hot pursuit" of enemy aircraft into Manchurian air-space, it was discouraged by the vehemence of the response (Canadian opposition was conveyed to American officials within two hours of the arrival in Ottawa of their inquiry).

Now that there was evidence that the Chinese were already in the field, Hume Wrong was instructed yet again to press upon the state department the need to keep United Nations forces well away from the northern areas and to exercise the greatest possible degree of military restraint. In advising an audience in Windsor, Ontario, on November 15 of his view that "nothing should be done in the establishment of a united and free Korea which would carry the slightest menace to Korea's neighbours," Mr. Pearson suggested that it was still possible that the Chinese were engaged only in "a protective and border mission," and a case could therefore be made for the United Nations attempting to get in touch with them "to find out their intentions." But it was much too late. On November 26, the Chinese "volunteers" launched a major offensive, and by December 15 the United Nations Command had been driven in a chaotic 120-mile retreat down the peninsula to lines located once again in the general vicinity of the 38th Parallel.

In thus so rude a fashion were the allied powers compelled to abandon their plans for a Korea unified and "democratized" by force of United Nations arms. All they could hope for now was an eventual securing of the peace, if necessary on terms reflecting no more than the restoration of the status quo ante bellum. But here, too, the Americans and their colleagues in the United Nations were prone to quarrel. For, in the case of the United States, the intervention of the Chinese had made the war more, not less, difficult to resolve. This was partly in consequence of the political pressures to which it gave rise at home, but more because in the American perspective it escalated the international significance of the crisis as a "Communist" challenge which could not safely be ignored. For the allies and the "neutrals," on the other hand, it strengthened immeasurably the argument that every effort should be made to contain the hostilities and to treat the issues involved as if they were reflective of nothing more than a localized breach of the international peace. From this vantage-point is was essential to restore the limited character of the U.N.'s objectives in the theatre, and to persuade the Peking regime that the security of Chinese territory was not under threat.

There ensued a complex series of negotiations among the Americans and other members of the United Nations, focusing on the question of whether discussions might usefully be initiated with the Chinese. The essence of the American position was that no progress could be expected until the military fortunes of the U.N. Command had improved at the front, and that concessions ought not to be granted in any event under military pressure. The British view, shared in general if not in detail by the Canadians among others, was that an intensification of United Nations military and other sanctions would harden, not soften, the Chinese position, and that Peking, therefore, ought to be approached instead in a spirit of accommodation. Certainly there could be little harm in making the attempt. If a cease-fire could be arranged, a conference in pursuit of a political settlement might shortly follow (the British, in fact, were prepared to make a number of the political concessions in advance, but the Americans would have none of this and the Canadians thought it futile to press them).

Confronted by these insistent demands, and convinced in any case that the Chinese would not agree to a cease-fire without advance political concessions, the Americans finally gave their blessing to an attempt "to seek an end to the hostilities by means of negotiation." They made it clear, however, that in the event the negotiations failed, a resolution labelling the Chinese as aggressors would be brought before the General Assembly for its approval.

The immediate result was the passage of a resolution in the General Assembly authorizing the creation of a Cease-fire Group to initiate discussions with the Communist Chinese. Its members included Nasrollah Entezam of Iran, Sir Benegal Rau of India and Mr. Pearson.

The history of the group's activities need not be recorded in detail here. Suffice it to say that the American requirement that a cease-fire precede, rather than follow, negotiations on the unification of Korea, the recognition of the Peking regime, and other political issues appeared to be unacceptable to the Chinese. At the same time, however, Peking's communications in response to the Cease-fire Group's inquiries were sufficiently ambiguous to lead a number of U.N. powers — notably Britain, Canada, France and several of the Arab and Asian states — to conclude that there was still room for manoeuvre.

In consequence, when the Americans ultimately introduced on January 20 a resolution in the General Assembly declaring that the Chinese People's Republic had "itself engaged in aggression in Korea," they encountered stiff resistance. In the meantime, the Canadians and the British had gone independently in search of a clarification of the Chinese position. A series of questions conveyed to Peking by Prime Minister Louis St. Laurent through New Delhi produced a reply which suggested that the mainland government might be prepared to consider at least a short-term, conditional cease-fire pending negotiation of some of the more immediately important political issues. Thus encouraged, the Asian powers, under the leadership of India, introduced an Assembly resolution calling for a forty-eight-hour adjournment of the Korean proceedings in order to permit further study. To the fury of the Americans, whose condemning resolution had been ready to come to a vote when the Chinese reply to Mr. St. Laurent's private inquiries arrived in New York, the Indian proposal was adopted. The American delegation subsequently complained with some bitterness that the Canadians had been negotiating with Peking behind their backs. Such was their resentment that Mr. Pearson was to recall the episode in later years as one of the most serious in the history of Canadian-American relations.

But, in the end, the Americans were to have their way. Peppered throughout the ensuing week by the pleas and propositions of diplomats representing the full spectrum of neutral and allied United Nations powers, they would agree only to minor modifications of the wording in their own draft. They were paying the piper, and they were calling the tune.

Since "the methods of peaceful negotiation" had not yet been "completely exhausted," Mr. Pearson confessed that he thought the measure "premature and unwise." But like the British, the French, and other sceptics in the Western camp, he ultimately voted in its favour. The demands of "allied unity," and the need to avoid alienating the United States entirely from the machinery of U.N. decision-making, were factors that he considered too important to ignore. In the utilitarian calculus of foreign policy, the strategy of constraining the Americans had passed, for Canada if not for India, beyond the point of productive return.

With the Chinese thus diplomatically condemned, the contest was left for a time with the military, and it was not until 10 July 1951, that armistice negotiations finally began. They endured for more than two years, and in them the United Nations played only a sporadic part. Even here, however, the pattern was the same, with the United States again the object of concerted diplomatic manoeuvres in which the Canadians assumed a prominent role. In the autumn of 1952, for example, the American authorities were compelled to accept a General Assembly resolution incorporating proposals for the repatriation of prisoners-of-war of which they did not entirely approve. Advanced initially by the Indians, it had been moulded only in part to American taste by the attentions of the Canadians, British and French, and it left Dean Acheson with so prolonged a sense of irritation that years later he was to write of Lester Pearson and India's Krishna Menon as "adroit operators" against whose proposals it had been necessary to maintain a constant guard.

Although little was achieved by the resolution at the time of its initial passage — it did not then appeal to the Chinese — it was later mobilized again in constraint of United States behaviour at the climax of the armistice negotiations in May and June of 1953, and the Americans were compelled once more to accede to its provisions. Within a month the war in Korea was over. The lines of demarcation had shifted a little, but the peninsula was as divided at the end as it was at the beginning.

Perhaps the most central feature of Canada's diplomacy throughout was the fact that its targets were friends rather than enemies. For the United States, the most important actors in the conflict were the North Koreans, the Chinese, and potentially, at least, the Soviet Union. The allied and neutral powers that were so active in the United Nations were relevant, too, but more as restive constituents than as primary targets of policy. They complicated America's diplomatic life;

they did not determine its central direction.

For the Canadians, on the other hand, these conditions were reversed. Since the "enemy" powers were clearly beyond the reach of Canadian influence, they could not be made the immediate object of Canadian policy. In the final analysis, their behaviour could be directly affected only by the United States. Hence, if the Canadians wished to modify the dynamics of East-West relations, they had little choice but to concentrate on the behaviour of the Americans, amplifying Canada's influence wherever possible by acting in concert with the governments of other powers. For the pursuit of such strategies, the United Nations was a convenient instrument.

THE DIPLOMACY OF COMPLICITY†

VICTOR LEVANT

It has now been more than a decade since forces loyal to the Provisional Revolutionary Government of South Vietnam entered Saigon and drove out the United States-backed regime of Nguyen Van Thieu. Vietnam has been reunified and the U.S. war in Indochina has come to an end. During the war, hundreds of thousands of Canadians marched, sat in, attended teach-ins, wrote their Members of Parliament, signed petitions, shouted obscenities, sang, spray painted walls, walked for peace, worked on draft resister support committees, harboured U.S. army deserters in their homes, prayed, fasted, and wept over the senseless slaughter of the Vietnamese civilian population. The reality of the Socialist Republic of Vietnam — allied to Moscow and with 170 000 troops stationed in neighbouring Cambodia — has, however, driven many former anti-war demonstrators into the closet, making them doubt the validity of their original perceptions and the value of their protest actions. The tragic spectacle of the Vietnamese boat people fleeing ethnic discrimination, financial ruin, and military conscription has silenced all criticism and swept our memories blank.

The amnesia which prevails about the war in Vietnam is unfortunate. Reprehensible as the actions of socialist Vietnam may be, they do not justify a retrospective rationalization of western actions between 1945 and 1975. In the United States, where the war in Vietnam provoked a national crisis of conscience, the significance of the war and the reasons

† Victor Levant, *Quiet Complicity: Canadian Involvement in the Vietnam War* (Toronto: Between the Lines, 1986), 1–6.

for the U.S. defeat remain a subject for debate. In Canada, by contrast, the war in Vietnam is treated at best as a matter of abstract historical interest. Yet Canada was deeply involved in the Indochinese conflict, and public outrage against Ottawa for its involvement was growing by the war's end; a comprehensive study of Canada's involvement in the Vietnam War is long overdue.

. . . Newly available evidence damages the image promoted of Canada as an impartial and objective peace-keeper, an innocent and, if possible, helpful bystander administering humanitarian aid to the victims of the Vietnam War. The same evidence fails to support a view of Canada as a colonial hinterland administered by a government subservient to Washington.

The picture that now emerges shows Canada to have been a willing ally in U.S. counter-insurgency efforts, sharing the same assumptions about the nature of the insurgency, the strategic geo-political importance of Indochina, and the value of trade and investment in Southeast Asia to the world market system. Canada geared its peace-keeping duties to the interests of the West, and its record on the international commissions to which it was appointed was characterized by partisan voting, willful distortion of fact, and complicity in U.S. violations of both the Geneva and Paris agreements. Canadian economic and social assistance to Vietnam was equally partisan, with bilateral aid being extended only to South Vietnam between 1953 and 1974. With the escalation of the war effort by the United States, Canadian aid became an integral part of Washington's policy of pacification.

Such behaviour is consistent with a government running a country integrated into the international free market system and ruled by an internal corporate elite that is international in scope, allied yet subordinate to the U.S. industrial and financial oligarchy. Far from being a hinterland economy run by U.S. branch-plant managers, Canada was an advanced industrial society during the period under study (1954 to 1975), with a highly concentrated economy ruled by a local elite based in banking, insurance, transportation, communications, and utilities that operated multinational corporations, exported capital overseas, and vied for its share of world trade and investment. On the other hand, there was also an inordinately high degree of product concentration in Canada's trade and few major trading partners, as well as massive foreign ownership of the resource and manufacturing sectors, with the usual resulting traits of massive capital outflows, a chronic deficit, and foreign monopolies over patents and licences.

Nominally a sovereign, liberal-democratic country, Canada was also subject to the exigencies of international and especially U.S. finance. The Canada-United States relationship was an unequal one. Canada-U.S. trade accounted for 70 percent of Canada's commerce and 20 to 25 percent of its gross national product, compared with 20 percent of

U.S. trade and 2 percent of the U.S. GNP. U.S. investment controlled 26 percent of all non-financial institutions in Canada. Canada's monetary and fiscal policies were tied to the U.S. Treasury, its exports were subject to the purview of the U.S. Department of Justice, its balance of payments was vulnerable to any movement of capital, and its manufacturing sector (especially the automotive and defence industries) was subject to U.S. Congressional re-examination. Within this context, Canada bore traits of both development and underdevelopment, dominance and dependence. Through the ideological link between the economic interests of the ruling indigenous elite and the governments in Ottawa that represented it, the reality of Ottawa's position was reflected in the principles that underlay its foreign policy pronouncements. These included:

- fear of communism;
- defence of the "free world" under U.S. leadership;
- acceptance of a junior partnership position in recognition of middle power status;
- a peace-keeping role in international affairs; and,
- "quiet diplomacy" in its approach to bilateral relations with the United States.

Canada's sensitivity to the stability of the world market system in general and its vulnerability to the United States in particular determined the boundaries for decision-makers in Ottawa. Definitions of national identity and interests and the parameters within which policy alternatives were considered were affected by these factors. A web of interdependence and repercussion formed the context within which reactions were anticipated, consequences determined, the accrued diplomatic credit calculated. As former Canadian diplomat John Holmes wrote:

> It is the restraints Canadians place upon themselves out of possible American attitudes which are the determining factor. These restraints are by no means inspired only by fear or the hope of favor. For the most part they are a natural consequence of the alliance diplomacy in which Canada has freely participated and the conviction that the maintenance of the strength and prestige of the United States is in the interest of the alliance in general and Canada in particular.[1]

Although Ottawa proclaimed that Canada had "no national interest in that part of the world," the documents reveal a definite Canadian stake in Southeast Asia at that time. Canadian trade and investment in

South Vietnam itself may have been insignificant, but Canada depended on Southeast Asia for crucial supplies of tin, rubber, chrome, jute, and coconut and palm oils. Canadian-Asian trade accounted for 10 percent of all Canada's trade, and Asia was also an important source of merchandise surplus and promising investments. Of particular value was Canadian trade with Japan, which in turn depended on Southeast Asia for 30 percent of its own commerce. Canada's third-largest trading partner after 1966, Japan was responsible for 81 percent of all Canadian-Asian trade and 84 percent of its merchandise surplus. Finally, the region was of strategic importance to Canada's primary economic partner and political ally, the United States, providing it with a series of air and naval bases, one-fifth of its trade, the highest rate of return on direct investment of any region in the world, and critical supplies of certain strategic materials. With export trade constituting 20 percent of Canada's GNP, the Canadian economy demanded the continued stability and expansion of the world market system.

The coincidence of interest between the Canadian and U.S. elites went beyond their common preference for the continued division of Vietnam. Canada also had a direct economic stake in the United States' prosecution of the war, which provided a catalyst for Canadian industrial expansion. As the war escalated, Canadian exports of copper, nickel, aluminum, zinc, lead, and oil fuelled the U.S. military-industrial complex; Canadian food, beverages, and clothing supplied U.S. troops; and Canadian-manufactured automotive parts were employed in U.S. trucks and tanks. As a result, Canada's balance of payments improved, unemployment fell, and the GNP increased dramatically. Of particular note was Canada's sale of $2.5 billion in war material to the Pentagon between 1965 and 1973. These sales were largely solicited by Ottawa through the Canadian Commercial Corporation and they provided 140 000 jobs, technological spin-offs for the civilian economy, and spill-overs aiding the establishment of a global arms industry.

Despite Ottawa's affirmations of "humanitarian and refugee relief" and "economic and social aid," Canadian aid was an integral part of U.S. counter-insurgency efforts aimed at maintaining South Vietnam within the western sphere of influence. Canada's aid program in South Vietnam under the Colombo Plan, its supply of French-speaking personnel, and its growing reputation in international peace-keeping made it an exceptionally valuable ally.

The effects of Canadian aid were multiple: they assuaged the barbarity of U.S. intervention while providing it with international legitimation, justified increased war appropriations in the U.S. Congress, and permitted the deployment of South Vietnamese funds directly into military expenditures. Contrary to Canada's pretensions of "nonmilitary assistance," Canadian medical aid was in fact administered by the Free World Military Assistance Program, sponsored by the Pentagon, co-ordinated by the U.S. State Department, and integrated into the Health-Defense Agreement of the Republic of Vietnam. Canadian participation in multilateral aid, whether through the Colombo Plan, the United Nations Development Program, the Mekong River Project or the Asian Development Bank, provided both the international legitimation requested by Washington and a way for the contributing countries to avoid the accusation of complicity in U.S. pacification programs.

Confidential documents reveal that the Canadian delegation on the International Control Commission (ICC) from 1954 to 1972, acting on Ottawa's instructions, willingly played a coordinated part in Washington's strategy of bolstering South Vietnam in defiance of the Geneva Accords. While Canada proclaimed impartiality and objectivity, it had a partisan voting record characterized by a presumption of Saigon's innocence and Hanoi's guilt. Canada committed itself to abide by the terms and intent of the Geneva Agreements, but its actionsshowed little respect for those agreements. Canadians serving on the ICC:

- acted as accessories in the U.S. Saigon Military Mission's "black psywar" in North Vietnam, fuelling the fires of the hysterical "Christ has gone south" campaign;
- exonerated Saigon from its obligations under the Geneva Agreements, especially its obligation to co-operate in holding an election to reunify the country in 1956;
- dragged their feet when Saigon violated provisions preventing reprisals against former members of the Viet Minh, and the illegal imprisonment of civilian detainees, but promptly condemned Hanoi for its violations concerning freedom of movement;
- obstructed controls of air- and seaports in South Vietnam;
- permitted the illegal existence of the U.S. Temporary Equipment Recovery Mission;
- aided and abetted the covert introduction of the arms and personnel of the U.S. Military Assistance Advisory Group;
- rationalized U.S. intervention for an international audience in the 1962 ICC special report;
- ran interference for the U.S. defoliant program in South Vietnam;
- transmitted U.S. threats to Hanoi;
- legitimated the U.S. air war over North Vietnam in their 1965 minority report;
- engaged in espionage for the U.S. Central Intelligence Agency and spotted for U.S. bombing missions over Hanoi and Haiphong.

Left-leaning nationalists in Canada consistently criticized Ottawa as a valet of Washington. However, the evidence does not suggest that an obsequious or fawning role was played by Canada within the ICC, nor does it suggest U.S. pressure or coercion. Canada was not appointed to serve on the commission by Washington, which preferred the old colonial power of Belgium. In fact, one of Canada's avowed goals was to mitigate rash and unilateral U.S. actions in the hope of preventing a split in NATO over the Indochina issue. When the possibility of an open breach of the Geneva Accords emerged, however, it was this same concern that led Canada to become an accomplice in covert violation of them. Top secret cables reveal that "quiet diplomacy" was less a method of raising criticisms without publicly embarrassing Washington than a means of deceiving both Canadian and international opinion about the extent of Ottawa's collusion. Ottawa's claims to impartiality and objectivity were not merely hypocritical; they were a shrewd tactic geared to mask Canadian complicity in the U.S. intervention strategy.

Canada's record on the International Commission for Control and Supervision (ICCS) in 1973 was an extension of its partisan activities on the earlier commission in spite of the Trudeau government's repeated promises of impartiality and objectivity. Assuming its role as a middle power, Canada assured President Nixon's "peace with honour" by providing an orderly retreat for the defeated U.S. armed forces. Canada fulfilled its protective function on the ICCS with creativity and ingenuity, and once again, its record was characterized by a partisan voting pattern, the distortion of fact, and anti-communist vituperation. Canada refused to condemn Saigon for preventing the establishment of the Joint Military Commissions as the Paris Peace Treaty required, condoned the continued existence of U.S. military bases, orchestrated a fraudulent missile crisis at Khe Sanh, fabricated reports on North Vietnamese infiltration of the south and on terrorist actions by the Provisional Revolutionary Government, refused to investigate the question of South Vietnamese political prisoners, and obstructed the very functioning of the ICCS through repeated adjournments. This policy was aimed at laying the blame for the breakdown of the Paris Agreement at Hanoi's door and at legitimizing massive U.S. assistance to the crumbling regime in Saigon.

Canada's support for U.S. counter-insurgency efforts in South Vietnam was a logical consequence of its position within the world market system, its dependence on the stability of that system for expanded trade and investment, the critical value of Southeast Asian resources, its fear of communist revolution, and its resulting concern for the prestige of the United States as the leader of the "free world." Canada's geo-political relationship to the United States and the structural integration of the Canadian and U.S. economies dictated the extent of Canada's commitment.

Notes

1. J.W. Holmes, "Focus on the Constant Dilemma," *International Perspectives* (May/June 1972), 10.

SECTION 4

ECONOMIC AND CULTURAL RELATIONS

Nationalism mixes pride and insecurity. Canadians have always had more than enough of the latter to go around, usually directed toward the economic and cultural dominance of the United States.

A case study of cultural nationalism written by Mary Vipond, of Concordia University, is important for its analysis of the forces arrayed against the entry into Canada of millions of copies of American magazines in the 1920s. Self-interest was part of it, of course, but so too was a highly negative view of the United States, which was displacing Great Britain as a factor in Canadian life and thought, robbing Canada of one of its chief claims to distinctiveness.

American capital, meanwhile, flowed readily into Canada most noticeably in the 1920s and after 1950. The higher tariffs associated with the National Policy had been seen traditionally as a method of stimulating foreign investment, and thus of building up domestic manufacturing and employment through the establishment of American branch plants. American capital sometimes led to American control, says Michael Bliss of the University of Toronto, but it was not until the 1957 report of Walter Gordon's Royal Commission on Canada's Economic Prospects that the question become a permanent fixture on the national political agenda. And not until the Vietnam-troubled late 1960s and early 1970s did a movement develop which sought to wrest control of Canada's economy from a United States that had lost its way at home and abroad. It was in this atmosphere that the Third Option was formulated and the Foreign Investment Review Agency constituted.

Irving Abella, a labour expert from York University, laments that there has not been enough nationalism in Canadian unions. At a crucial moment in Canadian labour history, the American Congress of Industrial Organizations (CIO) entered Canada, not as a result of imperialism or invasion but by the invitation of the Canadian working man.

Nationalism, clearly, is not everywhere. John Meisel is eloquent about the extent to which every Canadian is an American. Their symbols, realities and culture are in large part ours, and it is sometimes hard to imagine that the United States is a threat to national survival. For Meisel, however, the issue is precisely that. A former chairman of the Canadian Radio-Television and Telecommunications Commission, he chooses television and the broadcasting media to illustrate our cultural dependence. The dilemma is particularly worrying because of broadcasting's central position, not simply in Canadian culture but also in the development of our understanding of American ideas and values. In the face of an eccentric, fragmented, and hard-bargaining U.S. government and Congress, not to mention the American cultural industry itself, Meisel concludes that only clear and toughminded government and private sector action will prevent the further erosion and almost certain extinction of Canadian culture.

However Americanized we might be, no Canadian likes to think the United States matters too much. More than any cultural issue, free trade brings to the fore many of the old feelings of resentment and vulnerability, the old questions about control and survival. During the election campaign of 1988, which became a referendum on Canada's place in North America, the Council of Canadians' Mel Hurtig and the University of Ottawa's Duncan Cameron argued that the Mulroney trade agreement would transform the country into little more than a resource colony of the U.S. Opponents of free trade made much emotional headway with the charge that it threatened social programs and medicare; this was vigorously denied by the accord's negotiators, Simon Reisman and his chief deputy, Gordon Ritchie. Advocates of free trade liked to point out that the idea was supported by the royal commission headed by Liberal Donald Macdonald. However, the commission's executive director, J.G. Godsoe, insisted the agreement was not at all what the study had in mind. R.B. Farrell, a Canadian teaching at Northwestern University in the American midwest, warned that rejection of the deal would direct unprecedented protectionist pressures northwards. Although Farrell noted relatively little U.S. media interest in the Canadian campaign, almost every major new commentator had weighed in with an opinion by election eve. Like their politicians, the American media were firmly on the prime minister's side.

CULTURAL NATIONALISM†

MARY VIPOND

American popular culture poured into Canada in the 1920s, not for the first time, but at an unprecedented rate. Vast numbers of Canadians apparently delighted in the diverting, entertaining, cheap yet sophisticated products of the burgeoning American mass culture industry. A minority of English-speaking Canadian nationalists, self-styled moulders of public opinion and self-interested Canadian producers of similar products, however, campaigned aggressively against this "invasion" and struggled to create a competitive Canadian culture. One of their major offensives was against American magazines.

The American periodical industry expanded tremendously during the 1920s, sparked by improvements in printing technology and in business practices as well as by the growing market of a society with more leisure, education, and money.[1] As U.S. sales grew, so did Canadian. Over three hundred American publications (excluding newspapers) circulated in Canada in the mid-1920s; perhaps fifty million copies of American magazines were bought annually in Canada by 1926, and the number was steadily increasing.[2] The best sellers were the *Ladies' Home Journal* (with a circulation of 152 011 in Canada as of 30 June 1926), *Saturday Evening Post* (128 574), *Pictorial Review* (128 320), and *McCall's Magazine* (103 209).[3]

American publications outsold both British and Canadian in Canada by a wide margin. By 1929, for every dollar spent on British magazines

† Mary Vipond, "Canadian Nationalism and the Plight of Canadian Magazines in the 1920s," *Canadian Historical Review* LVIII, 1 (March 1977): 43–63.

in Canada, one hundred dollars was spent on American.[4] More worrying to Canadians, however, was the estimate that for every Canadian magazine printed, eight were imported from the United States.[5] The leading nation-wide Canadian magazines of general interest were *MacLean's Magazine* (with a circulation of 82 013 as of 31 December 1925), *Canadian Home Journal* (68 054), *Saturday Night* (30 858), and the *Canadian Magazine* (12 604).[6] Thus the combined circulation of the four leading Canadian magazines was considerably less than half that of the four major American magazines inside Canada. The crisis was apparent. How could the Canadian magazine industry meet American competition? How, indeed, could it survive?

This question concerned many groups, ranging from the IODE to the Canadian Authors' Association, from Boards of Trade to labour unions. Year after year they loudly bemoaned the "deluge" of American magazines "flooding" the country, and passed earnest resolutions calling for the rescue of the Canadian periodical industry. (Canadians always seemed to use aquatic metaphors — deluge, flood, tidal wave — to describe the influx of American popular culture. Perhaps most expressive of all was W.L. Grant, who remarked that American influences seemed to "seep in underground like drainage."[7]) Even the House of Commons discussed the magazine questions a couple of times during the decade — one of the few cultural matters to which the Honourable Members turned their attention in these years.

Those most interested in the problem, of course, were Canadian magazine publishers themselves, and they were the ones who took action during the 1920s. Indeed, that other groups became so concerned was at least in part due to the effectiveness of the publishers' lobby.

The decade began with a defeat for the publishers on an issue of perennial concern to them — postal rates. Despite their persistent lobbying since before the war, in June 1920 the Canadian House and Senate passed legislation raising the postal rate on second class matter (mainly newspapers and magazines) from a quarter of a cent to three quarters of a cent per pound, with the provision that it would increase to one and a half cents per pound on 1 January 1922.[8] The legislation in effect ended (or nearly ended) the "subsidy" Canadian publishers had been receiving from the government for years, for they were now required to pay close to the actual cost of the carriage of their papers. Not surprisingly, it aroused considerable resentment among the publishers, and significantly they immediately began to argue that the most important effect of the legislation would be to increase the advantage held by American publishers in Canada, for a large proportion of American magazines were trucked in to newsstands, and thus avoided all postal charges.

In the atmosphere of the impending postal rate legislation, the Magazine Section of the Canadian National Newspapers and Periodicals Association [CNNPA] held its first meeting on 4 May 1920. The CNNPA had been formed in 1919 by the subdivision of the Canadian Press Association. The Magazine Section consisted of the publishers of between ten and fifteen general-interest commercial magazines; it was dominated in the 1920s by the publishers of *MacLean's Magazine* (Colonel J.B. Maclean and his employees H.V. Tyrrell and G.H. Tyndall) and of the *Canadian Magazine* (W.F. Harrison and later Hugh C. MacLean, the colonel's brother).[9] Recognizing that they had lost on the postal rate issue, at this first meeting the magazine publishers decided that the federal government had to be made aware of the urgent need for encouragement and protection of the Canadian magazine industry. With dispatch those present agreed that they would attempt to persuade the government to impose some sort of tariff on American periodicals entering Canada. While not the first or last time such a duty has been advocated in Canada, this marked the commencement of the only concerted attempt ever made to force action on the idea.[10] On 15 May 1920 the members of the Magazine Section sent a memorandum advocating a tariff against American magazines to Sir Henry Drayton, minister of finance, and by the end of the year a delegation presented its case to the Tariff Commission.[11]

The members of the Magazine Section began their fight with high hopes, and felt that their presentation was well received in Ottawa. The 1921 budget, however, contained no mention of the desired tariff. There were other signs as well that the government was not as sympathetic to the publishers as it might have been. Not only did the postal rate increase come into effect but, under pressure from the newly-formed Canadian Authors' Association, the cabinet was beginning to sway toward amendments in the proposed Canadian Copyright Act which would work to the disadvantage of publishers. Despite these indications of less than complete co-operation on the part of the Union (now really Conservative) government, the worst blow of all, from the publishers' point of view, fell when the 1921 election brought into power a Liberal government intent on wooing the low-tariff Progressives — a government hardly likely to look kindly on any proposal for a new tariff, much less one on a medium of cultural communication.[12]

The publishers did not give up but revised their campaign in the light of the new political reality. At a meeting on 4 July 1922 they agreed "That the Magazine Section continue its effort to secure relief from its present impossible position by the placing of a duty on all foreign publications or on the advertising sections of them, or by the removal of duty on raw material coming into this country used in their manufacture."[13] Thus two options were to be put before the government simultaneously: either a tariff on all magazines entering the country, or a reduction or drawback of the tariffs and sales taxes which Canadian magazine publishers had to pay on their imported raw materials (especially paper) and processing equipment. Ontario and

Quebec publishers tended to prefer the first option; the publishers of western farm journals favoured the second as more consistent with their (and their readers') general anti-tariff stance. The two groups shared the goal of stimulating the Canadian magazine industry but disagreed as to the best means of achieving that objective. Throughout the early 1920s the Magazine Section (in 1922 it became the Magazine Publishers' Association of Canada or MPAC) pressed hardest for a tariff but the parent organization, the CNNPA, which included a larger and more diverse group of periodical publishers, stressed the drawback idea.[14] Despite their differences, the two groups shared resources and personnel, and for the most part carefully avoided denying the viability of the other's option.

From 1921 until mid-1926 the magazine publishers devoted their time and energy to seeking allies for their cause. The Canadian Manufacturers' Association, the principal pulp, paper, and ink manufacturers, the typographical unions, the Canadian Authors' Association, and the general public were all solicited for support. During 1923 at least twelve delegations went to Ottawa to approach members of parliament and government officials.[15] Useful contact was made with Conservative member Horatio C. Hocken, long-time imperialist and publisher of the Orange *Sentinel*, who offered to initiate a debate on the problems of the Canadian magazine industry in the House of Commons. The debate, on 5 March 1923, commenced with a general motion from Hocken "That, in the opinion of this House, it is desirable that measures should be adopted to encourage the publication of Canadian magazines and periodicals."[16] The response to the motion was unanimously favourable. Representatives of all parties bemoaned the sorry state of the magazine industry and called for its revitalization in order to build a Canadian national spirit. But controversy arose as to the best method of providing the necessary assistance. An amendment suggesting an end to the duty paid on all materials used in the production of Canadian magazines was rejected after several hours of debate; the original motion then passed without division.[17] The agreement of the House was virtually meaningless, however, for the motion had been decidedly vague in its wording. Nothing came of it; the budgets of the next three years were as silent on the subject as ever.

The Liberal governments for these years had several reasons for not acceding to the publishers' demands. Not only were the Liberals interested in attracting anti-tariff western voters but they were sincerely convinced that voters everywhere would punish a government which forced them to pay higher prices for the American magazines they read in such quantities, or which restricted freedom of access to the press. A certain antipathy toward some of those behind the publishers' campaign also played a role. Prime Minister King, for example, wrote to Newton MacTavish, former editor of the *Canadian Magazine*, in early 1926 to complain about magazines which criticized his government (specifically the *Canadian Magazine* under its new owner, Hugh C. MacLean): "So long as Canadian periodicals are used as media for helping to embarrass and destroy the Government of the day it is not a surprise to me that their owners find it difficult to enlist the sympathies of the Administration in their final troubles."[18]

For several years, then, the publishers bided their time, waiting until a more appropriate political climate prevailed in Ottawa. A few months after the 1925 election, with the Conservatives resurgent and King's Liberals desperately trying to hold on to a minority government, the publishers recommenced their campaign. Before any governmental response could be engendered, however, the unstable situation exploded in constitutional crisis; when the dust had settled the Liberals were firmly ensconced and the Progressives in disarray. Now, at last, however, the Liberals had set up an Advisory Board on Tariff and Taxation, designed in theory at least to provide non-political and objective advice on tariff matters to the cabinet. In September 1926 the MPAC and CNNPA submitted a joint formal request for a tariff on imported magazines to the minister of finance, J.A. Robb, and were accorded a hearing before the new Advisory Board. Colonel Maclean, John Atkins (newly appointed manager of the CNNPA), and H.V. Tyrrell (general manager of the MacLean Publishing Co.) made the trek to Ottawa for the first hearing on 28 October 1926.

Present at the hearing were the members of the Advisory Board (the Right Honourable George P. Graham, chairman, Hector McKinnon, secretary, Alfred Lambert, and D.G. McKenzie), Atkins, Maclean, and Tyrrell, several members of the Canadian Authors' Association, interested paper and ink manufacturers, labour spokesmen, and representatives of the Canadian Newsdealers' Association. The brief of the magazine publishers was read by John Atkins. It requested quite simply one of two alternatives, either a duty of fifteen cents per pound on advertising in imported magazines or a duty of ten cents per pound on the total weight of imported magazines or newspapers.[19] For the time being, the publishers were putting all of their eggs in the tariff basket.

Nine or ten arguments were introduced by the publishers in elaboration of their request. First, all the materials used by Canadian publishers, including paper, ink, engravings, and art work, and excepting only newspaper presses, were subject to both duties and sales taxes. Duties ranged from 10 percent on some machinery to 25 percent on paper, and sales taxes from 2.5 percent on paper to 5 percent on ink, engravings, and drawings. Many of these products were not even produced in Canada; Canadian publishers were *obliged* to import them and pay what was clearly simply a revenue tariff. Even those materials which the publishers did purchase in Canada, such as fine quality paper (only a small amount of which was imported), cost an amount "practically equivalent" to the U.S. price plus tariff and tax — that is, the publishers in effect had to pay the tariff even on domestic products. (This latter point was not explicitly voiced in the October brief for fear of offending paper-manufacturer allies, but it was used by the publishers both before and after that time.)[20] Meanwhile, the finished product of the American publisher entered Canada tax free. Because of this situation, the brief claimed, it would be to the "decided advantage" of the Canadian publisher to abandon Canada entirely, to set up his plants in Buffalo or Detroit, and then to ship his magazines into Canada duty-free for distribution. (A statement filed with the Advisory Board subsequent to the hearing showed that the approximate saving by printing two issues of *MacLean's* in Buffalo or some other U.S. city would be $3 161.91, the bulk of it on paper costs; over a year the publisher would save $37 942.92.)[21]

Secondly, the Canadian publisher was already operating under a severe handicap when trying to compete with American publications. The English-speaking Canadian market was very small (less than seven million) but from that the Canadian publisher had to pay all his overhead costs. Meanwhile American publishers, with a market of one hundred and ten million, could run off extra copies for the Canadian market "at nothing more than the cost of the extra paper and ink."[22] Thus American editors could afford to pay more for the best writers and artists, and lured Canadian talent away from Canadian magazines.

Thirdly, the brief raised the oft-emphasized question of the advertising which constituted as much as 60 percent of many imported magazines. Advertising matter, the publishers complained, was subject to a duty when it entered Canada in pamphlet or insert form; when it came inside a magazine, however, it entered free. American publishers used their Canadian circulation as a bonus for their advertisers. As a result more than four billion pages of "propaganda" for American products entered Canada free each year, creating crippling competition for Canadian manufacturers.[23] Moreover, branch plants in Canada were forced to advertise in American magazines, so their money did not go to Canadian publications. Because Canadian publishers could never attract advertising in the quantity that their American counterparts could, they were forced to rely to a greater extent upon their income from single-issue and subscription sales, which meant in turn that they could not lower their prices to competitive levels.

Fourthly, American publications, because of their number, crowded Canadian magazines off newsstands. "With their tremendous financial backing," the MPAC claimed, "the United States publishers are able to maintain large and efficient field forces, which constantly are influencing Canadian dealers to give prominence to their publications at the expense of Canadian magazines."[24]

Fifthly, while some American magazines were of high quality, those with the largest circulations were "cheaply printed on cheap paper, and devoted almost entirely to fiction that is sensational, suggestive,

and generally as demoralizing as the publishers dare make them [sic]."
Here Atkins enlarged upon the original brief in an aside. Canadian
publishers suffered from a "moral handicap" in this regard, he claimed,
for none of *them* would "stoop to profit by the publication of such
literature." He concluded with a reminder to his audience of the
deleterious effect of such "literary swill" on the youth of Canada, and
of the additional tragedy that American magazines contributed to
Canada's disturbingly high emigration rate by luring young Canadians
south by their portrayal of the benefits and pleasures of the American
system.[25]

Next, the brief turned to some positive considerations to support the
association's request, with stress on the immense advantages of a vital
magazine industry to Canada as a nation. First it pointed out the
economic benefits. An expanded Canadian magazine industry would
stimulate the Canadian pulp and paper industry, the engraving
industry, and many others. It would provide employment for many
Canadians, from lumbermen to authors, and would enhance government revenues through taxation and mailing charges. There were non-
material benefits to be derived from a healthy magazine industry as
well, the brief went on, for magazines enabled us "to build up a strong
Canadian literature, a matter of first importance to Canadian unity,
the preservation of Canadian tradition and ideals, and the development of a national consciousness."[26]

> In order to foster Canadian national spirit, national publications
> such as monthly and weekly magazines, and periodicals circulat-
> ing in both eastern and western provinces, are necessary. To
> retard the growth of Canadian national magazines and periodi-
> cals is to encourage north and south lines of influence instead
> of lines east and west, lines which will bring into being the same
> ideals of Canadianism in the western provinces, the central
> provinces and the maritime provinces. There is the particular
> danger of the people of the western provinces feeling that they
> are more or less cut off from eastern Canada, and we maintain
> that the establishment of magazines and periodicals with large
> national circulation will do much to bring the extreme West,
> particularly, in closer touch and sympathy with eastern
> Canada.[27]

The MPAC's claims were bolstered by numerous supporting statements from newspaper editorials, the IODE, the National Council of
Women, the Association of Canadian Clubs, the Canadian Authors'
Association, and the Ontario Chambers of Commerce. Some of the
most interested groups had sent representatives to the hearing. Tom

Moore, president of the Trades and Labour Congress of Canada, claiming to represent the majority of Canadian labour opinion, declared himself in agreement with the employers on this question, for a duty on imported magazines would create jobs in Canada.[28] He did however request that technical, religious, trade union, and fraternal society publications be exempt. Thomas Walsh (of the Federal Advertising Agency), C.R. Conquergood (representing printing ink manufacturers), A.C. Batten (of the Photo-Engravers Association), and Edward Beck (of the Canadian Pulp and Paper Association) also supported the idea of a tariff for the economic advantages it would bring. Conquergood mentioned the patriotic and moral benefits of the proposed tariff but Beck did not agree: "We regard the question wholly as an economic one," he remarked, and unrelated to "all the sentimental things that have been said here this morning." A.H. Jarvis, speaking for the Booksellers and Stationers of Canada, emphasized the problem of salacious literature coming in from the United States. Professor E.E. Prince, president of the Ottawa branch of the Canadian Authors' Association, presented a personal brief with which he claimed Canadian authors were in full accord. As far as he was concerned, American magazines were primarily commercial products; literary value was secondary to them. They ignored Canadian or British events or achievements, and thereby caused "denationalization" among Canadians.[29]

Thus three main arguments were used by the MPAC and its supporters before the Advisory Board. The primary one, appropriate to the circumstances of a tariff hearing, was that of economic advantage. The first sentence of the publishers' brief began: "The Magazine Publishers Association of Canada, representing an industry which employs thousands of Canadian workmen, pays hundreds of thousands annually in wages, uses hundreds of thousands of dollars annually in Canadian material, and contributes hundreds of thousands annually to the Canadian National Treasury, herewith respectfully presents . . . ."[30] The brief constantly reiterated this theme: a duty on imported magazines, as well as filling the government's coffers, would create investment opportunities and jobs in many Canadian industries. By reducing the circulation of American magazines in Canada by a probable 25 to 50 percent, the tariff would allow "Canadian and British" publications a fair share of display space on newsstands. In addition, the publishers argued, "leading American publishers would likely print Canadian editions, specially edited for Canada, in this country, employing Canadian labour and using Canadian raw materials."[31] The publishers' other arguments were less emphasized before the board but were used effectively to rally public opinion to their side. The first of these stressed that too many American magazines were salacious; a duty was necessary to supplement ineffective censorship laws. The final argument was the nationalist one: Canadian magazine publishers should be aided because Canadian magazines were essential to the preservation and growth of Canadian literature and thus of a strong sense of Canadian unity and identity. Economic self-interest, puritanism, and patriotism were thus combined in the publishers' plea.[32]

Not everyone present at the hearing supported the proposed tariff, however. The principal opponent was R.J. Deachman, representing the Canadian Wholesale Newsdealers' Association and also the American News Company Ltd. of Canada, which dominated distribution of magazines to retail outlets in both Canada and the U.S. Deachman, a journalist with his roots in rural Ontario, thus served as the spokesman for the special interest of those who profited from the volume of magazines sold, regardless of their origin. The Wholesale Newsdealers were much alarmed at the prospect of a large drop in their business if the price of American magazines was escalated by a tariff. At the later hearings Deachman also functioned as the representative of the Consumers' League of Canada, an organization formed in mid-1928 "to present to the Tariff Board and to the Public the point of view of the Consumers on matters of tariff and taxation." In this capacity Deachman regularly opposed all applications for higher tariffs before the board, and was as regularly accused by protectionists of serving as a front for American manufacturers.[33]

Deachman sliced into Atkins' brief with a scalpel-sharp tongue. First, he established that the MPAC represented only a small group — only eleven publications out of more than fifteen hundred in Canada. Then he forced Atkins to admit that he lacked any figures showing exactly how much Canadian magazines costs were increased by duties. Next he attacked Atkins' rhetoric. Atkins had talked about the danger of the estrangement of the West from the East because of the dearth of national magazines. Did he not really desire, Deachman asked, to bring the West more into line with the East? Then, switching ground, Deachman attacked one of the weakest points of the brief. If a tariff was necessary to keep out salacious American magazines, what did the MPAC think about similar material coming in from Britain? Was the whole moral question not just a camouflage? The only way to keep out immoral literature was by censorship. Clearly it was the competition, not the pornography, which Atkins and his associates feared. "Isn't it purely a question of dollars and not a question of morals?"[34]

Deachman then went on to ridicule some of the premises of the MPAC brief: "I find we are suffering from, I think it is, denationalization, suffocation of industry, increased emigration, millions in money lost to the country. It is rather a sad indictment, all due, apparently, to paying five cents instead of thirty cents for a copy of the Saturday Evening Post."[35] In fact, Deachman contended, the magazine publishers had merely made a series of completely unsubstantiated claims. Some information, indeed, seemed to suggest tendencies opposite to their statements. Despite the great increase in the number of American magazines circulating in Canada in the previous three or four years, for example, exports to the U.S. were steadily growing, as was Canada's general prosperity. Even Canadian national consciousness seemed not weaker but stronger than ever before.[36]

Deachman, then, was making two major points. First of all, the imposition of the tariff which the MPAC desired would harm Canadians by hermetically sealing them off from the rest of the world, restricting their outlook, and narrowing their minds. Far from being a problem, Deachman suggested, constant intercourse with the United States was of definite benefit to Canada:

> If you could drop the United States into oblivion tomorrow by an earthquake, the greatest sufferer in the world would be Canada. We would lose one of our greatest markets. We are not suffering but rather we are blessed by being alongside United States. Rich, powerful, energetic, capable, it provides an inspiration to us and a help for the development of our own country. Much of our capital comes from there, and not the least of the benefits we receive from the United States is that we are able to secure from them at relatively small prices life giving literature which on the whole can not be said to be uninspiring in its total effect upon the life of the people. I think we ought to be grateful for American literature instead of standing up here and saying we are suffering from it, and sometimes designating it as "swill."[37]

Canada, Deachman insisted, could be a world leader only if it maintained its openness and its contact with other races and other ideas and only if it did not become "hedged around with an intense partisan type of nationalism."[38]

Deachman's second point dealt more specifically with the actual proposal. He suggested that keeping out foreign periodicals by a tariff was primarily a device to allow the domestic publishers to raise their own prices, as had happened in other protected industries. The result would be not an increase but a drop in the consumption of Canadian publications. The application was in the interest of only a small group of people who were trying to shift the burden of sacrifice onto the shoulders of the Canadian public. "You are trying to fatten some [hogs] . . . by an excise duty on magazines," he accused the MPAC.[39] Quite simply, he said, there were two interests at stake — "the interest of a few publishers who want to get a higher price for their publications, and . . . the broader and fuller interest of the entire Canadian people."[40] Happily, the interests of the news companies Deachman represented coincided with the latter.

Even if one granted that Canadian magazine publishers did need help, and Deachman did in the end concede that, the imposition of a tariff was, he believed, the wrong way to assist them. In order to escape the tax American publishers would merely set up branch plants in Canada, as American companies had done in industry after industry already. But the publication of Canadian editions of American magazines, Deachman insisted, was nothing less than the "exploitation" of the Canadian people. A much more reasonable solution to the difficulties of Canadian publishers, he argued, would be a reduction in the duties they had to pay on the paper, machinery, and other equipment which they had no choice but to import. Then Canadian publishers would be able to reduce their prices and could sell all the more Canadian magazines to Canadians.[41]

Deachman was not alone in his opposition to the MPAC's application. The board received a total of 550 telegrams or letters of protest, most of them solicited by the American News Company from newsdealers. Typical of the telegrams was one from a Mrs. Williamson in Outlook, Saskatchewan, who wired: "If the legislation is passed it would absolutely ruin my business and deprive me of a means of livelihood." Others claimed that the tariff would be widely denounced by the "reading public" and that it could not "be tolerated by people in such a free country like ours [sic]." The representative of one Vancouver news company even suggested (presumably with tongue in cheek) that there was only one solution to the "American industrial literary invasion" — namely the banning of English and the endorsement of French as Canada's only official language.[42]

In the long run, the most important telegram of rebuttal which the board received came from R.D. Colquette, associate editor of the *Grain Growers' Guide*, who opposed the duty on the grounds that it would deprive the Canadian people of the opportunity to select from the "best British and American literature," but went on to urge that Canadian publishers be assisted by being allowed to import their materials duty free.[43] From this point on the opponents of the MPAC's application began to rally around the free trade position. They agreed that Canadian magazines should be given a fair chance to compete in the Canadian market, but firmly opposed any means of helping Canadian publishers which restricted the inflow of periodical literature from the rest of the world, including the United States, or which raised tariffs.

After a full day of testimony, the hearing adjourned so that the board could consider the evidence. Chairman Graham ended the session with a warning to the delegations that the board had no power to make decisions; it merely marshalled the facts for presentation to the minister of finance; the final decision would remain the cabinet's.

The publishers did not wait idly for the government's verdict, but used the opportunity to turn to a direct appeal to the Board of

Customs. The essence of their case before that board was that the tariff legislation of 1906 (Item 184) under which magazines were entering free in fact provided for free entry of *unbound* newspapers and magazines. This had been interpreted for years to include all magazines, on the grounds that to be "bound" meant to be durably bound with leather or cloth. Not so, argued the CNNPA. Clearly a magazine like the *Ladies' Home Journal* was bound — its covers were different from the inner pages and were firmly and permanently attached by stitching. The response of the Board of Customs to this manoeuvre of the publishers was, not surprisingly, negative. If you wish a tariff, they were told, go to the Advisory Board and get one applied — but don't expect us to provide a reinterpretation with such wide implications. Some months later, in mid-August 1927, the Board of Customs did concede a bit: one type of magazine — the "story" magazine, which contained nothing but fiction — *was* switched from Tariff Item 184 to Item 169 — that is, it was decreed bound and taxed like books at a rate of 10 percent (5 percent under British preference).[44]

So the members of the Magazine Publishers' Association returned to concentrating their energies on the main case before the Advisory Board. On 18 November 1926 they hastily wired the board that they were gathering additional data to back up their case. When it was ready, the initiated a second hearing, which was eventually held on 1 February 1927, with Atkins, Tyrrell, and Deachman again the main participants. At this hearing the publishers attempted to submit a "supplementary" brief proposing an alternative set of remedies for their plight (such as a 22.5–25 percent ad valorem duty with complete exemption for British and French publications and elimination of sales taxes on plant equipment, supplies, and raw materials), but it was ruled that this constituted a new application and must therefore follow the proper procedure of being submitted first to the minister of finance. Consequently, the second hearing consisted merely of amplification of the original application.

Many of the old arguments were voiced yet again. The Business Newspapers' Association presented a brief backing up the MPAC; petitions of support from 288 newsdealers and newsboys and from employees in various mechanical branches of the industry were put on record. (These petitions, which had been solicited by the MPAC, consisted mainly of forms filled out by newsboy members of *MacLean's* "Young Canada Boosters Club.") By this time the publishers had also gathered and now filed before the board comparative data which indicated that Canadian publishers were in a worse position than those of almost any other country. While very few nations imposed tariffs on magazines, normally their publishers were protected by the uniqueness of the national language. In some countries, such as Holland and Norway, all magazines were admitted free *except* those in the native tongue. Other countries, and most particularly the United States, used copyright legislation to safeguard their own publications. Canada was unique in the way it combined the lack of any copyright or tariff protection with propinquity to a giant neighbour of the same language.⁴⁵

It was at this February 1927 session before the Advisory Board on Tariff and Taxation that George Chipman, editor and managing director of the *Grain Growers' Guide*, became actively involved in the issue for the first time. Chipman was unable to attend the hearing owing to ill health, but shortly before it opened he sent a letter to the board reiterating the free trade position taken earlier by his associate, Colquette, and advocating a total rebate of duty on the supplies and materials used by magazine publishers. When informed by Hector McKinnon, the secretary of the Advisory Board, that his letter, by asking for *removal* of duties, must constitute a new application, Chipman sent in confirmation to the minister of finance that he did indeed wish to launch a new case before the board and asked that his letter remain on record as a deposition *against* the MPAC's case. By this action Chipman became, whether he wished it or not, the central figure in the publishers' campaign. The publishers' solidarity had broken, and the low-tariff position began to gain ascendancy.

Specifically, Chipman asked, in his letter and later in his formal application, for an end to both the duty and the sales taxes on twenty-six products used in the manufacture of magazines, including various kinds of paper, machines, ink, envelopes, engravings, drawings, and electrotypes. His argument ran as follows:

> We must remember that Canada has a population of approximately nine million people roughly divided into English and French speaking. It is utterly impossible to conceive that an English speaking population or a French speaking population of five million or less could maintain any large number or any wide range of high grade magazines. For that reason it would be nothing short of a national tragedy for the Canadian people to cut themselves off from the privileges which they now enjoy in the way of periodical literature without any possibility of it being replaced by home productions. It would be nothing more or less than a heavy tax or a prohibition upon the dissemination of knowledge.

But while we did not want to cut ourselves off from the world, Chipman went on, we did need our own national magazines too: "In order to build a self-reliant nation on the northern part of this continent it is essential that the Canadian people be provided with the utmost information upon Canadian problems. That we have problems of our own no one will doubt. That the development of high class magazines widely read throughout our nine provinces will assist in bringing about a better mutual understanding and the inculcation of common ideals no one will question. There is a great dearth of such magazines in Canada today."[46] Chipman stressed that while it was clear that the tariff on machinery not manufactured in Canada was purely for revenue, that on paper, the publishers' largest single raw material item, was protective. He claimed that his own paper, the *Grain Growers' Guide*, had had to switch from book paper to half-tone news (high quality newsprint) owing to the high cost of Canadian paper, while American publishers could buy their paper *cheaper* than Canadians (by almost exactly the amount of the duty) despite the fact that that paper was made from Canadian pulpwood. Why, he pointedly inquired, should the profitable and well-developed Canadian paper industry be protected by duties which were hurting a small and struggling industry? Why should the government attempt to make money at the expense of a vital national institution?[47]

Ten days later, on 23 February 1927, the CNNPA Board of Directors formally threw its full weight behind Chipman's application. The possibility of requesting a tariff drawback on supplies and raw materials as an alternative remedy had existed since the beginning of the struggle in 1920; by early 1927 it was the only option left, for the publishers had realized that they did not have the support of public or parliamentary opinion, and, more importantly, the finance minister had at last told them unequivocally that he had no intention of granting them the protective tariff they desired.[48] Thus the publishers were finally convinced that if they wished any sort of immediate relief they must turn to the free trade remedy. The switch to the new tack was not accomplished without some discord, however. The MPAC's old allies, the pulp and paper manufacturers, were furious, for they did not want to have to meet the competition of duty-free American paper.[49] More seriously, opposition to the new approach surfaced within the CNNPA itself. It was led by G. Grassie Archibald, publisher of the *Farmers' Guide* and, perhaps more significantly, of the trade journal, *Pulp and Paper Magazine*. Archibald stridently insisted that the decision to switch to the drawback remedy had been made by a clique within the CNNPA which did not represent the wishes of the members.[50] The conflict between the supporters of the two options had been stirring for some time; now it burst into the open. The Board of Directors of the CNNPA clamped down on Archibald quickly, refused to hold the special meeting he demanded, and reaffirmed that the association's immediate goal was a drawback of duty. The directors were careful to state, however, that this was not intended as a repudiation of the idea of a tariff against imported magazines. They affirmed: "The ground is taken that if the government decides that Canadian publishers cannot be protected, the minimum relief which our members have a right to expect is that the legislative handicaps which hamper our industry and compel us to pay duties and sales tax, directly and indirectly, be abated."[51]

The hearing on Chipman's request for a drawback was held on 18 November 1927. Rather than a complete drawback, he now asked for 99 percent (as this was simpler to administer) and he reduced the list of items involved to include only paper, engravings, electrotypes, drawings, ink, and machinery. Although apparently no complete transcript of this session has survived, it seems that the various groups concerned spent most of their time at each other's throats. The photoengraving industry objected to the application, and so, most strenuously, did the Canadian Pulp and Paper Association. In a lengthy brief the pulp and paper manufacturers emphasized how important the prosperity of their industry was to the Canadian economy and employment market, and accused the magazine publishers of taking advantage of their access to public opinion to arouse support for a measure really motivated by the desire for "private gain."[52] At this hearing the conflict between Archibald's Canadian Business Publishers' Association and the rest of the publishers became open and heated as well. Archibald continued to insist firmly that the publishing business was directly or indirectly supported by *all* of Canadian business, and therefore should, in its own self-interest, faithfully support "tariff stability" — that is, protection. The government now chose to ignore the magazine industry's internal quarrels, however. The paper manufacturers were given a final two weeks after the hearing to draft a complete reply to the publishers' case, which they dragged out (Chipman suspected deliberately) until well into January 1928. Shortly thereafter Chipman was asked to simplify his application once again to ease its passage. He reduced it to the two most important requests: drawback of duties on printing paper and machinery not manufactured in Canada.

The final result of the whole campaign was the granting in the 1928 budget of an 80 percent drawback on certain classes of paper used in magazine publishing. This did help the publishers, and both imports of book paper from the U.S. and the circulation of Canadian magazines increased significantly within a year.[53] The publishers, however, continued to press for an increase in the drawback to 99 percent and its application to *all* materials and equipment.

A little over a year later the Conservatives came to power and proved much more amenable to the type of tariff legislation the MPAC had wanted from the beginning. As of 1 September 1931 imported periodicals with over 30 percent advertising content were taxed at five cents per copy, those with 20–29 percent advertising at two cents, and those with less than 20 percent advertising came in free. Fiction, feature, and/or comic magazines were charged fifteen cents per pound.[54] The effects were immediate. Between 1931 and 1934 there was a large decline (perhaps as much as 60 percent) in the circulation of American magazines in Canada. Although this was probably partly a result of the depression (American magazines exempt from the duty lost Canadian circulation too), the circulation of the five leading Canadian magazines did rise by about the same amount. However, it is worth noting that the number of branch plant subsidiaries of American publishing firms was also very high between 1931 and 1935.[55] In the late 1930s the tariff was dropped again by the Liberals as one of the terms of the extensive Canadian-U.S. trade agreement. Since then the number of American magazines circulating in Canada has continued to climb. Recent governments have tended to attempt to assist Canadian magazines primarily by means of tax measures designed to make them more attractive to advertisers. Most recently these provisions have resulted in protracted debate over whether branch plant magazines like the Canadian editions of *Time* and *Reader's Digest*, which dominate the market, should be defined as Canadian or foreign. To date, the result is a split decision, and *Time* has ceased publication of its Canadian edition.

Several attributes of Canadian nationalism in the 1920s are revealed by the magazine publishers' campaign. First, the importance of self-interest to the nationalist cause is evident. The publishers were businessmen; magazines were their product. Their claim that they were "just as entitled to protection as the manufacturers of lamps or lingerie"[56] was well received by other Canadian businessmen whose products were supplied to the Canadian magazine industry or who wished to curtail the inflow of advertising for goods which competed with their own. Magazines were, however, more than simply an industry; they also helped to mould the minds of Canadians. On the one hand, the government's sensitivity to this fact stood the publishers in good stead, for it meant that Ottawa was particularly susceptible to the argument that "What is good for *MacLean's* is good for the country." On the other hand, the unique nature of their industry also militated against the publishers, for their opponents, in defending their own interest in maximum magazine sales, had little difficulty in convincing many English-speaking Canadians, liberal in spirit and accustomed to easy access to American periodicals, that a tariff against "ideas" was narrow-minded and parochial. To a considerable extent, however, the cultural aspect of the issue was merely a complication. On both sides, those who presented their cases before the Advisory Board on Tariff and Taxation were, above all, businessmen; principle and art were in the end less important to them than their balance sheets.

Secondly, it is clear that the publishers who initiated this campaign were pro-British and anti-American. Although their original application referred to the need for a duty on "all foreign magazines," certainly the publishers' statements before the Advisory Board indicated that they perceived only American magazines as a threat. When questioned at the hearing about this anomaly, Atkins expressed amazement that British magazines were considered "foreign" and immediately stated that the MPAC would favour an exemption of all British publications from the proposed tariff.[57] It apparently never occurred to Atkins that British publications might be dangerous either to the Canadian publishing industry or to the Canadian identity. His whole attention was concentrated on the American menace. This attitude was, of course, a realistic one. British magazines had such small circulations in Canada by the twenties that they indeed posed no danger to Canadian publishers; the Atlantic itself formed a trade barrier. His response also rested, however, in another assumption common to the publishers behind the demand for a tariff. For them, Canadian life and literature were not threatened by the tie with the Mother Country, but on the contrary reinforced by it. Indeed, one of the impulses behind the flurry of protest against American magazines during the war and immediately after had been concern about the "anti-British" material Canadians were reading in U.S. publications (particularly those of the Hearst empire) and resentment against the braggart American magazines which ignored the imperial war effort.[58] The magazine publishers recognized that Canadians would probably never again read British periodicals in large numbers; one of their objectives, then, was to replace them with Canadian magazines which retained a certain sympathy to the British point of view. As the MPAC informed the members of the House of Commons in a letter circulated just as their campaign commenced, they believed that it was their duty to try to counteract the prevailing tendency for Canadians to become "less British and more American."[59] These publishers, and their editors, often called themselves Canadian nationalists. In fact, however, they rarely distinguished between the British and the Canadian. They were Canadian nationalists of the most traditional type, defining Canada and differentiating it from the United States almost solely by its Britishness.

In contrast, some of the opponents of the tariff were lavish in their praise of the United States, its ideals and freedom, and paid not even lip service to the old theme of Canada's British heritage. They saw Canada's future as a North American nation, and happily subscribed to the progressive, liberal values which they believed the United States embodied. Both those who supported the tariff and those who opposed it agreed that Canada must become a stronger nation, and that a more vital magazine industry was essential to national growth and progress. They were all patriotic Canadians, but their perceptions of what Canada was and should be differed markedly. The eastern publishers were protectionist, Britannic, and conservative. Deachman and Chipman were liberals, free traders, and North Americans.[60] Just as their self-interest lay in different directions, so the patriotism of the two groups was manifest in different forms.

The Canadian magazine industry did face difficult, even unfair, competition from the United States in the 1920s. The publishers had as good a case for protection as had any manufacturers who claimed that their products should be "Made in Canada." In cultural terms as well, the publishers could make a very strong argument for the deliberate and artificial stimulation of their industry on the grounds that the press performed essential functions of self-definition and communication for the nation. The magazine publishers, however, were only partially successful in obtaining concrete concessions as long as Liberal governments remained in office. The Liberals, not surprisingly, responded to the tariff requests with their own political well-being in mind. Not only was the party's best interest to be found in a generally low-tariff stance, but its conviction that large numbers of Canadians desired cheap American magazines never died. The Liberal governments of the 1920s saw no point in legislating unpopular measures in order to help a few magazines which, while undeniably Canadian, were controlled by a small, powerful, and too often Conservative group.[61] The eventual granting of a drawback on duties on imported paper was a political masterstroke for Mackenzie King, for although it irritated Canadian paper manufacturers, it simultaneously placated the Liberal party's low-tariff wing and pandered to the nationalist sentiment of the decade. It also allowed the genuine liberals within the Liberal party to remain faithful to their belief, so nicely expressed by King himself in the House in 1931, that "thought is cosmopolitan. It should have no limitation with respect either to place or time. All advances that are made in civilization are the result of ideas, and in any way to preclude the possibility of a good idea having its opportunity of fruition to the full in any quarter is to retard the progress of civilization itself."[62]

In an oft-quoted remark, economist John Kenneth Galbraith replied to a question about the dangers inherent in the American economic domination of Canada by declaring: "If I were still a practising as distinct from an advisory Canadian, I would be much more concerned about maintaining the cultural integrity of the broadcasting system and with making sure Canada has an active, independent theatre, book-publishing industry, newspapers, magazines and schools of poets and painters. I wouldn't worry for a moment about the differences between Canadian or American corporations."[63] Canadian cultural nationalists have taken Galbraith's remarks to heart, and next to radio and television have focussed the greatest measure of their attention on the magazine industry's role in the struggle for cultural survival. The "magazine question" has not, however, been a simple one, combining as it has the problem of the commercialization of cultural media, the reality of English Canada's propinquity and similarity to the mass culture giant of the world, the question of the role of government in both the business and the cultural spheres, rivalries among competing interest groups, regions, and political parties, and conflicts between mass tastes and the nationalist goals of an élite. At its best, the debate on this issue has forced Canadians to probe to the roots of their assumptions about their nation and its culture and so to understand themselves better; at its worst the discussion has degenerated into obfuscating rhetoric and self-interested squabbling. The campaign of the Magazine Publishers' Association of Canada for a tariff against American magazines in the 1920s portrayed some of both the best and worst of the debate. The discussion continues in essentially the same terms in the 1970s; the issues the publishers raised continue to perplex and divide Canadians.

Notes

1. T. Peterson, *Magazines in the Twentieth Century* (Urbana 1964), viii, ix. The practice of financing magazine publication primarily from advertising revenues, which led to cuts in subscription rates in order to garner maximum circulation numbers, was well entrenched in the United States by the 1920s, but only beginning in Canada.

2. J.A. Stevenson, "The Campaign of Canadian Publishers for Protection," in *Canada and her Great Neighbour*, H.F. Angus, ed., (Toronto 1938), 154. See also C.W. Stokes, "Our Americanized News-stands," *Saturday Night*, XLI, 27 Feb. 1926, 2.

3. PAC, Canada, Advisory Board on Tariff and Taxation, Reference no 9, Exhibit H. "A.B.C. figures from A.B.C. Blue Book to June 30, 1926." See also ibid., Table A, which shows an unverified increase of over seventy percent in the Canadian circulation of the twenty-five leading American magazines between 1923 and 1926.

4. Canada, Dominion Bureau of Statistics, *Canada Year Book, 1932* (Ottawa 1932), 462.

5. Canada, Advisory Board on Tariff and Taxation, Reference no 9, Transcript of Public Hearing, 28 Oct. 1926, 5–6.

6. A.W. Thomas and H.C. Corner, eds., *The Canadian Almanac, 1926* (Toronto 1926), 404, 405. Note that these figures are unofficial. Other Canadian publications had circulation as large (for example, *The New Outlook, The Canadian Motorist*, and some of the farm magazines), but these were not magazines of general interest.

7. W.L. Grant Papers, Grant to Sir Maurice Hankey, 17 Nov. 1921, 2, Public Archives of Canada (hereinafter PAC).

8. Canada, House of Commons, *Debates*, 17 June 1920, 3761. The rate was slightly lowered (to one cent per pound) in 1927. *Debates*, 1 Apr. 1927, 1775–6, 2031–9.

9. W.H. Kesterton, *A History of Journalism in Canada* (Toronto 1967), 167; Canada, Department of Labour, Report on Organization in Industry, Commerce and the Professions in Canada (Ottawa 1926), 42. Colonel J.B. Maclean and his brother had adopted different spellings of the family name in a

period of rivalry in the late nineteenth century. See F. Chalmers, *A Gentleman of the Press* (Toronto 1969), 98–9.

10. See J. Weaver, "Imperilled Dreams: Canadian Opposition to American Empire, 1918–1930" (Ph.D. diss., Duke University, 1973), 338; I. Litvack and C. Maule, *Cultural Sovereignty: The Time and Reader's Digest Case in Canada* (New York 1974), 18.

11. Minute Books, 5 Mar. 1921, Periodical Press Association (hereinafter PPA), Magazine Publishers' Association of Canada (hereinafter MPAC).

12. The minister of finance in the Conservative government, Sir Henry Drayton, later claimed that but for the "accident" of 6 Dec. 1921 his party would have "protected the interests of Canadian magazines." Canada, House of Commons, *Debates*, 17 June 1922, 3112.

13. Minute Books, 4 July 1922, PPA, MPAC.

14. For example, see PPA, CNNPA Board of Directors Minute Books, 14 Dec. 1920, 17 and 28 March 1922.

15. Minute Books, 29 Feb., 1 Dec. 1924, 7 Jan. 1925, 4 June 1923, PPA, MPAC.

16. Canada, House of Commons, *Debates*, 5 March 1923, 826.

17. Ibid., 826–56. Hocken continued throughout his years in the House to bring up the magazine question almost every time he rose to his feet.

18. Mackenzie King Papers, Correspondence, vol. 135, King to Newton MacTavish, 29 March 1926, PAC.

19. Transcript of Public Hearing, 28 Oct. 1926, 21.

20. Advisory Board, Reference no 9, MPAC letter to members of House of Commons, 22 March 1926, PAC.

21. Transcript of Public Hearing, 28 Oct. 1926, 7, 6.

22. Ibid, 8.

23. Ibid., 10. It was on this point above all others that the publishers found allies among other manufacturers.

24. Ibid., 13.

25. Ibid., 14, 80–1, 20, 39.

26. Ibid., 15–16.

27. Ibid., 23.

28. Ibid., 28–33. The unions supported the publishers despite the fact that most Canadian magazines were printed in non-union shops. See Arthur Meighen Papers, series 3, vol. 134, "Bulletin of the Ontario and Quebec Conference of Typographical Unions," 20 Feb. 1925, 2, PAC.

29. Transcript of Public Hearing, 28 Oct. 1926, 56, 36–8, 43. The CAA had mixed feelings about how to aid Canadian magazines. In 1922 the annual conference, under the guidance of *MacLean's Magazine* editor J.V. McKenzie, had passed a resolution favouring a duty on the advertising matter in imported magazines. When the subject came up again at the 1926 conference, however, the association split into protectionists *versus* free traders, and the debate was so divisive that the organization chose to remain officially silent on the magazine question for the remainder of the decade. *Canadian Bookman*, IV, May 1922, 155; "Proceedings of Vancouver Convention," CAA *Authors' Bulletin*, no. 4, Nov. 1926, 15.

30. Transcript of Public Hearing, 28 Oct. 1926, 3.

31. Advisory Board, Reference no 9, "The Probable Effects of the Imposition of a Duty" [Oct. 1926], PAC.

32. Ibid.; Litvack and Maule, *Cultural Sovereignty*, 14.

33. Peterson, *Magazines*, 91. See also "The Consumers League as a Public Nuisance," *Willison's Monthly*, III, Dec. 1927, 257.

34. Transcript of Public Hearing, 28 Oct. 1926, 69–70, 74, 75–7, 80.

35. Ibid., 97.

36. Ibid., 100–3.

37. Ibid., 126–7.

38. Ibid., 104.

39. Ibid., 62, 73, 124–5, 78.

40. Ibid., 124.

41. Ibid., 112–3, 96–7.

42. Advisory Board, Reference no. 9, Rebuttal Correspondence, PAC.

43. Transcript of Public Hearing, 28 Oct. 1926, 68.

44. Advisory Board, Reference no. 9, Board of Customs file, PAC (Hocken also made this a frequent plea in the House. *Debates*, 29 Apr. 1926, 2927–34, 24 Feb. 1927, 604–7).

45. Ibid., Brief of Jan. 1927, Exhibit H.

46. Ibid., Transcript of Second Hearing, 1 Feb. 1927, 58; Reference no 9B, G.F. Chipman to the Hon. J.A. Robb, 16 May 1927.

47. See also "Taxes on Knowledge," *Grain Growers' Guide*, XX, 15 Dec. 1927, 7–8.

48. PPA, CNNPA Board of Directors Minute Books, 23 Feb. 1927; CNNPA advertisements in *Maclean's*, XLI, 1 Jan. 1928, 32; Canada, House of Commons, *Debates*, 17 July 1931, 3887.

49. PPA, CNNPA Board of Directors Minute Books, Transcript of informal meeting with paper manufacturers, nd; Minutes of 31 March 1927.

50. Advisory Board, Reference no 9, MPAC File, G. Archibald to T.J. Tobin, 21 Sept. 1927 (copy), PAC; Advertisement, *Grain Growers' Guide*, XX, 1 Nov. 1927, 62.

51. PPA, CNNPA Board of Directors Minute Books, 4 Oct. 1927; CNNPA Bulletins, Bulletin no. 200, 7 Oct. 1927.

52. For a partial record of this session see Advisory Board, Reference no. 9, "A Tariff Lesson," PAC reprinted from *Journal of Commerce*, 1 Dec. 1927, 1. See also ibid., Statement of Pulp and Paper Association to Advisory Board, 11, E. Beck to W.H. Moore, 11 Jan. 1928.

53. Ibid., file on "Book Paper," "Heavy Imports Indicate Canadian Paper Prices Are Too High," *Canadian Printer and Publisher*, Nov. 1929, 34.

54. Canada, House of Commons, *Debates*, 17 July 1931, 3878.

55. J.A. Stevenson, "Campaign of Canadian Publishers," 162; Litvack and Maule, *Cultural Sovereignty*, 26.

56. Andrew MacLean in the Toronto *Star*, 20 March 1926, cited in Weaver, "Imperilled Dreams," 340.

57. French magazines were later included for exemption as well. Transcript of Public Hearing, 28 Oct. 1926, 41–2, 79.

58. See H.L. Keenleyside, *Canada and the United States* (New York 1929), 362–76; J.A. Stevenson, "Canadian Sentiment toward the United States," *Current History*, XVI, Oct. 1930, 63.

59. Advisory Board on Tariff and Taxation, MPAC file, anonymous letter, 26 Oct. 1926, MPAC letter to members of House of Commons, 22 March 1926, PAC.

60. For more extensive comment on this dichotomy in the Canadian nationalism of the 1920s see M. Vipond, "National Consciousness in English-speaking Canada in the 1920's: Seven Studies" (Ph.D. diss., University of Toronto, 1974), passim.

61. Canada, House of Commons, *Debates*, 17 July 1931, 3889.

62. Ibid., 3880.

63. Cited in F. Peers, "Oh say, can you see?" in *Close the 49th Parallel etc.*, I. Lumsden, ed. (Toronto 1970), 13.

AMERICAN INVESTMENT†

MICHAEL BLISS

The Foreign Investment Review Agency was created in 1973–1974 in response to a wave of Canadian nationalist concern about the impact that direct investment by United States' firms was having on the Canadian economy. The concern was of relatively recent development, for at no time in Canadian history before the 1950s had there been serious alarm about foreign investment.

Traditionally there had been no barriers affecting the flow of capital in and out of Canada. In fact the rapid growth of the Canadian economy from colonial times through the mid-1950s had been fueled by constant imports of capital, first French, then British, then American. Foreign investment was both welcomed and actively sought as essential to the development of Canada's storehouse of natural resources. From the initiation of New France during the reign of Louis XIV through Canada's post-World War II economic boom, presided over by the "Minister of Everything," C.D. Howe, there were no significant variations in this attitude.

A strong sense of Canadian economic nationalism did develop in the years immediately following the creation (Confederation) of the modern Dominion of Canada in 1867. It took the form of a neo-mercantilist or protectionist desire to foster secondary manufacturing through the manipulation of tariff barriers. In 1879 the Conservative government of Sir John A. Macdonald responded to this sentiment by

† Michael Bliss, "Founding FIRA: The Historical Background," in *Foreign Investment Review Law in Canada*, ed. James M. Spence and William P. Rosenfeld (Toronto: Butterworths, 1984), 1–11.

a substantial upward revision to turn a large revenue tariff into an instrument to protect Canadian manufacturing. The new policy of tariff protection was labelled Canada's "National Policy." Although Great Britain was still Canada's largest trading partner, much of the protectionist rhetoric of the time focussed on the perceived ill-effects of imports of cheap American manufactured goods.

Substantial opposition to the costs of the National Policy led to intense political controversy. The Liberal party tended to favour freer trade, and flirted with the idea of returning to the high degree of continental free trade that had existed under a reciprocity treaty with the United States in the decade immediately before Confederation. The Canadian general elections of 1891 and 1911 were both fought mainly on the issue of Liberal "continentalism," i.e. proposals for reciprocal tariff reductions, versus Conservative economic nationalism rooted in the National Policy. In both elections economic nationalism was transformed into political nationalism as the Conservatives charged that free trade with the United States would be a prelude to U.S. control of Canada, perhaps through the ultimate "takeover," annexation. Such arguments struck a responsive chord on the part of a patriotic population. In both elections the continentalist option was decisively rejected.

The nationalist strategy of the National Policy was directed towards maximizing Canadian wealth by limiting the free flow of goods across national boundaries. The free flow of capital was not hindered. If anything, the proponents of the National Policy hoped that tariffs would attract foreign investment to Canada to help create the domestic manufacturing industries that were made possible by the protective barriers. The creation of Canadian branch-plants of foreign enterprises was actively encouraged because of their contribution to employment within Canada's borders. From the 1880s through the 1930s hosts of foreign-owned firms, mostly American-owned, established Canadian branches, in part because of the National Policy and such related tariff policies as the Imperial preferences which gave Canadian-made products an advantage in British and other Commonwealth markets. In this formative period of Canadian economic nationalism, then, a policy of hostility to the importation of foreign products was complemented by one of encouraging the importation of foreign capital.

Foreign capital also flowed into Canada to finance resource extraction, the development of the railway network, and the operations of national, provincial, and municipal governments. There were two particularly significant changes in the pattern of foreign investment between 1900 and the 1950s. First, the proportion of foreign investment originating in the United States grew almost constantly, rising from 13.6 percent in 1900 to 75.5 percent in 1950. British investment in Canada declined proportionately. Second, a substantial and growing amount of United States capital coming into Canada was in the form of direct investments, i.e. investments which involved an equity position. Moreover, foreign direct investment tended to be concentrated in certain sectors of the Canadian economy, notably manufacturing, mining, and the petroleum industry. By the late 1950s Canadians faced a situation in which more than sixty percent of their oil and gas industry was controlled by foreign firms (mostly American), more than fifty percent of their mining industry, and nearly half of all their manufacturing industries. Using finer divisions, it was possible to find examples of much greater American control, such as the 100 percent control of Canadian automobile manufacturing by Ford, Chrysler, General Motors, and American Motors.

Much of the foreign investment had taken place during the great 1945-1957 postwar boom in North America. American investors had poured money into what was perceived as a friendly neighbouring nation, culturally almost indistinguishable from the United States, rich in raw materials waiting to be processed to enrich the continental economy. The Liberal governments of the period pursued broadly internationalist policies, not only welcoming foreign capital, but also eschewing the protectionist mentality of the National Policy which had become discredited during the autarchy of the Great Depression and the ensuing international conflict. An American-born engineer, Clarence Decatur Howe, who held several economic portfolios in these Liberal governments, was widely seen as the mastermind of a strategy of holding the door wide open to foreign capital to fuel the Canadian boom. Such minor opposition as there was to this general policy before about 1955 centred in the miniscule Communist Party of Canada. A few Marxist nationalists argued that United States investment in Canada was tantamount to the expansion of imperial control. They were not given much attention.

Some Canadian business circles had always been hostile to or suspicious of foreign-owned firms, particularly when they had to face them in competitive situations. In the mid-1950s Walter Gordon, a management consultant with deep roots in the Toronto business community and strong personal contacts in the Liberal party, began voicing concern about the degree of American ownership in Canada. He was joined by a few other Canadian businessmen, including some Canadian-born executives of branch-plants, who began to worry about the possibility of poor corporate citizenship creating nationalist resentment. In 1956 there was an intense outburst of anti-American sentiment when the Liberal government, at C.D. Howe's insistence, determined to lend an American-controlled company the money needed to complete the building of the first trans-Canada natural gas pipeline. Howe believed that Canadians should be gratified to see the completion of a pipeline entirely on Canadian soil; instead, there was widespread native resentment at the prospect of Americans controlling the pipeline company.

The next year, 1957, the report of a federal Royal Commission on Canada's Economic Prospects, which had been chaired by Walter Gordon, injected the foreign ownership question permanently onto the agenda of Canadian politics. Its summary of the situation was a remarkable anticipation of the thrust of sentiment that ultimately culminated in the creation of the Foreign Investment Review Agency:

> In the course of the Commission's hearings, concern was expressed over the extent to which our productive resources are controlled by non-residents, mostly Americans. Many Canadians are worried about such a large degree of economic decision-making being in the hands of non-residents or in the hands of Canadian companies controlled by non-residents. This concern has arisen because of the concentration of foreign ownership in certain industries, because of the fact that most of it is centred in one country, the United States, and because most of it is in the form of equities which, in the ordinary course of events, are never likely to be repatriated. Some people think it is foolish to worry too much about the possible dangers of foreign investment in this country. However, the contrary opinions on this subject which we have mentioned do in fact exist and if a period of political or economic instability should occur, they might develop into demands for restrictive or discriminatory action of an extreme kind, the consequences of which would be unfortunate for all concerned.
>
> At the root of Canadian concern about foreign investment is undoubtedly a basic, traditional sense of insecurity vis-à-vis our friendly, albeit our much larger and more powerful neighbour, the United States. There is concern that as the position of American capital in the dynamic resource and manufacturing sectors becomes ever more dominant, our economy will inevitably become more and more integrated with that of the United States. Behind this is the fear that continuing integration might lead to economic domination by the United States and eventually to the loss of our political independence.[1]

The Gordon Commission's recommendations on the issue were very modest: that American-controlled firms in Canada give more job opportunities to Canadians, practise fuller corporate disclosure, and consider increasing the opportunities for Canadians to sit on their boards as well as take an equity position in their operations. Neither the proposals nor the statements of concern had significant impact on an academic and political community which was still largely committed to economic liberalism and the concept of a broad comity of interest between Canada and the United States. Between 1957 and 1963 the Conservative government of John Diefenbaker attempted a certain amount of nationalist posturing (promising, for example, to divert fifteen percent of Canada's trade from the United States to Great Britain — a practical impossibility), but instituted no significant policies affecting foreign ownership. It is noteworthy, however, that the final defeat of the Diefenbaker regime involved a sharp disagreement between Canada and the United States on defence policy (largely about commitments Canada had previously made to arm its forces with nuclear weapons). Shortly after Diefenbaker's defeat, a myth was created of a nationalist Prime Minister having been brought down by the power of United States influence on Canada.

Although the new Liberal government, headed by Lester B. Pearson, was ostensibly committed to restoring harmonious relations with the United States, its Finance Minister, Walter Gordon, had not wavered in his concern about foreign ownership. In his first budget, presented in 1963, Gordon attempted to levy a thirty percent "takeover tax" on the sale of publicly-held Canadian companies to foreign investors. The ill-considered and unworkable proposal, accompanied by other discriminatory taxes, aroused a storm of opposition both inside and outside the country. Within a few days Gordon was forced to abandon his nationalist measures, and, in his humiliation, nearly abandoned his job. In succeeding years as Finance Minister he clashed repeatedly with American investors and bureaucrats over issues ranging from the expansion of the Mercantile Bank in Canada to *Time* magazine's objection to protectionist legislation aimed at eliminating its cheap, profitable Canadian edition. The incidents all strengthened Gordon's antipathy to American influence on Canada. In a 1966 book entitled *A Choice for Canada* he wrote as follows:

> During the two and one-half years I held that office [Finance], the influence that financial and business interests in the U.S. had on Canadian policy and opinion was continually brought home to me. On occasion, this influence was reinforced by representations tationstationstationsfrom the State Department and the American administration as a whole. It was pressed by those who direct American businesses in Canada, by their professional advisers, by Canadian financiers whose interests were identified directly or indirectly with American investment in Canada, by influential members of the Canadian civil service, by some representatives of the university community, and by some sections of the press.[2]

In the changing Canadian climate of the middle and late 1960s Gordon's minority views were beginning to find a more receptive audience. United States involvement in Vietnam was beginning to have an immense impact reviving and reinforcing Canadians' sometime sense that there was not necessarily a complete community of interest between the two societies. An upsurge of Canadian nationalism, stimulated and expressed during the 1967 Centennial celebrations, was sometimes coloured by deep anti-American sentiments, including a fear that the United States was dominating Canada both economically and culturally. The academic and literary community devoured books with self-explanatory titles like *Lament for a Nation, Silent Surrender, The New Romans,* and *Close the 49th Parallel, Etc.: The Americanization of Canada,* and drew the authors' intended conclusions. The notion of Canada as an object of American "imperialism" became increasingly widespread, the nationalist view being that the country's history had been one of passing from colony to nation to colony again. The border began to take on new meaning, as many Canadian nationalists suggested that the customs' houses be supplemented by other kinds of barriers to free intercourse. The government of Canada's previous open-door policy of foreign investment began to be seen as a form of the old continentalist strategy, a policy of selling Canada to the United States. The historical and factual inaccuracies of these views were challenged with decreasing frequency.

The Pearson government responded in a piecemeal, pragmatic way to pressures generated by the new nationalism. From well before the 1950s there had been a minor tradition of protecting certain key sectors of the Canadian economy, such as broadcasting and the banking system, from substantial foreign ownership. In the mid-1960s several major pieces of legislation extended the key sector approach to other areas of the mass media. An attempt was also made to clarify the idea of "corporate citizenship" by developing federal guidelines to which it was hoped all foreign-owned companies would adhere. As well, as part of the agreement facilitating his re-entry into the Cabinet in 1967 (he had resigned in 1965), Walter Gordon was allowed to establish a special Task Force on the Structure of Canadian Industry. It was chaired by a young University of Toronto economist, Melville H. Watkins, and in 1968 produced the first government-sponsored study of the foreign ownership issue, entitled *Foreign Ownership and the Structure of Canadian Industry.*

The *Watkins Report,* as it came to be called, detailed the numerous benefits accruing to Canadians as a result of foreign investment, but also considered a wide range of possible costs. These included the extraterritoriality phenomenon caused by the application of foreign laws to subsidiaries operating in Canada, the limitations a multinational enterprise might place on its branches' ability to export or undertake research and development, and problems of transfer pricing and taxation. Acknowledging the difficulty of determining the precise effect of foreign investment, and offering no final assessment of its own, the task force did note that "No other country . . . seems prepared to tolerate so high a degree of foreign ownership as exists in Canada."[3] The group noted the policies of other countries, including France, Great Britain, and Japan, which seemed to screen all new foreign investments; but they did not go that far in their own recommendations. They supported a proposal Gordon had made in 1963 to found a Canada Development Corporation to mobilize Canadian capital to help forestall or even reverse the wave of foreign "takeovers," recommended other measures to improve Canadian entrepreneurship, called for direct action to block extraterritorial intrusion, and recommended that "a special agency be created to co-ordinate policies with respect to multi-national enterprise."[4]

The *Watkins Report* concluded with the suggestion that its recommendations be seen as comprising a "New National Policy," one which would replace the old National Policy as the vital strategy for maintaining the independence of the Canadian economy and increasing its efficiency. It was an appropriate genuflection to the Canadian past, for by 1968 it was clear that a new wave of economic nationalism was taking shape in parallel to that of the 1870s. This time, however, the concern would be to regulate the cross-border flow of capital in addition to that of goods.

By the late 1960s and early 1970s the concern about foreign investment, which was continually being stimulated by media publicity of dramatic American "takeovers" of Canadian companies, was often expressed in popular fears that the country was being sold out to Americans. Unless something was done soon, the argument went, the Americans would own everything and Canada would disappear. These fears ignored substantial evidence that Canada's dependence on foreign investment was actually beginning to decline, and perhaps had been declining for some time. "Canada's overall dependence on foreign capital relative to total Canadian capital formation has declined from the first decade of the century to the third to the seventh as domestic sources of savings have expanded," the Watkins group had noted, speculating that the decline would continue.[5] It has. This phenomenon, which will not surprise anyone familiar with European or American economic history, suggests that the new Canadian economic nationalism of the 1960s was rooted more in a revolution of rising expectations vis-à-vis capital formation than it was in rational perceptions of a real problem. The alarm Canadians felt about foreign ownership was not so much a function of its seriousness as a national problem, for that seriousness was decreasing, as it was a function of Canadians' growing belief that they could do something about it.

The federal government, now headed by Pierre Elliott Trudeau, was still not sure exactly what it wanted to do. In 1969 the Watkins recommendations and the problem were turned over to a junior minister, Mr. Herb Gray, for special study. Gray conducted his study during three years of intense nationalist ferment in Canada. The rising tide of cultural nationalism had engulfed the literary and academic communities, producing intense and often successful campaigns to subsidize Canadian publishing houses, protect impressionable Canadians from an excess of American television programs, limit imports of American professors teaching in Canadian universities, and juggle the tax laws to stimulate investment in Canadian motion pictures. In 1970 Walter Gordon and a number of influential friends, most of them based in Toronto, formed the Committee for an Independent Canada, as a nationalist lobby group. Melville Watkins of the Watkins report lobbied for action on his recommendations and then became converted to Marxist nationalist-socialism, becoming much more hostile to American "imperialism." Lobbyists for more money for scientific research were adding their state-subsidized voices to the clamour through reports and studies emanating from the newly-formed Science Council of Canada which blamed foreign investment for inhibiting the growth of indigenous Canadian research capacity. Considerable adverse media publicity was given to any American measures or proposals that seemed to hint at either continentalist designs on Canada (e.g. proposals to pool energy or water supplies), or U.S. nationalism (such as subsidized export schemes) which would justify a Canadian response in kind. The whole western world in these years was enduring a spasm of concern about whether or not the modern and mostly American multinational enterprise was susceptible to control by the citizens of the nationstate. The proponents of economic liberalism, whose views had previously dominated Canadian academic and political discourse, seemed to speak in softer tones, perhaps because their audience seemed to be constantly shrinking.[6]

By 1971 the left wing of Canadian politics, which included all of the New Democratic Party as well as a substantial segment of the governing Liberals, believed that taking action on foreign ownership question would be a first step towards the economic betterment of the country. Indeed, the idea that foreign ownership was a national problem, requiring some kind of action, had become an item of conventional wisdom across the spectrum of Canadian politics. Most politicians and other commentators used "foreign" and "American" synonymously. A 1972 Gallup poll revealed that 67 percent of Canadians believed the country had enough U.S. capital; in 1964 only 46 percent had shared that belief. From 1969 to 1972 the proportion of respondents agreeing that U.S. ownership of Canadian companies was "bad" for the economy had grown from 34 percent to 47 percent, "good" having decreased from 43 percent to 38 percent (the balance being undecided). Such divergence as there was in Canadian opinion on the issue now tended to be regional, with citizens of the prosperous Ontario heartland being much more in favour of limiting foreign investment than those in regions of low growth and high unemployment.

In 1971 the federal government created Gordon's Canada Development Corporation as a publicly-controlled vehicle to mobilize what was popularly thought of as an effort to "buy back" Canada. The chief recommendation of the *Gray Report, Foreign Direct Investment in Canada* (published in 1972; excerpts leaked to a nationalist magazine in 1971) was the establishment of a review mechanism or screening agency to oversee foreign direct investment in Canada. The recommendation was accepted in principle by the Trudeau government, which in 1972 introduced legislation to establish a process of reviewing foreign takeovers. The bill was still pending when Parliament was dissolved for a general election. In 1973 the government, now dependent for survival on parliamentary support from the leftwing and nationalist New Democratic Party, introduced a revised bill which would extend the review process to new investments in Canada as well as takeovers, and establish the Foreign Investment Review Agency to "advise and assist" the Minister of Trade and Commerce in administration of the act. Bill C–132, establishing the FIRA, received final approval by all parties in the House of Commons in November, 1973. In 1974 the agency began to function.

One of the more important criticisms levied against the bill during its passage came from those provinces which felt there should be a provision allowing a province to opt out from the operation of the act. These suggestions were not accepted. According to the 1973 *Canadian Annual Review*,

> The principal factor behind the federal government's decision to exclude any opting-out provision was its recognition that most provinces would have exercised the option of suspending application and thus have made a mockery of the federal legislation. It was believed that only Ontario and British Columbia would not have taken advantage of this option. What this indicated was that support of controls on foreign investment was not broadly based in Canada. The ultranationalists appeared to be concentrated in the large urban centres in southern Ontario and to a lesser degree in Vancouver.[7]

The *Gray Report*, which had fathered FIRA, is usually read as a much more nationalist document than the *Watkins Report*, the Gordon recommendations, or any previous study. And, of course, FIRA has been seen as an instrument created to foster an extreme form of Canadian economic nationalism, the "ultranationalism" referred to above. In this context, however, it should be noted that FIRA was conceived and created in a climate of such extreme nationalist agitation that it was in fact a relatively modest compromise proposal. Although some business commentators and economists argued that the whole concept of assessing the contribution of foreign investments to an economy was grounded in economic illiteracy, many Canadian nationalists wanted to go further. In 1970 the House of Commons standing committee on External Affairs, for example, had recommended that all companies operating in Canada be required, over time, to make 51 percent of their voting shares available to Canadians. This committee and other nationalists were also urging major extensions of the key sector approach, the idea of excluding foreigners from one industry after another. The legislation establishing FIRA was condemned as too little too late by most of the gurus of Canadian economic nationalism, including Walter Gordon and Melville Watkins.

In the context of the time, the *Gray Report* and its key recommendation were actually an attempt to straddle the fence. Gray and his advisers were caught between a body of Canadian opinion which, like free trade theorists of old, believed in maximizing the freedom of capital movements; and a new body of Canadian nationalist thought which, like the old protectionism, wanted to limit the flow and nature of imports. Although the thrust of the *Gray Report* was in the general direction of the new protectionism, it was still realized that firm judgments on the costs versus benefits of any fixed foreign investment policy were next to impossible. The key adjective echoing through the founding conception of FIRA is "flexible," and the *Gray Report* conceived its relationship to more direct nationalist policies as follows:

> A review process would be flexible. It could concentrate on that relatively small proportion of foreign investments which are of greatest concern to Canada at any point in time. It could focus on the key variable (e.g. research and development, industrial structure for economies of scale, and so on), which differs from industry to industry and from case to case. It could adapt to different industries and changing conditions over time, in light of increased efficiency and new technology which a particular investor might bring to Canada. As general economic policies and specific remedial measures involving capital markets, technology and management result in strengthening of indigenous capability in particular industries, the need for foreign direct investment could decline. A review, as opposed to a policy based solely on the designation of key sectors or the introduction of across-the-board ownership rules, would be flexible enough to take account of such changes in its negotiations.
>
> A review process can and ought to be used as an economically rational instrument. Unlike some of the alternative policies described below, it could avoid the costs to the economy which would result from protecting Canadian owners through

blocking all foreign direct investment; blocking all direct investment in a particular industry regardless of its terms or accompanying benefits such as new technology; or establishing fixed percentages or standards for exports, procurement, etc. without regard for the economies of individual industries or cases. The delineation of key sectors to be protected from foreign investment or the introduction of precise formulae covering such things as the extent of exports and the procurement of components would necessarily be arbitrary and thus potentially economically costly.[8]

The creation of FIRA, then, represented not so much a triumph of one view of the "problem" of foreign direct investment in Canada as it did a political shifting of much of the issue out of the realm of national politics and into the hands of a regulatory body. A regulatory body as flexible as FIRA was intended to be would shape its policies in response to changing perceptions of Canada's need for foreign investment. Given Canada's changing needs and the changing structure of the United States and world economies, there might even come a time in the future when, as one of the members of Watkins' task force later argued, the job might be to find ways of soliciting American capital.[9]

Notes

1. *Royal Commission on Canada's Economic Prospects, Final Report* (Ottawa: Queen's Printer, 1957), 390.

2. Walter L. Gordon, *A Choice for Canada* (Toronto: McClelland & Stewart, 1966), xix.

3. *Foreign Ownership and the Structure of Canadian Industry*, Report of the Task Force on the Structure of Canadian Industry (Ottawa: Privy Council Office, 1968), 363.

4. Ibid., 395.

5. Ibid., 114.

6. This point is expressed in a slightly different, sharper form by the authors of the standard history of Canada since 1945: "It was not businessmen who pushed the government from the benign acquiescence of the late sixties to the systematic screening and interventionism of 1971 and thereafter. The credit — if that is the word — belongs to three groups: nationalist sectarians among the intelligensia and their echoes in the media; like-minded people within the Liberal party and caucus; and eager officials, anxious to 'regulate' foreign-owned firms in the national interest. . . . In the background was an ever-increasing but unacknowledged echoing of American populist opinion, which

held that large business is Bad, multinational business is Worse, and [after 1973] oil companies are Worst of All." Robert Bothwell, John English, and Ian Drummond, *Canada Since 1945* (Toronto: University of Toronto Press, 1981), 416–16.

7. John Saywell, ed., *Canadian Annual Review of Politics and Public Affairs, 1973* (Toronto: University of Toronto Press, 1974), 337.

8. *Foreign Direct Investment in Canada* (Ottawa: Information Canada, 1972), 453–4.

9. Saywell, ed., *Canadian Annual Review, 1971*, 346.

THE ROLE OF THE UNIONS†

IRVING M. ABELLA

There has been very little written about the history of trade unions in Canada, but a good deal of what has been written should never have been; it has tended to confuse more than to elucidate. The purpose of my paper is not to condemn those who have written about the Canadian labour movement, but rather to question some of the basic premises which they have all unquestioningly adopted and which they have done much to perpetuate.

The history of the Canadian labour movement, at least as seen by almost all these authors, is based on three seemingly irrefutable truisms. Firstly, they all agree, as does almost everybody else who claims to know anything about the labour movement, that American unions had to move into Canada in order to create a strong, viable Canadian labour movement, that once we Canadians allowed in American industry, American unions necessarily had to follow. Thus the growth of international unionism was not only believed necessary, but beneficial as well, since Canadians were obviously not capable of building their own national union movement. Not one of these authors denies that American unions were absolutely essential in building the powerful trade-union organizations we have in Canada at the present time.

Similarly, it is the conventional wisdom amongst most knowledgeable Canadians that the contributions of the Communist Party to the

† Irving M. Abella, "American Unionism, Communism and the Canadian Labor Movement: Some Myths and Realities," in *The Influence of the United States on Canadian Development: Eleven Case Studies*, ed. Richard A. Preston (Durham, N.C.: Duke University Press, 1972), 205–25.

Canadian labour movement were largely, if not entirely, negative, that the Communists hurt the organization of labour in Canada more than they helped it, and that the Canadian labour movement would have progressed much more rapidly had it not been for Communist interference.

Finally, every student of the Canadian labour movement — almost without exception — concludes that, while the American Federation of Labor treated its Canadian affiliate, the Trades and Labor Congress, as an inferior dependant, the CIO's relationship with its Canadian affiliate, the Canadian Congress of Labour, was based on an assumption of equality between the two; in other words, the universal interpretation is that the CIO, unlike the AFL, recognized and accepted the autonomy of its Canadian affiliate, and indeed, encouraged the independent pretensions of the CCL.

These then are the three fundamental premises upon which the history of the Canadian labour movement has been built. So obvious and accepted are these axioms that few have questioned any one of them, let alone all three. For the rest of this paper, this is what I intend to do.

There are of course many reasons why American unions found Canada such a fertile territory for growth, but the primary reason, it seems to me, was that Canadian workers were so receptive. And why were they so hospitable? Simple because Canadian workers believed that American unions could do a better job for them than could Canadian unions. It wasn't that American unions were so imperialistic and aggressive; they were merely responding to pressing invitations sent by Canadian workers who had more confidence in the capabilities and strength of the American unions than they had in their own. But was this a feeling based on fact, or was it, as I suspect, based more on the typical Canadian belief that Americans can do things better than we can, that they are a more capable, aggressive people, and therefore that American unions could assure the "better life" the Canadian working man so desperately wanted, which was something he felt Canadian unions could not provide?

The most common explanation for the presence of American unions in Canada is that in a country the size and population of Canada, with the concomitant difficulties of communication, to create a strong nationwide trade-union movement would have been an impossibility. As Professor John Crispo, the recognized authority on international unionism in Canada, puts it, "Canadian unions lacked any substantial domestic base." "The weak industrial base of the country and the sparseness of the population," he adds, "made it extremely difficult for any sort of national trade union movement to establish roots." He also argues that the "growing American-based unions had much more to offer the Canadian worker" than did "fledgling" unions started by Canadians. The reason Canadian workers joined American unions, according to Professor Crispo, was that these unions "could supply financial aid and experienced personnel that would have taken many years to develop through Canadian resources alone."[1] This, of course, is the traditional analysis. Perhaps the time has arrived to test this hypothesis. And what better way to test it than to study in some detail how specific American unions came into Canada to see if this thesis is, in fact, valid.

Since Confederation there have been at least five major so-called incursions of American labour organizations into Canada. First to come in were the various craft unions such as the iron moulders and printers who arrived as early as 1859 and later, as affiliates of the American Federation of Labor, formed the Trades and Labor Congress. In the late 1860s and 1870s the railway brotherhoods crossed into Canada. The next wave came in the 1880s when the Knights of Labor began organizing in Canada. In the 1890s and first decade of this century the Western Federation of Miners and the International Workers of the World invaded the Canadian labour scene. And finally in the 1930s and 1940s the CIO entered Canada. In each of these periods, of course, Canadians joined these unions for various and quite different reasons. For purposes of this paper, however, I intend to look only at the most recent, and — I hope — the last, intrusion of a foreign labour centre into Canada, that of the CIO. Perhaps the conclusions that may be drawn from such a study could also throw some light on the reasons American unions came into Canada in earlier periods of our history.

The CIO came into Canada at a time when almost half the organized workers in Canada belonged to national unions — the Workers Unity League, the All-Canadian Congress of Labour, and the Catholic unions in Quebec. The other half were members of AFL unions affiliated with the Trades and Labor Congress. This, it seems, was the one time in this century for Canadians to regain control of their own labor movement, because never before nor ever again would national unions have that high a percentage of the organized workers of the country. But the arrival of the CIO doomed that hope. And the most ironical aspect of that arrival was that the CIO didn't even want to come.

From the beginning, CIO activity in Canada was more the result of the forceful demands and activities of the Canadian workers than of the plans of the CIO hierarchy in the United States. Taking their example from fellow workers in the United States, Canadian workers started their own organizing campaigns. They looked for leadership to the Trades and Labor Congress, but instead, received little more than advice to wait. Because they felt no Canadian union was in a position to undertake any large-scale organization, by default, therefore, they opted for the CIO.

The reaction of the CIO was something less than encouraging. Like those of the TLC, the CIO leaders also urged Canadian workers to hold back. John L. Lewis and his colleagues were much too involved in the hectic labour scene below the border to give the Canadian movement more than a passing thought.

But Lewis had not taken into account the growing demands of Canadian workers for organization. These were most evident in Ontario. With the worst of the depression over, industry after industry began announcing record profits and issuing optimistic reports for the new year. Workers, on the other hand, were still being paid depression wages and were growing increasingly more restless. With the example of the CIO sit-downs just across the border, it was only a matter of time before Ontario workers would rebel both against their deplorable working conditions and their overcautious union leadership.

Dismayed by the apparent apathy of the CIO, Ontario workers took matters into their own hands. All over the province tiny locals were springing up, calling themselves CIO. Naturally, the CIO in the United States had no knowledge of these locals. Throughout the province, a small group of dedicated men — most of them active Communists — were organizing for the CIO, though again, the CIO had never heard of them. Within a few months, the CIO found itself with scores of unions and thousands of workers it did not want, and even worse, did not know what to do with.

For the workers of Ontario the magic word was CIO. Wherever they heard it, they flocked; whoever used it, they trusted. Thus what Canadian organizers for eager Canadian unions had been unable to do, Canadian organizers for a reluctant American union succeeded in doing. Canadian workers obviously felt that the CIO magic would rub off on them; what the CIO was achieving for its members in the United States, it would also achieve for its members in Canada. Even though the CIO was not yet ready to expand into Canada, Canadian workers insisted. Thus a protesting CIO was dragged unwillingly into Canada. But even then it refused to do anything to help Canadian workers. It did not disown any of the unofficial CIO organizers in the country. On the other hand, neither did it assist them in any way. Indeed it was on the assembly lines of Oshawa and Sarnia, and not in the union offices in Washington and Detroit, that industrial unionism in Canada was born. It was not John L. Lewis nor any of his representatives who brought the CIO to Canada. It was the body-shop workers in Oshawa and the foundry workers in Sarnia who were responsible.

The first CIO sit-down strike in Canada occurred on 1 March 1937, at the Holmes Foundry in Sarnia. Actually, the strike had little to do with the CIO. Some seventy of the plant's workers — most of them recent immigrants from Eastern Europe — enraged both at the passivity of the CIO and at the company's refusal to negotiate with their new union, sat down at their machines. Within hours they were ruthlessly and bloodily evicted by a mob of Sarnia's "best" citizens, armed with such antiunion devices as crowbars, baseball bats, bricks, and steel pipes. The strike was soon broken, as were the arms, legs, and heads of many of the strikers. The strikers were at once arrested and convicted of trespassing; no charges were laid against the strike-breakers.[2]

The Ontario Premier, Mitchell Hepburn, immediately denounced the strikers and those "foreign agitators" who had led the strike. Unfortunately for the premier's case, there were no foreign agitators. All the strikers and their leaders were residents of the province of Ontario. No one from the CIO, nor indeed, from anywhere outside the province had been involved in this strike.

The famous Oshawa strike one month later marks the birth of industrial unionism in Canada. This two-week walkout by some four thousand workers of the General Motors plant in Oshawa was the turning point in Canadian labour history.[3] On their own these workers organized themselves into local 222 of the United Automobile Workers of America, a CIO affiliate. With some initial assistance from Hugh Thompson, a UAW organizer from Detroit, the workers forced the GM management to negotiate with their new union. When General Motors, on the insistence of Premier Hepburn, broke off negotiations, the union called a strike and shut down the plant.

For two weeks, despite the unyielding pressure from both the company and the provincial government, the workers held out. At times these pressures were almost irresistible. Hepburn was determined to keep the CIO out of Ontario, not so much because he was concerned with the violence associated with the CIO, but rather because he was worried that the CIO would organize the gold mines in Northern Ontario, and thus would jeopardize the enormous profits of the Ontario "mine barons" — all of whom were his cronies and amongst his closest advisers as well. When the federal government rejected Hepburn's request for a large contingent of the Royal Canadian Mounted Police to intimidate the strikers, the Ontario Premier founded his own police force of unemployed veterans and University of Toronto students. These were the infamous "Hepburn Hussars," or as they were known in Oshawa, "Sons of Mitches." Hepburn also attempted to deport Thompson and other CIO agents in the province, but aside from Thompson, who was a British subject and could not be deported, he could find no other organizers from outside the province. He sent messages to General Motors executives in Detroit urging them to hold firm. He even cabled Colonel McLaughlin, the president of the company in Canada, who was vacationing in a yacht somewhere in the Caribbean, to order his lieutenants in Oshawa not to negotiate with the union.

But Hepburn's efforts were in vain. The strikers were determined and eventually the company agreed to sign a contract with the new union. The achievement of the Oshawa strikers in fighting and defeating both the power of big business and government inspired workers throughout Canada. It gave the CIO the impetus it so desperately needed to begin organization in the mass production industries of the country. The agreement at Oshawa, but particularly Hepburn's peculiar behaviour, had suddenly turned the rather somnolent CIO organizing campaign into a violent crusade. The Oshawa strikers had won a great victory for themselves, but even more important, they had created for the CIO the psychology of success and enthusiasm needed for a massive organizing effort. What Akron and Flint had done in the United States, Oshawa was to do for Canada. It proved to be a landmark in Canadian labour history.

What is most significant about the Oshawa Strike is that it was conducted by Canadians without any assistance from the CIO. Although Hugh Thompson was ostensibly in charge of organization, most of the organizing was in fact done by Canadians. Whatever financial assistance the strikers were given came from churches and neighbours. Not one penny of aid came from the United States. Both the CIO and the UAW decided that they neither had the men nor the money to help the strikers. They also refused to call a sympathy strike of GM workers in the United States to support the strikers in Oshawa. Though the UAW had publicly promised to send one hundred thousand dollars, in the end all it delivered was its best wishes. Thus what the Oshawa strikers achieved, they achieved on their own.

In fact, I suppose it can be argued that the CIO connection was as harmful as it was helpful. Hepburn and his mine-owning friends were not so much opposed to the creation of a union in Oshawa as they were to the possibility of the CIO gaining a foothold in Ontario. When reports filtered down to Queens Park from the North that the CIO was organizing the mines, the determination of Hepburn and his cronies to crush the strike hardened. The CIO had, however, nothing to do with the increased labour activity in the North. All the organizing there was being done by a small corps of dedicated amateurs, none of whom had any official connection with the CIO. The General Motors Company agreed to a settlement in Oshawa not because of the threats of the CIO but because it desperately needed cars for the Canadian and Empire market, and these could only be built in Oshawa. Fear of losing these markets to Ford and Chrysler, rather than fear of John L. Lewis and Hugh Thompson, forced General Motors to recognize the union. Negotiations with the company were carried on solely by Canadians, Charlie Millard and J.L. Cohen, though, of course, Hugh Thompson was available to advise, although by the time the settlement was reached, he was back in the United States.

Thus the role of the CIO in the Oshawa Strike seems ambiguous. The strike was conducted, financed and settled by Canadians. The CIO played no actual role, except in the minds of Hepburn, the mine owners, and, perhaps most importantly, in the minds of the strikers themselves. Caught up in the mystique of the CIO, they believed the international connection was essential. Even though half the organized workers of Canada at the time belonged to Canadian unions, the workers in Oshawa and across the country seemed to think that only American unions could provide the necessary muscle to protect and forward their interests. It was this attitude, based more on sentiment than fact, which, more than anything else, has doomed national unions in Canada.

Through the victory at Oshawa was a victory for Canadians it was immediately hailed across the country as a great CIO triumph. Because Hepburn had defined the enemy at Oshawa as the CIO, the CIO was given full credit for a victory it had done little to win.

Following the Oshawa strike there was a massive CIO organizing campaign amongst the industrial workers of Ontario. CIO organizers went into the textile mills of Eastern Ontario, the steel mills in Hamilton, the rubber plants in Kitchener, and the gold mines in the North. But again none of these men were American; in fact they were not even official CIO organizers. Rather they were largely a group of young, militant radicals, most of them members or supporters of the Communist Party.

Long before the CIO had undertaken the organization of the mass-production industries, the Communists had maintained an elaborate framework of unions, both inside and outside the Workers Unity League. Some of these had existed only on paper but they had been built around a faithful and militant nucleus of experienced party members who knew how to chair meetings, make motions, give speeches, print pamphlets, mimeograph handbills, and organize picket lines — all indispensable when thousands of workers without previous trade-union experience flocked to union halls. As Tim Buck, the Communist leader, put it: "Our party had trained and developed a whole cadre of people who knew about unions and knew how to go about organizing them. And the party members, even though they didn't work in the industry, would go out distributing leaflets, helping to organize the union."[4] When the order was given in 1935 to disband the Workers Unity League, the Communist unions moved directly into the Trades and Labor Congress and most of the Party organizers began organizing for the CIO. Without their aid CIO efforts in Canada would have been vastly circumscribed, and conceivably even aborted.

The weeks following the Oshawa Strike were euphoric for the CIO. Scores of new locals were started in plants and industries that had never before been organized. Thousands of new members were organized. Unfortunately, these halcyon days turned out to be sadly evanescent. Many of the workers who had signed up with the CIO in the first flush of enthusiasm soon drifted away. By August 1937, CIO organization had come to a grinding halt.

The CIO failure following Oshawa was not surprising. With no funds and few experienced organizers organization campaigns were doomed.

The CIO hierarchy below the border was just too involved in its own projects to lend much assistance or thought to Canada. Of even more significance, however, the CIO had made the strategic decision that organization in Canada would have to be undertaken by Canadians themselves. As Sidney Hillman, the "theoretician" of the CIO put it, "Canada must develop its own leaders if it is to have a sound labour movement."[5] Both John L. Lewis and Hillman felt that organization in Canada would have to wait until there was a body of Canadian personnel large enough to carry out the job.

Both Lewis and Hillman were admitting the obvious: that CIO organization in Canada was almost entirely the work of Canadians; little help had been given in the past, and now even less would be given in the future. Canadian organizers for the CIO would again be on their own, though they could still use the CIO label. Yet the advantages of using the CIO name were dubious. Whenever and wherever the three magic letters appeared, employer and government resistance stiffened immeasurably. Canadian union organizers would probably have been more successful had they dropped the CIO affiliation — an affiliation which at the time provided little of benefit to the Canadian organizers and workingmen.

By the middle of 1938 and into 1939, with the economy rebounding, the future of the CIO revived and new, more successful, organizing campaigns were launched. Again these were staffed and financed exclusively by Canadians. Most of these men had one thing in common: they were members of the Communist Party. In fact, so influential was the Party in the UAW that the union's headquarters in Detroit would send the weekly edition of its newspaper to Communist Party headquarters in downtown Toronto to be distributed to the various UAW locals in southern Ontario.[6] Indeed the entire CIO operation in Ontario was run by Communists. Thus when the militantly anti-Communist Charlie Millard was appointed by John L. Lewis to co-ordinate CIO activities in Ontario he found himself surrounded in the CIO head office in Toronto by Communists. Only on Saturday morning, when the Party held its regular weekly meeting, did Millard have the office to himself, and even then a Party member stayed behind, in Joe Salsberg's words, "to keep his eye on things."[7] There was thus a direct pipeline from the CIO offices to Communist head-quarters; decisions made at the latter would shortly thereafter be made at the former, while those made at the former would instantly be known at the latter. It seems very obvious therefore that the Communists played a historic role in the development of the CIO in Canada. . . .

From the evidence available to me it appears that all the major CIO unions in Canada — the UAW, the United Steelworkers, the United Electrical Workers, the International Woodworkers of America and the Mine Mill and Smelter Workers — were organized and financed by Canadians with little, and often no help from their parent organizations in the United States. Indeed it seems that one American union, the United Steelworkers of America, survived its first few years of existence only because of the funds flowing in from Canada. Dues collected from the Steel local in Sydney, Nova Scotia, made it possible for the International to meet its financial obligations. Without the regular monthly payment from Sydney, there is some doubt whether Steel could have kept afloat, especially after John L. Lewis split with Steel's president, Philip Murray, and turned off the subsidies flowing from his Mineworkers union into Steel's coffers.[8]

The United Electrical Workers union was organized in Canada by C.S. Jackson, a Canadian. And indeed since 1939 all the organizing for the UE in Canada has been carried on by Canadians. Because both the parent organization in the United States and the Canadian affiliate were thought to be controlled by Communists, it was almost impossible for the leaders of both sections to meet together, since as suspected Communists, none could cross the border. Thus the UE from the beginning has been on its own, and in fact is now a larger and more powerful union in Canada than the American dominated and subsidized International Union of Electrical Workers.

The International Woodworkers of America was in fact largely founded by a Canadian, Harold Pritchett. A one-time organizer for the Workers Unity League, he resigned the presidency when he was expelled from the United States for his Communist connections. He then devoted all his energies to organizing the IWA in British Columbia, and was so successful that, until 1948, the B.C. section of the union subsidized the much smaller and poorer American section. All the organizing in Canada for the IWA was done by Canadians and much of the money they raised went to the United States to support IWA activities south of the border.

Finally, the Mine Mill and Smelter Workers was also the work of Canadians. In fact, the Sudbury local was the largest in the entire union and for a time it provided the bulk of the union's revenue. Such smaller CIO unions as the Textile Workers and the Packinghouse Workers were again largely organized by Canadians from Canadian funds with almost no assistance from American parent organizations.

What conclusions can be drawn from this description of CIO activity in Canada in the 1930s and early 1940s? If almost all the organizing for the CIO was done by Canadians, if almost all the money needed for this organization was provided by Canadians, and if all the leadership in the new unions was provided by Canadians, then who needed the CIO? What did the CIO do for Canadians that Canadians weren't doing for themselves? Was the CIO in fact necessary for the development of an industrial union movement in Canada?

I suppose the one deduction we can safely make is that, at the time, Canadian workers obviously believed that the CIO was necessary. For the Canadian workingman old traditions die hard. Because he felt that American unions had been essential in the past, despite the drastically changed situation of the 1930s he obviously believed they were still essential. Caught up in the "continentalist" ideology, and in the belief in the superiority of things American, Canadian workers were preconditioned to join American rather than Canadian unions; and having just suffered through a ravaging depression, they were understandably more concerned with material benefits than with national identity. They felt they had no choice but to join forces with their fellow workers in the United States. After all, their problems were the same, their traditions similar, and in many cases they worked for the same employers. Above all, the CIO seemed to have much more to offer than any Canadian union. It had the personnel, the large treasury, and, most important, the experience to provide Canadian workers with the organization they so urgently needed.

Or so Canadians thought. Yet in fact, the personnel, the treasury, and the experience were not provided by Americans but by Canadians. All the CIO provided was its name; and if this is all it provided then perhaps Canadians could have done the jobs themselves without any American assistance at all. If this is true for the CIO advance into Canada in the 1930s then perhaps it is also true of previous American union incursions into Canada. Perhaps international unions were, after all, not necessary for the development of a trade union movement in Canada. Perhaps, if the CIO example is the prototype, Canadians could have controlled their own unions right from the beginning. In any case, the nature of these earlier movements of American unions to Canada should be reexamined.

Surely it is also time to reexamine the contribution of the Communists to the Canadian labour movement. From my own research into the 1930s and 1940s it seems to me that on the whole their contribution was beneficial and perhaps even necessary for the development and growth of an industrial union movement in Canada.

. . .

Finally, let me deal with the relationship between the CIO and the CCL. Conventional wisdom has it that the relationship was between equals. As one noted student of the labour movement, Professor Paul Norgren, described it in 1951: "the CCL has been free of any domination by the CIO and the relationship between the two organizations has remained entirely amicable."[9] After his exhaustive study of international unionism in Canada, John Crispo concludes that the CIO "appears never to have had . . . designs . . . to interfere in the affairs of the CCL," and that the CIO fully sympathized "with Canadian aspirations for independence."[10]

Unfortunately these analyses are simply not true. Between the CIO and the CCL there was always a great deal of tension and animosity. One would have thought that the CIO should have stayed out of the

CCL's affairs, since the development of CIO unions in Canada was largely the work of Canadians. But right from the beginning the CIO was insistent upon showing the flag in Canada — the American flag that is. For a time it stubbornly refused to allow its unions in Canada to merge with the ACCL on the ground that they might sever their international connection. When the Canadian affiliates overcame this opposition the CIO then demanded that the newly created Congress devote all its energies to organizing workers into CIO unions. It also insisted that the CCL hand over to the appropriate CIO union its national and chartered unions, and to desist from organizing any more of these unions. This provoked a bitter squabble, since the CCL received most of its revenues from its national and chartered unions and not from its affiliated CIO unions, most of whose revenues went to the United States. Whatever funds dribbled back across the border from CIO headquarters in Washington to the CCL offices in Ottawa, the CIO insisted be used for solely CIO purposes. In addition, over Congress objections, the CIO demanded that the CCL accept as affiliates all CIO unions in Canada, and that all jurisdictional disputes among Canadian CIO unions be settled in the United States. After lengthy acrimonious disputes, the CCL usually — but not always — got its way on all these matters.[11]

They key man in warding off the designs of the CIO was the CCL's dynamic secretary-treasurer, Pat Conroy. He had been elected to this key position because he was a member of a CIO union — the United Mineworkers of America, but after a few short months in office he found himself spending a good deal of his time fighting the CIO. According to him, the aim of the CIO was to make the Canadian Congress of Labour its "satellite." Conroy felt that the Canadian labour movement had been for too long a satellite of American unions, and that it had finally arrived at a stage of its development where it needed a central labour body of independent decision-making authority.[12] It was his job, as he saw it, to give the CCL that authority.

On the other hand the CIO was not prepared to give the Congress that authority, at least not without a fight. To the CIO, the CCL was no different from any CIO state council; in other words the Canadian Congress of Labour in CIO eyes was no different than for example, the Nevada CIO Labor Council. It was for this reason that the CIO insisted at the founding convention of the World Federation of Trade Unions in London in 1945 that North America should have only one seat on the Executive Board, and that that seat should always be occupied by the United States. Conroy refused to support this measure on the sensible grounds that "no one could represent Canada . . . but Canada." Despite all the blandishments and ruses of the CIO, Conroy refused to budge. As the chief CIO delegate to the conference, Sidney Hillman, described it: "I came to London expecting trouble with the Russians. I have since discovered that I am to have more trouble with Canada, one of the CIO family, than anyone else in the Congress session."[13] Conroy got his way, and Canada was reluctantly given representation on the WFTU executive board.

Sometimes, however, the conflict between the CIO and the CCL took on ludicrous tones. In 1945, for example, when the CIO urged Congress unions in Canada to "communicate to their senators their support of Henry Wallace as Secretary of Commerce," Conroy pointedly responded that Canadians had no desire to interfere in American affairs "though the contrary could not be said for some Americans." In 1949, when the CIO urgently wired Conroy that "vigorous action from your state supporting President Truman's fight to win Senate confirmation of Leland Olds to Federal Power Commission" was needed at once, Conroy good-humoredly replied that since Canada had not yet been admitted to the American Union, "it . . . should meanwhile accept and recognize the sovereign status of United States and refrain from promoting Canadian Imperialist tendencies in the internal affairs of the American people." Finally in 1950, after the CIO office had sent a barrage of wires urging the workers in Conroy's "state" to send telegrams and letters to their senators voicing their strong opposition to the policies of the American Congress, Conroy's patience ran out. He informed the CIO that the Canadian Congress of Labour was not a "state federation and could not be treated like one," that the 49th parallel was not simply a state line but an international border, and that after ten years it was "about time" that the CIO realized that Canada could not be treated like an American state. This was something the CIO was extremely slow to accept.[14]

Unfortunately, Conroy's attempts to eliminate the interference of the CIO in Congress affairs failed. After ten fruitless years of effort, Conroy sadly lamented the Congress was now "left without any authority . . . thereby reducing it to the status of a satellite organization." As he complained to a CIO leader:

> My personal opinion is that I should resign from office, and let the Congress of Industrial Organizations and its International Unions take over the Congress. I am quite sincere in this, as I have been mulling the thought over for some time. The Congress is supposed to be an autonomous body . . . but . . . in matters of jurisdiction . . . the Congress is left without any authority, thereby reducing it to the status of a satellite organization at the mercy of its affiliated unions. These organizations choose to do whatever they want regardless of Congress desires, and in accordance with what their individual benefit may dictate they should do. . . . My own reaction is that I am completely fed up with this situation and within a few weeks it may be that I shall submit my resignation. . . . In short, the Congress

is either going to be the authority in its field, or it is not. If it is not to exercise authority, then the more quickly the Executive Council appoints someone to hold a satellite position, the sooner the Congress will know that it is a purely subject instrument, with no authority and a servant of the headquarters of International Unions in the United States. . . . This thought has been running through my mind for the last three or four years, and I have not arrived at it overnight. It is just that as the chief executive officer of the Congress, I am in an untenable position, and I am not going to work in that capacity.[15]

Eventually, in 1952, frustrated beyond endurance, Conroy resigned. With his resignation the last lingering hopes for a purely Canadian autonomous labour organization disappeared. The centralizing efforts of the CIO had triumphed over the nationalist aspirations of the CCL.

It is worth noting, I think, that to most rank and file union members the conflict between national and international unionism was entirely irrelevant. It was amongst the leadership and not the rank and file that this battle was fought. The average union member, as almost all studies of the labour movement have shown, plays an unimportant role in the affairs of his union. Only at times when his own economic well-being is at stake — during strikes and collective bargaining negotiations — does he take more than a passing interest in the activities of his union. This was especially true of the unionist in the 1930s and 1940s when his immediate, and indeed sole concern was to achieve financial security.

American control of their unions did not concern union members as much as higher wages, better working conditions, and job security, all of which seemed dependent on the muscle provided by the American connection. Since most of them were working for American-owned companies, why should they be overly concerned if their unions were also American controlled? This attitude of the Canadian worker, more than anything else, allowed the Canadian labour movement to be controlled by foreigners, the only country in the western world where this is the case. In more pointed words, perhaps we have American unions in Canada largely because of the colonial mentality of the Canadian workingman, a mentality, I might add, that was fully shared by the Canadian businessman. At the crucial times in the history of the Canadian labour movement, the Canadian workingman opted for American over Canadian unions, and refused to support Canadian leaders who were attempting to limit American control. In other words, the Canadian workingman has the union movement he deserves: large, powerful, rich, paternal, and American-dominated.

Notes

1. J. Crispo, *International Unionism: A Study in Canadian-American Relations* (Toronto, 1967), 12–14.

2. For a more complete study of this incident, see I.M. Abella, "The CIO, the Communist Party and the Formation of the Canadian Congress of Labour, 1936–1941," *Canadian Historical Association Historical Papers* (1969), 113–115.

3. Ibid., 115–119.

4. Transcript of an interview with Tim Buck, 3 Oct. 1960, United Electrical Workers Archives, Toronto, 8.

5. Quoted in *Financial Post*, 30 Oct. 1937.

6. Interview, J.B. Salsberg.

7. Ibid.

8. Interview, Charles Millard; Philip Murray to Charles Millard, 18 Feb. 1940, United Steel Workers Archives, Toronto.

9. Paul Norgren, "The Labour Link Between Canada and the United States," in *Canadian Labour Economics*, ed. A.E. Kovacs (Toronto, 1961), 37.

10. Crispo, *International Unionism*, 111–112.

11. See I.M. Abella, "Lament for a Union Movement," in *Close the 49th Parallel*, ed. I. Lumsden (Toronto, 1970), 75–92.

12. See, e.g., Conroy to Millard, 12 Jan. 1942, Canadian Labour Congress Archives, Ottawa.

13. Memo from Conroy to Mosher, 18 Mar. 1945, ibid.

14. Haywood to Conroy, 24 Jan. 1945; 10 Oct. 1949; 10 Apr. 1950; Conroy to Haywood, 1 Feb. 1945; 11 Oct. 1949; 2 May 1950, ibid.

15. Conroy to Millard, 21 Apr. 1950, ibid.

ESCAPING EXTINCTION†

JOHN MEISEL

Much has been written, and even more said, about what constitutes the Canadian character, what identifies the quintessential Canadian. A definitive answer continues to elude us, but two features clearly emerge as dominant elements in the make-up of both French- and English-speaking members of our family: we are constantly brooding over who we are, what gives us our Canadian character, and what makes us different from other nationals. Most other nationals never think about such things, or take the answers for granted. Secondly, we share a keen awareness of, interest in, and concern with all things American, that is, with the United States of America. Popular culture, sports, politics, even tourist attractions south of the border are part of the mental map of most Canadians and are frequently as important to us, if not more so, than corresponding indigenous realities. Inside every Canadian, whether she or he knows it or not, there is, in fact, an American. The magnitude and effect of this American presence in us all varies considerably from person to person, but it is ubiquitous and inescapable.

The economic dependence of Canada on the United States only exacerbates this state of affairs. Economic issues usually arouse the greatest interest and controversy; they are viewed from a variety of perspectives, depending on current problems and fashions. Right now, everyone is "atwitter" about sectoral free trade, and it is an awesome

† John Meisel, "Escaping Extinction: Cultural Defence of an Independent Border," in *Southern Exposure: Canadian Perspectives on the United States*, ed. D.H. Flaherty and W.R. McKercher (Toronto: McGraw-Hill Ryerson, 1986), 152–67.

matter, to be sure. But other aspects of our uneasily shared and separated lives are equally important. We shall deal with one of these and shall take a leaf out of the economists' book by also adopting a sectoral approach. The sector explored in this essay is our culture and our cultural relations, particularly one manifestation of them.

You may think that the wording of the title — "Escaping Extinction" — is a trifle hysterical and that to link Canadians, even if only potentially, to the dinosaur, the passenger pigeon, or the dodo ignores the fact that there is a dance or two left in us yet. But it was chosen after reflection which was certainly measured and . . . also mature. The greatest threat to Canada lies in the possibility (some might even say probability) that, as the result of the strong presence of American influences, our cultural development may be stunted. United States styles, ideas, and products are never far away. There is, alas, a well-grounded fear that as a consequence, our perceptions, values, ideas, and priorities will become so dominated by those of our neighbours that the distinctiveness of Canada will, to all intents and purposes, vanish. The danger is greater with respect to anglophones than francophones, but even the latter have cause for alarm.

Canada's cultural vulnerability vis-à-vis the United States is manifest everywhere. Book publishing, the periodical press, film production and distribution, comic books, the record industry, theatre, dance, popular and so-called classical music — all have been dominated by foreign influences in Canada. The indigenous product has had an exceedingly hard time getting started and surviving. This was so, in English Canada at least, largely because of the absence of a suitable native infrastructure and of an indigenous tradition, and because of the easy accessibility of, first, British cultural goods, and later, United States counterparts. The facts are only too well known, even if the solutions do not always leap readily to mind.

No form of cultural activity so clearly displays Canada's cultural dilemmas, and their implications for Canadian-American relations, as the field of communications. This critical and ever more important area is immensely complex. It encompasses such diverse aspects as transborder data flows, the transnational character of satellite footprints, the allocation of scarce slots for communications birds in the geostationary orbit, and the implications of one country's being dependent on another with respect to computer hardware and software. More important still, it embraces the field of broadcasting, the focus of our concerns in this essay.

All of broadcasting, but television in particular, has the most far-reaching effect on the minds of individuals and therefore on the nature of human society. Television is by far the most popular of all the media, engaging, on the average, the attention of Canadians for more than three hours a day. Children spend more time before the little screen than in the presence of teachers. Dominant perceptions of ourselves, of others, of this country and its neighbours, of desirable lifestyles, of national and world affairs, of different ethnic, religious, and social groups, of the diverse regions at home and abroad — perceptions of all these things are profoundly influenced by the programming available and watched on television. No wonder then that this medium is a uniquely powerful force in the socialization of individuals and in the formation of collective attitudes, values, and aspirations.

And television is, as we all know, predominantly, even overwhelmingly American. This fact is of absolutely central significance in the state and development not only of Canada's culture but also of the country's perception of, and relations with, the United States. It is, therefore, imperative that we understand fully why we are so dependent on our neighbour and what we can do to ensure that the electronic media serve the best individual and collective interests of Canadians.

There are at least six major factors explaining why Canada is so vulnerable to the television world of the United States. First, the physical proximity of so many Canadians to the United States border places a vast majority of the population within the reception area of American signals with the aid of only a cheap rooftop antenna. New technologies, particularly cable, and, more recently, satellites, have placed almost the whole of the country within reach of American programming. Secondly, 80 percent of Canadians speak English and therefore have no problem in savouring the goodies produced south of the border.

Thirdly, the American entertainment industry is the most vital and vivacious in the world. Growing largely out of the enormously successful and widely applauded American film industry, television programs and stars have found easy acceptance everywhere. American television has from the beginning, and until the advent of the Public Broadcasting System (PBS) in the late 1960s, been conceived as a commercial medium whose major role is to deliver audiences to advertisers. The content has therefore been designed, and with consummate skill, to appeal to the largest possible audiences. While this may leave something to be desired aesthetically, or in terms of the educational potential of the medium, it has unquestionably produced immensely popular shows. The format and type of drama originated by the American entertainment industry have in the most recent era created a new universal art form which is claiming something close to a worldwide audience. Successful genres of drama as typified by "Dallas," for example, have not only led to imitations domestically and massive sales in scores of countries, but are actually being copied in communities that in no way resemble the United States. America, having given us the western, has now presented the world with a vastly popular new theatrical form claiming widespread acceptance.

The fourth cause of Canada's vulnerability to United States television is probably the most telling. It concerns the economics of television programming and particularly of drama production. It costs about one million dollars to produce a one-hour show like "Dallas." American networks can afford this expense, because it can be amortized in their vast and rich domestic market. Having paid for themselves at home, these programs can then be offered to foreign (including Canadian) purchasers for from 3 to 6 percent of their cost.[1] Although the money spent on a program certainly does not guarantee its quality, it is impossible to present, consistently, shows comparable to the best American dramas without spending very large sums on them. But the size of the Canadian market does not permit the same investment in indigenous productions as is possible in the United States. Even the CBC can only afford to offer its English viewers less than two hours of original Canadian drama a week. The rest of the time the insatiable hunger for entertainment of our audiences can only be met from foreign sources or old stock.

As for the private broadcasters, their involvement in the production of Canadian drama is insignificant. One reason is obvious: they can acquire the rights to wildly popular American shows for very much less than the cost of comparable Canadian ones. It therefore makes very little *economic* sense for commercial broadcasters to try to program Canadian dramas.

The importance of this matter cannot be exaggerated. Fifty percent of Canadian viewing hours are devoted to drama, but only 4 percent of the available shows in this category are Canadian. Films, soap operas, situation comedies, and television plays are at least as important in influencing perceptions and values as public affairs, and yet the menu offered our viewers in this most popular type of programming is almost totally foreign, in part because of the facts just described.

Historical antecedents are also responsible for the strong presence in Canadian homes of American programs. They are the fifth factor we need to note. Television made its way south of the forty-ninth parallel in the 1940s: "The year 1948 is commonly accepted as the turning point when TV emerged as a mass medium and the United States networks changed their emphasis from radio to television."[2] Canada only authorized the new medium in 1952, after the release of the Report of the Massey Commission.[3] In the first instance, only the CBC and its affiliates provided service, but in the early 1960s CTV was licenced and provided an alternative source of programs in many parts of the country. Television broadcasting was, of course, regulated in hopes that the broadcasting system would, in the words of the 1958 Broadcasting Act, be "basically Canadian in content and character."

Viewers who bought sets before the inauguration of the CBC's service were able to watch United States shows, and this, in a sense, established expectations and patterns which could not be ignored later. Both the CBC and the private broadcasters realized that they would only win and hold viewers, so many of whom could receive signals from south of the border, if they themselves offered many of the most popular American programs; the appetite for these, therefore, became deeply ingrained. Free marketers argue that in commercial broadcasting it is the viewers' tastes which determine programming. In fact, of course, the reverse normally occurs. The shows available shape tastes, and in our case it was essentially American television fare which formed the preferences of Canadian audiences.

This brings me to the sixth factor accounting for our vulnerability to American cultural influences. It would be foolish to ascribe the popularity of entertainment provided by CBS, NBC, ABC or PBS to its being crammed down reluctant Canadian throats. On the contrary, a great many Canadians have an avid thirst for most things American and feel perfectly at home surrounded by them. This applies not only to anglophones but also to francophones, as their mass annual exodus to Florida, among other things, shows. The fact that these sentiments are induced in part by the hype emanating from Hollywood and the United States entertainment industry makes the Canadian empathy no less genuinely felt.

Although we have inadequate evidence to permit firm assertions, it looks as if the affinity for our neighbour's culture is not shared equally among all groups of Canadians. A mass/élite dichotomy is evident, with the better-educated, higher-income groups being more sensitive to Canadian-American cultural differences and more interested in indigenous cultural products. One consequence of this phenomenon is that the more low-brow an American cultural activity, the wider its appeal in Canada. Similarly, it is largely Canadians with middle- and upper-class backgrounds and with middle- and highbrow tastes who are concerned with the health and viability of Canadian culture. A nationalist foreign cultural policy is therefore more likely to appeal to a minority of the population.

Canadians not only like American programs, they also believe that they are entitled to have full access to them. They may not share their southern neighbours' conviction that they have an inalienable right to carry a gun, but they make up for it by insisting that they must not be deprived of all the gun-play being shown on American television. This strongly held view compelled the Canadian Radio-Television and Telecommunications Commission (CRTC) to allow Canadian cable systems to carry the programs of American stations, and it has weakened the government's will to block the widespread pirating of American shows carried on satellites. Not only individuals and companies but also municipalities, sometimes supported by Members of Parliament and provincial governments, have resorted to the unauthorized reception of United States signals, many of which, as I just noted, are meant to be available only to bona fide subscribers. There is, in short, an enormous interest in United States programming which reflects the liking of countless Canadians for the United States and the responsiveness among them to the diverse facets of American life.

The result of being so exposed to other people's electronic offerings is that it is extremely difficult for our own programs to be made and to be aired. Many of our most gifted writers, performers, and technicians are consequently forced to find work abroad, where they come to reflect the realities and perspectives of another country. Under these circumstances it becomes extremely difficult for very large numbers of Canadians to know the highly textured and varied character of their own land and to allow their imaginations to roam at home rather than abroad. This makes it hard not only to recognize one's own national interest but also to pursue it. American popular culture, and particularly television, is thus an immense Trojan horse enabling foreign concerns and priorities to infiltrate our very minds and beings.

Lest that martial metaphor of the Trojan horse give rise to a misunderstanding, I hasten to add that the nationalist, pro-Canadian stance espoused here in no way reflects an anti-American sentiment. Although the overall quality of American television may not fully satisfy, many of its programs are good. In any event, Canadians should not be deprived of the opportunity of watching whatever they please from abroad so long as a reasonable chance is provided for their own shows to be available. This, in a nutshell, is the problem: given the potent forces favouring the foreign product and the latter's plentiful supply, what can be done to create conditions in which Canadians can make genuine choices between foreign and domestic offerings? When only 4 percent of drama available is Canadian, such a choice simply does not exist.

Canada has laboured hard and long in an effort to find a solution to the dilemma. No less than six Royal Commissions and special committees of inquiry, as well as seemingly endless parliamentary probings, have struggled with the problem, and we are still without a sure-fire remedy.[4]

The issue has both domestic and international dimensions. Students of international affairs now draw important distinctions between the field of *international* relations, which focuses on the interaction between states speaking through their governments, and *transnational* relations, which deal with all manner of individual, corporate, and other contacts across boundaries. Our broadcasting conundrum has both transnational and international aspects, as well as purely domestic elements. To examine it is, in fact, a nearly perfect means of exploring the perspectives the two countries adopt toward each other, since it touches on virtually every facet of their political, social, economic, and cultural characteristics, and how these affect the relations between them. Canadian broadcasting policy is, in other words, and contrary to what one might at first surmise, a singularly suitable and apposite subject to be tackled in a collection of essays on Canada's perspectives on the United States of America.

The centrepiece of Canada's broadcast policy has always been an act of Parliament. The most recent version, that of 1968, as amended several times since, contains a description of what the Canadian broadcasting system should be. It states unequivocally that radio frequencies are public property and hence implies that they should be used in a manner promoting the public interest. The act nevertheless recognizes that Canadian broadcasting undertakings constitute one system, comprised of both public and private elements. This system, it is asserted, should be owned and controlled by Canadians, "so as to safeguard, enrich and strengthen the cultural, political, social and economic fabric of Canada." Another clause specifies that programming should use predominantly Canadian creative and other resources. The act also provides for two of the major actors on the broadcasting scene: a nationally-owned broadcasting corporation (the CBC) and "a single independent public authority" (the CRTC) which is to regulate and supervise the system according to the objectives enunciated in the act.

Underlying these and many other provisions is the assumption that broadcasting should not respond merely to the dictates of the market but that it should serve certain national interests, some of them related to the strengthening of a sense of Canadian nationality and identity. This concern with community goals rather than the profit motive (substantially at variance with the American pattern) is also reflected in the act's specifying that when a conflict emerges between the private and public elements, it shall be resolved in the public interest, "but paramount consideration shall be given to the objectives of the national broadcasting service."

The act accomplished three things: it set the goals of the Canadian broadcasting system (in greater detail than is suggested by my summary); it provided the objectives and mandate of the CBC; and it created a powerful regulatory agency independent of the government of the day.

Although the relative position of the CBC had been declining in English television since the creation of the private networks, the act reaffirmed its primary role in the system. It also charged it with special responsibilities in providing "for a continuing expression of Canadian identity." And it has certainly been the CBC which has played a key role in providing such Canadian drama as has been available. The private broadcasters for the most part tended to focus on producing news, public affairs, sports broadcasts, and some inexpensive light entertainment. In so far as television drama is concerned, they have relied virtually exclusively on the purchase of popular American shows, a programming policy which, to a lesser extent, even the CBC itself has had to emulate.

The reasons for the CBC's recourse to American drama and such programs as "Hockey Night in Canada" are instructive. As I have already noted, one way that Canadian broadcasters have used to attract audiences is to present popular American shows. Thus, for instance, "Dallas" is brought to us by our very own public corporation. Furthermore, only part of the CBC's income is derived from government subsidies. It must recover some of its expenses from advertising revenues.[5] This is said to have several advantages. First, it is an inescapable necessity in so far as the CBC's affiliates are concerned. These private stations, which operate in places where the public broadcaster does not own an outlet, depend for their survival on the sale of commercials. Secondly, advertising provides useful information and thus is seen by many business people and consumers as an essential service. Finally, income derived from sources other than parliamentary votes is considered to be some protection against possible political interference.

There are, of course, disadvantages. Advertising sometimes distressingly interrupts dramatic lines in a story and thus destroys its artistic effect. Many of the potentially most loyal CBC viewers were disgusted by the corporation's use of commercials during the showing of "The Jewel in the Crown" in 1984, and forsook the CBC for PBS, which had scheduled the series for a later showing without the maddening interruptions. The commitment to present lucrative sports events all too frequently compels the postponement of "The National" news and "The Journal" and thus appears to interfere with what some perceive to be a main part of the CBC's mandate. Some also argue that the advertising revenue adds little to the network's independence.

From the perspective of this essay, the most intriguing aspect of the CBC's and the private broadcasters' reliance on United States programming is that American cultural products are, in an important way, paradoxically used to diminish America's cultural influence.[6] Viewers display considerable loyalty to the station to which they are tuned. It is therefore argued that audiences attracted to Canadian stations by United States programs will continue being tuned to Canadian news, sports, and other programs which are offered by the CBC because of its policies, and by many private broadcasters because of the need to live up to the CRTC's Canadian content regulations.

The CBC has another excellent reason for purveying foreign shows, sports, and all manner of other programs. The Broadcasting Act enjoins it to provide "a balanced service of information, enlightenment and entertainment for people of different ages, interests and tastes covering the whole range of programming in fair proportion." This immensely broad mandate makes it imperative that the service cover a bewildering array of productions. When it is remembered that it must do this in both of our official languages, that it operates four superb radio networks, a northern service, and an international shortwave agency, and that it reports parliamentary debates via satellite, it becomes apparent that the CBC is among the world's largest and most active broadcasters.

Although like all big and aging structures the CBC has organization-al problems and confronts formidable internal challenges, it has made and continues to make absolutely Herculean contributions to the broadcasting and cultural scene in this country. This is evident at two levels: the quality of its programs is, for the most part, extremely high; and its increasingly successful efforts are making Canadian program-ming available during the prime viewing hours. Compared to the record of the private broadcasters, its performance in this area is phenomenal.[7]

In addition, the program sales arm of the company, CBC Enterprises, is having increasing success in selling Canadian productions abroad, including the United States. The latter is particularly encouraging. American audiences, no doubt because of the timid and unventure-some habits of the commercial networks, have amazingly parochial tastes. Except for PBS viewers, who comprise only a very small propor-tion of the United States viewing public, Americans are not attracted to foreign shows. It is well known that some Canadian films and TV plays have had to have their Canadian features, such as place and street names or the presence of Canadian banknotes, Americanized before they became acceptable to United States buyers. The fact that such programs as "As It Happens," on radio, and "Seeing Things," "The Wayne and Shuster Show," "Empire, Inc.," as well as other CBC productions on television are being heard or viewed abroad indicates that the CBC may be able to benefit from the growing world television market. Still, realistically, one must recognize that the successes so far have been modest and that the costs of major Canadian drama produc-tions are not likely to be recouped through exports. We shall have to continue to a very great extent finding domestic means of paying for our own television production.

If Parliament intended the CBC to be the principal player in our broadcasting bands, then the CRTC was to be the principal conductor. It has, as the act suggests, licensed broadcast undertakings and has supervised the overall system in an effort to ensure that the goals enun-ciated by Parliament are realized. Judgment of how successful it has been is by no means unanimous. Some see the regulatory agency as an overbearing ogre imposing élite tastes and unrealistic demands on a potentially enterprising but shackled industry. Others consider it to be a supine slave of the private broadcasters. On balance, it is proba-bly fair to say that it has fought fairly tenaciously for Parliament's goal of a predominantly Canadian broadcasting system but that its efforts have often been blunted by some fundamental characteristics of the Canadian environment.

The CRTC has not been aggressive in ensuring the primacy of the CBC within the system and it has been rather lenient with respect to the Canadian content goals. Because of the staggering difficulty of defining the key terms, it has also largely avoided implementing the act's injunction that "the programming provided by each broadcaster should be of high standard."

Still, the CRTC's impact on what is available on the air has been very considerable and salutary. In the 1970s, the insistence, fiercely attacked by the broadcasters, that 30 percent of the music played on AM radio be Canadian, created a Canadian record industry and poses no serious problems to the licences. The benefits to Canadian musicians, and hence to their audiences, have been enormous.

Although Canadian content regulations on television are less successful, they have nevertheless made a considerable difference to the availability of Canadian programs on our stations, particularly private ones. In essence each broadcaster must, on the average, present Canadian programming during 60 percent of the daily schedule and during at least half of the evening hours. The CBC is governed by more stringent requirements but has for some time exceeded these by a fairly wide margin. One result of the regulations has been that high quality news, public affairs, and sports are widely available on all Canadian stations. Variety, light entertainment, and drama, on the other hand — categories which are expensive to produce — have been woefully neglected by the private sector. With only rare exceptions, domestic children's shows have also been overlooked. To meet the Canadian content quotas, many stations have also resorted to inexpensive quiz shows and similar fillers, usually exhibited at low viewing times. This kind of programming and the allocation of inadequate resources to the rare production of Canadian drama have contributed to the low esteem enjoyed, by and large, by Canadian programs. Despite the indifferent reputation of domestic production in the minds of many, when good quality shows or mini-series are available, they attract very significant audiences.[8]

It is probably no exaggeration to say that the most powerful factor in the back of the CRTC's mind has been the need to protect the Canadian element in our broadcasting system. The presence of the United States is therefore of major importance in the evolution of Canadian broadcasting policy. Examples abound, but I shall mention only two. Knowing full well that Canadian broadcasters, particularly in the private domain, cannot produce Canadian programs unless their revenues are ensured, the Commission has defended the economic viability of its licensees whenever this was compatible with the terms of the Broadcasting Act. Thus rules were developed forcing cable systems to provide simultaneous program substitution when a United States and Canadian station carry the same show at the same time. Accordingly, a subscriber watching a program on an American station, which is available at the same time on a Canadian channel, would see the same material, including the advertisements, as one tuned to the Canadian source of that program. The purpose is, of course, to protect the advertising revenue of the Canadian broadcaster.

The other reason for the never absent awareness of the "United States factor" in Canadian broadcasting on the part of the Commission is that a majority of Canadians can, as we have noted, receive United States signals "off air," that is, without cable, and that to prevent Canadian cable systems from carrying United States stations is impossible in the current climate of opinion. Thus *too* stringent Canadian content regulations and other prescriptions giving our programming a distinctive flavour and quality could easily drive audiences into the arms of the American networks and out of reach of Canadian broadcasters and of the CRTC altogether. Thus the limits of what we can do in this country are set not only by ourselves but also in a very real sense by our neighbours. And when I say this, I mean not only the United States government but also private companies and individuals.

So far, in our survey of what has been done to give Canadians a choice between watching United States and indigenous television, we have caught a glimpse of the Broadcasting Act and its pivotal creatures: the CBC, private broadcasters, and the CRTC. But other instruments are required, farther removed from the parliamentary umbrella. The most remote, in this sense, is educational television. Under conditions laid down by the CRTC in response to a cabinet directive, educational television services were established in several provinces by agencies legally at an arm's length distance from the provincial government. Some of these, like the Knowledge Network in British Columbia, are devoted exclusively to instructional purposes but others, notably TVOntario and Radio Québec, have defined their mandate very broadly. In some of their activities these networks resemble PBS, and they certainly cater in part to adult audiences. Although they carry a good deal of foreign programming, their schedules also provide considerable Canadian content. Substantially different from the commercial networks, they furnish viewing opportunities which are not otherwise available. Their children's services are excellent, but they do not add materially to the availability of Canadian dramatic shows for adults.

As we have seen, the Broadcasting Act focuses on the CBC, the private sector, and the CRTC as the chosen instruments for the realization of a successful policy. But the intractable nature of the problems, particularly in the light of technological innovation, has made it imperative that other agencies and measures come to the rescue. Some have been on the scene for a while, but others have emerged only as the result of growing difficulties. Among the former, the National Film Board (NFB) is a well-known and widely acclaimed producer of fine Canadian programs. For reasons which must be related to internecine rivalries, NFB programs have not been shown as frequently on Canadian television as they have, in recent years, on PBS. Neither the private broadcasters nor the CBC have utilized the rich store-house of Film

Board footage to the extent possible, although at least one Quebec cable system does make effective use of it and the CBC has done much better than the private networks. Co-productions between the CBC and the NFB have become increasingly common lately and have resulted in some first-rate programs.

Beyond this, the federal government has developed a number of initiatives designed to strengthen Canadian program production and the general health of the television industry. Three deserve our special attention: the negotiation of international agreements facilitating co-productions between Canadian and foreign companies, the Canadian Broadcast Production Development Fund, and the famous (or infamous, depending on which side of the border you stand) Bill C–58. The first of these can be dispatched quickly. Ottawa has actively sought to enter into agreements with a number of governments, under the aegis of which Canadian and foreign partners would be able to benefit, in their production of films and television programs, from joint investments, in sharing larger markets, from access to their respective television outlets under preferred conditions, and from otherwise reinforcing one another's efforts to maintain a healthy domestic production industry. While many of the signatories are francophone countries, the scheme is by no means confined to them. The United States is, for obvious reasons, not included, and neither is Britain. In the latter case union agreements make such accords unacceptable.

The Canadian Broadcast Production Development Fund was announced by the then Minister of Communications, Francis Fox, when he launched his new broadcast policy in 1983. Its goal was to provide fairly substantial sums of money annually to private production companies and independent producers for assistance in the creation of drama, children's, and variety programs. A pump-priming feature required that for every dollar provided by the fund, the producer must raise at least two dollars elsewhere. Thirty-five million dollars were provided at the start, but the sum was to rise to $60 million by the fifth year. By that time, therefore, the fund was expected to inject $180 million for the production of programs in neglected categories.

Half of the monies available each year were to be allocated to productions intended for exhibition by private broadcasters and the other half by the CBC. The fund was to be administered by Telefilm Canada, the new name given to the Canadian Film Development Corporation. It was also announced that the cost of the project to the government was to be raised from the imposition of a 6 percent tax on Canadian cable companies. Since the latter pay no royalties for the programs they deliver to their subscribers, this was deemed to be a fair arrangement, inducing the profitable cable industry to contribute to Canadian production. Canadians were to be given the opportunity to see indigenous programs meeting certain requirements by means of a redistributive arrangement drawing on funds collected from companies which derive their income to a large extent from distributing the services of the American networks.

This ingenious scheme got off to a good start and led to the commissioning of some promising Canadian programs. The CBC made ample use of the opportunity from the start; it committed about $23 million by commissioning new programs from independent producers. The private broadcasters, however, whose record in the production of Canadian drama, variety, and children's programming had for so long been generally shameful, still showed less interest, even with the new incentives, and put up only $10 million. The program is now in a state of crisis because cuts in the CBC budget announced by Marcel Masse, the new Minister of Communications, prevent the Corporation from making further use of the fund in the immediate future. The government is in the process of trying to revise the terms of the program so as to rescue it from oblivion.[9]

By far the most controversial initiative of the federal government in support of Canadian cultural development, including broadcasting, was its Bill C–58. This piece of legislation received extensive publicity, largely because of its impact on the Canadian editions of *Reader's Digest* and *Time*. President Carter personally intervened against the measure. The conversion of *Maclean's* into a weekly would not have been possible without it. But the bill's most far-reaching impact on Canadian-American relations results from its effect on a small number of American television stations situated near the border.

Introduced in 1975, Bill C–58 sought to stop or reduce the hemorrhaging of Canadian advertising funds from Canada into the United States. Broadcasters to be protected were, for the most part, in the Toronto, Vancouver, and Montreal areas. American stations just across the border allegedly deprived the Canadian broadcasters of substantial revenue by accepting, and even aggressively soliciting, Canadian advertising beamed at Canadian viewers. Some stations were apparently established for the primary purpose of milking the Canadian market. The legislation, actually an amendment to the Income Tax Act, intended to put an end to this by no longer accepting the cost of TV commercials placed by Canadian advertisers on American stations as a tax-deductible business expense. It has been estimated that Canadians spent about $21.5 million on United States television advertising in 1975. This represented roughly 10 percent of all Canadian television advertising. By 1978, as the result of the legislation, the revenue of American border broadcasters had dropped to $6.5 million.[10]

The American reaction could not have been fiercer. It is no exaggeration to say that the border broadcast dispute, which still festers on, has been the most threatening irritant in Canadian-American relations. It also illumines some significant differences between the two countries. The affected United States broadcasters lobbied as best they could to have the legislation rescinded, but without success. Since then, some heavy guns have become involved on both sides of the border. Henry Kissinger raised the matter with Alan MacEachen, then Secretary of State for External Affairs.[11] Congress retaliated by passing legislation which severely restricted income tax deductions allowed Americans who attended conventions in Canada. The revenge apparently cost Canada hundreds of millions of dollars in lost tourist income.

This measure was ultimately annulled, but matters did not stop there. It was proposed that punitive changes should be made to the United States-Canada automotive agreement if Bill C–58 was not rescinded. Legislation was introduced in Congress by Senator Barry Goldwater intended to prohibit foreign ownership of cable if no reciprocal rights are granted — a provision which would have hit several large Canadian companies with cable franchises in the United States. Presidents Carter and Reagan both urged Congress to pass legislation which would mirror Bill C–58. The most serious attempted retaliation was contained in an amendment to the 1982 Senate mirror bill, which would deny United States business tax deductions for the purchase of Telidon, Canada's videotext system. A successful move in this direction would seriously harm the future of Canada's high-tech industry, which is expected by some to play a pivotal role in the country's economy in the emerging information society.

Why has this dispute assumed such a virulent character? After all, a loss of some $15 million annually in revenue is trifling between countries whose trade exceeds $70 billion a year. As sometimes happens in the relations between states and neighbours, the controversy, though quite insignificant in many ways, encapsulates some extraordinarily sensitive issues which arise from fundamental assumptions and values central to both societies. It also reveals how political structures sometimes create problems as well as solve them.

The Canadian position grew out of few central assumptions: Canadian cultural life was being threatened by the massive advantages that American cultural products derived from the huge scale of the American market. Measures needed to be devised to create an environment in which Canadian creativity could flourish and which would provide Canadians with their own cultural goods.

With respect to broadcasting, it was assumed that programming must be predominantly Canadian, and that for this to happen adequate resources must be available. A serious drain of such resources, particularly in the major markets, weakens the economic viability of the licensees and therefore their ability to live up to their commitments, particularly with respect to Canadian content. Something had to be done to protect them. Tax policy was seen as an acceptable means for achieving these ends.

Although economic measures were being used to promote national goals, the purposes of the enterprise, in so far as the government of

Canada was concerned, were cultural and were related to the preservation of a distinct Canadian identity. It was of course also the case that Canadian broadcasters affected by the new measures would derive economic benefits from them.

Two major concerns animated the violent American reaction. The border broadcasters were outraged by what they saw as the unfairness of the Canadian action and they, and less immediately involved Americans, objected on the grounds that Canada was interfering with the free flow of information and with the salutary and efficient operation of the free market.

Canada's broadcasting system, so it was argued, benefited in no small measure from the free availability of American network programs. The Canadian cable industry, in particular, sold subscriptions to the American channels without paying any compensation, and its rapid and vast growth rested on its ability to deliver these highly popular offerings. Canadian practices of commercial or signal substitution were seen as contributing to piracy. The ability to benefit from selling time to Canadian advertisers on the same footing as Canadian stations was therefore considered a fair compensation for the contribution made to Canada by the American stations.

It was further affirmed that the benefits of the Canadian tax provisions would not achieve their intended goal: Canadians would continue watching the American stations, and there was no assurance that the advertising revenue accruing to the Canadian companies would find its way into greater Canadian content. This train of thought was echoed in 1981 by Ted Rogers, one of Canada's leading cablecasters: "there has never been a public accounting by the privileged few companies," he asserted, "who financially benefited from this . . . legislation. There should be such a public accounting. . . . If the cash flow gain to these relatively few private companies is not going to produce enhanced Canadian programming — then the bill should be repealed."[12]

It is doubtful whether the cause of the border broadcasters would have received so much support in the United States, and for so long, had there not been a matter of deep-seated principle involved. A very large number of Americans, inspired in part by the First Amendment, have a passionate and absolute commitment to the free flow of information. No matter that this ideological position often miraculously coincides with crass self-serving economic interests and that, domestically, it is occasionally compromised by the mundane claims of competing interests; the free-speech rhetoric arouses ardent and genuine support among most Americans. To interfere with the transfer of information, as directed by the whims of the market, is to impose authoritarian and reprehensible restraints inimical to human freedom. It is this deeply ingrained terror of interference with freedom of speech which has led to the tragic misreading of the MacBride Report and of the New World Information Order and the related United States withdrawal from UNESCO, and which has also given the border broadcasters ideological support.[13]

There were other aspects of course. Senator Patrick Moynihan, in explaining his "strengthening amendment" linking the mirror legislation to the sales of Telidon, noted that "the Canadians have made the issue a major test of our will to protect United States service industries faced by unreasonable and unfair discrimination by a United States trading partner. . . . The border broadcast issue is indeed a test of our trade law."[14] So the problem is not seen merely as one of abstract principle but also as one possibly setting a precedent with respect to international trade and even property rights. But whatever the instrumental and egotistical motives for retaliation, and whatever the desire of certain politicians to cater to the interests of their constituents, the ideological drive and concern is not only genuine but also paramount.

What lessons can Canadians derive from this ongoing battle other than that, when the undefended border is concerned, a snowflake may grow into an avalanche? The first is that despite many similarities and affinities, profound disparities exist between our two countries. In so far as these relate to broadcasting, they have been admirably summarized by Theodore Hagelin and Hudson Janisch, on whose study of Bill C–58 I have drawn heavily in the foregoing discussion. Canadian and United States domestic communications policies, they say, "differ both in their ends and their means. Canadian policy seeks cultural development; United States policy seeks consumer choices. Canadian policy relies on program content regulation and a strong public broadcasting system to achieve its objectives. United States policy relies on structural, or industrial, regulation and a strong commercial broadcasting system to achieve its objectives."[15]

A major consequence of these differences is that when disagreements occur between the two countries, which is inevitable, both deep-seated ideological and mundane egotistical forces are likely to come into play. And, as the history of religious wars has so painfully taught us, disputes in which self-interest is bolstered by articles of faith are devilishly hard to resolve. Secondly, Americans, though in many ways among the most generous people in the world, can also be inordinately tough bargainers. In international relations and transnational dealings, they nearly always play hardball and rarely give 2.54 cm. Thirdly, because of the size of the country, its power and outlook, Americans are not always well informed about prevailing conditions and the philosophical preoccupations existing among others. Even the most enlightened find it hard to understand Canada's cultural nationalism. They cannot see why we would not wish to embrace joyously all manifestations of American civilization and why anyone should be afraid of it, or why it should pose any dangers. After all, they see it as benign, unassuming, and universally valid.

This lack of understanding is exacerbated at the official level by the complex and fragmented nature of the United States governmental structure. The imposition by the United States Constitution of the separation of powers has something to do with the highly differentiated character of Washington's organizations, but there are other reasons. The following bodies are involved in formulating international broadcasting policy: several "desks" in the State Department, the Federal Communications Commission, the National Telecommunications and Information Agency, the Office of the United States Trade Representative, various committees of each branch of Congress, and a special co-ordinator with ambassadorial rank attached to the Department of State. The proliferation of agencies leads to specialization, which may prevent the adoption of a holistic view on policy matters. It is, for instance, highly likely that the perception of Bill C–58 by officials involved in trade policy will completely ignore the cultural dimension of the legislation, and so fail to see its purpose and the importance attached to it by the Canadian government.

Finally, the absence of cabinet government bestows awesome powers on Congress. Since party discipline there is relatively weak, it is not at all uncommon for various regional interests to cohere on policy packages servicing specific local groups. Logrolling is rife, and the wishes of fairly small groups like those of the border broadcasters, for example, can be combined with others for the sake of forcing relatively unimportant or even unwanted policies on the nation. There is some evidence that not all the retaliatory motions against Canada introduced in the legislature had the support of the United States administration and that the latter does not favour the practice of linking one particular international issue to others which may be quite unrelated to it.

The insights obtained by our examination of the United States position on the border broadcasting dispute are instructive with respect to the theme of this essay — how to avoid cultural extinction in the face of the bubbling American presence next to and inside us.

At one level, the battle is obviously international and involves the usual armoury of weapons employed whenever our interests in Washington are at stake. A thorough knowledge of the American system and of American politics is required, as well as the willingness to engage in the power plays which determine American policy. There has been a change in this respect in recent years. Canadians no longer recoil from hiring lobbyists and from playing the game according to the local rules. The infinite subtleties and variations of American ideas, positions, and strategies must be fully understood and then utilized in the deployment of our plans. A Centre for American Studies can play a vital role in this context.

But although our problem is in a sense truly international or at least in the domain of transborder relations, its solutions are essentially domestic. No amount of pressure on Washington or even on American industry is going to sensibly diminish the inexorable American cultural influence. We need to review our attitudes to our country and its cultural traditions and opportunities. The quality of our cultural production must be enhanced so as to enable it to hold its own. This has implications for the educational system and for the organization of our economy. A review of broadcasting policy is in order in the light of current conditions. It appears that the government is gearing up to another attempt (the fourth since 1968) to produce a new Communications Act. Some of the matters touched upon in this essay must be borne in mind while this process takes place.

Public broadcasting needs to be strengthened rather than weakened, and its appropriate place and form reaffirmed. Likewise, the regulatory process awaits streamlining and adjustment to guide us effectively into the next century. Other governmental measures cry out for examination, as does a searching look at what must be done by the private sector if we are to maintain our national identity.

As in so many other areas, the prime ingredient in the escape from extinction is to recognize the problem realistically and then to have the will to act upon it. Ironically, whether we have these qualities, whether we can muster the force needed to defend ourselves effectively, depends in no small measure on the extent to which we have already become Americanized. If we trust the market to pull us through, if we fail to pursue the public interest through both public and private means, then, I fear, we are lost.

Notes

1. Pierre Juneau, "Public Broadcasting and the New Technological Environment: A Canadian View," Speech given at Luxembourg, 16 July 1983 (Canadian Broadcasting Corporation), 9–10.

2. Frank W. Peers, "Canada and the United States: Comparative Approaches to Broadcast Policy," in Canadian-U.S. Conference on Communications Policy, *Cultures in Collision: The Interaction of Canadian and U.S. Television Broadcast Policies* (New York: Praeger, 1984), 20.

3. *The Royal Commission on National Development in the Arts, Letters and Sciences* (Massey) (Ottawa: Printer to the King's Most Excellent Majesty, 1951).

4. *The Royal Commission on Radio Broadcasting* (Aird, 1929); *The Royal Commission on National Development in the Arts, Letters and Sciences* (Massey, 1951); *The Royal Commission on Broadcasting* (Fowler, 1957); *The Advisory Committee on Broadcasting* (Fowler, 1965); *The Federal Cultural Policy Review Committee* (Applebaum-Hébert, 1982); *The Task Force on Broadcasting Policy* (Caplan-Sauvageau, 1986).

5. In 1983–1984, the parliamentary appropriation was over $736 million and the advertising revenue came to almost $180 million. Canadian Broadcasting Corporation, *Annual Report 1983–1984* (Ottawa), 50.

6. This holds for English Canada much more forcibly than for Quebec. Most of the argument of this paper in fact applies to English broadcasting more than to French, but the general tendencies visible in the former are also in evidence, albeit to a lesser degree, in the latter.

7. That this encomium is deserved does not diminish the need to examine the structure and performance of the Corporation most carefully. There clearly are some serious problems requiring solution.

8. See A.W. Johnson's, "Canadian Programming in Television. Do Canadians Want it?" Address to the Broadcast Executive Society, Toronto, 19 Feb. 1981, for compelling evidence on this point.

9. Since this paper was delivered, new rules have been developed which have revived the program. Private broadcasters have made more extensive use of the scheme since it has been re-defined.

10. Arthur Donner and Fred Lazer, *An Examination of the Financial Aspects of Canada's 1976 Amendment to Section 19.1 of the Income Tax Act (Bill C–58) on U.S. and Canadian TV Broadcasting* (Ottawa: Department of Communications, 1979). Cited by Theodore Hagelin and Hudson Janisch in "The Border Broadcast Dispute in Context" in *Cultures in Collision*, 62.

11. Hagelin and Janisch, *Cultures in Collision*, 52.

12. Leslie R. Arries, Jr., "The Position of the Border Broadcasters," in *Cultures in Collision*, 147.

13. International Commission for the Study of Communications Problems, *Many Voices, One World* (Paris: UNESCO, 1980).

14. Hagelin and Janisch, *Cultures in Collision*, 54.

15. Ibid., 56.

A CONTRACT FOR ECONOMIC INTEGRATION†

MEL HURTIG AND DUNCAN CAMERON

In the dead of the night, a truckload of men pulled up to Fleck Manufacturing in Huron Park, Ont., dismantled the equipment, loaded the truck, and moved the operation to Mexico.

Workers making $7 an hour had turned down an offer of an hourly increase of 22 cents, so the company opted for Mexico, where wages begin at 69 cents an hour and many workers earn $4.50 to $6.50 a day. The plant closing left more than two hundred Canadians, mostly women, without work.

Fleck Manufacturing is owned by James Fleck, author of *Canada Can Compete*. A member of the Business Council on National Issues (BCNI), and of the International Trade Advisory Committee established by the Mulroney government to make recommendations on trade policy, he is a strong supporter of the free trade deal. And, in the context of the agreement, his action represents a sound business decision; it makes more sense for industry to locate where the cost of production is lowest.

Another strong supporter of the agreement is Robert Campeau. Speaking to the fifty-ninth annual meeting of the Canadian Chamber of Commerce in September, he said: "Within the next decade . . . we will see the development of a great North American market, forged

† Mel Hurtig and Duncan Cameron, "No Longer Will Canada Make Economic Sense," *The Globe and Mail* (Toronto), 14 November 1988, A7.

by two strong economies, with Mexico providing a significant part of the process, with their great labour pool."

There are now more than eleven hundred plants with some three hundred thousand workers in the Maquiladoras, Mexican free-trade areas adjacent to the U.S. border. A recent U.S. customs memo makes it clear that the United States intends most of the Maquiladoras production to qualify as "of U.S. origin."

In the great debate about the future of our country, probably the most important single question is where new investment will locate if the trade agreement is implemented, if investment, tariff, and other barriers are eliminated and corporations are granted "national treatment" on both sides of the border.

Some 37 percent of the work force in Canada is unionized, compared with only 17 percent in the United States. Manufacturing wages are higher in Canada. There are far better (but altogether more costly) fringe benefits here. Many U.S. states have either no minimum-wage laws at all or minimum wages far below those in Canada. Most Canadian provinces have average hourly wages above those of most U.S. states.

Offices, factories, and warehouses in Canada are more expensive to build and maintain. Transportation costs to the major markets in North America are considerably higher. Because of our social programs, taxes are higher in Canada for both executives and workers, as well as for corporations. U.S. federal labour standards are but a pale shadow of those in Canada. U.S. states with populations totalling seventy-five million have anti-union "right to work" laws. In the southern United States the climate is much less severe, the operating costs are much lower.

If the agreement is implemented and trade and investment barriers are wiped out, why would new Canadian investment locate in Canada? As former federal cabinet minister Eric Kierans has put it so well: "Would you prefer to locate in the United States and ship 90 percent of your sales to Camden, New Jersey, and 10 percent to Bramalea, or locate in Bramalea and ship 90 percent all the way to Camden?" As a Labatts vice-president put it: "The logical business step will be to put operations in the largest population centres ... it would be much more efficient to be located in Michigan or New York."

Most U.S. industries already produce enough to flood the Canadian market with no new capital investment. Weston Foods president David Beatty, discussing possible effects of the agreement earlier this year, said: "There is excess capacity in the United States; there are larger scale facilities in many segments; momentum will be to supply from the U.S. home base; you don't put the plant at the end of a spoke of the wheel, but at the hub; you don't choose Winnipeg, you choose Raleigh, North Carolina. There will be a clear tilt toward U.S.-based manufacturing. The tilt is against the Canadian plant."

Most Canadians now oppose the trade deal. And for very good reasons.

No other government in the world would treat its energy future as though it were an offering at a continental "potlach." No nation with such an enormous amount of foreign ownership would have agreed to never again review most new foreign takeovers. No other government would agree to compensate its trading partner before establishing a new Crown corporation or agree it would never adopt a national policy for the services sector.

No other government would have negotiated such a comprehensive agreement without first obtaining a formal definition of what constitutes unfair trading. No other nation would have agreed to give up so many crucial economic levers for so little in return.

There are dozens of disasters in this agreement, and not room to do them justice here. But by now, most Canadians have a pretty good idea of the immense potential dangers for our standard of living, compared with the overstated and uncertain benefits.

There is one fundamental irony in this great debate about the future of our nation. Between 1985 and 1987, Canadians were being warned — by Peter Lougheed, Donald Macdonald, the BCNI, and right wing economists . . . — that the sky would fall if we did not take the "leap of faith" through the "window of opportunity."

We were the only nation in the world without access to a market of one hundred million; protectionism in the United States was running rampant; there was a flight of capital; investment would dry up and jobs would be destroyed. The nation would be impoverished. Over and over we heard politicians and professors and continentalist think-tanks tell us there was *no other choice*. And besides, the United States will make us The Chosen People.

Yet, without the strangling, straitjacketing, Reisman-Mulroney deal, Canada created more new jobs than all three hundred and twenty million people in the European Community combined. We had a better trade growth rate than any of the world's major trading nations. We had huge trade surpluses with the United States, well beyond our fondest expectations. Domestic and foreign investment soared and unemployment dropped to its lowest level in seven years.

The sky was not falling at all. So, the prophets of doom have changed their message. The new message, if you can imagine, is that those opposed to the deal are fearmongers. Ironic in the extreme.

The multilateral process of the General Agreement on Tariffs and Trade has served us well in the past. Why abandon the most important assets we have — the economic, social, political, and cultural tools that will allow us to continue to develop our society as we choose, one decidedly different from our giant neighbour to the south? Why tie the hands of future generations of Canadians?

We do not agree with those who say they are "willing to pay the cost of being Canadian." There is no such cost. Rather there is the benefit of living in a relatively peaceful, non-aggressive, and non-violent society where the poor and the sick and the elderly and other disadvantaged are better cared for. And where freedom of opportunity to develop the way *we* wish is not constrained by a so-called "trade" deal that, in reality, is a contract for economic integration that will turn Canada into a de-industrialized warehouse economy and little more than a resource colony of the United States.

The election a week from today is the most important in our history. If the Conservative party gains 148 or more seats, the nation will proceed toward integration with the United States. On the other hand, 147 or fewer Tory seats will mean Canada sets forth on a totally different course, with infinitely greater freedom and opportunity in the future.

No threat to social programs†

GORDON RITCHIE

It is important to understand the facts about the claim that the Canadian-U.S. free trade agreement would undermine Canada's universal social programs, including medicare, and the health-care systems Canadians cherish.

In short, there is nothing in the free trade agreement that limits Canada's capacity to run the kind of health-care system it chooses and to finance it through a universal medicare program.

It is that simple. There are no ifs, ands, buts, or maybes. The proof is there in black and white.

The critics have made two major allegations. First, they have said our universal social programs, notably medicare, are vulnerable under the agreement. This is not true. Second, they have said that the agreement gives Americans the right to open, acquire, control, and manage health-care facilities in Canada. This is also not true.

The agreement and its implementing legislation are completely silent on the issue of universal social programs. Why? Simply because, under the General Agreement on Tariffs and Trade, under existing Canadian law and under existing U.S. law, a program that is generally available cannot be considered a subsidy.

That means that, even without free trade, Canadian senior citizens

† Gordon Ritchie, "Grasping at Straws to Make Their Case," *The Globe and Mail* (Toronto), 14 November 1988, A7.

and those in need of medical care can rest assured: universal social programs, such as medicare, cannot be successfully attacked by U.S. protectionist interests, unless the Americans were prepared to pervert the application of their own laws or amend them in contravention of GATT codes.

That is where the free trade pact comes in. The situation under the agreement is exactly as it is today — the existing laws continue to apply — with some vitally important further protections. Under free trade, if the Americans were to flagrantly misapply their laws to call medicare a subsidy, Canada would haul them before a binational panel of Canadian and U.S. experts. That panel would have no choice but to find that the Americans have acted wrongly and to order them to drop their case — an order that would be binding under U.S. law.

If the Americans were to go so far as to change their laws to pretend somehow that universal social programs were subsidies — which is virtually unthinkable — then the agreement would again come to our defence. Canada would haul them before a binational panel. Again, that panel would have no choice but to find that the Americans had acted wrongly, contrary to the rules of the GATT and the objectives of the agreement, and order them to clean up their law. The Americans would have no choice but to do just that, unless they were prepared to tear up the agreement.

Much has been made of the fact that the free trade agreement makes reference in an annex to "health-care facilities management services." It is alleged that this means that Americans would have the right to set up, to acquire, to own, and to operate health-care facilities in Canada. Nothing could be further from the truth.

The agreement provides that, for those services — and only those services — explicitly covered by the agreement, all existing restrictions remain intact. Where those restrictions permit the Americans to set up shop in Canada, however, the regulations must apply equally to Canadians and Americans, except where differential treatment is justified on health and safety or other grounds.

Canada and the provinces remain perfectly free to continue to run a publicly operated health-care system. If, however, Canadians decide to permit certain facilities to be commercially operated, we are still under no obligation to permit Americans to own and operate such facilities or to provide services to those facilities, including management services for health-care facilities.

If however, we do decide in our regulations to permit such commercial facilities to contract out their "facilities management services" to Americans, then the regulations that apply to these U.S. services must be just as tough as those that apply to Canadian services.

This means that Canadians remain entirely free to decide how we want our health-care system to operate, to run the system through our governments or through non-profit institutions if we want, and to regulate the system as tightly as we want, even if we decide to allow commercial involvement in the system.

Clarifying these misunderstandings has prompted some critics of the deal to concede that the agreement contains nothing that would dismantle medicare or open up our health-care system to U.S. commercial operations. However, their fallback position has been to claim that there is nothing in the agreement that would prevent future governments from yielding to pressures to dismantle the system. Indeed, it is suggested that a future Canadian government in the course of negotiations to define subsidies under the agreement (or presumably under the GATT) may reverse field and agree to sacrifice our universal social programs.

On the other hand, it is claimed that Americans may argue that ours is such an efficient system, delivering a high quality of care at lower cost than theirs, that it gives us an unfair advantage and should be dismantled. On the other hand, and often in the same breath, it is claimed that Canadian businessmen may argue that ours is such an expensive system that it imposes an unfair penalty upon our industries and should be dismantled. The contradiction in these arguments is obvious.

More important, this has nothing to do with the free trade agreement but everything to do with Canadian social policies. For many years, there have been critics of our system in both Canada and the United States who have argued that our system should be cut back or dismantled entirely. Their views have been rejected by Canadian governments and, indeed, by the vast majority of Canadian business leaders. The point is simply this: it is a matter for Canadians to decide; it is no business of the Americans, and it has no place in an international trade pact.

We are justly proud of our health-care system, financed through our universal medical-care program. We react strongly against anyone who would seek to weaken this system — as various federal and provincial governments have learned from experience. This is a legitimate concern that may figure prominently in the choices Canadians make about who is to govern them and how they are to govern.

These are matters for Canadians, and Canadians alone, to decide. They have absolutely nothing to do with the trade agreement.

ONLY HALF A TRADE AGREEMENT†

J.G. GODSOE

If the Tories form a majority government after Monday's election and
the free trade deal goes ahead, it is virtually certain that Prime Minister Brian Mulroney will have to cancel it within the next two or three
years.

To find out why he would have to kill his own creation, we must look
at the deal itself. It is only half a trade agreement. It gives each country
increased access to the other's market through lower trade barriers,
but it does not deal with how stable and secure that access will be.
What the agreement does not deliver are two key issues for Canada
— binding arbitration of trade disputes and a common book of rules
defining unfair trade practices and subsidies.

Under this agreement, the Americans have seen their major
concerns addressed. They obtained access to the Canadian financial
market, Canadian resources and the service sectors. Canada also won
lower barriers for exports to the United States.

But Canada was unable to restrict the U.S. definition of unfair trade,
nor did it win bilateral binding arbitration. Small wonder there was
virtually no dissent over the deal in the Senate or House of Representatives.

If the present deal is implemented, the next two or three years will
see U.S. firms continue to initiate trade disputes against Canadian

† J.G. Godsoe, "Free Trade May Go Ahead But it Won't Last for Long," *The Globe
and Mail* (Toronto), 18 November 1988, A7.

competitors. The deal does not impair U.S. potential to harass Canadian exporters. It won't be long before there is a hue and cry from those hurt by U.S. trade action. Business will press Ottawa to get back to the table and deal with these issues in round two of the trade talks.

The difficulty facing Canadian negotiators, however, is that they will have nothing left to offer. In view of the present debate over the costs and benefits of the first stage of the deal, it scarcely seems imaginable that the negotiators will be allowed to put anything of great value on the table.

On the other hand, the United States has nothing to gain in round two. The Americans do not want any restrictions on the U.S. definition of unfair subsidy or trading practices. Nor do they want a binding bilateral dispute tribunal that would make substantive decisions. They didn't settle for either point in round one; why should they give in during round two?

Because we have nothing left to offer, we will have to exercise the only power left, termination.

That the Mulroney-Reagan deal is only half a trade agreement should not surprise an astute reader of the Macdonald Commission report. Advocates of the trade agreement have frequently cited the commission. Commentators have even credited the commission with convincing Mr. Mulroney to pursue free trade. It did strongly recommend opening negotiations with the United States on a free trade arrangement, and produce the first comprehensive analysis of the nature of such an agreement.

However, a key point has been missed. The commission's analysis and recommendations were very specific. There was never any doubt that a free trade agreement could be either a benefit or a disaster. The difference would depend on its terms.

The commission's analysis is far more helpful to opponents of the trade deal than to its supporters. Mr. Mulroney's negotiators failed to fulfil the key criteria for a successful agreement as spelled out in the report — a strong initiative in multilateral trade negotiations under the General Agreement on Tariffs and Trade, not a deal with the United States.

Multilateral negotiations were to remain the "central theme" of Canadian trade policy. More secure access to major markets, including the U.S. one, a better opportunity for further processing our natural resources before export and an improved framework of international rules were to be some of the objectives of our leadership role in the GATT round. Negotiations with the United States were to be pursued within the context of our GATT position. A U.S. deal was not to replace the GATT negotiations.

There were sound reasons why Canada should have negotiated only with the United States in the overall GATT context. Macdonald Commission studies had shown that Canada did better with the United

States when both had others to negotiate with. U.S. trading partners profit by hanging together.

Second, the commission recommended that there be no "linkage" between free trade and any other issues. Free trade is concerned with lowering trade barriers. We were particularly concerned about cultural and defence issues being linked with trade. It never occurred to the commission that a trade agreement would encompass some of the non-trade issues the Mulroney-Reagan deal covers. Under a GATT trade agreement the Americans should gain no special right to energy resources.

The commission expressly recommended against any broader agreement such as a common market or economic union and against linking such non-trade issues with trade. In its view, trade was about barriers, not about a continental energy policy.

Third, the commission placed considerable stress on the resolution of trade disputes with the United States. We had been through a protracted period of trade harassment based on the very political U.S. system. Decisions there seemed to be made by a home-town jury, and it had become impossible to stabilize trade when no one knew who would be hit next.

While Canadians wanted increased access to the U.S. market, the key item was how stable and secure that access would be. How could you justify to your shareholders major investments in plant, equipment, intellectual property and technology and training for a competitive North American market if you could not be assured that the trade route would stay open?

The commission saw that it was essential in any trade agreement to shift the enforcement of trade actions away from national tribunals to a bilateral body that would make the actual decision. For trade disputes such as safeguard actions ("unfair trade") and anti-dumping and countervailing-duty proceedings ("unfair subsidies"), the justness of the complaint would be decided by an impartial body with equal representation from both countries.

The Mulroney-Reagan agreement does not do this. It sets up several bilateral bodies, but the only one with any power is a bilateral tribunal with only a very technical review power. It can decide whether the U.S. government followed its own procedures correctly. It has no role in saying whether those procedures were fair to Canadian exporters or whether the decision itself was wrong.

Implementing the agreement would not only be contrary to the Macdonald Commission's recommendations, it would set off intensive negotiations over the real agenda. Canadian negotiators have stated there was no time to conclude any agreement on the definition of "unfair trade" and what regional development of other economic or social support programs would be in jeopardy.

The United States well knows that we have used all our cards. It makes little sense to suggest that it will ditch its very ad hoc and politically responsive trade-dispute process with no convincing reasons. The only way to ensure U.S. attention would be the prospect that the agreement would be terminated.

In short, what else is there to offer the Americans except agreement that at least some of our government-support programs are to be classified as unfair trade subsidies? Surely the most ardent advocate of the current agreement must concede that. The focus will then shift to what regional-development and other support programs will have to be discontinued at least for export industries. This is the measure of failure of the free trade deal.

THE PRICE OF REJECTION†

R. BARRY FARRELL

The U.S. media have given very little attention to the free trade agreement or to the Canadian election. The average American probably knows more about Wayne Gretzky's trade to the Los Angeles Kings than any other current Canadian story.

However, there is a small but powerful sector of the U.S. public that is interested in Canada — and it should not be neglected in the Canadian debate.

The newly elected 101st Congress will be protectionist. The idea that Canadian rejection of the free trade agreement would simply return things to the way they were two or three years ago is wrong. More likely, it would make the situation worse than it was in 1981–1982, when U.S. trade and investment left Canada and the United States exerted strong political and economic pressure against this country.

It is amazing that many Canadians seem to have little understanding of the protectionist sentiment that gripped the last Congress and will be even more powerful in the new one. Without the defence of a trade agreement Canadians can expect to feel the weight of that protectionist sentiment in a way they have never felt it before.

As one U.S. business leader put it: "I think there will be a trade war between our two countries, when, instead, we could have worked together to benefit both sides."

† R. Barry Farrell, "Expect a Very Rocky Road if Canada Backs Out Now," *The Globe and Mail* (Toronto), 18 November 1988, A7.

Why more protectionist pressure against Canada? Many U.S. businessmen, politicians, officials, and opinion makers have said privately that they view the free trade deal as better for Canada than for the United States. Others view it as an equally good arrangement for both sides.

In a U.S. election campaign full of politicians' references to "the export of American jobs," U.S. supporters of the deal did everything they could to keep Americans bored about Canada and to keep the agreement out of partisan political debate. They also feared any comments about the agreement that could be misinterpreted in the Canadian election campaign and cause a reaction like the anger at the unfortunate U.S. shakes and shingles decision. Every effort was made by the U.S. administration to keep free trade on the back burner.

While the agreement was being negotiated, the administration and its supporters were able to argue against taking protectionist action against Canada, saying it might sabotage the legislation in Canada. It would also, they said work against a broader strategy of free trade agreements with other countries, a pattern that began with the U.S.-Israeli free trade agreement.

If the agreement with Canada is "torn up," all such pressures are off. The Bush administration will have every reason to distance itself from a trade relationship with Canada, which will appear to have been a futile quest of the previous administration. Canada will be the object of all the protectionism of the new Congress.

Also to be considered is James Baker, the next secretary of state. As treasury secretary under Ronald Reagan, Mr. Baker was important in running political interference and securing the U.S. passage of the trade agreement before the U.S. election campaign was in full swing. It is hard to imagine that he will be too inclined to use his influence to hold back protectionist pressures against a country that has rejected an agreement on which he worked so hard.

From a U.S. perspective, it is wrong to say that, since 80 percent of Canadian-U.S. trade is already duty free, the failure of the agreement will leave the 80 percent untouched.

Virtually every area of Canadian sales to the United States about which U.S. politicians can decry the "export of American jobs" will be vulnerable. This could range from high-tech machinery to energy, lumber, steel, agriculture, fish and services.

For example, more often than not, U.S. experts now consider the auto pact much more favourable to Canada than to the United States. It would be illusory for Canadians to assume that it could remain untouched without being shielded by a comprehensive trade agreement.

There are other areas of Canadian activity that could well suffer. One is the present freedom of Canadian investment in the United States. The large Canadian investment in the United States is perceived to be growing. An obvious area is real estate. Without the special relationship the free trade agreement would give it, Canada should expect to be included in multilateral U.S. protectionist actions against such countries as Japan, Taiwan, and West Germany.

One additional set of considerations is very important. Many U.S. backers of the agreement base their support on their concern about the consequences of trade blocs being formed elsewhere in the world, notably in the Pacific rim countries and Western Europe. Even though the Canadian deal may be seen as more advantageous to Canada than the United States, they want Canada and the United States to be co-operating in the face of competition from the new economic blocs.

With its two most highly developed and economically powerful countries working together, North America could create its own economic bloc and thus be less vulnerable to those forming elsewhere.

From this perspective, the Americans feel they are making two major concessions. First, under the agreement Canada will be the only country in the world with such free access to the U.S. market.

Second, Canada will have a special defence against U.S. protectionism in all the areas where the new Congress is in the mood to move. This defence applies even to the auto pact, which some Americans now consider a bad agreement — one that, without the specifics agreed upon in the trade deal, should be renegotiated, if not scrapped.

In honesty, probably no one can predict with confidence or accuracy the consequences of the complicated set of arrangements that would go into effect with the free trade agreement. The long and tedious negotiations were undertaken by representatives of both sides whose competence and interest in securing the maximum advantage for their respective countries can hardly be questioned. They saw the agreement as the best possible political and economic compromise, a necessary response to new conditions.

If the agreement is rejected, very bad times are ahead for the relationship between Canada and the United States. We have seen such times before. Canadian business and Canadians in general will suffer.

Further Reading

This book should be seen as a companion to another in the New Canadian Readings series, J.L. Granatstein's *Canadian Foreign Policy: Historical Readings* (Copp Clark Pitman, 1986). A number of the Granatstein selections are relevant to our subject and the references at the end of the readings in his volume and this one are a source of much bibliographic information. It is also worth consulting J.L. Granatstein and Paul Stevens, *A Reader's Guide to Canadian History*, II (University of Toronto Press [hereinafter UTP], 1982), as well as the Canadian Institute of International Affairs' *A Bibliography of Works on Canadian Foreign Relations* (4 vols. to date; CIIA, 1973–1987), which lists works from 1945.

There are remarkably few broad historical surveys of Canadian-American relations. The point of departure is C.P. Stacey, *Canada and the Age of Conflict: A History of Canadian External Relations* (2 vols.; Macmillan and UTP, 1977–81), which runs from 1867–1948. Bearing more directly on the two countries are H.L. Keenleyside, *Canada and the United States: Some Aspects of their Historical Relations* (Knopf, 1929; revised edition with G.S. Brown, 1952); E.W. McInnis, *The Unguarded Frontier: A History of Canadian-American Relations* (Doubleday, Doran, 1942); and E.E. Mahant and G.S. Mount, *An Introduction to Canadian-American Relations* (Methuen, 1984). W.R. Willoughby canvasses the institutional aspect in *The Joint Organizations of Canada and the United States* (UTP, 1979). A lighter view is provided by Laurence Martin, *The Presidents and the Prime Ministers, Washington and Ottawa Face to Face: The Myth of Bilateral Bliss, 1867–1982* (Doubleday, 1982).

John Barlett Brebner's *North Atlantic Triangle: The Interplay of Canada, the United States and Great Britain* (Yale University Press and Ryerson, 1945) was the flagship volume of the Carnegie Institute's *The Relations of Canada and the United States*, an ambitious 25-volume collection by Canadian and American scholars published from 1936–1945. This undertaking, described by Carl Berger in *The Writing of Canadian History* (Oxford University Press, 1976), includes studies of history, diplomacy, politics, industry, labour, opinion, and migration. Other series of note are *Canada in World Affairs* (14 vols.; Canadian Institute of International Affairs, 1941–1985); James Eayrs, *In Defence of Canada* (5 vols. to date; UTP, 1964–1983); B.W. Tomlin and Maureen Molot, eds., *Canada Among Nations* (4 vols. to date; Lorimer, 1985–1988); and *Documents on Canadian External Relations* (11 vols. to date; Department of External Affairs, 1967–1989).

For the period before 1945, there are a number of valuable specific studies: Kenneth Bourne, *Britain and the Balance of Power in North America 1815–1908* (Longman's, 1967); Richard A. Preston, *The Defence of the Undefended Border: Planning for War in North America 1867–1939* (McGill-Queen's University Press, 1977); S.F. Wise and R. Craig Brown, *Canada Views the United States: Nineteenth Century Political Attitudes* (Macmillan, 1967); Guildo Rousseau, *L'image des Etats-Unis dans la littérerature Québécoise* (1775–1930) (Naaman, 1981); D.C. Masters, *Reciprocity, 1846–1911* (Canadian Historical Association, Booklet 12, 1961); R.D. Cuff and J.L Granatstein, *Canadian-American Relations in Wartime: From the Great War to the Cold War* (Hakkert, 1975; 2nd edition is entitled *Ties That Bind*, Samuel Stevens, Hakkert, 1977); Yves Roby, *Les Québécois et les investissements américains* (1918–1929) (Les Presses de l'Université Laval, 1976); C.P. Stacey, *Mackenzie King and the Atlantic Triangle* (Macmillan, 1976); R.N. Kottman, *Reciprocity and the North Atlantic Triangle, 1932–1938* (Cornell University Press, 1968); Ian M. Drummond and Norman Hillmer, *Negotiating Freer Trade: the United Kingdom, the United States, Canada and the Trade Agreements of 1938* (Wilfred Laurier University Press, 1989); C.P. Stacey, *Arms, Men, and Governments: The War Policies of Canada 1939–1945* (Queen's Printer, 1970); S.W. Dziuban, *Military Relations Between the United States and Canada 1939–1945* (U.S. Department of the Army, 1959); and J.L. Granatstein, *Canada's War* (Oxford University Press, 1975).

The origins and nature of the Cold War remain a matter of controversy. The perspectives of J.W. Holmes, *The Shaping of Peace: Canada and the Search for World Order 1943–1957* (2 vols.; UTP, 1979–1982) and L.B. Pearson in his memoirs, *Mike* (3 vols.; UTP, 1972–1975), I and II, should be contrasted with Cuff and Granatstein's *Ties That Bind* and their *American Dollars – Canadian Prosperity: Canadian-American Relations, 1945–1950* (Samuel-Stevens, 1978), and Denis Smith, *Diplomacy of Fear: Canada and the Cold War, 1941–1948* (UTP, 1988). Three excellent Cold War case studies are Joseph T. Jockel, *No Boundaries Upstairs: Canada, the United States, and the Origins of North American Air Defence, 1945–1958* (University of British Columbia Press, 1987); Escott Reid, *Time of Fear and Hope: The Making of the North Atlantic Treaty, 1947–1949* (McClelland and Stewart, 1977); and Denis Stairs, *The Diplomacy of Constraint: Canada, the Korean War, and the United States* (UTP, 1974). Robert Bothwell and William Kilbourn discuss the most controversial of all politicians in *C.D. Howe* (McClelland and Stewart, 1979). J.L. Granatstein's lives of Norman Robertson, *A Man of Influence* (Deneau, 1981), and of *The Ottawa Men* (Oxford University Press, 1982) include the Cold War and much else.

The modern period from the late 1950s on is treated in J.L. Granatstein, *Canada 1957–1967* (McClelland and Stewart, 1986); Neil A. Swainson, *Conflict Over the Columbia* (McGill-Queen's University

Press, 1979); H. Basil Robinson, *Diefenbaker's World: A Populist in World Affairs* (UTP, 1989); two volumes of oral history by Peter Stursburg, *Diefenbaker: Leadership Lost 1962–1967* (UTP, 1976) and *Lester Pearson and the American Dilemma* (Doubleday, 1980); J.B. McLin, *Canada's Changing Defence Policy, 1957–1963* (Johns Hopkins Press, 1967); Pearson's *Mike*, III; *Walter Gordon: A Political Memoir* (McClelland and Stewart, 1977); Paul Martin, *A Very Public Life*, II (Deneau, 1985); Richard Gwyn, *The 49th Paradox* (McClelland and Stewart, 1985); and Stephen Clarkson, *Canada and the Reagan Challenge* (Lorimer, 1982; revised edition, 1985). Robert Bothwell and J.L. Granatstein are completing an analysis of Trudeau foreign policy (UTP, forthcoming).

The debate over American investment in the Canadian economy is reflected in A.E. Safarian, *Foreign Ownership of Canadian Industry* (McGraw-Hill, 1966) and Karl Levitt, *Silent Surrender: The Multinational Corporation in Canada* (Macmillan, 1970). On Vietnam, as their titles indicate, Victor Levant, *Quiet Complicity* (Between the Lines, 1986) and Charles Taylor, *Snow Job* (Anansi, 1975) are very critical of Canadian diplomacy and diplomats. Douglas A. Ross, *In the Interests of Peace: Canada and Vietnam, 1954–1973* (UTP, 1984), takes a different view.

On the environment, see John E. Carroll, *Environmental Diplomacy: An Examination and a Prospective of Canadian-U.S. Transboundary Environmental Relations* (University of Michigan Press, 1983) and D.C. Piper, *The International Law of the Great Lakes* (Duke University Press, 1967). William R. Willoughby gives an overview of *The St. Lawrence Seaway* (University of Wisconsin Press, 1961). For unions, consult John Crispo, *International Unionism: A Study in Canadian-American Relations* (McGraw-Hill, 1967) and Irving M. Abella, *Nationalism, Communism, and Canadian Labour: The CIO, the Communist Party, and the Canadian Congress of Labour, 1935–1956* (UTP, 1973). Frank W. Peers describes the role of broadcasting from 1920–1968 in *The Politics of Canadian Broadcasting* (UTP, 1969) and *The Public Eye* (UTP, 1979).

Books of essays, some scholarly and some not, abound, and they can be useful, inter alia, as a guide to contemporary views on both sides of the border. Examples are the American Assembly's two collections, *The United States and Canada*, the first ed., J.S. Dickey, the second ed., C.F. Doran and J.H. Sigler (Prentice Hall, 1964 and 1984); H.G.J. Aitken, et al., *The American Economic Impact on Canada* (Duke University Press, 1959); Andrew Axline, et al., eds., *Continental Community? Independence and Integration in North America* (McClelland and Stewart, 1974); Stephen Clarkson, ed., *An Independent Foreign Policy for Canada?* (McClelland and Stewart, 1968); Ian Lumsden, ed., *Close the 49th Parallel etc* (UTP, 1970); Annette Baker Fox, et al., eds., *Canada and the United States: Transnational and Transgovernmental Relations* (Columbia University Press, 1976); E.J. Feldman and Neil Nevitte, eds., *The Future of North America: Canada, the United States, and Quebec*

Nationalism; J.W. Holmes, *Life With Uncle* (UTP, 1981); and W.T.R. Fox, *A Continent Apart* (UTP, 1985).

A substantial literature on free trade already exists. Richard G. Lipsey and Robert C. York, *Evaluating the Free Trade Deal* (C.D. Howe Institute, 1988) review the agreement in some detail. M.M. Bowker, *On Guard for Thee* (Voyageur, 1988) prosecutes; John Crispo, ed., *Free Trade: The Real Story* (Gage, 1988) is the case for the defence.

Finally, three journals, *International Journal*, *The American Review of Canadian Studies*, and *International Perspectives* have frequent articles on the relationship. The CIIA publishes a regular booklet series, *Behind the Headlines*.

An honest attempt has been made to secure permission for all material used, and if there are errors or omissions, these are wholly unintentional and the publisher will be grateful to learn of them.

Gordon T. Stewart, " 'A Special Contiguous Country Economic Regime': An Overview of America's Canada Policy," *Diplomatic History* VI, 4 (Fall 1982): 339–357. Reprinted by permission of Scholarly Resources Inc.

John English and Norman Hillmer, "Canada's Alliances," *Revue Internationale d'Histoire Militaire* LIV (1982): 31–52. Reprinted by permission of the Commission Internationale d'Histoire Militaire.

Robert Bothwell and John Kirton, " 'A Sweet Little Country': American Attitudes Toward Canada, 1925–1963," *Queen's Quarterly* 90, 4 (Winter 1983): 1078–1102. Reprinted by permission of the journal and authors.

J.L. Granatstein, "Free Trade Between Canada and the United States: The Issue That Will Not Go Away" in *The Politics of Canada's Economic Relationship with the United States*, ed. Denis Stairs and Gilbert R. Winham (Toronto: University of Toronto Press, 1985), 20–54. Reprinted by permission of University of Toronto Press in co-operation with the Royal Commission on the Economic Union and Development Prospects for Canada and the Canadian Government Publishing Centre, Supply and Services Canada: Study 29, © Minister of Supply and Services Canada, 1985.

Department of External Affairs, "Defence Agreement Between Canada and the United States of America" (NORAD), 12 May 1958; L.B. Pearson, "Canada, the United States, and Vietnam, *Statements and Speeches* 67/8, 19 March 1967; Mitchell Sharp, "Canada-U.S. Relations: Options for the Future," *International Perspectives*, Department of External Affairs, special issue, (Autumn 1972): 1–24; Mark MacGuigan, "The Canadian Perspective on Foreign Investment and Energy Questions," 30 September 1981, *Statements and Speeches* 81/24, 1981; Denis Stairs, "Canada and the Korean War: The Boundaries of Diplomacy," *International Perspectives*, Department of External Affairs (November–December 1972): 25–32. Reprinted with permission of the Minister of Supply and Services Canada.

House of Commons, Debates, 2nd Session, 19th Parliament, Nov. 12, 1940, 55–57, Apr. 28, 1941, 2286–2289; Debates, 4th Session, 21st Parliament, May 7, 1951, 2751–2756; Debates, 2nd Session, 33rd Parliament, Aug. 30, 1988, 19049–19058. Reprinted by permission of the House of Commons of Canada.

Danford W. Middlemiss, "Economic Defence Co-operation with the United States 1940–63" in *Acceptance of Paradox: Essays in Honour of John W. Holmes*, ed. Kim Richard Nossal (Toronto: Canadian Institute of International Affairs, 1982), 86–109. Reprinted by permission of the publisher.

Kenneth M. Curtis and John E. Carroll, *Canadian-American Relations: The Promise and the Challenge* (Lexington, Mass.: D.C. Heath, 1983), 27–37. Reprinted by permission of the publisher.

J.L. Granatstein and R.D. Cuff, "Looking Back at the Cold War: 1945–54," *Canadian Forum* LII (July 1972): 8–11. Reprinted by permission of the authors.

Victor Levant, *Quiet Complicity: Canadian Involvement in the Vietnam War* (Toronto: Between the Lines, 1986), 1–6. Reprinted by permission of the publisher.